W9-APT-484

Methods Toward a Science of Behavior and Experience

WILLIAM J. RAY
Pennsylvania State University

RICHARD RAVIZZA
Pennsylvania State University

Wadsworth Publishing Company
Belmont, California
A Division of Wadsworth, Inc.

ISBN 0-534-00947-6

Psychology Editor: Kenneth King
Production Editor: Helen Sweetland
Managing Designer: Detta Penna
Designer: Rick Chafian
Copy Editor: Carol Reitz
Technical Illustrations: Innographics
Cartoons: Sidney Harris

Cover: *Omega VI;* Alexander Liberman, (1912–); acrylic on canvas; 79¾ x 60 inches. The Art Museum, Princeton University, Princeton, New Jersey. Gift of the artist.

Printed in the United States of America

4 5 6 7 8 9 10—85 84 83

Library of Congress Cataloging in Publication Data

Ray, William J 1945–
Methods toward a science of behavior and experience.
Bibliography: p.
Includes index.
1. Psychological research. 2. Psychology, Experimental. I. Ravizza, Richard, joint author.
II. Title. BF76.5.R38 150′.72 80-29596
ISBN 0-534-00947-6

ACKNOWLEDGMENTS

Chapter 4. Pages 77–79: The interview with Lance Shotland is used by permission of Lance Shotland. Page 81: The interview with Nora Newcombe is used by permission of Nora Newcombe. Pages 88, 89: Portions of sample pages appearing in Box 4.2 and on the following page from *Psychological Abstracts,* copyright 1979 by the American Psychological Association, are reprinted by permission of the publisher. Page 91: Portion of a sample page in Box 4.4 from *Science Citation Index,* 1978 Annual, copyright 1979 by the Institute for Scientific Information, is reprinted by permission of the publisher.

Chapters 5 and 7. Pages 101, 102, and 144–145: The quotation and Figures 5.1 and 7.1 from J. D. Bransford and M. K. Johnson, "Contextual Prerequisites for Understanding," *Journal of Verbal Learning and Verbal Behavior,* 1972, *11,* 717–726, are used by permission of Academic Press and J. D. Bransford.

Chapter 6. Page 123: The random number table in Box 6.1 is reprinted with permission from William Beyer (ed.), *Handbook of Tables for Probability and Statistics,* Second Edition, 1968; copyright The Chemical Rubber Co., CRC Press, Inc.

Chapter 11. Pages 240–242: The ten *Ethical Principles in the Conduct of Research with Human Participants,* copyright 1973 by the American Psychological Association, are reprinted by permission of the publisher. Pages 244–245: The editorial in Box 11.1 from E. F. Loftus and J. F. Fries, "Informed Consent May Be Hazardous to Your Health," *Science,* 1979, *204,* 4388, copyright 1979 by the American Association for the Advancement of Science, is reprinted by permission of the publisher and Elizabeth Loftus.

Chapter 12. Pages 256, 258, 261, 264, 266–267: Quotations from D. J. Gaul, W. E. Craighead, and M. J. Mahoney, "Relationship between Eating Rates and Obesity," *Journal of Consulting and Clinical Psychology,* 1975, *43,* 123–125, copyright 1975 by the American Psychological Association, are reprinted by permission of the publisher and W. E.

Craighead. Pages 257, 261–263: Quotations from R. L. Shotland and M. K. Straw, "Bystander Response to an Assault," *Journal of Personality and Social Psychology,* 1976, *34,* 990–999, copyright 1976 by the American Psychological Association, are reprinted by permission of the publisher and R. L. Shotland. Pages 258–259: The quotation from K. Ravizza, "Peak Experiences in Sports," *Journal of Humanistic Psychology,* 1977, *17,* 35–40, is reprinted by permission of the publisher and the author. Pages 268–269: The checklist in Box 12.1 from R. R. Holt, "Experimental Methods in Clinical Psychology," in B. B. Wolman (ed.), *Handbook of Clinical Psychology,* McGraw-Hill, 1965, is reprinted by permission of the publisher.

Chapter 13. Pages 290–291: The quotation in Box 13.2 from L. Thomas, *The Medusa and the Snail,* Viking, 1979, is reprinted by permission of the author.

To Adam & Lauren & their mommie, Susan (wjr)

a child is the most superb research scientist we can get
Buckminster Fuller

To my parents, who gave me their roots and their love (rr)

CONTENTS

Preface xv

Introduction xviii

CHAPTER ONE What Is Science? 1

Introduction 1
Science as a Way of Knowing 3
Tenacity 3
Authority 4
Box 1.1 Galileo: The Transition from Authority to Empiricism 5
Reason 6
Common Sense 6
Science 6
The Scientific Approach 7
Box 1.2 Newton's Rules of Reasoning 8
Early Approaches 9
Summary Interlude 16
Studying Psychological Behavior and Experience Processes 16
Behavior: An Inroad to the Subjective Experience of Subjects 19
The People Who Do Science (Soon to be You) 21
Summary 22

CHAPTER TWO Introduction to the Methods of Science 24

Introduction 24
Naturalistic Observation 26
Naturalistic Observation—Summary 28
Experimental Method 29
Definitions in the Experimental Method 30
Uses of the Experimental Method 34
Logic and Inference: The Detective Work of Science 35
Validity 36
Propositional Logic 37
Box 2.1 Think Square 38
Scientific Observation: The Raw Data of Science 41
Box 2.2 Philosophy of Science: Sir Karl Popper 42
Box 2.3 Philosophy of Science: Thomas Kuhn 44
Evaluating Scientific Research 45
Communication in Science 46
Summary 47

CHAPTER THREE Description of Behavior through Numerical Representation 49

Introduction 49
Scales of Measurement 49
Nominal Measurement 50
Ordinal Measurement 51
Interval Measurement 52
Ratio Measurement 52
Pictorial Description of Frequency Information 53
Frequency Distribution 53
Descriptive Statistics 56
Measures of Central Tendency 56
Mean 56
Median 57
Mode 57
Measures of Variability 59
Pictorial Descriptions Using Measures of Central Tendency 65
Conclusion: Descriptive Statistics 67

Overview 68
Summary 69

CHAPTER FOUR Developing the Hypothesis 71

Introduction 71
Making Our Hypotheses about Reality Concrete 72
Making Our Hypotheses Logical 75
The "I Wonder What Would Happen If" Hypothesis and Inductive Reasoning 75
The "I Bet This Would Happen If" Question and Deductive Reasoning 77
Ideas Come from Everywhere 77
Intuition and Revelation 82
Box 4.1 Strong Inference: John Platt 83
The Scientist's Guide to Having an Idea 85
Tools for Library Research 86
Journals 86
Psychological Abstracts 87
Box 4.2 Psychological Abstracts 88
Index Medicus 89
Box 4.3 Index Medicus 90
Science Citation Index and Social Science Citation Index 91
Box 4.4 Science Citation Index 91
Creating Testable Research Hypotheses and the Problem of Measurement 92
Conclusion 95
Summary 96

CHAPTER FIVE Testing the Hypothesis: A Conceptual Introduction 98

Introduction 98
The Context of Experimentation: An Example 101
Statistical Interpretation 103
Types of Variation 107

Box 5.1 Type I and Type II Errors 107
Systematic Factors Not Related to the Independent Variable 110
Threats to Internal Validity 111
History 111
Maturation 112
Testing 112
Instrumentation 114
Statistical Regression 114
Selection 114
Mortality 115
Selection-Maturation Interaction 115
Diffusion or Imitation of Treatments 116
Summary 117

CHAPTER SIX Control: The Keystone of the Experimental Method 119

Introduction 119
Control Achieved through Subject Assignment and Subject Selection 120
Box 6.1 Random Number Table 123
Procedures for Subject Assignment: Matching, Counterbalancing, and Randomization 127
Control Achieved through Experimental Design 131
Control as Related to the Logic of Experimentation 136
Summary 139

CHAPTER SEVEN Applying the Logic of Experimentation: Between-Subjects Designs 140

Introduction 140
Between-Subjects Design: Terminology 141
Completely Randomized Design 141
Multileveled Completely Randomized Designs 142
Factorial Design 147
Factorial Designs: The Logic of Experimentation and the Interaction Effect 152

Eight Possible Outcomes of 2 × 2 Factorial Experiments Showing Different Combinations of Significant and Nonsignificant Main Effects and Interactions 160
The Interpretation of Subject Variables with Factorial Designs 165
Advantages of Factorial Designs 167
Summary 167

CHAPTER EIGHT Extending the Logic of Experimentation: Within-Subjects and Matched-Subjects Approaches 170

Introduction 170
Within-Subjects Designs 171
- An Illustration of Within-Subjects Research 173
- Advantages and Disadvantages of Within-Subjects Designs 175
- Repeated Measures 177

Mixed Designs 178
Matched-Subjects Procedures 179
- Matching as a Control Procedure 180
- Matching as an Experimental Procedure 181

Summary 184

CHAPTER NINE The Ecology of the Experiment: The Scientist and Subject in Relation to Their Environment 186

Introduction 186
Ecology 187
Experimenter Factors 189
- Biased Data Collection 189
- Biased Interactions with Subjects 193
- Some Ways to Avoid Experimenter Bias 194

Subject Factors 195
- *Box 9.1 Recommendations for Research* 196

Placebo Factors 199
Demand Characteristics 200
Cultural and Social Bias 203
Summary 204

CHAPTER TEN Quasi-Experimental, Single-Subject, and Naturalistic Observation Designs 205

Introduction 205
Quasi-Experimental Designs 208
Time Series Design 208
Interrupted Time Series Design 210
Multiple Time Series Design 212
Nonequivalent Before-After Design 215
Ex Post Facto Design 216
Single-Subject Designs 218
Case Study Design 218
Box 10.1 A Patient with Bilateral Temporal Lobe Damage 220
Reversal Design 221
Multiple Baseline Design 223
Naturalistic Observations 224
Concerns While Making Naturalistic Observations 226
Data Collection 226
Data Analysis 228
To Conceal or Not to Conceal; To Participate or Not to Participate 228
Strengths and Weaknesses of Naturalistic Observation 230
Summary 231

CHAPTER ELEVEN Ethics 232

Introduction 232
Ethical Consideration of Psychological Experimentation 233
The Rights of the Scientist and the Subject 234
The Experiment as an Ethical Problem 236
Ingredients of the Initial Scientist-Subject Dialogue 237
The Rights of the Subject and the Responsibility of the Experimenter 238
What Is Harmful to a Subject? 239
The American Psychological Association Ethical Guidelines 239
Internal Review Committees 242
Deception Studies 243
Box 11.1 Informed Consent May Be Hazardous to Your Health 244

Obedience-to-Authority Research 245
It's Not a Crime the Way I See It 248
Bypassing the Bypass 250
Debriefing—When Is Enough Enough? 251
The Subject as Colleague 252
Summary 253

CHAPTER TWELVE Sharing the Results 254

Introduction 254
Communication with Other Scientists: The Scientific Article 255
Preparing Your Article 255
Abstract 256
Introduction 256
Method 259
Results 263
Discussion 264
Box 12.1 Preparing a Research Proposal 268
Publishing Your Article 269
What Makes a Good Article? 271
Summary 275

CHAPTER THIRTEEN Beyond Method 276

Introduction 276
Beginning with a Question 278
Limitations to Finding Answers 279
Our Tools 280
Box 13.1 Philosophy of Science: Imre Lakatos 280
Our Shared View of the World 281
Psychological Limitations 282
Science as a Complex Human Process 283
Value in Science 285
Relevance 287
Science as a Means of Transcendence 288
Box 13.2 Lewis Thomas on the Nature of Science 290
Summary 293

Appendix A Guidelines for Nonsexist Language in APA Journals 295

Appendix B Printed Article 305

Appendix C Article Manuscript 307

Bibliography 317

Index 323

PREFACE

We live in a time when books on science are setting sales records. Yet, at many universities, the experimental course remains one that students dread and put off until the last minute. This seems strange to us, since many of our colleagues are excited about what they do in psychology and approach research with excitement and a real desire to know. This makes us think that, in the process of teaching experimental psychology, we have often neglected to include our own experience in psychology, especially the reasons why we attempt a science of behavior and experience in the first place. Thus, one of our major goals in writing this book is to introduce the student both to the basics of doing science and to the spirit that motivates many scientists.

One idea we try to convey to the student from the very beginning is the relationship of science and philosophy. We do this not only through the introduction of propositional logic in Chapter 2, but through a discussion of individuals who have shaped our ideas about science. For example, in the first two chapters, the student is introduced not only to Newton's rules of reasoning, but to the views of Karl Popper and Thomas Kuhn on how science works. We also show the student how some approaches to science, such as the use of strong inference and the development of a research program, have allowed certain fields to move at an accelerated rate. Likewise, we show the student that science cannot be done without reference to values. We do this not only in our discussion of the ecology of the experimental situation in Chapter 9 and our discussion of ethics in Chapter 11, but throughout the text.

However useful, abstractions alone do not teach the student about science as it is practiced, much less how to practice science themselves. Thus, we also emphasize the concrete. In our discussion of descriptive statistics in Chapter 3, we teach students how to read graphs and how to plot them. In Chapter 4, we include detailed information on how to use major library reference works, such as *Psychological Abstracts, Index Medicus,* and *Science* and *Social Citation Indexes.* In Chapter 11, we not only teach the student how to write up an experiment, but include a valuable checklist both for writing up an article and for presenting a research proposal. Because of our desire to make science concrete for the student, we have included interviews with active psychologists on how they first obtained the ideas for their studies. These interviews are followed by a discussion of how to turn an idea into a testable hypothesis.

In order to help faculty members teach this course, we have made a special effort to define and illustrate what we know to be general problem areas for students. For example, the concept of interaction effect is not only illustrated with research examples, but numerous possible outcomes are graphically represented for the student to see. We have also carefully walked the student through the interpretation of interaction effects and explained why an interaction effect must be interpreted before a main effect. These discussions have been facilitated by our explanation of the concept behind the F-ratio. Beginning in Chapter 5 and continuing throughout the rest of the text, the logic of the F-ratio is used in our discussions of experimental control and variation. By emphasizing the factors that influence either the numerator or the denominator of the F-ratio, students are able to conceptually grasp what factors will influence their acceptance or rejection of the null hypothesis. We gave special attention to two other problem areas for students: the meaning of *causation* in science, and the use of the terms *error* and *chance* in relation to experimentation.

By using the title *Methods Toward a Science of Behavior and Experience,* we wanted to convey a sense of not only where experimental psychology has been but where it might be going. We expand on this idea in the final chapter of the book, in which we discuss the potential for a scientific psychology. We point out that psychology was once almost a battleground for those who were interested in behavior and those interested in experience. But today, with scientific studies of attention, awareness, consciousness, and communication between species, we see a new group of scientists who are interested in both behavior *and* experience, not only in others but in themselves.

This book grew out of our discussions concerning our experience of science and the role it presently plays in psychology. At this time we would like to acknowledge individuals who joined us in these discussions at various times. We especially appreciate the time Dale Harris spent discussing with us his perspective on the history of the experimental movement in psychology. We also appreciate the willingness of Lance Shotland, Nora Newcombe, and Carolyn Sherif to discuss with us how their ideas came about and how they began their important research programs.

Many people played a role in the development and preparation of this text. Our manuscript would still be unfinished if it hadn't been for the efforts of our secretaries, Esther Strause, Joy Creeger, Anna Mary Madden, Kathy Leitzell, Nancy McGinnis, and Ellie Meals, who had to suffer through the various drafts and deadlines required to produce a book. We are deeply indebted to John M. Knight for his careful and thorough reviews, and we appreciate the comments and suggestions of the publisher's readers: Robert T. Brown, Dennis Cogan, Paul Eskildsen, Henry Gorman, Alan C. Kamil, Elizabeth Lynn, Henry Morlock, Nancy Oley, Howard B. Orenstein, Ronald R. Rossi, Mark S. Sanders, Kathryn Schwarz, Barbara Tabachnick, W. Scott Terry, and Sheila G. Zipf. We hope we have not lessened the book in our inability to implement all of their suggestions. Additionally, we would like to thank Les Herold of California State College at San Bernardino for inspiring our imaginations with the thought provoking title. We found the production staff at Wadsworth to be excellent and wish to thank them for their efforts. In particular, we would like to thank the production editor, Helen Sweetland, for her careful attention to detail and concern for perfection in the process of transforming a manuscript into a book. And, finally, we would like to thank Ken King, the psychology editor at Wadsworth, for his commitment to this project, as well as his dedication to quality publishing.

Since one of us is a physiological psychologist and the other a clinical psychologist, we each gave much from our respective backgrounds and talents to this book. Because we each put much of ourselves into this project, we simply flipped a coin to determine first authorship. For us, the real life and spirit of this book lies in the interactions that we had with one another and with those acknowledged above, with our students who patiently read early drafts, and, equally important, with you, our readers, as we wrote the text. We hope that you may be able to use this book in a similar way and to continue this discussion of psychology, science, and experience.

State College, Pennsylvania

INTRODUCTION

You are about to begin a voyage of wonder and curiosity, of questionings and doubts. Historically, it is a voyage that humans began many generations ago and that young scientists like yourselves embark on every day. It is a voyage into the nature of ourselves and the world in which we live. It is a voyage with a particular focus: science. For some of you, science may offer a new way to view the world. Learning about science, like learning anything new, will offer added perspective, which can in turn lead to a very real expansion of your own consciousness. For those of you already familiar with science, this book offers a deeper exploration of the science of behavior and experience. It is important to emphasize from the onset that learning about science is an expansion of what you already are. It is an *option,* an alternative that you are free to use or not to use as you explore and interact with our world. You choose how and when to use it. In fact, after taking this course, you may decide it is not a way you wish to view the world at all and you may never use it again!

Some beginning students are hesitant to explore science because they believe it is cold, antihumanistic, and even antireligious. They believe it separates us from our beliefs, our faiths, our feelings, and ourselves. This is a serious and limiting misconception. Many of our colleagues in all fields of science are as open to humanistic and spiritual traditions as they are to science. We believe that science—a science of behavior and experience—will some day assist us in a profoundly deep exploration of the inner teachings of all our great humanistic and spiritual traditions. This task of helping all of us more fully explore and understand our own potential may be the major function of science in the future evolution of human consciousness.

Our voyage into the science of behavior and experience begins by stressing that there are many childlike qualities that we hope will always remain part of us. Genuine laughter, spontaneous play, intimacy, curiosity, and creativity are some childlike qualities that form the very foundation of mature human experience. In a similar way, the scientific method we are about to explore has firm roots in the simple way a child goes about exploring its world. With this in mind, we begin our exploration of science by viewing ourselves as children who wish to explore. The world awaiting the child includes not only the outside world but also the child's own psychological experience. Through this child, which is one aspect of ourselves, we approach the question of how we go about performing a science of behavior and experience. We will watch the child search for knowledge and mature into three distinct aspects, which we can define as actors in our drama of psychological inquiry.

The first aspect or role is that of the *scientist.* This is the role that you are reading this book to learn about. It is the active role in our drama. The task before you is to learn how the scientist goes about doing science. In this book we will watch the child learn the role of the scientist. We will come to see that many activities of present-day, mature scientists are only extensions of the way we approached the world as children. As you learn about this role, you will learn the type of questions scientists ask, the type of answers that they accept, and the manner in which knowledge is approached and verified. You will also learn how to assume this role for yourself and begin your drama of experimentation.

The second aspect or role is that of the *subject.* This is the passive role in our drama. The subject is the particular organism that the scientist chooses to study. In fact, it is the various experiences and behaviors of the subject that form the content of psychology. The paradox for scientists interested in the study of human behavior and experience is that although the subject matter is "out there" in the subjects we study, because we are also human, it is at the same time "in here" in us. In a very real sense, as we study other people and animals, we also study ourselves.

The third role is that of the *witness.* This role is not always recognized, yet in many ways it is the most important because it maintains a balance between the scientist and the subject, the active and passive aspects of this process. The witness, who is also us, stands back and watches the scientist do science and the subject behave and experience the world. One task of the witness is to teach that both the scientist and the subject are *limited* because each sees the world from his or her own perspective.

As the witness teaches us that there is a broader perspective from which we can appreciate both viewpoints simultaneously, we begin to mature and realize the richness of the scientific process and the wonder of knowing reality. In this vein, it is the role of the witness to remind us that the experience and understanding of life require more than just a description of miles of blood vessels, reinforcement schedules, and chemicals interacting with each other. It is the witness who asks whether the science of the scientist is relevant, ethical, and generally worth doing. But most important, it is the witness who brings together the procedures of the scientist and the experience of the subject and allows them to have a relationship in the first place.

Once we have developed these aspects of ourselves—the scientist, the subject, and the witness—we will be in a better position to understand the strengths and weaknesses of using science to study ourselves. Until that time, we would like to suggest that you neither accept nor reject the scientific approach but rather that you *allow* that it may have something to offer you. That is, you can allow yourself to become actively involved in trying to solve problems and answer questions using this method while remaining free to remember the problems and limitations of the scientific approach. As in anything else, it is only through active involvement that you will come to understand fully what the method has to offer. Let us now begin the drama of science with a problem—how did we as children come to know the world?—and from this develop methods for a science of behavior and experience.

CHAPTER ONE

What Is Science?

INTRODUCTION

Science is above all a human activity. One obvious meaning of this is that science is done by people. A second and equally accurate meaning is that all people do science in some form. After all, the methods of science are basically simple extensions of the ways all people learn about their world. Science in many ways is very similar to how we have been learning about the world since we were infants. Consequently, because each of us has been using it in one form or another since we first began toddling about and discovering our world, you already know much more about the scientific method than you think you do.

Watch a young child. When something catches his or her eye, the child must examine it, study it, observe it, have fun with it. Next, the child wants to interact with it, touch it, feel it. From passive observations and active interactions, the child slowly learns about the world. Some interactions are fun: "If I tip the glass, I get to see the milk form pretty pictures on the floor." Other interactions are not much fun: "If I touch the red circles on the stove, my fingers hurt!" From each interaction, the child learns a little more about the world.

Like the child, scientists are exploring the unknown and sometimes the known features of the world. Although most scientists have mastered the effects of spilling their milk, all basic research strategies are based on one simple notion: *To discover what the world is like, we must experience it.* To have an idea about how the world is, is simply not enough. Instead, like the child, scientists experience the world to determine whether their ideas accurately reflect reality. Direct experience is our most important tool because it alone allows us to bridge the gap between our ideas and reality.

In general, there is not one scientific method any more than there is one art or one education or one religion. Yet there is a general process that is called *science.* This process consists of experiencing the world and then drawing general conclusions (called *facts*) from observations. Sometimes these conclusions or facts may be descriptive and represented by numbers. For example, we say that it is 238,000 miles to the moon or that the average human heart rate is 72 beats per minute. Other times these facts may be more general and describe a relationship or a process. For example, we say that it is more difficult to learn a second language after puberty than before, or that as we age we hear fewer high-frequency sounds. Whatever the topic, the known facts about a particular subject are called *scientific knowledge.*

Many conceptions of science picture a man or woman in a white lab coat laboriously writing down numbers and later mulling about in a cluttered office trying to make theoretical sense out of the findings. This concept may be accurate, but it is not a total picture of science. In addition, we will stress another aspect of science. This aspect takes place when the available facts are viewed in light of human value. It is this aspect of value that allows us to see one set of numbers as more relevant or potentially more useful than another. This combining of fact and value results in a humanistic approach to scientific understanding. Scientific understanding helps us to see the *how* and *why* of the world, and thereby to understand nature in a fuller perspective. In many cases, this understanding raises new questions, which in turn can be answered by using science to examine the world. In other cases, these new facts may be applied in real-life settings (technology) and make life easier for everyone. Thus, at its best, science begins and ends in human experience.

In the Introduction we described three actors in the drama of science: the subject, the scientist, and the witness. In our study of behavior and experience, it is the scientist who experiences the world and then formulates general facts or conclusions that describe it. The subject is the particular psychological experience of whatever organism we are studying. In the case of studying human consciousness, the subject will also be some aspect of ourselves. Finally, the witness provides the perspective, the concerns for value, and the relation of science and its facts to other aspects of human life.

SCIENCE AS A WAY OF KNOWING

Some students fall into the trap of viewing science as the best way, or even the only way, to study behavior and experience. If you find this happening to you, beware! Nothing is further from the truth. To emphasize this, we offer science to you as merely one way of examining human nature. There are others. Art, philosophy, religion, and literature are all extremely fruitful ways or channels through which we can gain new ideas about human behavior and experience. In the past, psychology has drawn on many of these traditions and will surely continue to do so in the future.

Having a fruitful source of ideas, whether it is our literary, spiritual, scientific, or artistic traditions, is an important part of understanding behavior and experience. However, a second and perhaps even more important aspect of learning about psychology is the process of deciding whether or not a new idea is accurate. In contrast to other ways of knowing, science offers not only a fertile source of new ideas but also a powerful method for evaluating the ideas we have about reality. For example, suppose you go to a lecture by a well-known spiritual leader and he says that if you meditate twice a day you will be happier. Here is an instance where you are confronted with a new idea that may have a very important impact on your life. Yet, because some time and effort are involved, you are hesitant to try meditation unless you know it will be profitable. So you are faced with the task of evaluating the suggestion and deciding whether or not meditation is for you. How do you decide this? In the remainder of this section, we will examine several ways people commonly decide whether or not to accept new ideas about the world. For a more detailed discussion of these ways of accepting belief, we suggest you consult the work of the American philosopher Charles Peirce (see Cohen & Nagel, 1934; Kerlinger, 1973). Obviously we are biased and believe the best way to go about accepting new ideas is to use science to first evaluate them and then use the results to help make a decision.

Tenacity

Charles Peirce uses the term *tenacity* to refer to an acceptance of a belief because "we have always known it to be this way." People say "women are bad drivers," "you can't teach an old dog new tricks," or "science is always beneficial." These statements are repeated over and over again and accepted as true, yet they are never examined and evaluated. Unfortunately, this is an all-too-common method of accepting information. You may notice that some television advertising and political election campaigns use this technique when they present a single phrase or slogan repeatedly. Even an empty phrase repeated often enough becomes "true." As has been said, if you tell people something often enough, they will believe it. As a way of learning about the world, there are two problems with this method. First, the statement may be just an empty phrase and its accuracy may never have been evaluated. Even though the statement gains wide acceptance, it is primarily because of familiarity. Second, tenacity offers no means for correcting erroneous ideas, and this is its greatest problem. That is, once information based solely on tenacity is widely accepted, it is very difficult to change. Social psychologists have shown that once a person accepts a belief without data to support it, the person will often create or make up a reason why it is true; the person may even refuse to accept new information that contradicts this erroneous belief. In the case of the meditation example, a decision to meditate simply because it is "known to be beneficial" would be acceptance based on tenacity. Accepting ideas about experience and behavior simply because they are familiar to us or widely believed by others is an extension of the childish behavior of the three-year-old who just copies the words and behaviors of his or her parents. For the child this is a useful way to learn about the world, but for the rest of us it is very limiting.

Authority

A second way we may accept a new idea is because some authority figure tells us it is so. Acceptance based on authority is simple, since we have only to repeat and live by what we are told. In many cases, referring to an authority, especially in areas we know nothing about, is not only useful but also beneficial. When we were young, our parents often used the method of authority for directing our behavior. Health care and education in many places were based almost exclusively on authority. If a famous physician or educator said it was true, everyone considered it true. Even today, we often rely on the judgment of an authority whether we are going to physicians, psychologists, scientists, or stockbrokers. Likewise, religious training as it is taught today relies on the authority of the church for establishing correct religious procedures. Although authority brings with it a stability that allows for consistency, it is not without problems. The major problem of accepting authority as the sole knower of truth is that authority can be incorrect and thus send people in the wrong directions. For example, as long as the world accepted the viewpoint that the world was flat or that the earth was the center of the universe, no one thought to look for America or to study the orbit of the earth. Consequently, it is very important to have some idea of the basis of the authority's claims. Are they based on opinion, tradition, revelation, or direct experience? How valid are these sources of information? In the meditation example, if you decided to meditate simply because this well-known spiritual leader advised it, you would be basing your decision solely on his authority. Box 1.1 discusses the transition from authority to experimentation in the beginning of modern science.

Box 1.1 *Galileo: The Transition from Authority to Empiricism*

Galileo represents for many scientists a symbol of change in the rules of evidence. Before the time of Galileo, intellectual questions were solved by referring to authority, usually the authority of the church. The church of this period in turn looked to the Greek philosopher Aristotle for answers to "material" questions—what today we call *natural science.*

Suppose a person wanted to know which of two balls would hit the ground first if dropped from a tall building. To the time of Galileo, the method of answering this question would be to refer to Aristotle's theory, which stated that the world is made up of four types of elements—earth, air, water, and fire. Each element, according to Aristotle, acts according to its own nature. To answer the question of which of two bodies would hit the ground first, one would reason that the two objects, composed of the element "earth," would seek to return to earth and thus fall down. If one object weighed more than the other, it would be reasoned that this heavier object contained more of the element "earth" than the lighter one and would naturally fall faster. Thus, it would be concluded that the heavier body would hit the ground before the lighter one. No one would have thought actually to drop two objects from a tower and *observe* which hit the ground first. Answers were always given in terms of authority.

Galileo began a revolution that was to challenge authority. He successfully replaced the method of authority with that of experimentation. The movement to experimentation was greatly aided by Galileo's own inventions such as a telescope, a thermometer, an improved microscope, and a pendulum-type timing device. Each of these devices allowed people to experiment and to see for themselves the answers to questions of nature. After establishing that balls rolling down an inclined plane act similarly to falling objects, Galileo successfully challenged the authority of Aristotle concerning two falling weights. With Galileo's work, a new science based on observation and experimentation had begun.

Reason

Reason and logic are the basic method of philosophy. Reason is often in the form of a logical syllogism such as: *All men can't count; Dick is a man; therefore Dick can't count.* We all use reason every day as we try to solve problems and understand relationships. However, useful as it is to be reasonable, reason alone will not always produce the appropriate answer. Why is this so? One potential problem in the reasoned approach is that our original assumption must be correct. If the original assumption is incorrect or at odds with the world in which we live, then logic cannot help us. For example, the syllogism that concluded that Dick can't count is logically valid even though it is based on the absurd premise that all men can't count! The weakness of using reason alone is that we have no way to determine the accuracy of our assumptions. Thus, we can have situations in which our logic is impeccable, but because our original assumption was inaccurate, the conclusion is silly.

Common Sense

Common sense offers an improvement over acceptance based on tenacity, authority, or reason because it offers an appeal to direct experience. Common sense is based on our own past experiences and our perception of how we think the world is. One problem is that our experiences and perceptions of the world may be quite limited. Whereas common sense may help us deal with the routine aspects of our daily life, it may also form a wall and prevent us from understanding new areas. This can be a problem particularly when we enter realms outside our everyday experience. For example, people considered it against common sense when Einstein suggested that time was relative and could be different for different people. Likewise, it was considered against common sense when Freud suggested that we did not always know our own motivations or when Skinner suggested that the concept of free will is meaningless for most individuals.

Science

The final way we will discuss in which people accept new ideas is through science. The philosopher of science, Alfred North Whitehead (1925), suggested that there are two methods for what he called the "purification of ideas" that are combined in the scientific method. An idea is evaluated and/or corrected through (1) dispassionately observing by means of our bodily senses (for example, vision, hearing, and touch) and (2) using reason to compare various theoretical conceptualizations based on experience.

The first method is a direct extension of the commonsense approach just described. Unlike a given individual's common sense, however, science is open to *anyone's* direct experience. Presumably any observation made by one scientist could be verified by any other individual with normal sensory capacities. To aid individuals in repeating the observations of others, some scientists (see Bridgman, 1927) have emphasized the importance of *operational definitions* in research. As you will see in the next chapter, operational definitions direct *how* observations are to be made and *what* is to be observed and measured.

The second method is a direct application of the principles of logic. In this case, however, logic is combined with experience to rule out any assumptions that do not accurately reflect the world. This blend of direct sensory experience and reason gives science a self-corrective nature, which is not found in other ways of accepting ideas about the world. This means that scientific conclusions are never taken as final but are always open to reinterpretation as new evidence is gained. In other words, the method of science includes a feedback component by which conclusions about the world can be refined over time. It is the refining of ideas through both experimentation and reason that allows science to be a fruitful method for knowing about the world. Box 1.2 on pp. 8–9 describes Sir Isaac Newton's rules of reasoning in science. In many ways these rules are as applicable today as they were 300 years ago.

THE SCIENTIFIC APPROACH

In this chapter we will acquaint you with the scientific approach through various informal illustrations, examples, and stories. Then in Chapter 2 we will more formally discuss the methods of natural observation and experimentation. Among other things we will emphasize that a major characteristic of science is a reliance on information that is *verifiable through experience.* That is, it is possible for different individuals in different places and at different times using a similar method to produce the same results.

Once you know the methods of science and have actually used them in a variety of situations, you will be in a position to evaluate science as a method of knowing about the world that includes the behavior and experience of yourself and others. More important, you will be in a position to decide whether it is the way you choose to understand your world. First, however, let us begin to understand what science is by looking at three early efforts to better understand the world. Although these efforts attempted to be systematic, today we would call them pre-experimental or quasi-experimental. That is, in none of these recounts was an actual experiment conducted. Our purpose is to ask you to focus on the manner in which the problem was resolved. Try to see how the solution was sought, particularly the efforts to be systematic, and what errors were made. You might also recall instances from your own life when you attempted to solve problems in similar ways.

Box 1.2 Newton's Rules of Reasoning

Born the year after Galileo's death, Newton represents the beginning of modern science as we know it. Where Galileo had fought with philosophers of his day and was tortured by the church for his belief, Newton was able to live in a new age in which science through experimentation and reason began to bear fruits.

In the 1680s Newton's classic work, *Principia,* was published (Newton, 1969 reprint). Designated by the historian of science Gerald Holton (1952) as "probably the greatest single book in the history of science," this work described Newton's theories concerning time, space, and motion as well as his rules of reasoning for science. Science, called *natural philosophy* by Newton, is based on four rules of reasoning. These rules, created more than 300 years ago, are still useful for helping scientists to reason and develop hypotheses.

Rule 1

We are to admit no more causes of natural things than such as are both true and sufficient to explain their appearances.

To this purpose the philosophers say that Nature does nothing in vain, and more is in vain when less will serve; for Nature is pleased with simplicity, and affects not the pomp of superfluous causes.

Today we refer to this rule as the law of parsimony. The rule simply states that natural events should be explained in the simplest way possible.

Rule 2

Therefore to the same natural effects we must, as far as possible, assign the same causes.

As to respiration in a man and in a beast, the descent of stones in Europe and in America; the light of our culinary fire and of the sun; the reflection of light in the earth, and in the planets.

This rule reflects Newton's belief in a natural order, which requires that the same gravity causes stones to fall in America and in Europe.

Rule 3

The qualities of bodies, which admit neither intensification nor remission of degrees, and

EARLY APPROACHES

The first example concerns extrasensory perception (ESP). Do you think research on ESP is new? Think again, for the story we are about to relate took place in 447 B.C., more than 2,400 years ago.

According to the historian Herodotus (1942 trans.), Croesus, the king of Lydia, became concerned as the Persian army became more powerful because Lydia was located between Persia and Greece. King Croesus knew the Persian armies to be strong and thus did not want to attack them unless it was certain he would win. He needed someone who could foretell the future. As an enlightened consumer, Croesus wanted to know that the information he received was true. To determine this, he constructed a test of the oracles who were said to foretell the future best. The test went as follows:

---

which are found to belong to all bodies within the reach of our experiments, are to be esteemed the universal qualities of all bodies whatsoever.

For since the qualities of bodies are only known to us by experiments, we are to hold for universal all such as universally agree with experiments; and such as are not liable to diminution can never be quite taken away. We are certainly not to relinquish the evidence of experiments for the sake of dreams and vain fictions of our own devising; nor are we to recede from the analogy of Nature, which is wont to be simple, and always consonant to itself. We no other way know the extension of bodies than by our senses, nor do these reach it in all bodies; but because we perceive extension in all that are sensible, therefore we ascribe it universally to all others also.

Newton continues a long discussion of this principle. Briefly, it states that what we learn from our experiments can be applied to other similar structures outside the reach of our experiments. For example, the same properties such as gravity and inertia should apply to the moon and other planets as they apply to stones and other objects we experiment with.

Rule 4

In experimental philosophy we are to look upon propositions inferred by general induction from phenomena as accurately or very nearly true, notwithstanding any contrary hypotheses that may be imagined, till such time as other phenomena occur, by which they may either by made more accurate, or liable to exceptions.

This rule we must follow, that the argument of induction may not be evaded by hypotheses.

This rule simply states that theories obtained from experiments should be considered true or approximately true until new experimental evidence shows the old to be incorrect. Ideas developed from experiments should not be changed just because we like another hypothesis better.

These four simple rules have directed science for the past 300 years. In this century they have been applied to the social and behavioral sciences as well.

Croesus's assistants were to go out into Greece and Libya where famous oracles lived. The assistants were to visit each oracle on a specific day and at a specific time and ask the following question: What was the king doing at that moment? Since the king told no one what he was actually doing at that moment, he reasoned that only a true oracle capable of ESP could answer correctly. The assistants all returned to the king and reported their answers. Only one oracle—the oracle at Delphi—knew the correct answer. In fact, according to Herodotus, this oracle answered the question before it was even asked. The king had been making lamb stew.

Although the king had the beginnings of a scientific approach to experience, he had not yet learned the role of chance in science or the nature of the language of science, as we shall soon see. Trusting his research, the king honored the oracle and asked the important political question whether he should go to battle against the Persian armies. The oracle replied that in such a contest, "a mighty empire would be destroyed." This was all the king needed to assemble his armies and attack. When the battle was completed, a mighty empire had been destroyed as the oracle had predicted. The problem for the king was that the empire destroyed was his own and he was a prisoner. As we shall discuss in later chapters, the king, like many others after him, failed to realize that the initial "correct answer" of the oracle may have been only a lucky guess. Likewise, he did not realize that the language of prediction must be quite precise in directing our attention toward possible outcomes that can be tested.

Let us look at another attempt to understand the world, this one dating back almost 2,000 years. In the second century A.D., Galen, a well-known physician, described a woman who complained of insomnia (Mesulam & Perry, 1972). The problem was to determine the factors that led to the insomnia. Galen first decided that the problem was not mainly physical. Following this determination, he began to notice the woman's condition during his examinations. It happened that during one examination, a person returning from the theater mentioned the name of a certain dancer, Pylades. At this point Galen observed that the woman's pulse increased along with a change in her facial color and expression. What did Galen do next? To answer his questions as to what was affecting the woman, he began to experiment. In his own words,

> The next day, I told one of my following that when I went to visit the woman he was to arrive a little later and mention that Morphus was dancing that day. When this was done the patient's pulse was in

> no way changed. And likewise, on the following day, while I was attending her, the name of the third dancer was mentioned, and in like fashion the pulse was hardly affected at all. I investigated the matter for a fourth time in the evening. Studying the pulse and seeing that it was excited and irregular when mention was made that Pylades was dancing, I concluded that the lady was in love with Pylades, and in the days following, this conclusion was confirmed exactly (Galen, 1827 trans.).

Galen went past observation and began to ask, "I wonder what will happen if I do this?" He performed what we would now call a *single-subject experiment* (see Chapter 10). It is important for you to notice that Galen checked to determine that it was not the name of just any dancer that produced a change in pulse rate or even just a man's name. Thus, he sought to discover what factors brought on an irregular pulse by examining a number of alternatives. From this investigation, he concluded that only the name of one particular man repeated on different occasions produced the effect.

Let us consider one more story, which took place in Europe 200 years ago. A physician named Semmelweis faced a serious problem when he noticed that healthy women who had just given birth to healthy children were dying. The women died of a condition that included fever, chills, and seizures. Although there were numerous theories offered, which included bad diet, unhealthy water, and even the smell of certain flowers, Semmelweis knew that other women in the same hospital who ate the same food, drank the same water, and smelled the same flowers did not die. Consequently, Semmelweis reasoned that it was not the food, water, or flowers. Yet the fact remained that only women giving birth died of this condition.

Semmelweis became aware of a crucial clue when he learned that an assistant who had accidentally cut his hand during an autopsy had later died of the same symptoms as the mothers. What was the connection between the death of the assistant and those of the mothers? Was there any connection at all? Semmelweis reasoned that the autopsy laboratory where the assistant had worked might be the cause of the mysterious deaths. To evaluate this notion, he traveled to other hospitals and recorded what physicians did just before delivering babies. From these observations, he learned that when the physicians who delivered the babies came directly from a pathology lecture in which diseased tissues were handled or from performing an autopsy, the death rate was highest. He suggested that it was the physicians who were transferring the diseases from the pathological tissue to the healthy mothers, just as the assistant had accidentally infected himself with the knife cut.

As you might imagine, the physicians of the day were outraged at the suggestion that they were the cause of death. Semmelweis found further evidence by demonstrating that in those hospitals where there was an option for a birth by either a midwife or a physician, the mothers with the birth by midwife survived at a much greater rate. In a rather dramatic, though not totally controlled experiment, Semmelweis is said to have placed himself at the door to the delivery ward and forced all physicians who entered to wash their hands first. The number of deaths decreased dramatically. Although not everyone accepted the report of his findings, the data spoke for themselves and modern medical practice has been shaped by this event (Glasser, 1976).

These three stories—of Croesus, Galen, and Semmelweis—show the beginning of a scientific approach to human problems. Croesus faced the problem of how to evaluate information offered by various oracles. To do this, he devised a test—an evaluation of the sources to decide which one he would use to direct his behavior. But we do not consult oracles today, you might argue. This may be true, but we do develop far-reaching social programs and treatments. For example, is "Sesame Street" a useful means for teaching disadvantaged children? In terms of psychotherapy, would you gain more by just talking with your favorite professor rather than going to a clinical psychologist? If you want to avoid heart attacks, do you change your diet, run four miles a day, meditate, or just do nothing? To answer these questions, we, like Croesus, need to perform evaluation research, and the methods of science offer us one approach.

Croesus's experience also reminds us of two potential pitfalls to knowing about the world. These are the roles of chance in the events we observe and the need for unambiguous statements. Croesus's single question to the oracle might have been correctly answered by a lucky guess. To decrease the chance of a lucky guess, Croesus might have asked the oracles several questions. In essence, such a safeguard would have constituted a *replication* (repeating a procedure under similar conditions) of his experiment. Today simple replication of a new finding is a powerful way to decrease the likelihood that it is a fluke. In retrospect, Croesus also surely recognized that he misinterpreted the oracle's ambiguous answer about the battle. To minimize the chances of ambiguities, scientists carefully and systematically define their words as precisely as possible.

Galen faced a different problem. He wanted to learn why a particular woman did not sleep. To do this, he first observed the woman; that is, he just spent some time with her and noticed what happened. Once he realized that the woman's heart reacted to a dancer's name, he began to test his observations. Galen at this point moved to a more sophisticated process than Croesus's simple consultation with a fortune-teller. Galen sought evidence for a causal relationship by examining the woman directly. In this he anticipated a major shift concerning how we know about the world. Very briefly, Croesus sought his answers from authority. The authority of his time was the gods, who spoke through the oracles. A more empirical approach would have been for Croesus to develop a system of spies and scouts to provide information about the Persians' strength based on direct experience. In contrast, Galen went beyond the ungrounded opinions or guesses of available authorities and relied on his direct experience. Galen's appeal to direct experience reflects an alternative approach to knowing and in a real way reflects an alternative level of consciousness toward which modern science has evolved. Indeed, for several generations now science has been rebuilding our knowledge and understanding of the world in terms of direct experience.

In all likelihood, the actual choice of basing our actions on evidence from experience or on unfounded opinion has probably been with us in some form for thousands of years and presently confronts *each of us* countless times each day. Yet basing one's actions on direct experience of the world sometimes initially appears time-consuming and more difficult than simply consulting some expert or acting on a hunch. In the long run, because our actions invariably take place in the world, the wiser alternative is to base actions on experiential knowledge of the "real situation." For you, this may mean beginning to resolve those nagging career decisions by attempting to get some part-time or even volunteer job experience to find out whether you enjoy the job as much as you thought. Frequently students base their career decisions solely on their own hunches or their parents' opinions. Because it is difficult to get direct experience of many jobs, we often encourage our students to take time off and try out some of their ideas. Mere opinion of others provides a convenient answer, but in the long run, as Croesus found out, reality prevails. We hope the experiences you have in this course, particularly the experimental aspects, will help you decide whether you enjoy "doing science." So use this course as a way of learning about science and yourself as well.

In the third story Semmelweis had a different problem to solve. Why were some healthy women dying after giving birth? To solve this problem, he examined a number of factors. *He observed the patients with a definite purpose in mind.* He asked: How are these women being treated that is different from the way other patients are treated? That is, he sought to determine what was unique to these patients. Was it diet? Flowers? Doctors? What was it? Then an unexpected event occurred; an autopsy assistant died. This gave the clue that led to the solution of the problem. To digress, we want to suggest that science not only is a method that scientists engage in to solve problems and learn about the world, but also is a procedure that allows for unexpected events to play a part, whether in the form of accident or human error. That is to say, one of the rich aspects of science includes unpredictability, serendipity, and what is often called "luck." Keep in mind, however, that luck can work either way, as Croesus found out.

In thinking about Semmelweis's work, notice how he used logic and simple common sense to design his tests so that his observations would lead to a better understanding of the problem. In some cases Semmelweis tried to determine *what was causing* the mothers' deaths. For example, because the laboratory assistant died of similar symptoms, Semmelweis reasoned that perhaps he died of the same cause. Semmelweis's observation that more deaths occurred after doctors handled diseased tissue led him to reason that perhaps the cause was somehow related to the diseased tissue. In other cases he tried to rule out *factors that were not responsible* for the deaths. For instance, because women patients who did not die ate the same food and drank the same water, Semmelweis reasoned that these were not possible causes and could be eliminated from further consideration.

There was nothing particularly extraordinary about any of these conclusions. In fact, they reflect the simple common sense we all possess. What was exceptional was that Semmelweis saw relationships that others overlooked. When simple common sense and reason are combined with direct sensory experience, a desire to understand reality, and the courage to accept new facts, science emerges as a powerful means of asking questions about reality.

Our final aspect of Semmelweis's work is that his desire to know and understand led to the development of a series of investigations that approached the problem from several directions. Once he had gained the clue from the death of the assistant, he set out to answer his question through a series of observations. First, he saw how the new mothers in his hospital were treated differently than other women; that is, he observed that they were *not* given different food or flowers or treated by different doctors. Second, he allowed himself to consider a possible connection between the death of an assistant and the death of the mothers. Third, he went to other hospitals to determine whether his ideas or hypotheses were limited to his hospi-

"TREADMILLS! MAZES! THERE MUST BE MORE TO LIFE THAN THIS."

tal or whether they were true for other hospitals as well. Fourth, he concluded that the problem was that the physicians handled diseased tissue and then delivered babies without washing their hands, even though this was an unpopular idea. Fifth, he performed an indirect test of his theory by comparing the difference in death rates caused by physicians who handled diseased tissue and midwives who did not. Sixth, he began a direct test of his theory by insisting that physicians wash their hands as they came onto the delivery ward. The power of Semmelweis's procedure was not in any one test of his ideas, since it is almost impossible for any single procedure to answer all questions in science. The power was that he began with a problem and followed it through to the end by means of a series of observations.

SUMMARY INTERLUDE

Let's pause for a moment and review what we have covered so far. In the preceding sections we described the scientific approach to problem solving. We began with children learning about the world through interacting with it. In particular, we suggested that this leads to science as a way of knowing through direct experience. We characterized science as a process for drawing conclusions that describe the world. We further discussed science not as a sacred ritual to be worshiped but as the simple extension of the way children and all of us learn about our world.

We then gave an overview of science by relating the stories of Croesus, Galen, and Semmelweis. We pointed out the manner in which aspects of these stories anticipated important issues in present-day behavioral science. These correspondences included the need for unambiguous statements, the need for testing what does not affect behavior as well as what does affect behavior, and the importance of a series of tests or research studies for zeroing in on the solution to a problem. We wanted you to see that science combines experience, reason, and desire to answer questions about reality. Furthermore, this approach to solving problems is not new and represents a way of solving problems that we *all* use to some extent every day.

STUDYING PSYCHOLOGICAL BEHAVIOR AND EXPERIENCE PROCESSES

In the preceding discussion we emphasized that scientists use direct sensory experience to determine whether their ideas about the world are accurate.

This appeal to sensory experience is crucial for two reasons. First, it represents a genuine attempt to pause and observe the external world. Second, reliance on sensory experience means that not only scientists but also *any other person* with normal sensory capacities and training can observe the particular behavior under study. The fact that anyone can use his or her own sensory experience to verify the raw data of any scientist provides a strong and essential safeguard that our observations of the world remain as free as possible of the unintended, or even intended, biases of any one particular scientist. This process of relying on direct sensory experience to verify our ideas about reality is referred to as *empiricism.* Empiricism is the traditional approach for psychology.

Yet, as the title of this book implies, we are dealing with two worlds in our study of behavior and experience. One is the objective, physical world in which anyone can observe appearance and *behavior.* The other is the subjective world of personal psychological *experience,* which is, of course, completely private. Science, whether it be biology, physics, chemistry, psychology, sociology, or zoology, focuses on the objective world of appearances and behavior. In the behavior of people, molecules, internal organs, or electrons, that which is observed and measured by science is observable objects in the real world. Psychology has continued this tradition, and many studies you will perform and read about will consist of the observation and measurement of human behavior. However, since the subject matter of psychology focuses in part on humans, psychology is faced with a greater challenge. Not only can we observe humans behave, but we can also ask them about their inner experiences, whether they be thoughts, feelings, or sensations. Furthermore, because we share the same presumably normal array of psychological processes, we can also observe our own behavior and experiences.

This diversity offers us a challenge. The challenge is to explore and understand scientifically the experiences as well as the behaviors of ourselves and others. E. F. Schumacher (1977) emphasized this diversity when he pointed out that the possibility of using experience and behavior to study psychological processes in ourselves and others leads to four possible fields of knowledge. For our purposes, we will consider these as four possible ways of studying psychological processes. These ways are summarized in Table 1.1.

Let us consider this table for a moment. The first cell (1) is that with which we are all immediately acquainted. This is our private experience of being who we are and living in our world. It is unshared subjective experi-

Table 1.1 Four Ways of Studying Psychological Processes

	Inner Experience	*Outer Appearance (Behavior)*
"I" (self)	1	3
"You" (others)	2	4

ence open to no one but ourself. However, as we will suggest to you later, it may be possible to explore this space scientifically and in a systematic manner. The second cell (2) is the inner world of all beings other than ourselves. We, of course, have no direct experience of the subjective world of others. This cell asks those intriguing yet unanswerable questions such as: What does it feel like to be you? Do my cats experience the world as I do? Do you and I both see a red apple as the same color? A person would have to possess mind-reading or clairvoyant abilities to experience what another person is experiencing. The third cell (3) asks the question: What do I look like in the eyes of others? Some aspects of psychology such as psychotherapy or skills training (for example, sensitivity training) focus on helping people become more aware of their own subjective experiences. The therapist achieves this by observing clients' behaviors and giving feedback that enables them to become more aware of their own subjective experiences. The fourth cell (4) focuses on those behaviors of other people or animals that anyone can directly observe, measure, or objectify. This is the traditional domain of modern science. The methods we will describe in this book fall into this fourth cell. It is these facts, generated by observing the behavior of others, that make up our scientific knowledge of psychology.

But what about the subjective experiences of our subjects? Can't we study these subjective experiences *directly*? No! Unless you possess clairvoyant abilities (cell 2), direct study of the psychological processes of others is impossible. To resolve this impasse, modern psychology rarely even attempts to study psychological processes directly. *Instead, we study behavior not as an end in itself but as an indirect way of learning about the subjective experiences of our subjects.* That we use behavior to study subjective experience indirectly is an important idea. Consequently, it will be helpful to step back and discuss the idea at length.

BEHAVIOR: AN INROAD TO THE SUBJECTIVE EXPERIENCE OF SUBJECTS

As we mentioned in the preceding section, the only way we currently have to study empirically the psychological processes of others is to observe their behavior. Yet their behavior is not their subjective experience. We are faced with the crucial problem of how to make subjective psychological experiences observable so that we can use the scientific method to study them. The traditional way to resolve this impasse is to study the experiences and perceptions of subjects indirectly. We use objective behavior, which can be observed and studied by anyone, as a means of making indirect inferences about psychological experience and awareness. *Thus we use the overt behavior of our subjects to study indirectly their subjective world.*

By using this procedure, scientists have asked such questions as: Do pigeons see colors? Does test-taking anxiety improve or impair performance? Are dreams like daytime thinking? Do thoughts change the sensation of pain? What determines what you see? To better understand how scientists answer these and other questions, let us examine one problem in more detail.

Assume you want to know whether an animal sees colors. How would you go about it? You cannot directly experience what the animal experiences in the presence of color; you must find a method for asking the animal. You must accept that you can never scientifically answer the question directly, but you can answer indirectly. That is, you begin by reasoning how the animal's behavior would be different if it could see colors from how it would be if it could not. You could create a situation in which being able to experience color is necessary for the animal to solve a certain problem.

One way this problem has been approached by some psychologists is through the use of a Skinner box. A Skinner box is designed for use with small animals such as rats or pigeons; it contains a lever on one wall near a food dish. Most Skinner boxes are electrically automated so that a single press or a certain number of presses on the lever causes food to be dropped into the dish. You could program the delivery system in such a manner that the animal would receive food each time the lever was pressed when a green light was on. When either a blue light or no light was on, the animal would not receive food for pressing the lever. How do you think the animal would respond if it could see colors? How would it respond if it could not see colors? Let's look at the table at the top of the next page.

	COLOR LIGHT		
	Green	*Blue*	*Light off*
Food for lever press in each condition?	yes	no	no
Expected behavior if:			
-animal experiences color	?	?	?
-animal doesn't experience color	?	?	?

Imagine yourself as an animal for a second, and we think you will see how we could use the animal's behavior to tell us whether it can distinguish green from blue. If, as an animal, you could see colors, then you would soon learn to press the lever only when the green light was on and not to press the lever when either the blue light or no light was on. What if you could not see colors? When would you press the lever? You would probably quickly learn not to press the lever when no light was on. But what about when there was a green or blue light on? If you could not see colors, you would never distinguish between the blue and the green light. Thus you would probably press anytime either light was on. If we made systematic recordings of your behavior (lever pressing) over a period of time, we would be able to predict whether or not you could discriminate a blue light from a green one. We might then set up other discrimination problems (red versus blue, yellow versus green, and so forth). From this information, we could *infer* indirectly whether you could see colors. In solving this problem, we utilized two techniques for inferring the experience of our subjects. The first is to create a situation in which different behaviors require different experiences. The second technique is to imagine yourself as the subject and role-play the responses to gain an experiential perspective.

As you can see, the scientific study of experience rests on the assumption that the subject's behavior is a manifestation of what he or she is experiencing. If we are studying human emotions, we may assume that aggressive attacking behaviors are related in some way to an experience of anger in our subjects. In a similar way, if we are studying factors that facilitate the experience of joy in preschool children, we might use increased laughter as evidence that joyful experiences have actually taken place. In these cases we use the behavior of our subjects (aggressive attacks and laughter) to study their subjective experiences of anger and joy. Seen in this light, *behavior and experience are two sides of the same coin*. In the case of anger, for example, the subject's feeling of anger is the internal and unseen experiential aspect, and the subject's aggressive attacks are the external and observable behavioral aspects. In a preceding section, we saw Galen infer his patient's love for Pylades when he observed her behavioral and physiological reactions to his name. In a similar way, Semmelweis never saw a physician carrying germs into the delivery room. Indeed, at that time germs could not even be seen! Yet, using indirect evidence, Semmelweis was able to pinpoint the unobservable yet very real cause of the mothers' deaths.

This use of objective behavior to study subjective experience is by no means new to you. We are all very good at "reading" the psychological states of people from their behavior. If your professor walks into class with a scowl, you immediately assume he or she is experiencing some sort of negative emotion. Once again, notice how the way we scientifically study the subjective experiences of our subjects reflects the way we have been making inferences about the subjective experiences of other people since we were young children.

It should be stressed that the use of objective behavior and appearances to study indirectly unobservable phenomena, such as subjective experience, is not unique to psychology. It is a common feature of all sciences. For example, in physics we discuss the *construct* "gravity," yet we never see gravity. Instead, we observe the movement of objects toward the earth and make inferences about gravity. Nor do we study magnetism directly, but we do observe the movements of iron filings, iron bars, charged particles, and various types of gauges and make inferences about magnetism. A construct is merely a concept used in a particular theoretical manner that ties together a number of observations. In a nutshell, many major constructs of science such as gravity, time, evolution, electricity, genetic transmission, learning, and even life itself are discussed and examined indirectly through their manifestations in the physical world. Thus in science we use the observation of physical events to make inferences concerning not only the physical world but also the unseen processes that underlie them.

THE PEOPLE WHO DO SCIENCE (SOON TO BE YOU)

We want to remind you, as we did at the beginning of the chapter, that science is a human activity. A third meaning of this statement is that we do science with the support and communication of other scientists. Because a group of people shares our search and values, it is possible for scientists to work together as a larger body of searchers after truth. Sometimes scientists communicate with each other in almost a storybook manner, and new discoveries and formulations are the result of the work of many different individuals. At times, the opposite is the case. As if in a race, the individual scientist competes against other scientists and even against scientists as a group to be the first to make a discovery.

Remember, doing science is just one role or activity of the people who do science. Scientists are people, and as people they do what people everywhere do. They love and hate. They have good ideas and they have bad ideas. They have thoughts and feelings. Some may want attention and fame, and others may want to be left alone. Scientists feel lonely and sad as well as happy and gregarious. Science is not a means for avoiding what is human within us, although some scientists as well as persons who do not do science certainly do this. Science is merely a systematic way of using experience to test our ideas about the world.

At times in our history, we have forgotten that scientists are human. We have thought of scientists as *objective,* without feeling, and oblivious to the human condition in general and to what is going on around them in particular. To be sure, there have been instances when this sort of thing has happened. In these irresponsible persons, however, it is the failure of the witness and not of the scientist or the subject that is the basis of the problem. We will develop this idea further at a later time.

The message we wish to emphasize now is that in the final analysis, the human sensitivity of scientists adds life and spirit to the scientific enterprise. Thus, what is unique about science is not that it is performed by superhuman individuals in an all-out search for knowledge but almost the opposite. What is unique about science is not the individuals who are scientists, but the methods and the relationship of the people who do science with these methods.

SUMMARY

In this chapter we described the scientific approach to problem solving. We suggested that science surpasses the alternative methods of learning about ourselves by providing a fertile source of new ideas *and* a powerful method for evaluating these ideas. We reviewed several ways (based on the work of Charles Peirce) of deciding whether or not to accept new ideas. Tenacity, authority, reason, common sense, and science were all discussed, in terms of their strengths and weaknesses, as methods through which people accept new ideas. Because of its self-corrective nature derived from the application of direct sensory experience and reason, we argued that science is a very fruitful method of knowing about the world.

An overview of early scientific approaches followed. The stories of Croesus, Galen, and Semmelweis revealed some important issues and aspects of contemporary behavioral science. These issues include the need for unambiguous statements, the need for testing factors that do and do not affect behavior, and the importance of a carefully designed series of observations. We tried to stress that science combines experience, reason, and desire to answer questions about reality.

Empiricism, the traditional approach to psychology, was defined as the process of relying on direct sensory experience to verify ideas about reality. We suggested that outer appearances (behavior) as well as inner experiences are worthy of scientific exploration in psychology. Schumacher (1977) emphasized this issue in his discussion of the four possible fields of knowledge. One of these fields of knowledge involves facts generated by observing the behavior of others. This was earmarked as the domain of modern science in general and of psychology in particular. We concluded that the subjective world of our subjects can be studied indirectly by carefully observing their overt behaviors and drawing inferences from them. We further emphasized that what is unique about science is its methods and the relationship of the people who do science with these methods.

CHAPTER TWO

Introduction to the Methods of Science

INTRODUCTION

Most of us remember how different our first few weeks of college were from anything we had known before. Remember how you expected your roommate or your professors to act, and how you reacted when they did not act that way? If you stop and think about your first reactions to college, you can see that there were three aspects of these experiences. First, there was an idea or expectation concerning what was about to happen in college. Second, there was the actual experience of what did happen during those first few weeks, and it was probably quite different, at least in some respects, from what you had expected. Third, there was the resulting reorganization of your ideas about college and the potential impact of this experience on your life.

The methods of science closely parallel these three aspects of your experience. First, scientists begin with an idea or expectation. As you will learn, a formally stated expectation is called a *hypothesis*. The scientist simply says, "I expect this to happen under these conditions," and thus states the hypothesis. Second, scientists look to experience to evaluate the accuracy of their ideas or expectations about the world. That is, they try to find or create the situation that will allow them to observe what they are interested in studying. Through observation and experimentation, scientists can begin to evaluate their ideas and expectations about the world. As mentioned in Chapter 1, learning about the world through observation and experimentation is an example of *empiricism,* which means nothing more than accepting sensory information as valid. Third, based on their observations and experiments, scientists seek to draw conclusions or inferences about their ideas and expectations. They reorganize their ideas and consider the impact of the new information on their theoretical conceptualizations.

As mentioned earlier, science is simply a way of determining what the world is really like. In its simplest form, the scientific method consists of asking a question about the world and then experiencing the world to determine the answer. When we begin an inquiry, what we already know about our topic leaves us in one of two positions. In some cases, we know relatively little about our topic and, consequently, our ideas and questions are very general. For example, what causes mental illness? What factors make a fruitful marriage? If relatively little is known about a particular phenomenon, it is frequently useful simply to watch the phenomenon *occur* naturally and get a general feeling for what is involved by simply describing what naturally occurs. This scientific technique is called *naturalistic observation.* On the other hand, if we already know quite a bit about a given phenomenon, a general description of this sort would probably not add much new information. Instead, we would gain more by seeing how some single factor affects the phenomenon we are studying. To do this, we begin to interact with the phenomenon. *If I do this, what will happen?* For example, will a rat learn to press a lever faster if it is given food each time it presses or only on every fifth press? As our knowledge grows, we may even get to the point where we can formulate specific predictions. *If I do this, I bet this will happen!* These two scientific methods in which we interact directly with the phenomenon we are studying are examples of the *experimental method.*

Before we continue, we want to emphasize that there is no set number of methods for doing science. Methods are developed in response to specific questions. Often our area of study determines which methods we use. For example, in sciences such as astronomy and zoology, scientists often use *post hoc* (after the fact) methods; like Darwin, they might ask how a certain species came about. Clinical psychologists use similar methods when they speculate on the development of personality or the origin of mental illness. Other areas of psychology rely on single-subject approaches since the problem they are studying may be rare, such as a specific brain disorder. We will discuss these and other approaches to research later in this book. For the present we will focus on two main approaches to research: naturalistic observation and experimental manipulation. We do not want to leave you with the impression that these are the only two ways to organize research; that is not the case. However, these two approaches do use very different strategies for answering questions in science and thus it is informative to examine them in some detail.

Let us consider the relationship between the scientist and the subject in each of these methods. With the naturalistic method, it is the job of the scientist to be passive and observe carefully the activity of the subject. In this method, the scientist does not try to change the environment of the subject. The subject simply goes about its normal activity in its normal way and the scientist watches, preferably without his presence influencing the subject's behavior. In this way, the scientist gains a detailed description of some aspect of the subject's natural behavior. In contrast, when using the experimental method, the scientist is more active and the subject is restricted in activities. The scientist intentionally structures the situation so that she can study the effect of a particular factor on the subject's behavior.

If you have not noticed already, let us pause and remind you that each of these methods is a simple extension of the way a child explores its world. A common way children and scientists begin to explore a new phenomenon is first simply to watch it occur naturally for a while. As a second step, we continue to learn by beginning to interact with the phenomenon. Once we understand the relationship involved in a particular phenomenon, we can use it profitably in our everyday lives. It works for the child, and it works for scientists, too, although on a more complex level. Consequently, to provide you with a more accurate conception of how the scientific method is an extension of our everyday activities, we will examine two fundamental scientific strategies at this time: the *naturalistic observation* technique, which is akin to the child's observing a phenomenon, and the *experimental method,* which is akin to the child's interacting with the phenomenon to learn more about it. Let us now turn to a more detailed discussion of each method.

NATURALISTIC OBSERVATION

Imagine that it is 20,000 years in the future and you have been sent to a strange part of the galaxy to study a particular species that has been described by astronauts as "cultural apes." Assume you could arrive there and remain undetected. How would you go about your mission? . . . Right! Because you know virtually nothing about these cultural apes, the method of naturalistic observation would be an efficient way to get a general idea of what these alien beings are like.

As many others who have studied animals in the wild on nineteenth- and twentieth-century earth, you might set up a "blind" such that you would not be detected and observe the behavior of these aliens. Often with animals in the wild, scientists try to find a place where the animals come together, such as a watering hole, and set up an observation post near this place. After some preliminary observations, you find that these cultural apes come together every morning in large structures. Consequently, you set up your observation within one of these structures. Assuming you remain undetected, what would you do next?

The answer is simple yet deceptively difficult to do. *You just watch.* To just watch is difficult because it might be compared to watching a movic in a foreign language that you do not understand. It is easy to see that there are interactions between the actors in the movie, yet you can only guess what they mean. In the beginning, the most difficult part of just watching is not to guess constantly. Until you have observed a similar interaction repeatedly, you can easily color or even distort what you are seeing by your expectation that it is a certain way. After much observation, you may begin to notice certain patterns of behavior by the aliens. For example, they may say "hello" each time they meet and "good-bye" each time they leave each other. One hallmark of naturalistic observation is the discovery of patterns in the behaviors of different organisms.

An important part of the naturalistic technique is to record what you observe. At one time, the only method of recording was to reduce the observations to written notes or hand-drawn pictures, much in the same manner as Darwin did when he went to the Galapagos Islands. Today, however, we can record our observations on audio or video tape. Of course, individual scientists are still an important part of the process, since they select what will be recorded and thus determine the observations for later analysis.

Once we have observed many instances of the typical behavior of this alien species, we can withdraw from our observation post and begin to analyze our recorded observations. It is at this stage that we can begin to make summary statements that characterize the natural ongoing behavior of these aliens.

Coming down to earth, let's consider the work of one scientist who has used the naturalistic method in his research. Several years ago Nikolaas Tinbergen (who later received the Nobel Prize for his research) became interested in autistic children. Because little was known about the overall behavior of autistic children, Tinbergen began by using the *naturalistic observation* method and simply observed autistic children (Tinbergen & Tinbergen, 1972). Autistic children do not communicate with others. Often they just walk around making sounds to themselves or even literally hit their heads against a wall. As Tinbergen watched these children, he observed that there was a pattern to their abnormal behavior in that the behavior appeared most often when these children were in an unfamiliar social situation. Even a smile from a stranger might be followed by an attempt to withdraw from the situation. Tinbergen was also interested in how autistic children were different from normal children. To understand these differences, Tinbergen observed normal children and also children with varying degrees of autism. He found that there were different facial expressions displayed by the autistic children as compared with the normal ones. Thus, the naturalistic method offered a starting point for describing differences between autistic and normal children.

Another scientist who has utilized the naturalistic method of observation is Konrad Lorenz (Lorenz also received the Nobel Prize for his behavioral research). In the following passage, Lorenz (1952) describes the behavioral interactions in a colony of birds called jackdaws:

> A jackdaw sits feeding at the communal dish, a second bird approaches ponderously, in an attitude of self-display, with head proudly erected, whereupon the first visitor moves slightly to one side, but otherwise does not allow himself to be disturbed. Now comes a third bird, in a much more modest attitude which, surprisingly enough, puts the first bird to flight; the second, on the other hand, assumes a threatening pose, with his back feathers ruffled, attacks the latest comer and drives him from the spot.

Naturalistic Observation—Summary

In summary, there are four characteristics of this method. First, the idea of noninterference is of prime importance. It is the task of scientists using this method not to disrupt the process or flow of events that is going on before them. In this way we can see things as "they really are" without influencing the ongoing phenomenon. Second, this method emphasizes the invariants or patterns that exist in the world. For example, if you could observe yourself in a noninterfering manner, you might conclude that your moods vary with the time of day or with particular weather patterns or even with particular thoughts. Third, this method is most useful when we know relatively little about the subject of our investigation. It is most useful for observing the "big picture" and emphasizing a series of events, rather than isolated happenings. Fourth, the naturalistic method may not shed light on those factors that cause the behavior being observed. It provides a *description* of a phenomenon; it does not answer the causal question of why it happened. To determine causal relationships, we use the experimental method. This method emphasizes scientists' ability to manipulate important aspects of the topic under study. Through the manipulation, scientists are better able to understand and describe important aspects of our world.

EXPERIMENTAL METHOD

As we suggested, you already know a great deal about the experimental method. Indeed, each of us has used it in one form or another to explore our world since we were small children. From these early interactions, we expand our knowledge of the world by learning causal relationships about the world. The experimental method is a direct extension of this way of gaining knowledge about causal relationships. Like the child, the scientist begins to interact with the phenomenon he or she is studying: *If I do this, what will happen?* From these interactions, the scientist gains increased understanding of the phenomenon under study. To test this understanding further, the scientist asks: *Was what happened really because of what I did?*

To give you a more accurate feeling for how the scientist learns from interacting with the environment, consider the following line of fictitious research. Assume that the makers of a children's brand of cereal, which we will call Roasty-Toasties, want to claim that their cereal helps children to grow when it is eaten for breakfast. In their enthusiasm to demonstrate the claim and thus add "scientific evidence" to their television commercials, the company designed the following experiment. A group of children were given daily a bowl of Roasty-Toasties with cream, bananas, and sugar. After several months each child was weighed. It was found that they gained an average of eight pounds each. Obviously, the weight increase was due to the nourishing breakfast and, consequently, the company recommended this breakfast for all children. Well, what do you think? Do you see any problems? When a thoughtful scientist heard the results, he admitted to their appeal but added that he was confused about several things. One thing that bothered him quite a bit was that the children also ate lunch and dinner. Consequently, he pointed out, the weight gain may be due to the food eaten at these other meals.

Dismayed that they had not thought of that, the company designed a new experiment. This time it used two groups of children whose average

age and weight were the same. One group received the recommended cereal with cream, bananas, and sugar; the other was given scrambled eggs. Both groups ate approximately the same foods for lunch and dinner. Several months later each child was weighed. It was found that there was an average gain of five pounds in the group who received the recommended breakfast cereal and an average gain of only one pound for the children who ate eggs for breakfast. Needless to say, the company was excited and assailed our thoughtful scientist with the new findings confirming the earlier results. The scientist pointed out that he was even more impressed than before. However, he grew silent again, looked up, and meekly said, "Could the weight gain be due to the cream, sugar, and bananas and not to the revolutionary new cereal?" Although the company was confident that the results were due to the cereal, logically, the scientist was right. The entire effect could have been due to the cream, sugar, and bananas and not to the cereal.

Crushed by the scientist's keen insight, the company returned to the laboratory to plan its next experiment. After much debate, it decided to do the following experiment. As before, one group received the cereal with cream, sugar, and bananas for breakfast, but now another group received equal amounts of cream, sugar, and bananas each morning. Once again lunch and dinner were approximately the same for both groups, as were their weights at the onset of the study. The company was confident of replicating the earlier findings, so after several months they weighed each child. Much to their dismay, it was found that children in both groups gained five pounds. The group that received cereal did not gain more weight than the other group.

Definitions in the Experimental Method

The goal of the third study was to determine whether eating cereal affected the growth of a child. The *hypothesis* or idea being tested was that eating the new cereal causes growth. To test its hypothesis, the company gave its cereal to one group of children and not to a second group. The group that received the cereal was called the *experimental group*. The group that did not receive the cereal was called the *control group*. A control group is a group that is treated exactly like the experimental group except for being given the cereal. In this case, the control group was used to assess growth from all other possible factors *except* the cereal. The study can be characterized as in Table 2.1.

Table 2.1 Design of the Final Roasty-Toasties Study

	Pretreatment Weight (Before the Study)	*Treatment*	*Posttreatment Weight (After Treatment)*
Group 1 (experimental)	50 lb.	cereal with cream, bananas, and sugar	55 lb.
Group 2 (control)	50 lb.	cream, bananas, and sugar without cereal	55 lb.

In this experiment we are evaluating a cause-and-effect statement. If the hypothesis is correct, then we assume that the cereal is the cause and growth is the effect. If the hypothesis is incorrect, then the cereal is the cause and no growth is the effect.

In any experiment we must define the terms in the hypothesis so that it can be tested. To minimize possible confusion, the crucial terms in the hypothesis are clearly defined in reference to concrete operations. This sort of definition is called an *operational definition* and, as you will see, it forms a crucial link between our ideas and the world. Kerlinger (1973) suggests that there are two types of operational definitions. The first type relates to measurement and may specify both *how* observations are to be made and *what* is to be observed and measured. For example, in a study that measures anxiety during certain types of tasks, it would be necessary to define operationally how anxiety was measured. That is, did the anxiety score result from self-report measures, physiological measures such as heart rate, or observation of a specific behavior? The second type of operational definition refers to experimental manipulation. This type of operational definition describes how experimental procedures are to be followed. For example, in a study that examines the effects of praise on change in psychotherapy, it would be necessary to define operationally both what praise is and under what conditions it is to be given and withheld. In one sense operational definitions function like a recipe for a cook. In the same way that it would be difficult to follow a recipe that said only "heat eggs, milk, and flour," it would be impossible to understand an experiment that said only "anxiety hurts performance." For a complete understanding, it would be necessary to specify (that is, operationally define) what measure of anxiety was used and how the measurement of performance was made. Thus, one of the first tasks in developing a research study is to specify the operational definitions related to measurement and experimentation.

In the cereal experiment, the researchers had to define operationally both the eating of the cereal (suspected cause) and growth (suspected effect). The suspected causal agent in an experiment is called the *independent variable* or *treatment*. An independent variable is said to be "independent" because it is defined by the experimenter before the experiment begins and is thus completely independent of anything that happens during the experiment itself. In other words, in a possible causal relationship, the independent variable is seen to precede the suspected effect.

Turning now to the suspected effect, the aspect of the world that the experimenter feels will be affected by the independent variable is referred to as the *dependent variable*. The dependent variable gets its name because if a causal relationship does exist, its value will *depend* on or be caused by the independent variable. In the present experiment, the researchers hoped that growth would be enhanced by eating their new cereal. However, because there are many aspects of growth (physical maturation, height, weight, intellectual or emotional maturation), the task of deciding which aspect to measure is difficult. Notice that their final decision to define growth operationally in terms of weight is quite arbitrary and ignores other aspects of growth that might be evaluated.

The difference in the magnitude of the dependent variable for the control and experimental groups is called the *treatment effect*. The only difference between the experimental and control groups should be the independent variable or treatment. If we are certain of this, then any difference in the magnitude of the dependent variable is said to be due to or *caused* by the independent variable. If there is more than one difference between the two groups (two suspected causal factors or independent variables), then we would not know which is responsible for any treatment effects we may observe. (Note that there are more complex experimental designs, called *factorial designs,* that allow us to investigate the effects of two or more independent variables in the same experiment. This class of designs will be discussed in Chapter 7.)

If we suspect that some unintended causal factor may also be operating, then, as we mentioned earlier, the truth or validity of the experiment is seriously threatened and the entire experiment must be questioned. In the second experiment, the fact that the control group did not receive cream, bananas, and sugar constitutes a potential alternative explanation for the group's growth. Whenever two or more independent variables are operating, the unintended (those not chosen by the experimenter) independent variables are referred to as *confounding variables.* In the second experiment, the cream, sugar, and bananas were confounding variables.

Before we continue, we would like to clear up some confusion experienced by a number of people when the word *caused* is used. In psychology when we speak about an independent variable causing a change in the dependent variable, we mean that these two variables reflect a consistent association. That is, with every change in the independent variable, there comes a related and predictable change in the dependent variable. This means that the idea of causality in science is generally a conclusion or judgment made concerning the relationship between the independent and dependent variables. If research shows us that each time we change one aspect of a situation, then a predictable change follows in another aspect, we usually say that the first aspect caused a change in the second. If, as we repeat an experiment in varying situations and under different conditions, the same relationship between the independent variable and the dependent variable continues to hold true, then we have more confidence in our judgment of causation.

Another way to discuss causation is to see what conditions are required for the occurrence of an event. In particular, we discuss *necessary* and *sufficient* conditions. A necessary condition, as the name implies, is the situation that *must* occur. For example, it is necessary to be a woman to become pregnant. However, just being a woman does not make you pregnant. To do this, we must also show a *sufficient* condition. A sufficient condition is a condition that *can* occur, and when it does occur it always produces the effect. For example, we say that fertilization through intercorse is a sufficient condition for producing an embryo and that feeding milk to a child is a sufficient condition for producing growth. However, these may not be necessary conditions. For example, other substances fed to the child will also produce growth. Thus, if we were looking for *The Cause* of growth, we would reject the idea that milk causes growth, since the administration of milk does not represent both a necessary *and* a sufficient condition for growth. However, as we suggested earlier, when we use the word *cause,* we do not mean *The Cause*—the one and only cause—but rather the case in which two events (the independent and dependent variables) are systematically connected in a variety of situations. Thus, saying that milk causes growth is consistent with the way *cause* is used in science.

Uses of the Experimental Method

Having described the experimental method, it is important to emphasize that psychologists frequently use this method either more or less rigidly depending on how much they already know about the phenomenon they are studying and the types of questions they want to ask. In some cases, following an extensive library search for relevant information, a scientist may realize that almost nothing is known about a particular phenomenon and simply wonder what effect a given treatment will have on subjects' experience. Given this situation, the scientist can use the experimental method in either of two ways. First, when we really have no idea what the effect of the independent variables will be, we are sometimes content to give the experimental treatment to a single group of subjects and then informally observe the subjects to get some idea of what aspects of behavior were affected by the independent variable. This initial exploratory use of the experimental method is frequently employed in the initial stages of biofeedback experiments, psychotherapy research, and drug evaluation studies, for example. Strictly speaking, this way of gaining information is not an experiment because it does not involve a control group or test specific hypotheses. It is no more than a simple demonstration that may provide either (1) clues to fruitful independent variables for more refined analysis or (2) potential attributes of behavior that should be reflected in the future selection of dependent variables.

The second way we use the experimental method as an exploratory tool occurs when we have some idea which aspects of behavior will be affected by the independent variable and, consequently, have a reasonable idea what sort of dependent variables and control group(s) we should use. Yet we do not understand the phenomenon well enough to make a specific prediction. In this way, our understanding of the phenomenon is progressively refined by a more detailed search for causal factors (independent variables that produce treatment effects) and by a more accurate estimate of their influence (measured by the dependent variables) on the phenomenon under study.

At other times, when we actually know a great deal about a particular topic, we can move beyond the exploratory uses of the experimental method. In these cases we are able to formulate specific predictions that reflect a more detailed theoretical understanding of the phenomenon. Because we have a clearer understanding, we are able to *refine* our independent and dependent variables and our use of control groups so that we can more precisely isolate the causal relationships involved in our phenomenon.

Whether we use the method of naturalistic observation or the experimental method, the task before us is to make inferences about human experience from the behaviors we observe. These inferences are generally related back to our hypothesis or some larger theory we wish to evaluate. Thus, after we look to the world through these methods, we are faced with the task of deciding how to evaluate new information we receive in the light of both the methods used and our theoretical perspective. To accomplish this task, we use reason and logic. In particular we ask whether the results of our methods as well as our conclusion are valid. In the next section we will focus on the question of validity and differentiate among some common types of validity. We will also summarize briefly the structure of propositional logic. We present this discussion to aid you as you begin to evaluate your own research and that of others.

LOGIC AND INFERENCE: THE DETECTIVE WORK OF SCIENCE

Perhaps you have heard the story of our friend from Boston who got up every morning, walked outside his house, walked around in a circle three times, and yelled at the top of his voice. His neighbors, being somewhat curious after days of this ritual, asked the purpose behind his strange behavior. The man answered with some certainty that the purpose was to keep away tigers. "But," the neighbor replied quite frankly, "there are no tigers within thousands of miles of here." To which our friend replied, "Works quite well, doesn't it?"

Consider this story for a moment. What is wrong with our friend's method for keeping away tigers? It works, doesn't it? Why not? How could we demonstrate to our friend that his yelling is not causally related to the absence of tigers? One strategy might be to point out that the absence of tigers might have come about for other reasons, including that there are no tigers roaming in the greater Boston area. In technical terms we would say that the absence of tigers was a *necessary* condition but not a *sufficient* condition for showing that yelling *caused* the tigers to stay away. Our friend's reasoning was insufficient because it left many other plausible explanations of the obvious absence of tigers unevaluated.

Logic is particularly important in science as an aid to answering the question: What question should my experimental study answer to test my ideas about the world? That is, logic can help us to answer questions of *inference*. Inference refers to the process by which we look at the evidence available to us and then use our powers of reasoning to reach a conclusion. Like Sherlock Holmes engaged in a mystery, we attempt to solve a problem based on the available evidence. Did the butler do it? No, the butler could not have done it because there was blond hair on the knife and the butler had black hair. But perhaps the butler left the blond hair there to fool us. Like a detective, scientists try to determine other factors that may be responsible for the outcome of their experiment or to piece together available information and draw general conclusions about the world. Also, like the detective, the scientist is constantly asking: Given these clues, what inference can I make and is the inference valid? Logic is one method for answering these questions.

Validity

Logical procedures are also important for helping us to understand the accuracy or *validity* of our ideas and research. Validity means true and capable of being supported. In psychological research we are particularly interested in two general types of validity (Campbell & Stanley, 1963). The first is *internal validity*. The word *internal* refers to the experiment itself. Internal validity asks the question: Is there another reason that might be used to explain the outcome of our experimental procedures? Students are particularly sensitive to questions of internal validity when it is time for final exams. They are able to make a number of alternative suggestions as to what the test actually measures and why it does not measure their knowledge of a particular subject. Like students, scientists look for reasons (threats to internal validity) why a particular piece of research does not measure what it claims to measure. In the case of our friend from Boston, the absence of tigers near his house could have reflected a long-standing absence of tigers in his part of the world rather than the effectiveness of his yelling.

The second type of validity is *external validity*. External validity refers to whether a particular set of research results can be applied in another setting. This is often called *generalizability*. Remember the story of Semmelweis. His finding that the deaths of the mothers was the result of the physicians handling diseased tissue was true not only for his hospital but for all other hospitals as well. Thus, in answering the question of external validity for the work of Semmelweis, we would conclude that his answers could be generalized to other hospitals with other women and not just to his own original setting. Now consider the story of Galen. We would not fault his research concerning why the woman did not sleep, but we would say that it lacked external validity or generalizability. Although the insomnia of one particular woman was due to a particular male dancer, it is not true that all people who suffer from insomnia react to male dancers, nor are they all in love. In summary, internal validity refers to the internal consistency or logic of the experiment that allows for the results to be meaningful. External validity, on the other hand, refers to whether or not the results from an internally valid experiment can be applied in other situations and with other subjects.

We logically design our research to rule out as many alternative interpretations of our findings as possible and to have any new facts be applicable to as wide a variety of other situations as possible. Unfortunately, in many real-life situations where external validity is high, it is impossible to rule out alternative interpretations of our findings. In a similar way, in laboratory settings where internal validity is high, the setting is often artificial and in many cases our findings cannot be generalized beyond the laboratory. Consequently, in designing and conducting research, one goal is to maximize *both* internal and external validity. In the next section we will introduce you to propositional logic. However, before you begin this section, we suggest that you try to solve the problem presented in Box 2.1. The problem relies on logical approaches you will learn about in the next section.

Propositional Logic

In the previous section, we introduced the terms *internal* and *external validity* and emphasized the scientist's attempt to rule out alternative explanations. In this section, we will emphasize the way in which a scientist relies on the rules of formal logic to both *deduce* and *induce* valid conclusions. As a starting point, keep in mind that deduction (to deduce) is the process by which one moves from a general theory to particular data, whereas induction (to induce) is the process by which one moves from a particular set of data to a general theory or concept.

If one were to begin with the premise and from this *deduce* the consequences, this would be called the *deductive* approach to knowledge. One uses deductive reasoning when saying, "If it is true that schizophrenia is genetically determined, then we should find greater similarity in the existence of the disorder (either presence or absence) between twins than between strangers." On the other hand, if one were to begin with the consequent and then *induce* the premise, this would be called *inductive* reasoning. Inductive reasoning might be of the form: "I just saw a monkey use sign language and ask me for food; therefore, it is true that monkeys can communicate with humans." In summary, deductive reasoning goes from theory (the premise) to data (the consequent), whereas inductive reasoning goes from data (the consequent) to the theory (the premise).

Suppose a friend said to you, "You know, all experimental textbooks are really dull." You might respond, "That's not true, I am reading one right now that is really interesting." (Well, what did you expect we would have you say?) In terms of logic, you were showing your friend a simple way to disprove the statement "All experimental textbooks are really dull." That is, by finding an exception to a statement, you can show it to be false.

Let's look at this procedure in a formal way. You begin with a premise—"All experimental textbooks are really dull." From this premise, a

---

Box 2.1 Think Square

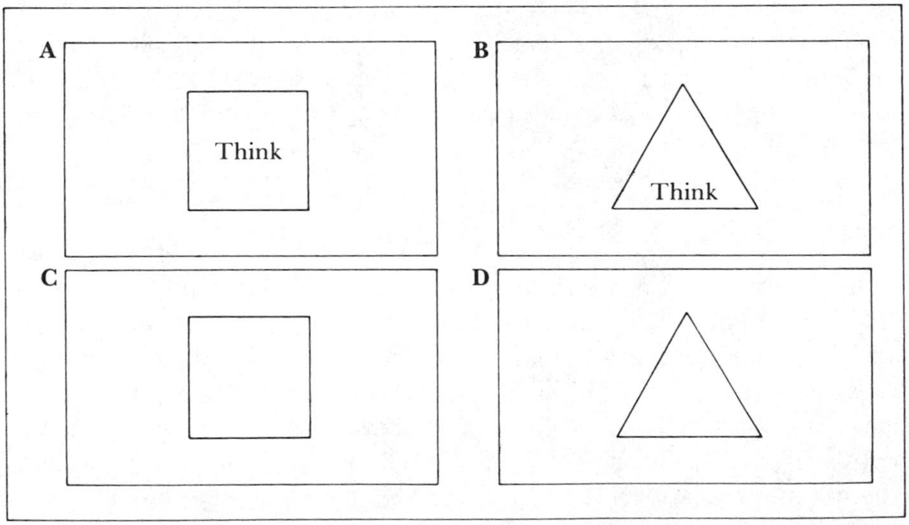

Assume that there are four cards. Each has a square with or without the word "think" on one side and a triangle with or without "think" on the other side. Which of the

---

After Wason (1977).

logical consequence follows. The consequence would be that given an experimental textbook, it would be really dull.

Technically, this type of reasoning is referred to as *confirmatory reasoning* or *modus ponens.* Confirmatory reasoning is nothing more than a true premise leading to a true consequent. This is abbreviated as: If p, then q (if the premise, then the consequent). Suppose we have an instance where q is correct; what does this say about p? That is, if I can find a single experimental textbook that is dull, does that demonstrate the truth of the statement "All experimental textbooks are dull"? The answer is, of course not, because there may be other experimental textbooks that are exciting! Technically this type of reverse confirmatory reasoning is referred to as *affirming the consequent.* Although it is an invalid form of logic, one sees it used almost daily. The cartoon on p. 43 offers one example of this form of reasoning. Consider another example. A person may tell you a story about how she knows someone who is more than 100 years of age and meditates. Therefore, she concludes that meditating makes you live longer. This is an

---

cards would you have to turn over to determine whether EVERY CARD THAT HAS A *THINK* SQUARE ON ONE SIDE HAS A TRIANGLE WITHOUT *THINK* ON THE OTHER?

We will make a prediction based on previous experience that you chose cards A and D. You may be in good company since many people choose these cards, but you were wrong. However, you were right when you chose card A. As you correctly reasoned, card A must have a triangle without "think" on the other side for the statement to be true. However, if you turn over card D, which we did when we first tried the problem, you missed the point of the statement. The statement talks about what is opposite a "think" square and says nothing about what is opposite a triangle. The other card that we needed to turn over to solve the problem was card B. We needed to demonstrate that the negative of the statement was not true; that is, we needed to demonstrate that there was not a "think" square with a "think" triangle on the other side. Still confused?

We begin with the premise that all "think" squares have empty triangles on the other side, which we sought to test. We then move to the real situation in which there are four cards. In these four cards we see a "think" square and thus can test the truth of the statement just by turning it over. Now comes the problem. We have tested all the "think" squares (card A), so what do we do next? If it is true that all "think" squares have empty triangles on the other side, then it must also be true that no card with a "think" triangle has a "think" square on the other side. Once we realize this, we know that we must look at card B and test this assumption. Thus the correct answer is cards A and B.

invalid argument of logic, since any single case does not prove that the same is true for an entire group. The premise may indeed be correct in the real world, but we cannot make that conclusion logically from single cases. We believe this point is so important that we will repeat it. It is an invalid form of logic to conclude from a true consequent that the premise is true. If you begin with the idea that beer makes you creative and attempt to prove this by finding a creative person who drinks beer, then you have produced an invalid argument referred to as *affirming the consequent.* As you think about this, you should be able to see that a single study can never *prove* any theory. Research results may support (that is, not refute) a theory, but they cannot prove it (show the theory to be logically true).

Let us take another situation in which the premise is shown to be incorrect. What can we conclude from this? Someone might say that if we show the premise "All experimental textbooks are dull" to be false, then it follows that all experimental textbooks are not dull. Right? Wrong! It might turn out that some textbooks are dull and some are not. Thus a false premise does not necessarily lead to a false consequent; that is, if p is not true, it does not follow that q is not true also. To reason in this way is invalid and referred to technically as *denying the antecedent.* Although this is invalid logic, we still hear individuals suggesting that since Carl Rogers's theory (or Fritz Perls's or B. F. Skinner's or Sigmund Freud's) has been shown to be incorrect, then the therapy is not effective. His therapy may be very effective but just not for the theoretical reasons he suggested.

This brings us to the last situation where we have a false consequent. What does this have to say about the premise (if q is not true, then p is ?)? If q is not true, then p is also not true. In our example, if we can find one experimental textbook that is not dull, then it is not true that "All experimental textbooks are dull." This is a valid form of argument and is referred to technically as *disconfirmatory reasoning* or *modus tollens.* To see how *modus tollens* reasoning might be applied to testing scientific theories, read Box 2.2.

To summarize, we discussed four forms of propositional logic of the form "if p, then q" where p is the premise and q is the consequent. These four forms are presented in Table 2.2.

Having presented logical inference in its ideal form, we want to remind you that logic is a tool of the scientist. Like the experimental method, logic is an approach to knowledge designed to help us evaluate and direct our research questions. Because of the complexity of the world in which we live and the limits of our own minds to perceive this complexity precisely,

Table 2.2 Forms of Propositional Logic

1. A true premise leads to a true consequent and is called *confirmatory* (modus ponens).
   Example: If "All species are shaped by evolution" is true, then humans (a species) are shaped by evolution.
2. A false premise *does not* lead to a false consequent, and to argue so is a mistake called *denying the antecedent.*
   Example: If "All people are sexually motivated" is false, it does not mean that no one is sexually motivated.
3. A true consequent *does not* lead to a true premise, and to argue so is a mistake called *affirming the consequent.*
   Example: If behavior therapy works in a given case, it does not follow that the theory of behavior therapy is true.
4. A false consequent does lead to a false premise and is called *disconfirmatory* (modus tollens).
   Example: If there is one person over 65 who is productive, then the premise "no one over 65 is productive" is false.

we find ourselves as scientists using a combination of both inductive and deductive approaches to knowledge in our science as well as in our lives. We often use deductive and inductive approaches as a means of gaining information, which becomes a clue as we attempt to interact with and understand the world in which we live. Logic offers us a means of evaluating the inferences we draw from these clues. Logic helps us to understand the limits to our claims of certitude. Quite often logic helps us to see that we do not know enough to make any claim. In this manner logic tends to make the scientific process conservative in its claims. It does not follow that our research topics, our ideas, or our theories also need to be conservative, however.

SCIENTIFIC OBSERVATION: THE RAW DATA OF SCIENCE

Have you ever heard the question: If a tree fell in the middle of the forest without anyone around, would there be any sound? This question reflects a philosophical problem in science that was solved in physics at the beginning of this century. Until that time, the notion of physicists was that they study *events* in the world. The job of the scientist in this earlier world view was to be the passive observer and accurately watch events that take place either in the real world or in experiments. There was no thought that the process of observing might influence the perception of the very events being observed.

According to modern physics, scientists do not record events. Instead, scientists record their *observations* of events. They record their experience of the world and consequently base their science on these perceptions. This development amounts to a simple acceptance of the fact that in science we can get no closer to the world than our observations of it.

Let's return for a moment to the child who is discovering the world for the first time. Imagine for a moment that you are that small child who is still crawling and cannot stand up yet. As you go around your world, what do you see? What do you know about objects and events that take place

---

Box 2.2 Philosophy of Science: Sir Karl Popper (Falsification Approach)

Popper has devoted much of his career to answering the questions: What is science? and How is science performed? Although these questions may at first seem easy to you, consider such areas as astrology and Marxism. Could these approaches be considered scientific? Why not?

Falsificationism is the name given to Popper's description of how science is performed. Falsificationism suggests that science should be concerned with disproving or falsifying theories through logic based on observation. How is this accomplished? First, a scientist must create a consistent falsifiable hypothesis. A falsifiable hypothesis is one that can be shown to be false. For example, the hypothesis "It will rain in Tuscaloosa, Alabama, on Tuesday, December 23, 1997" is a testable hypothesis. Likewise the hypothesis "All objects regardless of weight will fall to earth at approximately the same speed" is a testable hypothesis. However, a hypothesis such as "ESP (extrasensory perception) exists" is an untestable hypothesis. Even the hypothesis "Gravity exists" is untestable. It may be true that both ESP and gravity exist, yet until the hypothesis is stated in a form that can be falsified, the hypothesis is not testable. Second, once a scientist has a falsifiable hypothesis, the task is to develop a test of the hypothesis. Third, the hypothesis is tested. Fourth, if the hypothesis is shown to be false, a new bold hypothesis is developed.

Using this model of science, Popper emphasizes science as a process for the elimination of false theories. You may also compare Popper's model for science with the discussion on propositional logic presented in Chapter 2 as well as with Box 2.1 on problem solving. If you study the section on logic and accept the suggestion that all psychological research is inductive in nature, you must then conclude with Popper that the major role of science is the falsification of incorrect theories. This line of reasoning also leads one to conclude that science, particularly psychology, never *proves* a hypothesis. Science, according to Popper, only shows that the hypothesis is not false.

Note: Although the falsification position is the way Popper is usually discussed, his recent writings emphasize research programs rather than single theories.

"IT MUST BE ACUPUNCTURE. MY TOOTHACHE IS GONE."

more than three feet above the ground? Some events you may know by their sound, like a passing car or your father's electric razor. Other events you may recognize only by smell, like the cooking of bacon or the bleach being added to the wash. Other events you could know only from the sensation involved, such as your father or mother picking you up and throwing you in the air and catching you. Suppose someone could talk with you at this age and asked you to describe what the world was like, how would you do it? What would you say? How would the adult that you were talking to react to your description? Would she say it was a true, accurate, and acceptable view of the world?

As you begin to answer these questions, you see that your description as a child was from your own perspective. You may also realize that it is difficult to say whether this account was true or false. From your viewpoint

---

Box 2.3 Philosophy of Science: Thomas Kuhn

When Newton said, "I stand on the shoulders of giants," he was referring to those individuals who came before him and on whose work he was able to build his scientific system. Many of us have similar ideas when it comes to the progression of science. We think that each new discovery is simply added to old discoveries with the result being a gradual accumulation of knowledge.

In 1962, Thomas Kuhn suggested that this view is wrong. Kuhn proposed that science actually goes through a series of revolutions. Following each revolution, a new system or method for performing science is instituted. The new system or world view is referred to as a *paradigm* or set of assumptions, which guide scientific activity until a new revolution and paradigm shift take place. The stable period between revolutions is referred to as *normal science.* Normal science is the process of problem solving, which most of us think of when someone uses the term *science.* Normal science for Kuhn is always science performed in relation to a particular paradigm.

As an example of the role of paradigms, assume you were a map maker before the time of Columbus. You would draw your maps as if the world were flat, since that was the accepted belief. You, as a map maker, would never think to question this belief; it was a given in your task of drawing maps. Then in the Middle Ages, there was the map maker's version of a scientific revolution. The paradigm shifted to that of a world that was round. As a map maker, you would now draw the world as if it were round and you would continue with this system until a new revolution came along. This, of course, was the replacing of the earth as the center of the universe with the sun as the center. In the same way that map makers work in relation to present-day assumptions and beliefs about the world, Kuhn suggests that scientists also work in relation to a set of beliefs or paradigms until these are replaced by a revolution.

---

as an adult, it was incomplete. In the same way that the view of a child's world is relative to where and when the child lives and observes the world, the view of the scientist and consequently the *facts* of science are *relative* to the current notions of working scientists and the instruments they use to make observations (see Box 2.3). The current notions concerning science and accepted methods, which encompass a philosophical way of seeing the world, are referred to as a *paradigm*. Although there is much debate as to the exact meaning of the word *paradigm,* most scientists understand it to mean shared beliefs, which include topics to be studied and the types of answers that will be given. For example, the current scientific paradigm in psychology emphasizes the importance of quantitative measurement. Thus scientific psychology, as you will learn it, directs you toward topics that can be measured quantitatively.

Not only are the results and conclusions of our research relative to our current notions of science, but they may also relate to our own psychology. Consider the role of the experimenter (soon to be you) in the psychological experiment. Do you think your own state (hungry, sad, tired, excited, and so forth) could influence the data of an experiment? That is just one of the factors we will consider later in this book. The important point now is to realize that the state of the experimenter is relative and important. Since the scientist is not passive but is *actively* searching for answers, then he or she can actually influence the event being recorded by the very manner in which the observation is being made. Although you may not fully realize it yet, the scientist can actually change the world and our understanding of it. Thus, the scientist is more than a passive observer; he or she is a real actor in the drama of science.

EVALUATING SCIENTIFIC RESEARCH

Regardless of the amount of work involved in scientific research, an extremely important aspect of *any* research endeavor is whether or not the final product is worthy of being reported to the scientific community. We must ask whether our conclusions are *accurate,* whether they are capable of being *replicated,* and whether they have *relevance* to others. In this book we will emphasize four ways to ensure the high quality of our research. The first is through impartial systematic observation using logically sound experimental design. Since the experimental method is the most powerful class of research design presently available, we will emphasize this technique in the initial chapters of this book and later discuss some other scientific approaches. The second way we ensure meaningful research is through statistical description and inference. We will show you how statistics help us decide whether our results are due to some causal agent or merely to chance. The third method of quality control is through reason and logic. In discussing logic, we will emphasize types of validity as well as types of propositional logic and how they help us evaluate research. The fourth and final way is by emphasizing perspective and context. In particular we will suggest that you view your conclusions from the perspectives of the scientist, the subject, and the witness. Although this book emphasizes the perspective of the scientist, it is important to remember the experiences of the subject as well as the perspective of the witness if our conclusions are to have meaning. We believe that through these four ways of evaluating research you can come to understand science and maintain the high level of excellence that a science of behavior and experience requires.

COMMUNICATION IN SCIENCE

Unlike the child who is busy learning about the world, the scientist must share what he learns about the world with other people, especially other scientists. More than 2,000 years ago, Aristotle emphasized this when he taught that science had two parts: inquiry and argument. In modern terms, inquiry is represented by the research itself, which answers our questions about the world, and argument refers in part to the scientist's responsibility to inform others of his findings. Consequently, we design our research, record our observations, and summarize our findings in a manner that others can understand. For a scientist to answer a question only in terms that she can understand would not be complete science because it is not shared knowledge. The final product of mature science is and has always been a communication that summarizes a conclusion about the world and is directed to both scientists and nonscientists.

Learning to communicate in science may be compared to learning a foreign language. One of your first tasks is to learn the vocabulary of science. You need to understand what a scientist means by a certain word. Initially, you may say that is easy since most scientists speak English anyway. That may be true, but it can also be a problem since English words have slightly different or even totally different meanings when used in the context of a scientific statement. For example, suppose you were reading a newspaper article concerning a new discovery in subatomic physics. The article is about particles with "color" and "charm." If you were to talk to a physicist, you would find that "color" and "charm" have nothing to do with colors or with the particles being appealing. These words have special meaning for the physicist. Likewise in psychology, common words may be used in a special or technical way. For example, B. F. Skinner discusses "negative reinforcements" as applied to people, yet "negative reinforcements" have nothing to do with punishment as many people think. Likewise, Carl Jung invented the words "extrovert" and "introvert," which have a technical meaning very different from the way they are used in newspapers and magazines. Even as common a word as "sex" was used scientifically by Freud in a manner almost as different as the terms "color" and "charm" are used by the physicists. Sound confusing? At first the language of science may seem strange. Yet, as with any language, once you learn some words and phrases, you can begin to understand what is going on. This understanding will be useful not only to those of you who pursue careers as scientists, but also to all of us in our daily interactions with the world as we try to understand what we read about science and strive to become more educated consumers. The point to be made is that you have in front of you a twofold task. First, you must seek to understand how words are used in research in a technical way. You cannot just assume that because you have heard the word you must know its meaning. Second, in your own report writing you must seek to define your words and ideas in as precise a way as possible such that others can understand and follow what you are saying.

SUMMARY

In this chapter we emphasized that scientists have various methods available for making decisions and evaluating their ideas. Initially, we discussed the method of naturalistic observation as a means of observing and learning about the world. We then emphasized the experimental method as a way of achieving control over a situation and determining causal relationships between variables. Whatever method of science we use to generate new facts, we are always faced with the question of validity. In research we are interested in two types of validity—internal and external. Internal validity refers to the question of whether or not there are alternative explanations such as confounding variables that might lead us to suspect that our inferences are faulty. External validity involves the generalizability of our findings; that is, would similar results be found using other subjects with different experimenters in other locations? At this point we introduced propositional logic as a tool the scientist can use in deductive and inductive reasoning.

We again emphasized that science as we know it reflects a history of the observations of events that take place in the world. Since it is a record of observations, it is important that we be sensitive to the factors that can influence this record. Some of these will be discussed later in the book. As an analogy we reminded you of the world as seen through the eyes of a child. Although scientists are no longer children, they still see the world from a certain perspective, which is generally called a paradigm. Unlike the child, however, scientists have agreed to describe their observations of the world formally in scientific publications. We thus ended the chapter by stressing the importance of clear communication and precise language in science.

CHAPTER THREE

Description of Behavior through Numerical Representation

INTRODUCTION

Behavior can be described in many ways. In naturalistic observation studies, descriptions may consist of simple lists of behaviors or behavior sequences. An ethologist, for example, might describe the detailed movements in the feeding behavior of some common fish. In experimental studies, behaviors are usually expressed in more quantitative terms. Some examples of these measurements are the number of millimeters an observer overestimates the length of a line in a visual illusion experiment, the number of words recalled in a memory experiment, the change in heart rate experienced from watching an emotionally laden film, and the results of an IQ test taken under different conditions.

SCALES OF MEASUREMENT

Unlike a rose, a number is not always a number. A number may be used in a variety of ways. Sometimes numbers are used to identify particular objects or events, as when a friend tells you she lives at 45 Glenn Road. Sometimes numbers are used to mean "more than," as when a child says that a bike must cost a million dollars more than a candy bar. We adults do the same thing when we tell someone that we woke up in the middle of the night and stayed awake for hours. Numbers can also be used to specify an exact relationship or unit of measure. We know that twenty-five cents is half of fifty cents and that the difference between seventy degrees and ninety degrees is the same as the difference between thirty degrees and fifty degrees. Thus, a given number may convey different types of information depending on how it is used. The type of information a number conveys also determines how that number may be used mathematically.

The most common way of classifying the type of information that a number conveys is through scales of measurement. There are four basic scales of measurement: *nominal, ordinal, interval,* and *ratio.* These scales correspond to four properties of our number system. These properties are identity, magnitude, equal intervals, and an absolute zero point. These basic properties are identified with each of the four scales in Table 3.1, which we will expand upon in this section.

Nominal Measurement

Nominal (sometimes called *categorical*) measurement occurs when subjects are simply placed into different categories. This form of measurement is a

Table 3.1 Scales of Measurement

Levels	*Mathematical Operations*	*Mathematical Properties*	*Examples*
Nominal	None	Identity	Phone numbers, numbers on uniforms, races, brands of soup, employment statuses, diagnostic categories (schizophrenic, paranoid, neurotic, etc.)
Ordinal	None	Identity, magnitude	Class standing, weekly college football polls
Interval	Addition, subtraction	Identity, magnitude, equal intervals	Temperature (Fahrenheit or Celsius), scores on intelligence tests, scores on personality adjustment inventories
Ratio	Addition, subtraction, multiplication, division	Identity, magnitude, equal intervals, absolute zero point	Length, weight, time, reaction time, number of responses made by a subject

classifying or naming activity, which is the origin of the term *nominal.* For example, you can classify your subjects as men or women, as right-handed or left-handed, as liberal or conservative. The differences between categories are of kind (qualitative) and not of degree (quantitative). In many research problems, it is sufficient to determine simply whether the number of individuals in a given category varies as a function of some treatment in which you are interested. For example, you might want to determine whether the percentage of people willing to try a new product is altered by a particular type of advertising. In this example, your behavioral measure would simply be whether or not an individual is willing to try a new product. Numbers can sometimes be used as nominal categories. For example, the numbers on baseball jerseys, telephone numbers, and zip codes illustrate nominal uses of numbers. Notice that numbers used in nominal measurement have no mathematical properties other than providing categories. For example, it does not make sense to say that the first baseman on the baseball team is twice as good as the second baseman simply because their uniform numbers are 14 and 7, respectively.

Ordinal Measurement

In the case of ordinal measurement, there is usually a single continuum that underlies a particular classification system. College football standings, pop charts, and class standings are widely used examples of ordinal measurement. In a psychological experiment, you may divide your subjects on the basis of creativity and end up with three categories: noncreative, creative, and highly creative, which can be given the values 1, 2, and 3. These scores reflect an underlying continuum: the *relative amount* or *magnitude* of creativity. An ordinal scale represents some degree of quantitative difference, whereas a nominal scale does not. Ordinal scales can be obtained whenever you rank subjects or events along a single dimension. With ordinal measures, you are making statements only about order; the differences between consecutive values are not necessarily equal. Notice that numbers used in ordinal measurement have no mathematical properties other than providing categories and rank. Nothing is implied about the intervals between the categories. For example, in the case of the top 20 ranked football teams, there is no assumption that the difference in excellence between the number 1 and 4 football teams is the same as that between the number 6 and 9 football teams. Furthermore, it does not make sense to say that the number 1 and 4 teams equal the number 2 and 3 teams.

Interval Measurement

For interval data, the scale values are related by a single, underlying quantitative dimension (like ordinal data) and *also* there are *equal* intervals between consecutive scale values. Equal intervals mean that there are equal amounts of the quantity being measured between every two successive numbers on the scale. Thus, on an interval scale, the interval between 1 and 4 equals the interval between 6 and 9. The household thermometer is an example of an interval scale. The degree lines are equal distances apart and, consequently, reflect equal volumes of mercury so that the difference between twenty degrees and forty degrees is equivalent to the difference between fifty degrees and seventy degrees.

Because interval measurement is based on equal units, it provides more information than do either ordinal or nominal measurements. Furthermore, it is amenable to a wide variety of mathematical operations not permitted with nominal and ordinal measures. For example, the arithmetic mean can be computed for interval data. Thus, it makes sense to compare the mean temperatures in Atlanta and Portland, whereas a mean involving ordinal data simply does not make sense.

Ratio Measurement

For ratio data, scores are related by a single quantitative dimension (like interval or ordinal); they are also separated by equal intervals (like interval) *and* there is an absolute zero. The most common ratio scales are found in the measurement of the physical attributes of objects, such as weight or length. There is no length shorter than zero inches, no weight lighter than zero pounds. Simple reaction time is one example of a ratio scale. Ratio measurement permits all the numerical properties, and with this type of data we can do the greatest number of mathematical manipulations (addition, subtraction, multiplication, and division). Thus, with a ratio scale it makes sense to say that a subject with a reaction time of one second responded twice as fast as a subject with a two-second reaction time. However, with an interval scale it does not make sense to say, for example, that sixty degrees is twice as warm as thirty degrees.

When confronted with the actual task of deciding what sort of measurement best characterizes your data, don't panic! It is easy to spot nominal data becausc one can readily determine whether the categories are quantitatively related or not. Furthermore, for our purpose, it usually does not matter whether a given set of data is ratio or interval. The occasionally hard decisions involve whether the data are ordinal or interval. For example, scores on questionnaires or intelligence tests are frequently viewed as either interval or ordinal data because it is usually not clear whether equal intervals are involved.

PICTORIAL DESCRIPTION OF FREQUENCY INFORMATION

Frequency Distribution

A useful way to begin analyzing the results of any experiment is to convert your numerical data to pictorial form and then simply look at it. One way to depict the results of an experiment is to draw a frequency distribution; that is, simply plot how frequently each score appears in your data. Suppose you were interested in dreaming. One initial baseline measurement might be to ask twenty subjects to write down their dreams for a week. To get an idea of how often people dream, you might begin your analysis by seeing how many dreams each subject recalled. Table 3.2 shows the number of dreams each subject remembered dreaming.

Table 3.2 Hypothetical Dream Study

Subject	*Number of Dreams Recalled*	*Subject*	*Number of Dreams Recalled*
1	1	11	7
2	4	12	1
3	5	13	2
4	2	14	5
5	0	15	6
6	2	16	5
7	0	17	2
8	6	18	6
9	1	19	7
10	3	20	5

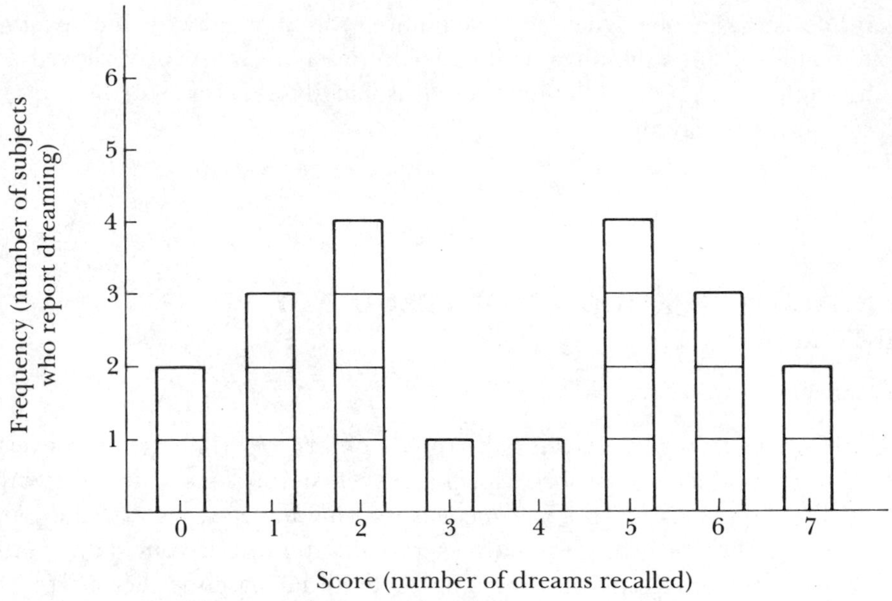

Figure 3.1 Bar graph of dream data.

Figure 3.1 shows a frequency distribution for these data. The vertical or y-axis (ordinate) labeled *frequency* is the number of subjects who fall into each category, and the horizontal or x-axis (abscissa) is the number of dreams recalled. This type of graph is referred to as a *bar graph.*

In Figure 3.1, the two blocks above a 0 score mean that two people reported no dreams during the entire week. Thus, we simply count squares and learn that three people reported only one dream, four people reported two dreams, and so forth. Since the measurements along the x-axis may be treated as interval data, we could also present them in the form of a *frequency polygon.* A frequency polygon of the dream data is presented in Figure 3.2.

Upon closer inspection, it appears that measurements from most subjects tended to be clustered either to the left or to the right on the x-axis. This means that for these twenty subjects at least, dreams were recalled either relatively infrequently (one or two dreams) or relatively often (five, six, or seven dreams). This particular type of distribution, in which the subjects tend to fall into two groups, is called a *bimodal distribution.*

Some common types of distributions you might encounter are illustrated in Figure 3.3.

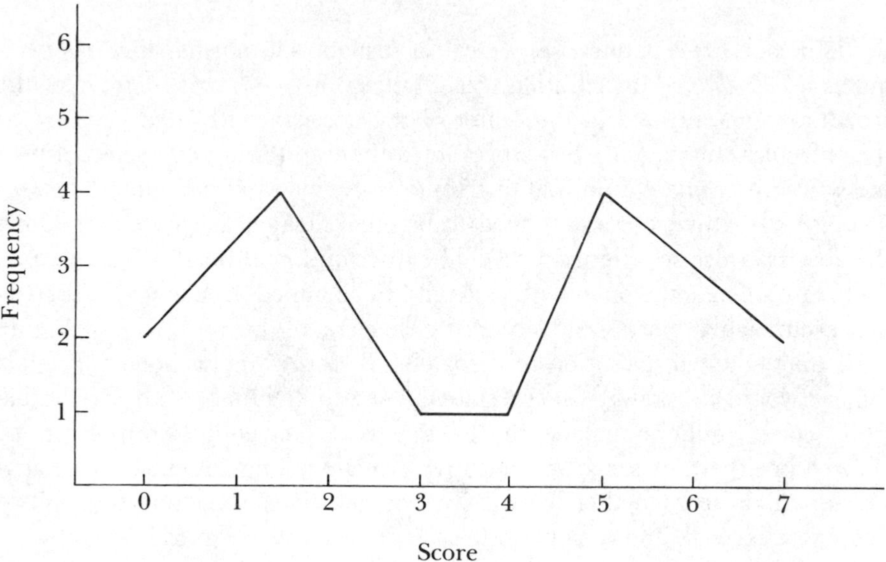

Figure 3.2 Frequency polygon of dream data.

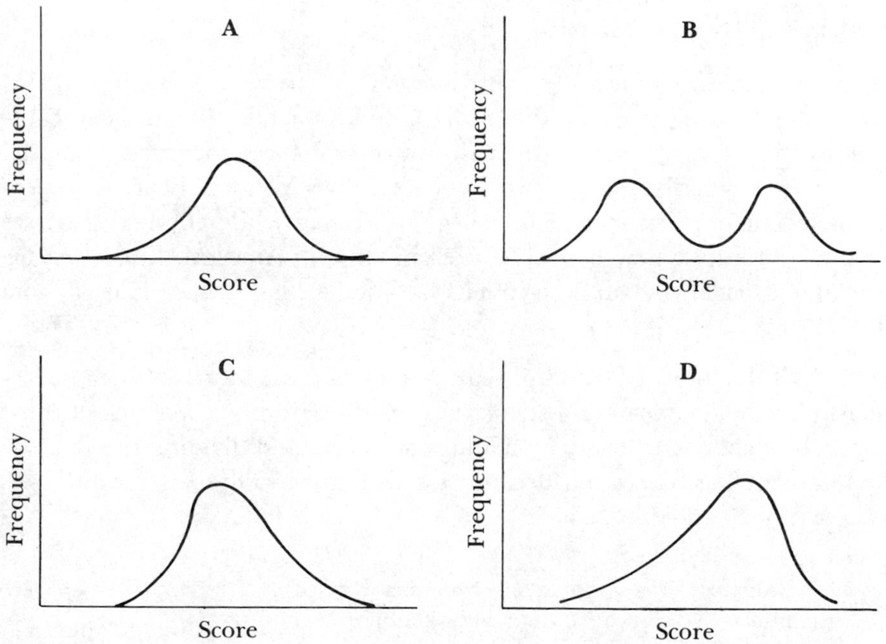

Figure 3.3 Four types of frequency distributions are shown: A, normal; B, bimodal; C, positively skewed; and D, negatively skewed.

For our present purpose, we call a distribution *normal* if it approximates a *bell-shaped* distribution (see Figure 3.3A)—that is, if most of the scores are concentrated in the center of the abscissa with relatively few at the extremes. Intelligence test scores for a thousand randomly selected people will approximate a normal distribution. As we saw in Figure 3.1, a *bimodal distribution,* the scores tend to be concentrated at two points along the abscissa (also see Figure 3.3B). The distribution of heights for an equal number of men and women will also tend to be bimodal. A *skewed distribution* occurs when more scores occur at either end of the abscissa (see Figure 3.3C and D). A distribution of verbal SAT scores among honors English majors would be skewed since relatively few individuals with low verbal SAT scores would be included in this group. A skewed distribution can be skewed in either a positive or a negative direction. The direction of the gentle slope indicates whether it is positive or negative. A slope to the right is positively skewed, and a slope to the left is negatively skewed.

DESCRIPTIVE STATISTICS

Measures of Central Tendency

There are three measures of central tendency that we will discuss in this section. These are the mean, the median, and the mode. If you listen carefully to the television news, you will notice that these measures are used frequently to describe the way we "typically" live. You will hear one report discussing the median income of college professors while another discusses the mean price of a new house in different cities in America. Less often we hear about modal (mode) descriptions, although this measure is used from time to time.

Mean Of the three measures of central tendency, the *mean* is the most frequently used. The mean of a set of scores is the arithmetic average of those scores. It is obtained simply by adding the scores and dividing the total by the number of scores. In our dream data, a total of 75 dreams recalled was reported by 20 subjects.

$$\text{Mean} = \frac{\text{sum of scores}}{\text{number of scores}} = \frac{\text{number of dreams recalled}}{\text{number of subjects}} = \frac{75}{20} = 3.75$$

average number of dreams recalled per subject.

In this particular example, 75 divided by 20 equals exactly 3.75. However, other times the answer may give us a recurring decimal, which must be rounded off to a given number of decimal places. For example, if the total score for 7 subjects was 100, the mean would equal 100/7, or 14.285714285714. . . . The simple rule used by most researchers is to round up if the number is greater than or equal to five and to round down if it is less than five. In this case, if we were to round to four decimal places the mean would be 14.2857, whereas if we were to round to two decimal places the mean would be 14.29. We will follow this rounding rule for any calculation performed in this book.

Median The *median* of a set of scores is the middle score—that is, the score that has an equal number of scores both above and below it. To calculate the median of a set of scores, simply list all the scores and the median will be the middle score or, in the case of an even number of scores, the score halfway between the two middle scores. In our dream data, the two middle scores are 4 and 5. Consequently, the median is 4.5

A slight problem in calculating the median is encountered when the median interval contains a large number of scores. In this case, we must interpolate such that an equal number of scores lie above and below the median. This procedure will not be required in this book and is discussed in various statistics books such as McCall (1980, pp. 64–66).

Mode The *mode* is simply the most frequently occurring score. The only mathematical calculation required to compute the mode of a distribution of scores is to count the frequency of each score. The score that occurs most frequently is the mode. If there are two scores with the same frequency, we simply report two modes. For example, the dream data presented earlier had two modes: one at 2 and one at 5 dreams recalled.

Given these three measures, you may be wondering which provides the best estimate of central tendency. As is often the case, there is no clear-cut answer. The appropriate choice varies with the particular frequency distribution and the intent of the researcher. For example, as Figure 3.4A indicates, for a normal distribution, the mode, median, and mean all have the same value.

As you can see from Figure 3.4B, in a skewed distribution, the mean is affected by extreme scores. For example, before you take a job in a company where the mean salary is $100,000 a year, you might want to find out the median salary. A mean of $100,000 could simply be produced by ten people making $10,000 each and one person making $1,000,000

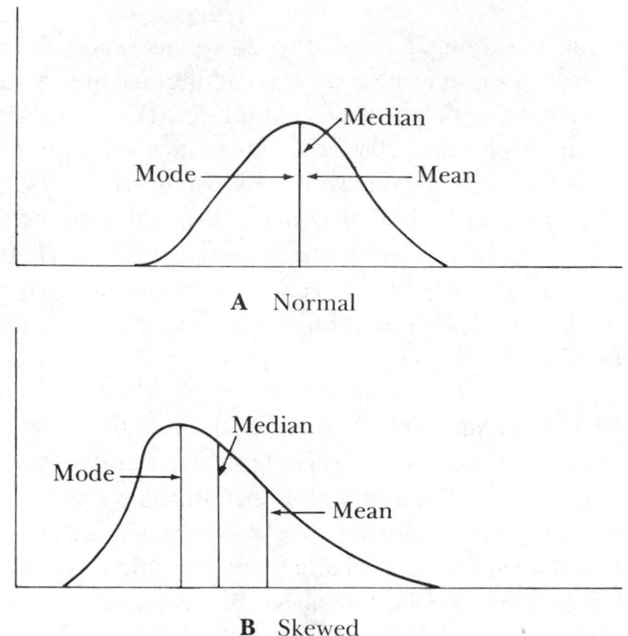

Figure 3.4 Mean, median, and mode of a normal distribution (A) and a skewed distribution (B).

(1,100,000/11 = 100,000). If you were a stock market analyst concerned with how much a company pays out in salaries, however, the mean would be the appropriate measure. In other words, if you are interested in the scores of a total group, then the mean is the most appropriate measure. However, if you are more interested in a representative score for any given individual, then the median is more appropriate.

In psychological research, we tend to use the mean most often since it gives the best description of the group as a whole. However, we must make sure that the data are in the appropriate scale of measurement before we use the mean.

Technically speaking, the mean can be used only with interval or ratio data since it requires the addition of numbers. The median can be used with ordinal, interval, or ratio data since it uses the ordering of the data. The mode can be used with nominal, ordinal, interval, or ratio data since it requires only classification.

In summary, the measure of central tendency that you use depends on both the type of data you have (nominal, ordinal, interval, or ratio) and the question you are asking. Thus, in the final analysis, you must use your judgment to determine which measure of central tendency to use.

Measures of Variability

As we have seen, a measure of central tendency gives us some information concerning a set of scores; however, it does not give any information about how the scores are distributed. To obtain a more complete description of a set of data, we use a second measure in addition to the measure of central tendency. This is a measure of *variability.* Measures of variability are merely attempts to indicate how spread out the scores are. We can also refer to this variability as *dispersion.* One common measure of dispersion is the *range,* which reflects the difference between the largest and smallest scores in a set of data. The actual computational formula given for the range in most introductory statistics books is the largest score minus the smallest score. In the dream data presented earlier, the range is 7 ($7 - 0 = 7$). This is technically referred to as the *exclusive range* (Keppel & Suafley, 1980). Although the computation is easy, the range tells us only about the two extreme scores; it provides no information about the dispersion of the remaining scores.

Let us now demonstrate this graphically. Consider the following two sets of data for group A and group B.

Group A	*Group B*
2	2
3	5
4	5
5	6
6	6
7	6
8	7
9	7
10	10

In these two distributions, the ranges are the same (8) and the means are the same (6), yet the actual shapes of the distributions are very different (see Figure 3.5). The scores in group B appear more concentrated in the center of the distribution, yet our estimate of range does not reflect this. To

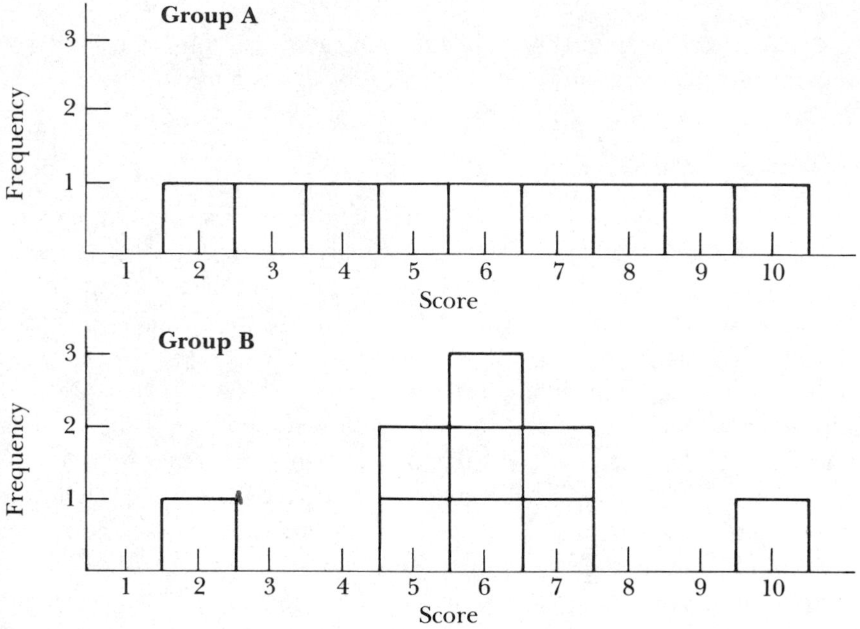

Figure 3.5 Two different distributions with the same range and mean but different dispersions of scores.

provide a more sensitive estimate of the dispersion of *all* the scores, a second measure of the variability of data is used. This measure is called the *variance.*

Simply stated, the variance is an estimate of how much each score varies from the mean. One way to estimate the dispersion of *all* the scores would be to subtract each score from the mean and then add these deviations and divide the total by the number of scores. Unfortunately, for both technical and practical reasons, this approach does not give us the type of information we need. Since the sum of the positive deviations is always equal to the sum of the negative deviations from the mean, adding these deviations gives a sum of zero. Instead, we square each deviation, add the squares, and then divide the total by the number of deviations. This gives us an estimate of how much each score varies from the mean. From this we arrive at the definition of *variance: the average of the squared deviations from the mean.* In order to determine variance, we must first calculate what is called the *sum of the squares;* that is, we add the numbers squared. The sum of the squares is often abbreviated as SS. The first formula for SS that we will show you is called the deviation method:

Sum of squares = sum of squared deviation scores = $\Sigma(X - \bar{X})^2$.
Thus,

$$SS = \Sigma(X - \bar{X})^2$$

where Σ = sum of, X = individual score, and $\bar{X}$ = mean of scores.

The deviation method is a useful teaching device because it requires that you compute the actual deviations for each score. The method is cumbersome, however, and once you master the concept, you might want to consider a second way to calculate the sum of squares. This is called the *computational formula* and is sometimes used simply because it requires less work, particularly on hand calculators. The formula is:

$$SS = \Sigma X^2 - \frac{(\Sigma X)^2}{N}$$

where X = individual score and N = number of observations.

In the tables on pp. 62 and 63, the sum of squares of a set of data is calculated by both the computational and the deviation methods. The difference in SS for the two methods reflects the rounding of the data to two decimal places during computation.

If you remember the definition of variance—the average of the squared deviations from the mean—you will realize that we must now determine the average of the sum of squares. However, in determining the variance, we divide either by N for a description of a single population or $N-1$ for inference to a larger group (see inferential statistics on page 68).

$$\text{variance} = \frac{\text{sum of squares}}{\text{number of scores minus 1}}$$

$$= \frac{SS}{N - 1}.$$

The denominator in this ratio is technically referred to as the degrees of freedom, abbreviated df. Thus, the variance formula becomes:

$$\text{variance} = \frac{SS}{df}.$$

Although a formal discussion of degrees of freedom is beyond the scope of this presentation, the basic idea is simple. Degrees of freedom refers to the number of scores that are free to vary. To illustrate this, imagine that you and two friends are eating out and you are waiting for your order to come. One of you orders chicken salad on rye, another orders a yogurt and fruit cup, and the third pastrami on white bread with mayonnaise. The waiter comes with the food, but he has forgotten who ordered what. From his standpoint, he has a number of degrees of freedom in that he can place the dishes in any of several different combinations. However, if you were to remind him that you ordered chicken salad and the friend on your right the yogurt, this would limit his degrees of freedom. How many would he now have? Right, he would not have any; that is, once you had fixed the order in two of the three selections, the third was determined and not free to vary. Thus, the general idea behind the term *degrees of freedom* reflects how many scores are free to vary. In a computation with N scores, once we

Deviation Method

Individual Scores, (X)	*Deviation,* $(X - \bar{X})$	*Deviation*^{2}, $(X - \bar{X})^2$	
1	−2.75	7.56	
4	0.25	0.06	
5	1.25	1.56	$\bar{X} = 3.75$
2	−1.75	3.06	
0	−3.75	14.06	$SS = \sum(X - \bar{X})^2$
2	−1.75	3.06	
5	1.25	1.56	$= 93.70$
6	−2.25	5.06	
1	−2.75	7.56	
3	−0.75	0.56	
7	3.25	10.56	
1	−2.75	7.56	
2	−1.75	3.06	
5	1.25	1.56	
6	2.25	5.06	
5	1.25	1.56	
2	−1.75	3.06	
6	2.25	5.06	
7	3.25	10.56	
5	1.25	1.56	
	Sum $(\sum) = 0$	Sum $(\sum) = 93.70$	

know the mean, $N-1$ scores are free to vary. See if you can work out why this is true.

Returning to our previous example in which the sum of squares equals 93.75, we determine variance by dividing this by the number of scores (20) minus 1. Thus,

$$\text{variance} = \frac{\text{SS}}{\text{df}} = \frac{93.75}{19} = 4.93\ .$$

This calculation formula for variance would now appear as follows:

$$\text{variance} = \frac{\Sigma X^2 - \frac{(\Sigma X)^2}{N}}{N - 1}\ .$$

Computational Method

Individual Scores (X)	$(X)^2$
1	1
4	16
5	25
2	4
0	0
2	4
5	25
6	36
1	1
3	9
7	49
1	1
2	4
5	25
6	36
5	25
2	4
6	36
7	49
5	25
Sum (Σ) = 75	Sum (Σ) = 375

$$\text{SS} = \sum X^2 - \frac{(\sum X)^2}{N}$$

$$= 375 - \frac{(75)^2}{20}$$

$$= 375 - \frac{5{,}625}{20}$$

$$= 375 - 281.25$$

$$= 93.75$$

At this point, let's return to the two sets of data in Figure 3.5 (see p. 60). We saw that even though these distributions look quite different, the range for each distribution is the same. Granting for the moment that variance is a more sensitive measure of dispersion, let's see whether it provides a more useful tool for describing the dispersion about the mean of a group of scores. The tables below and on p. 65 show the calculation of the variance for each of these samples using the deviation method.

Thus, group B has less variance than group A and, consequently, this supports our earlier subjective analysis, which indicated less variability or dispersion in group B than in group A. Because variance uses squared scores, however, the variance does not describe the amount of variability in the same units of measurement as the original scores; that is, a variance of 6.67 exceeds the greatest absolute deviation in either sample! Consequently, many researchers prefer simply to use the square root of variance as their estimate of variability. The square root of the variance is called the *standard deviation* (SD) and is calculated by taking the square root of the variance. Thus,

$$\text{standard deviation} = \sqrt{\text{variance}} \ .$$

Group A	$(X-\bar{X})$	$(X-\bar{X})^2$
2	−4	16
3	−3	9
4	−2	4
5	−1	1
6	0	0
7	+1	1
8	+2	4
9	+3	9
10	+4	16
	$\Sigma = 0$	$\Sigma = 60$

$$\text{Variance} = \frac{\Sigma(X - \bar{X})^2}{N - 1} = \frac{60}{8} = 7.5$$

Group B	$(X-\bar{X})$	$(X-\bar{X})^2$
2	−4	16
5	−1	1
5	−1	1
6	0	0
6	0	0
6	0	0
7	+1	1
7	+1	1
10	+4	16
	$\Sigma = 0$	$\Sigma = 36$

$$\text{Variance} = \frac{\Sigma(X-\bar{X})^2}{N-1} = \frac{36}{8} = 4.5$$

To illustrate:

$$\text{Group A variance} = 7.5,\quad SD = \sqrt{7.5} = 2.74.$$

$$\text{Group B variance} = 4.5,\quad SD = \sqrt{4.5} = 2.12.$$

As stated previously, by making this transformation we return to the original units of measurement.

PICTORIAL DESCRIPTIONS USING MEASURES OF CENTRAL TENDENCY

In addition to using numerical descriptions of data such as frequency counts, measures of central tendency, and variance, it is usually helpful to use graphs to describe our results pictorially.

In psychology we have borrowed graphing procedures from other fields such as mathematics, and we use many of their conventions. For example, the independent variable is placed on the x-axis and the dependent variable on the y-axis. There are two main types of graphs used: line graphs and bar graphs.

Line graphs are used when the independent variable represents a point along a continuum. For example, you could graph the data from a study of the effects of room temperature on running rates in rats as follows:

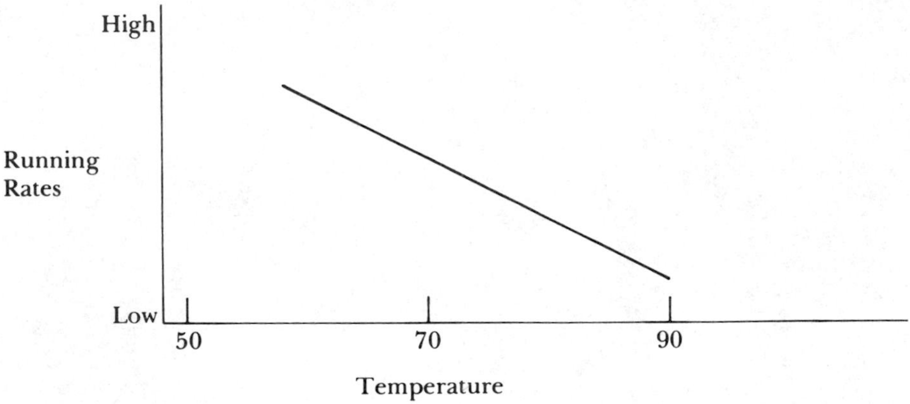

Bar graphs are used to depict information that is categorical. For example, the results of a study that examined the effects of different forms of therapy could be illustrated as follows:

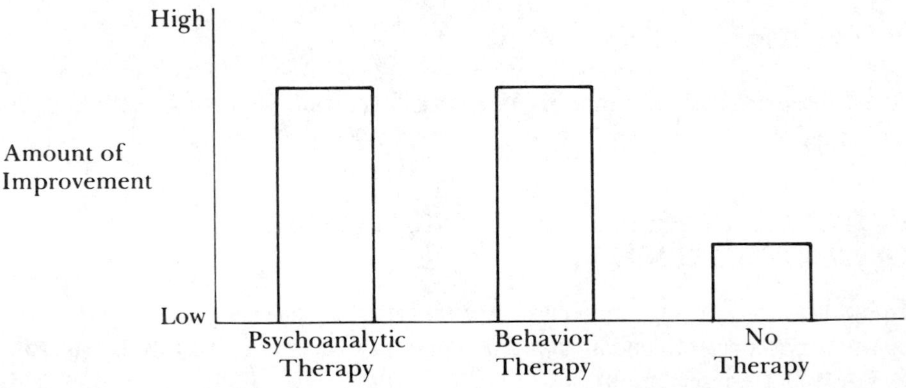

It would not be appropriate in this case to draw lines since these types of therapy do not lie along a continuum, although it would have been appropriate if the independent variable had been the amount of a particular drug given, since dosage levels of the *same* drug would form a continuum.

CONCLUSION: DESCRIPTIVE STATISTICS

A primary responsibility of any researcher is communication. The purpose of descriptive statistics is to describe the distribution of scores in a given experiment. However, in selecting a descriptive statistic, we must keep in mind that the appropriate statistic depends on the mathematical properties of our data. Table 3.3 indicates the appropriate descriptive statistic for the four major types of measurement.

For nominal data, each score falls into a single category. Thus, to describe our results we can only compare the number or percentage of subjects in each category. For example, several years ago we were interested in determining whether rats preferred to climb up or down a forty-five-degree incline when placed halfway up the incline. To answer this question, we set up an incline made of wood with a wire mesh floor (to increase traction). Then we placed an animal facing either to the right or to the left halfway up the incline and noted whether the animal moved up or down the incline. We repeated this procedure with twenty rats and found that eighteen of them moved up the incline, one moved down, and one failed to move. In summarizing our results, we simply stated the percentage of animals in each of three categories—that is, 90% moved up, 5% moved down, and 5% remained stationary.

In the case of ordinal data, things are a bit more complex. Typically

Table 3.3 Appropriate Descriptive Statistics for the Four Major Types of Measurement

Type of Measurement	*Appropriate Descriptive Statistic*
Nominal	Number or percentage of subjects in each category
Ordinal	Number or percentage of subjects in each group above median rank
Interval	Mode, median, or mean and standard deviation score for each treatment condition
Ratio	Mode, median, or mean and standard deviation score for each treatment condition

the effect of the independent variable is determined by comparing the rankings of the experimental and control subjects. As pointed out earlier, with ordinal data there is often no reason to believe that the differences between consecutive ranks are equal. Consequently, strictly speaking it is *not* permissible to add the ranks of subjects in each group to obtain mean rankings for each group. Probably the best way to describe the outcome of an experiment involving ordinal data is to indicate the number or percentage of subjects in the experimental and control groups that are above the median rank. As we will see later, we can then use inferential statistics to determine whether the number in each group above the median is due to chance or to our independent variable.

For experiments involving interval and ratio data, our descriptive statistical analysis is more involved than merely determining the number or percentage of subjects in each category, or the number above the median for each group. Interval and ratio data possess the additional mathematical property of equal intervals between scores, which enables us to add and subtract scores. For the purpose of describing our results, this additional property means that we can use two additional types of descriptive statistics. The first type is measures of central tendency, which convey information on where the center of the distribution lies. The second is measures of the range of scores or variability, which convey how concentrated the obtained scores are about the center of the distribution.

OVERVIEW

We have tried to give you only a brief overview of descriptive statistics in this chapter. For a fuller discussion of particular techniques, we recommend that you consult introductory statistics books (e.g., Runyon & Haber, 1977; McCall, 1980; Ferguson, 1976; Guilford & Fruchter, 1978).

In all the statistics discussed in this chapter, the goal was the description of a certain set of numbers in and of themselves. There are other types of statistics upon which we also rely in psychology. They are referred to as *inferential* statistics. When we use inferential statistics, we seek to make an inference from the behavior of the subjects in our experiment to a large group of subjects. In the cereal experiment described in Chapter 2, the purpose of the study was to show that the cereal did (or did not) affect the growth of children in general, and not just the actual children who were used in the study. Because we are inferring from one group that has been tested to a larger group that has not been tested, there is always some probability connected with our inference; that is, we can never know for sure that the same effect would be found with the larger group if we were able to test all of them. Thus, most statements that we make concerning psychological research findings carry with them the chance that they might be wrong. But we are getting ahead of ourselves. In later chapters, we will expand upon this idea to help you understand the conceptual use of inferential statistics. Although we will introduce you to this conceptual understanding, particularly as it is related to the F-ratio, we will not develop or calculate any specific tests.

Our purpose in this book is to give you a conceptual understanding of psychological experimentation, and we believe that this purpose is best served in the absence of excessive calculational formulas. For those who require inferential statistics in their research, we suggest they consult one of the introductory statistics books (e.g., McCall, 1980; Runyon & Haber, 1977; Ferguson, 1976; Guilford & Fruchter, 1978). For a book that combines the underlying logic of experimentation with the calculational formulas, we recommend Keppel and Suafley (1980).

SUMMARY

In this chapter we discussed scales of measurement; our discussion included definitions of nominal, ordinal, interval, and ratio data. We drew distinctions between these forms of measurement in terms of their respective mathematical properties; examples of each were provided. In nominal measurement, differences between categories are qualitative but not quantitative. This is a form of classifying data only. With ordinal data, there is a single underlying continuum that reflects the amount or magnitude of the variable being measured. For interval data, the scale values are related by a single quantitative dimension and there are equal intervals between successive scale values. For ratio data, the scores are related by a single quantitative dimension with equal intervals between successive scale values, and there is also an absolute zero point.

We discussed the value of a pictorial description of any set of data. We gave frequency distributions, frequency polygons, and bar graphs for a set of data to clarify the similarities and differences between these methods of data presentation. We also described normal and bimodal distributions, and examples of positively and negatively skewed distributions were presented graphically.

We then dealt with descriptive statistics and began with a discussion of the three measures of central tendency known as the mean, median, and mode. The mean is computed by adding the individual scores together and dividing the sum by the number of scores. The median of a set of scores is the middle score, and the mode is simply the most frequently occurring score. We stressed that the mean is most frequently used in psychological research because it minimizes sampling error. Measures of variability such as the range and variance were discussed in detail, and we provided examples of exactly how each of them is derived numerically. Variance is an estimate of how much a score varies from the mean. The standard deviation is the square root of the variance.

We concluded with a summary of the various scales of measurement and the descriptive statistics that are appropriate to use with each type of data.

CHAPTER FOUR

Developing the Hypothesis

INTRODUCTION

Imagine that your instructor in this course has just announced that you are to begin an *experiment* of your own and that you are to start right *now.* What do you do? Where do you begin? This chapter is specifically intended to answer these questions and to help you begin your first experiment. As Lewis Carroll once said, the best place to begin is at the beginning.

As with any other human activity, excellence and enjoyment in research begin with genuine interest in some topic. When confronted with their first experiment, many beginning students panic and forget that research begins with interest. Consequently, your first task is simply to sit back and let your interests emerge. Some of you have already done this and are aware of your interests in various areas of psychology. For most of you, however, strong interests have not yet begun to emerge. One way to facilitate this process is to begin exploring various areas of psychology and watch yourself to see what you are interested in.

For example, you may look through your introductory psychology book and see which areas grab your attention. Once you realize the areas that interest you, you might go to the library and look through some textbooks or other books specifically devoted to these areas. You might also talk with psychologists who live in your community and learn more about what they do and what type of questions they ask. However, if no interests emerge, beware; you might want to consider changing majors or even taking a few semesters off. If you have made a mistake in selecting psychology as a major, it is better to try to find areas that do interest you now than after you graduate. It can be very boring to work in an area in which you are not internally motivated by strong personal interest.

As you watch your interests unfold, keep in mind that the interests of even the most dedicated person are not constant. They fluctuate from day to day, sometimes strong and sometimes forgotten. Over a period of years, a scientist may change interests many times. Indeed, some scientists even decide not to be scientists anymore. The key idea here is that interests can be a valuable guide to enable us to enjoy our interactions with the world.

When researchers are interested in a given topic, they learn all they can about it. They go to the library and read about the topic. They talk to other researchers about it. They actively think about the topic. After a time, many researchers find their topic spontaneously arising in their thoughts as they take showers, fall asleep, and eat breakfast. Like a child playing with a new toy, scientists consider their topics from ever-changing perspectives. Some researchers even amuse themselves by trying to describe their topic as if all their ideas about it were backward. The main idea is that they *play* with their thoughts to gain new perspectives on their topic.

MAKING OUR HYPOTHESES ABOUT REALITY CONCRETE

The essence of a scientific experiment is to see whether our ideas about the world are accurate. In its simplest form it is an interface, a meeting point, between our ideas and reality, between our psychological world and the physical world. This distinction is one aspect of the distinction we made in Chapter 1 between experience (psychological world) and behavior (physical world). To bridge this gap successfully, we must first realize that our intellectual ideas or hypotheses about the world are personal experiences just like our emotions or sensory experiences. They cannot be shared directly with other people no matter how hard we try. They are private knowledge. Yet science, at least in its present form, is objective; its conclusions can be seen and checked by *anyone*. This raises a dilemma: How can we scientifically evaluate our completely private ideas about the world? One answer is to define or represent our private ideas in terms of specific behavior or concrete activities that anyone can witness or repeat. These representations of psychological events in the physical world are called *operational definitions*. An operational definition gives our idea a concrete meaning in reality. For example, the idea that watching violence on television increases aggression is certainly a reasonable and potentially important notion. Yet before we can test it, we must define exactly what is meant by violence on television. Is a program with an unseen murder more violent than an exciting boxing match? Should the violence be rated by how many minutes it is on the screen, by the particular type of crime, by how much blood you see, or by a combination of all three? Likewise, to perform this research we would need to devise some measure of aggression. Let's take another example. Assume we wanted to test the idea that psychotherapy is effective. Before we could do that, we must define what psychotherapy is and what could be considered a measure of effectiveness. We would have to adopt operational definitions.

An operational definition takes a general concept such as aggression or effectiveness and places it within a given context; that is, *it redefines it in terms of clearly observable operations that anyone can see and repeat.* For example, we might define aggression as the number of times a child hits a toy doll after watching a violent television show. Likewise, we might define effectiveness in psychotherapy as measured by a score on a personality test. We could also use the number of days that a person stays out of a mental hospital as an operational definition of the effectiveness of psychotherapy. In each of these cases we have redefined an idea in terms of specific operations. We define an idea (psychological world) in terms of operations (physical world) that are required to produce the phenomenon (physical world) the idea (psychological world) represents. Circular? Of course; that is what science is all about—movement back and forth between our ideas and physical reality. Operational definitions make it possible to tie our ideas and hypotheses to objects and operations in physical reality.

One problem we face with operational definitions is that a given concept may be defined in several possible ways. Similarly, a given operational definition guarantees only a single instance of the original concept. Although we all realize that the grade you receive on a multiple-choice final exam is a narrow facet of all you may have learned in a college course, it is, strictly speaking, an adequate operational definition of your performance. Suppose we were interested in studying the effectiveness of a new form of psychotherapy on severely depressed individuals. Regardless of the research design we use, one task we would face is operationally defining the dependent variable: depression. Before beginning our research, we know that depression can manifest itself in a variety of ways (see Figure 4.1). Each of these ways can then become the focus of an operational definition of depres-

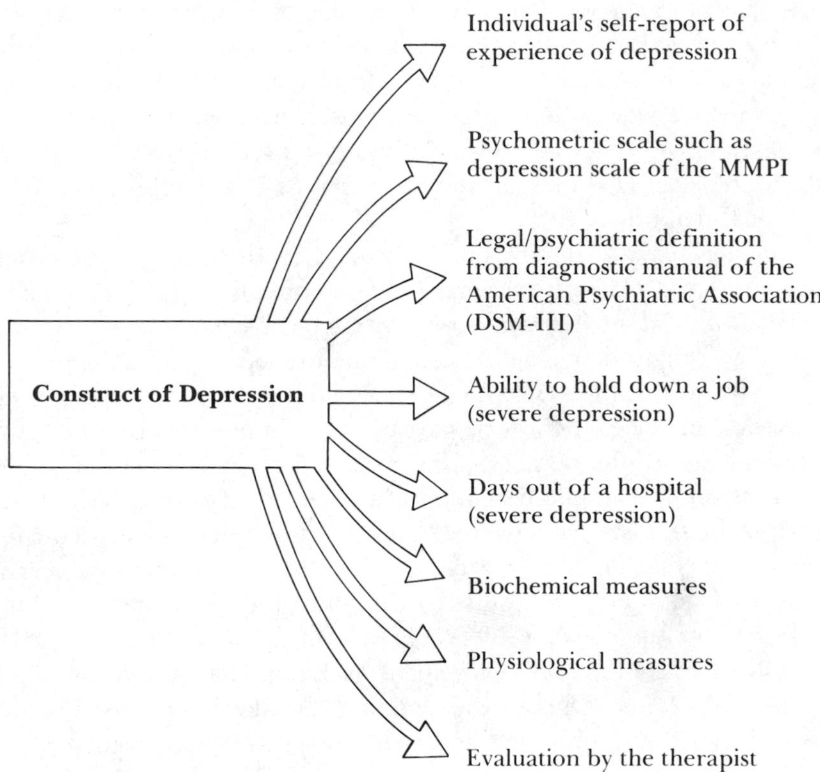

Figure 4.1 From any one global construct, there are several possible operational definitions depending on the questions asked and the type of population studied (for example, college students or mental hospital patients).

sion. For example, we know that the biochemistry of depressed patients undergoes certain changes, so these characteristics would constitute an adequate operational definition of depression. We also know that therapists generally agree on which patients are depressed. So we might operationally define the degree of depression in our subjects by the estimates of various therapists. However, the question of which operational definition is best is tricky. Ideally, it is safest to use several operational definitions. In this case, we might define depression as a certain score on some depression test plus a depressed rating by a therapist and the subject's subjective report of feeling depressed. If this battery of operational definitions is not possible, then at least we should select one that is known to be correlated with others. In selecting operational definitions, remember that they are always arbitrary. For example, we would probably all agree that going for 24 hours without food is an adequate operational definition of hunger. Yet people who fast frequently report no feelings of hunger even after several days of fasting.

MAKING OUR HYPOTHESES LOGICAL

As mentioned in Chapter 2, when we begin our experiment we are in either of two positions concerning what we already know about a research area. In some cases we already know a great deal and can use the experimental method to test specific predictions and hypotheses. Hypotheses of this type take the form "I bet this will happen if." In other cases we know relatively little and use the experimental method as an exploratory tool. Hypotheses of this type take the form "I wonder what will happen if?" As it turns out, the types of logic underlying these two types of hypotheses are fundamentally different.

The "I Wonder What Would Happen If" Hypothesis and Inductive Reasoning

If we are working in a relatively new area and know little about the phenomenon we are studying, we have no clear ideas from which to make specific predictions. In this case we use either naturalistic observation or the experimental method to generate new data from which we can begin to formulate a preliminary notion about how the phenomenon is organized. This process of generalizing from a specific instance or even several new facts to a more general idea is called *inductive reasoning* (see Figure 4.2). Thus we use inductive reasoning to increase our knowledge by generalizing new facts to a new understanding. For example, we use inductive reasoning when we observe a chimpanzee using sign language to communicate with a person and conclude: Chimpanzees can communicate with humans. We are generalizing from a specific event to a general idea about how the world is. The danger with this form of logic is overlooking causal factors that may be responsible for the effects we observe. For example, a person may know

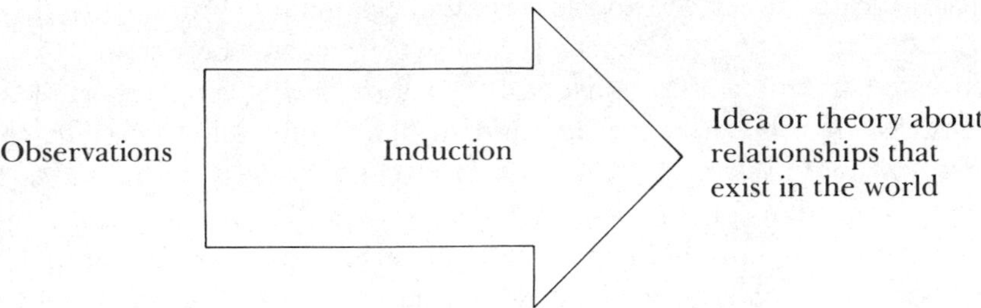

In the early stages of studying a phenomenon, scientists move from observations to theory. Some philosophers of science such as Karl Popper believe that psychology is at this stage and thus induction remains the main experimental method of psychological research.

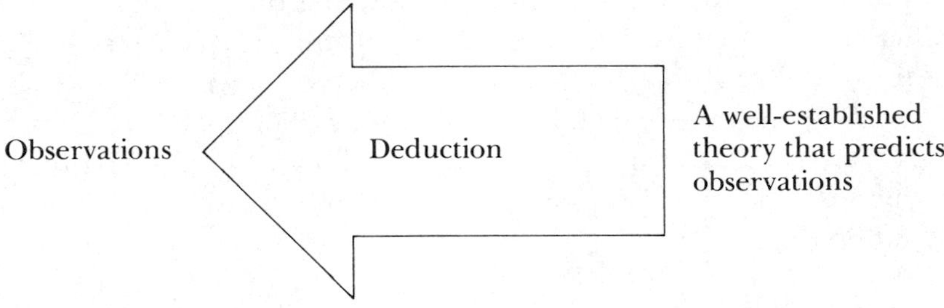

Once a comprehensive theory is developed, predictions can be made from the theory and tested through experimentation. Classical physics is a clear example of a science that uses this procedure.

Figure 4.2 Inductive and deductive relationships between observations and theory.

someone who is 106 years old and eats yogurt. From this observation, he may conclude that yogurt makes people live longer. This is an invalid use of inductive reasoning since there may be any number of other factors that contribute to this person's longevity. As mentioned in Chapter 2, the *internal validity* supporting this conclusion is questionable.

The "I Bet This Would Happen If" Question and Deductive Reasoning

If we already knew a great deal about a particular phenomenon and had formulated a clear-cut idea or theory, then we might *deduce* a specific hypothesis to predict how unexamined but related phenomena operate. In its simplest form, deductive reasoning takes the form of an if–then statement: If my idea about the world is correct, then this cause should produce the following effect. For example, we use deductive reasoning when we say: If it is true that schizophrenia is genetically determined (general idea about world), then we should find a greater incidence of the disorder between twins than between strangers (specific consequence of heredity). The terms of the hypothesis could be operationally defined, an experiment could be conducted, and a decision made about the accuracy of this particular hypothesis. If the hypothesis is supported, then this new fact strengthens the confidence we have that schizophrenia is genetically determined. If it is not supported, then we have reason to question our idea that schizophrenia is genetically determined. Regardless of the outcome, our deduction is logically correct in that if schizophrenia is genetically determined, then we should find a greater incidence among twins than among strangers because twins are known to be more genetically similar than strangers. It only remains to determine empirically whether this logically correct deduction accurately reflects the world. To decide this we use the experimental method.

IDEAS COME FROM EVERYWHERE

Every experiment begins with an idea. These ideas can come from anywhere. As we shall see, we may get our ideas from other people, newspapers, television, other scientists, students, ourselves, or just "out of the air." One of our colleagues, Lance Shotland, is a social psychologist who was discussing bystander behavior with his class. Their conversation turned to factors that influenced whether one person will help another in times of trouble. This particular discussion raised questions that led him to conduct a series of studies. Suppose we let him tell how his idea developed.

> While teaching social psychology I got interested in why people don't seem to act when men attack women. For a long time I gave the standard explanation of why people don't help. What happened was that students in the class began to give me other explanations to ac-

count for why people don't help. The questions from students gave me the idea that the standard explanation may not be the total answer. What I did was go back to an actual situation in which a woman named Kitty Genovese was killed in front of over thirty people in the streets of New York without anyone calling the police or giving aid. The story is that at 3:00 A.M. a woman named Kitty Genovese arrived home and parked her car in a parking lot across from her home. She walked across the street from the parking lot and started to walk toward her home. She became uneasy as she was walking since someone was walking toward her and she didn't like the way he looked. She became extremely uneasy and turned around and started to walk toward a police telephone. She never reached the police callbox. He overtook her and stabbed her. She screamed, "OH MY GOD, I HAVE BEEN STABBED." With that scream, windows were opened, people's heads came out, and lights came on. The people shouted. With that, the man got scared and ran off. He then jumped into his car and drove away. A bus then came by and people got out of the bus. People in the houses then closed their windows and went back to sleep. She apparently was not helped by anybody. She managed to crawl to another building and the man came back and overtook her and stabbed again. Again she screamed. Again, windows opened and lights came on. Again the people shouted and the man again ran off. The third time, he came back again and this time he killed her. The entire event took over a half an hour.

This is a true event that happened in New York City in 1964. No one who looked out of the apartment windows had done anything that was effective except to scare him off. To have been really effective, the people would have to have helped her, but no one bothered to do that. At that time, the New York papers said "What's going on in New York?" and talked about apathy. A couple of psychologists named Latane and Darley decided to research the question of bystander intervention. In their research, Latane and Darley concluded that numbers in themselves may not be important and in fact people in large crowds may leave it to others. These psychologists called this "diffusion of responsibility." Also, the fact that other people are not intervening gives others the feeling that they are not really seeing the situation correctly. Well, this is what I always told my class and my class felt there were other things going on. So I returned to a book that was composed of interviews with the people who watched the Kitty Genovese murder. In this book, *Thirty-eight Witnesses,* I read the bystanders' own accounts of what was going on. One of the things they said was that they were scared. I really don't know why because they were safe in their homes. But also what they seemed to say was that they thought it was a lovers' quarrel. I became interested in that and what I did was to go to *The New York Times* and I started to search through several years looking for cases where men were attacking women and what I found is that it

> does occur with fair frequency since *The New York Times* generally does not report crime news. Another case happened in the middle 1970s. There was a situation where a man raped a woman in full view of some thirty people. They watched the whole thing. They didn't do anything and it was only a half a block away from a police station. Again, what you find from interviews was that the people thought it was her boyfriend. I began to wonder if this was the controlling factor in the behavior of the bystanders. What I did was to test this. I also went further and wondered what bystanders assume if they don't know the relationship between people. The first thing I wanted to test was if bystanders perceive a relationship between a woman and her attacker, will they intervene less frequently than if it is a situation where a strange man is attacking a strange woman?

At this point, Dr. Shotland had an idea, an educated guess, which stemmed partly from his students' dissatisfaction with the standard explanation and partly from his reading of first-person accounts of crimes. His idea was that one of the important factors that determine whether a woman would be helped or not is related to whether the man and woman are perceived to have a relationship. As a social scientist, Dr. Shotland wanted to test this idea in an experiment. Before he could design the experiment, however, he had to restate the idea in a statement or hypothesis that could be tested in a scientific manner.

What were the steps that Dr. Shotland needed to go through before he could begin an experiment? These are outlined in Figure 4.3. We have already discussed the first two steps: (1) being interested in a topic and having an idea, and (2) considering and thinking about the topic from different perspectives. The third step is the formulation of the initial question when Dr. Shotland wondered whether the perception of the relationship was important for a woman to be helped. The fourth step is when he reformulated this question into a research hypothesis.

The specific research hypothesis that Dr. Shotland sought to test was: If bystanders perceive a relationship between a woman and her attacker, they will be less likely to intervene than if the victim and the attacker are perceived to be strangers. To test this hypothesis, Dr. Shotland designed an experiment in which a staged fight took place between a man and a woman. Suppose you were a subject in the experiment. What would you do if you walked out of a classroom and saw a man and woman fighting and yelling at each other? Do you think you would act differently if the woman yelled, "I don't know why I ever married you" than if she yelled, "I don't know you"?

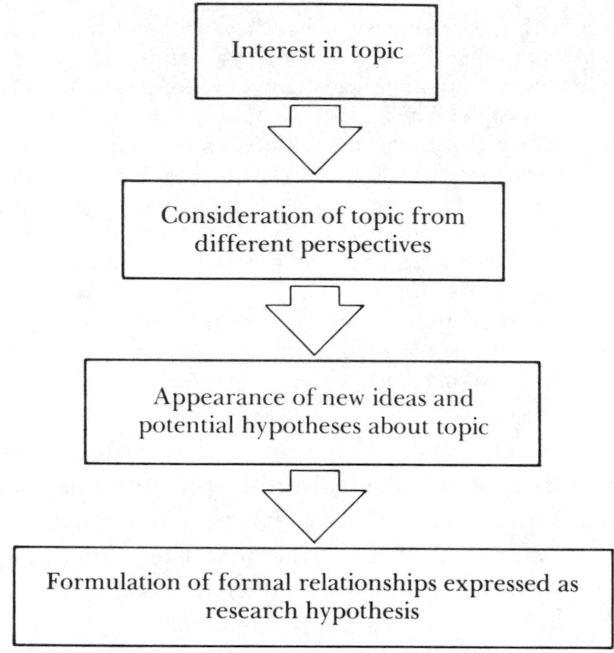

Figure 4.3 Steps involved in formulating a research hypothesis.

In this study what would be the dependent and independent variables? To help you answer this, let's reexamine the structure of a research hypothesis. When a researcher sets up a hypothesis, it is of the general form—if I do this (independent variable), then this will happen (dependent variable). What did Dr. Shotland do in his study? What did he manipulate? He manipulated the perception of the relationship between the man and the woman. In one condition the man and woman were portrayed as married ("I don't know why I ever married you") and in the other as strangers ("I have never seen you before"). Thus the independent variable (that variable under Dr. Shotland's control) was the relationship between the man and the woman. What was the dependent variable; that is, what was measured? What was measured was whether or not the subject who was a genuine bystander in the experiment intervened. A good question at this point is: What do you mean by "intervene"? Dr. Shotland operationally defined intervene as any one of four activities: (1) called the police on a nearby phone, (2) asked a person working nearby to help, (3) shouted at the man attacking the woman, or (4) tried to stop the fight. Now that you know what was measured, an extremely important question arises: How was the dependent variable measured? In this study Dr. Shotland used a very simple procedure; he just counted the number of people who did or did not intervene in the staged fight.

Before we leave this study, let us quickly look at part of the results. How do you think the study came out? As predicted by his hypothesis, in the condition in which there was an apparent marriage relationship, 20% of the subjects intervened, whereas in the stranger condition, 80% of the subjects intervened. It should be pointed out that Dr. Shotland did not stop at this point but performed additional studies that controlled for alternative explanations of the data (Shotland & Straw, 1976). The entire article illustrates well how scientists perform research, control for alternative explanations, and modify their studies as new information comes to light.

Let us now turn to another researcher and see how she obtained her ideas. The researcher is a developmental psychologist, Nora Newcombe.

> It all began in graduate school when I shared an office with another woman. One day she asked me what I thought about studying how children go about saying what they want. That is, how they express imperative intent (for example, saying, "Bring me some orange juice"). I thought that was a very interesting idea. It is interesting to me because there is a theoretical position presented by Robin Lakoff that adult men and women differ in how they express imperatives. She stated that women are more tentative and unsure. According to Lakoff, women say things like "Would you please open the door" rather than "Open the door" or even hint by saying "It's hot in here" rather than "Open the window." Assuming Lakoff was right, I thought it would be interesting to see if children already showed this type of sex role differentiation. But first I wanted to test Lakoff's theory with adults. You see, Lakoff is a linguist and had presented her ideas in the form of a theory but had never tested them in a scientific manner. That is, she never collected data from men and women to see if their speech styles indeed did differ.
>
> Another woman, Diane Arnkoff, and I began our research at this point. We did what seemed most straightforward, which was to bring people in and ask them to talk with each other. We brought people in two at a time, either two men, or two women, or a man and a woman. We did this because we thought it was probably important to determine not only if men and women differed in their speech styles but also whether they differed according to whether they were talking to a member of the same sex or opposite sex. In our first study, the people didn't know each other. We gave them a set of topics to talk about, but also told them they could talk about anything else they liked. We then turned a tape recorder on and left them for fifteen minutes.

By performing this study, Dr. Newcombe sought to test the general idea that men and women speak differently, especially when asking for something or giving commands.

Again, if we look at the general pattern of *if I do this, what will happen?*, we can see that Dr. Newcombe paired men-men, women-women, and men-women and then observed the outcomes. *What* was measured is the next question we ask. The general dependent variable was speech styles, which was operationally defined in relation to Lakoff's theory. Specifically, the number of qualifiers (such as "you know," "kinda," "I guess," and "maybe") and the number of indirect statements (such as "it is really cold in here, isn't it?") were noticed. The next question is *how* were these measured. Dr. Newcombe used two measures. The first was to count the number of qualifiers and indirect statements spoken during the fifteen minutes of recording. Can you imagine some other factors that might influence this measure? You probably realized that one very important factor would be the actual amount of time a person spoke. That is, if one person in the pair spoke almost all the time and the other one said little, then it would be difficult to draw conclusions from the frequency numbers alone. Thus, Dr. Newcombe used a second measure, which was the number of qualifiers divided by the time that a person spoke. Likewise she measured the number of indirect statements divided by the time that a person spoke. What did she find? She found that there were no differences between the speech styles of men and women as operationally defined.

Thus far we have described the manner in which two particular scientists came upon research ideas. However, we want to point out that few researchers perform just one study; rather, they conduct a series of studies in which they can clarify their ideas (see Box 4.1). Also, as we hope you begin to see, scientists are people and as people they differ in the manner in which they discover and develop ideas. Some individuals learn from their classes, some from talking to other people, some from reading the work (scientific or not) of others, and for some the ideas just seem to come out of the air.

INTUITION AND REVELATION

Depending on the particular century in which you live, ideas that seem to "pop" into your mind have been considered as voices of God, meaningless chatter, nonscientific, mystical as well as meaningful, an activation of the right hemisphere of the brain, or an example of psychological intuition.

This should suggest that we really do not know much about the working of our brain, especially when it comes to our own thought processes. At this point in our understanding of the process of science and how we obtain our ideas, we are much like the little baby in the first chapter who watches and tries to see the world. Although we do not know where spontaneous ideas come from, we can observe some examples in which spontaneous or intuitive ideas have influenced the course of science and the work of individual scientists.

Box 4.1 Strong Inference: John Platt

John Platt proposes that certain fields of science have progressed very quickly because of the adoption of a certain method. This method he refers to as *strong inference.* Strong inference is characterized by the following four steps:

1. Devise alternative hypotheses.
2. Devise a crucial experiment (or several experiments) with alternative possible outcomes, each of which would exclude one or more of the hypotheses.
3. Carry out the experiment so as to get clear results.
4. Return to step 1 with further refinements of the supported hypothesis.

Assume you lived during the time of Galileo and wanted to apply this procedure to the study of falling weights. A simple example would be to drop two weights and hypothesize that if the heavier hit first, then Aristotle would be supported, whereas if they hit at the same time, Galileo would be supported. Once it was determined that Galileo's hypothesis was supported, then a scientist could begin further refinements of the theory. Platt likens the procedure of strong inference to climbing a tree where each choice point is dependent on the previous one taken. Platt sees strong inference not only as a method for rapid progress in science but also at the heart of every scientist's thinking.

> Obviously it should be applied as much to one's own thinking as to others'. It consists of asking in your own mind, on hearing any scientific explanation or theory put forward, "But sir what experiment could *dis*prove your hypothesis?"; or on hearing a scientific experiment described, "But sir what hypothesis does your experiment disprove?" (Platt, 1964, p. 352).

Platt's procedure of strong inference emphasizes the problem-solving aspects of science and the search for adequate theoretical conceptualizations. It can also serve as a heuristic to help one determine whether his or her ideas about the world are stated in the form of a testable hypothesis. To help you understand this procedure better, take the hypothesis you are presently developing and ask how you could use the ideas of strong inference to create a line of research in which to test your ideas.

One of the most famous stories of an idea just popping into the consciousness of a scientist is that of Albert Einstein. When asked how he came upon ideas and solved problems, Einstein replied:

> The words or the language, as they are written or spoken, do not seem to play any role in my mechanism of thought. . . . The above mentioned elements are, in any case, of visual and some of muscular type. Conventional words or other signs have to be sought for laboriously only in a secondary stage (Koestler, 1964, p. 171).

In other places, Einstein speaks of having a body sensation concerning the answer to a problem, or he says that ideas just came to him while sailing. However, he goes on to state that often the translation from the body state to scientific notation required years. Einstein's image of a man riding on a beam of light proved to be one intuitive vision that changed science. Although this vision came in one instant, Einstein spent considerable time working this out and communicating it to other scientists.

Another interesting example of ideas coming from unexpected places is the case of the German chemist Kekulé in 1865. Kekulé was sitting in a chair watching the fire when he fell asleep and later reported the following dream.

> Again the atoms were gambolling before my eyes. This time the small groups kept modestly in the background. My mental eye, rendered more acute by repeated visions of this kind, could now distinguish larger structures, of manifold conformation; long rows, sometimes more closely fitted together; all twining and twisting in a snakelike motion. But look! What was that? One of the snakes had seized hold of its own tail, and the form whirled mockingly before my eyes. As if by a flash of lightning I awoke (Koestler, 1964, p. 118).

This simple dream of a snake biting its own tail led to the idea of a circular ring of carbon atoms, which led to research that changed the field of organic chemistry. Through this dream, Kekulé came to suggest the idea that certain chemical compounds are best described as closed rings. Not bad for a night's work, you might say!

Lest you conclude that the best thing for you to do is go sailing as Einstein was fond of doing or take a visionary nap in the middle of class, let us remind you that the insights of these scientists were preceded by years of intensive work in their respective areas of interest. Furthermore, their insight or idea had to be translated into the language and workings of science. This requires not only effort on the part of the scientist but also adequate preparation for understanding the insight in the first place. What can you do to help your ideas along and to prepare yourself for the insights and ideas that lead to new research?

THE SCIENTIST'S GUIDE TO HAVING AN IDEA

In the 1920s Graham Wallas became interested in how scientists solved problems. Because very little was known about this process, Wallas began by reading the works of famous scientists, particularly Helmholtz and Poincare. Wallas (1926) concluded that the scientific process could be described in four stages. The first stage is the *preparation* stage. This is the stage in which a person becomes interested in a problem, learns all she can about it, and examines it from varied perspectives. Although we do not know why we become interested in the topics that we do, at some point one topic or idea becomes more interesting to us than others. It was at this stage that Dr. Shotland became interested in the alternative reasons his class gave for why people would not help a woman who is being attacked. This initial stage begins with the scientist's interest and then involves assembling available information on the subject. As you might imagine, assembling available information to get an accurate picture of a research area may take many trips to the library and may involve reading and rereading many crucial articles. As you remember, Dr. Shotland not only talked with his class but also read all he could about bystander behavior and went to eyewitness accounts to hear other people talk about the event. Now you have prepared yourself, but you still do not know what question to ask. What do you do? Actually, the answer is nothing.

The next stage described by Wallas is called the *incubation* stage. This is the stage in which Einstein goes sailing or Kekulé takes a nap. This stage is very close to meditating on a topic but not thinking about it. One common report is that these new ideas frequently appear spontaneously and catch us by surprise while we are thinking about something else. Brain researchers use the metaphor of letting the right hemisphere take over. Using Wallas's terms, the incubation stage may involve the right hemisphere, whereas the initial survey of the area was primarily left-hemisphere activity (Ornstein, 1977). Keep in mind also that the incubation stage may take years, as it did in cases like Einstein.

The third stage of the process described by Wallas is called *illumination*. It is at this point that the idea or solution begins to emerge into consciousness. This emerging idea could take the form of the dream of Kekulé or the bodily sensations of Einstein or even just an idea that comes out of nowhere. In this stage one sees a new answer that was not seen before or even a totally different method of viewing the world. It would be like growing up in the Middle Ages and being taught that the world was flat. Then all of a sudden one day you change and see a picture of a round world.

For a scientist, seeing the picture is not enough, and this brings us to the fourth stage—*verification*. This is when you test your idea or hypothesis to see whether it fits the real world. The verification stage is what the remainder of this book is all about. Yet we consider it very important that you also realize that there are some very human aspects to doing science, which involve learning everything you can about a topic that interests you, then mulling all this information over and over, and finally permitting yourself to find your answers in strange places.

In trying to understand how scientists obtain the ideas for their experiments, keep in mind that they are already familiar with much of the published work in their areas of interest. At this time in your development, you do not have that advantage. Consequently, an essential first step for all of you is to spend time in the library becoming familiar with various content areas in which you might be interested. To facilitate this process, the next section of this chapter describes several resource tools psychologists commonly use to explore new areas of interest.

TOOLS FOR LIBRARY RESEARCH

Journals

Sometimes a person is interested in a general area and would like to learn more about it before he attempts to perform an experiment. For example, beginning psychology students may say they want to study biofeedback or

ESP or what makes someone go crazy. Where can they go for more information? They could, of course, go directly to experience and attempt to learn more about the topic from the world itself. They could also read what others have written on the topic in either books or journal articles. You can look up books in the card catalog in your library or in a book called *Books in Print,* which lists all the currently available books that can be ordered from a bookstore. You may also search for journal articles on your topic. Most scientists publish their scientific work in journals. A journal is nothing more than a collection of experiments and other articles written by scientists. There are journals for most areas of psychology; for example, there is the *Journal of Experimental Psychology, Journal of Abnormal Psychology, Developmental Psychology, Journal of Humanistic Psychology, Journal of Applied Behavioral Analysis,* and others. Your reference librarian will help you find out which journals your library carries. If you go to the library, you will notice that the articles in a journal, like a newspaper, may be on different topics within a given area. In general, journals serve as a type of newspaper for scientists, telling of the latest experiments that have been performed in each general area of psychology. But if you want articles on a given topic, what do you do? You look in one of the major indexes for the specific area you need. The major indexes that cover psychological research are *Psychological Abstracts, Science Citation Index, Social Science Citation Index,* and *Index Medicus.*

Psychological Abstracts

Psychological Abstracts is published each month and an index volume is published every six months. There are also cumulative indexes covering a number of years. Let us give you an example to illustrate the use of *Psychological Abstracts.* Suppose you had read about biofeedback in the newspaper and wanted to learn about the research concerning biofeedback. How would you do this? Simply go to the most recent index issue of *Psychological Abstracts* and look up the term "biofeedback." You will find two listings: one for biofeedback and one for biofeedback training. Looking at the sample page of *Psychological Abstracts* in Box 4.2, you see a large number of articles. Where do you begin? It depends on what type of question you are asking. If you want only general scientific information, a good place to begin is with a review article. *Psychological Abstracts* notes when the article is a literature review. Notice about halfway down the second column the following citation:

> Biofeedback training, visceral learning and modification, therapeutic implications, literature review, 10455

Box 4.2 Psychological Abstracts

Psychological Abstracts is published by the American Psychological Association and includes summaries and listings of recent research of a psychological nature. At the end of each six-month period, an index is published for the preceding six months. Following is a portion of a sample page from the index for the second half of 1979. The number at the end of each listing corresponds to a specific abstract in the monthly issues of *Psychological Abstracts*.

Biofeedback *SUBJECT INDEX* **Biofeedback Training**

biofeedback & cognitive-behavioral treatment, myofascial pain dysfunction syndrome, 16–34 yr olds, 6707
biofeedback hardware, book, 32
biofeedback, voluntary control of sexual arousal, unmarried college females, 7988
biofeedback vs instructions & adaptation control, systolic blood pressure control, 2990
cognitive & interpersonal considerations, biofeedback treatment of hypertension vs psychotherapeutic approach, 1456
continuous tumescence feedback & contingent erotic film, voluntary facilitation of erection, men with psychogenic erectile dysfunction, 1630
dichotic stimuli with varying amounts of articulatory feature similarity & EMG feedback, frontalis muscle activity & subvocal muscle activity, right handed Ss, 13087
EEG biofeedback & computer analysis, brain region interactions, cats, implications for experimental design for biofeedback research, 10052
EMG biofeedback & progressive relaxation training, relaxation, tense & anxious vs heterogeneous male alcoholics, 6688
EMG biofeedback, regulation of stuttering, adult stutterers, 6770
false heart rate feedback, sexual arousal, pedophiles, 1610
feedback time & schedule, EMG response, hospitalized males, 7995
frontalis muscle EMG biofeedback vs transcendental meditation muscle tension & locus of control, college students, 5397
hypnosis vs electromyographic biofeedback vs Jacobson progressive relaxation, prefrontal muscle contraction headache, patients, 14063
increased vs decreased vs constant vs noncontingent reinforcement of frontalis muscle activity, verbal decision making task performance, male college students, 3005
information frequency & feedback timing, instructed heart rate speeding, 534
locus of control, dropout from biofeedback treatment program, alcoholics, 6889
manipulation of pulse rate with biofeedback, subjective rating of marihuana intoxication, female 19–30 yr old experienced marihuana users, 5452
nonveridical heart rate feedback & anxiety, electrodermal responses & verbal reports to emotionally laden stimuli, female college students, 10449
progressive relaxation & contingent biofeedback vs no feedback, systolic & diastolic blood pressure & heart rate, college students, 2989
relaxation training vs biofeedback, children, 6713
right vs left ear input [illegible] stimulus & bio[illegible]back informatio[illegible] cerebral lateraliz[illegible] volunt[illegible] heart rate. [illegible]

biofeedback & relaxation techniques, control of essential hypertension, literature review, 11486
biofeedback assisted muscle relaxation, anxiety & cognitive processes, physical rehabilitation patients, 6656
biofeedback involving frontalis EMG feedback &/or peripheral temperature feedback, muscle contraction headache, patients, posttreatment followup, 14271
biofeedback mediated relaxation training, primary process manifestations in free association, 8968
biofeedback mediated relaxation, depression & anxiety, heroin addicts in methadone maintenance program, 9395
biofeedback monitored relaxation training, writing performance, college students, 516
biofeedback signals & signal aversiveness & reformation value, frontalis muscle relaxation acquisition, patients & normal Ss, 9129
biofeedback thermal training, retainment of biofeedback handwarming skills, 18–24 yr olds, 519
biofeedback training, control of surface skin temperature & response specificity, college students, 13077
biofeedback training, detection of sexual arousal at lower levels of excitation, women, 14229
biofeedback training involving blood volume pulse & frontalis muscle EMG, control of temporal artery vasoconstriction & muscle activity, 2 female 34 & 54 yr olds with combined migraine-muscle contraction headaches, 11516
biofeedback training, treatment of spasmotic torticollis, 60 yr old male, 6627
biofeedback training, visceral learning & modification, therapeutic implications, literature review, 10455
biofeedback training &/vs brief individual psychotherapy, gastrointestinal disorders, college students, 1433
biofeedback vs hypnosis, tension headaches, 14029
biofeedback &/vs relaxation training, psycho-physical measures of stress manifestations, nursing & retirement home residents, 1647
biofeedback &/vs relaxation training, treatment of psychosomatic & functional disorders, literature review, 9144
biofeedback vs voluntary control, heart rate & subjective cold tolerance, 18–25 yr old males, 535
continuous beat vs VR heart rate biofeedback schedules vs no feedback, heart rate & skin conductance & blood pressure & EMG, male college students, 522
description of response vs relaxation training vs directed imagery as adjuncts to biofeedback training, subsequent hand temperature control, 5389
[illegible]G alpha biofeedback training & unusual experiential states, [illegible]rlying variables [illegible]2924
[illegible]edbac[illegible] [illegible]ntrolled relaxation [illegible] college

If we now look up the number 10455 in the abstracts, we find the following:

10455. **Miller, Neal E.** (Rockefeller U) **Biofeedback and visceral learning.** *Annual Review of Psychology,* 1978, Vol 29, 373–404. —After a clarification of what biofeedback is, methodological and substantive findings in biofeedback research are reviewed in terms of 3 basic scientific issues: (a) the visceral and other responses believed to be unmodifiable that actually can be modified by instrumental training procedures; (b) the types of learned effects involved (indirect or direct); and (c) the law and parameters governing the learned modification of such responses. Implications for therapy are also considered for each area. (218 ref)

This tells us that Neal Miller of Rockefeller University wrote an article entitled "Biofeedback and visceral learning" published in the *Annual Review of Psychology* in 1978. The specific reference is volume 29, pages 373–404. The abstract tells us what information is covered in the article and that the article includes 218 references (218 ref). From reading the abstract, you can see whether the article covers the information you are interested in or relates to the question you are trying to answer. In addition to abstracting literatures, *Psychological Abstracts* includes research articles, some books, and Ph.D. dissertations.

Index Medicus

Whereas *Psychological Abstracts* reviews articles published in journals that are of interest to psychologists, *Index Medicus* performs the same function for medical journals. Most of the time, topics of interest to psychological researchers, such as Dr. Shotland's research on bystander intervention, are not found in *Index Medicus.* However, if the topic also deals with treatment factors such as with biofeedback, one can find articles in *Index Medicus* that are not reviewed in *Psychological Abstracts.* If we were to look up "biofeedback" in the July 1978 issue, we would see two references that were not reported in *Psychological Abstracts.* The first refers to an article in the *American Journal of Occupational Therapy.* By looking up the initials AJOT in the index, we find the name of the journal. *Index Medicus* does not provide abstracts but only lists the original article by title, authors, and journal. The second reference is to an article on respiratory feedback published in a German journal. You can determine that the article is in German by the (GER) at the end of the article and by the name of the journal: *Zeitschrift für Psychosomatische Medizin und Psychoanalyse.* As with *Psychological Abstracts,* at the end of the year *Index Medicus* publishes a complete listing of articles for the entire year. An example of an *Index Medicus* listing of biofeedback articles for 1979 is shown in Box 4.3.

Box 4.3 Index Medicus

Index Medicus is published by the National Institutes of Health of the U.S. government. Although the index covers medical journals most fully, areas of psychology related to the health sciences are also included. Unlike *Psychological Abstracts, Index Medicus* does not present a summary of the article but, as the name implies, serves as an index to articles in a given area. Following is part of a page referring to biofeedback work from the 1979 *Cumulated Index Medicus.* Each listing begins with the title of the article, the authors, and then the journal name. The journal name is abbreviated such that the *Journal of Consulting and Clinical Psychology* would appear as *J Consult Clin Psychol.* All abbreviations used appear in a special table in *Index Medicus.*

1979 **CUMULATED INDEX MEDICUS**

board meeting: Center's Board identifies key issues, reorganizes, starts task forces. **Hosp Prog** 60(1):28-9, Jan 79
In vitro fertilization: a moratorium is in order. Diamond EF. **Hosp Prog** 60(5):66-8, 80, May 79
In vitro fertilization: legal and ethical implications. Horan DJ. **Hosp Prog** 60(5):60-5, May 79
Bioethical issues and the moral matrix of U.S. health care. McCormick RA. **Hosp Prog** 60(5):42-5, May 79
Creation, the eschaton, and bioethics. Moraczewski AS. **Hosp Prog** 60(9):61-3, 94, Sep 79
All the President's bioethicists. Annas GJ. **Inquiry** 9(1):14-5, Feb 79
Bioethics and informed consent in American health care delivery. Barkes P. **J Adv Nurs** 4(1):23-38, Jan 79
Nephrology and bioethics. Berman LB, et al. **JAMA** 241(13):1402-3, 30 Mar 79
The role of the nurse in the bioethical decision-making process. Lumpp F. **Nurs Clin North Am** 14(1):13-21, Mar 79
Symposium on bioethical issues in nursing. Shriver EK. **Nurs Clin North Am** 14(1):1-81, Mar 79
Books on bioethics--a commentary. Jonsen AR. **Pharos** 41(3):39-43, Jul 78

BIOFEEDBACK (PSYCHOLOGY)

Biofeedback, mediated biofeedback and hypnosis in peripheral vasodilation training. Barabasz AF, et al. **Am J Clin Hypn** 21(1):28-37, Jul 78
A biofeedback service by nurses. Putt AM. **Am J Nurs** 79(1):88-9, Jan 79
Biofeedback of accommodation to reduce functional myopia: a case report. Trachtman JN. **Am J Optom Physiol Opt** 55(6):400-6, Jun 78
Bioconverter for upper extremity rehabilitation. Brown DM, et al. **Am J Phys Med** 57(5):233-8, Oct 78
Electromyographic biofeedback in the reeducation of facial palsy. Brown DM, et al. **Am J Phys Med** 57(4):183-90, Aug 78
Biofeedback training of knee control in the above-knee amputee. Fernie G, et al. **Am J Phys Med** 57(4):161-6, Aug 78
Effect of ··ctromyographic feedback and static stretching on ar induced muscle sorenes Glynn GH, et

the recent experimental literature. Williamson DA, et al. **Biofeedback Self Regul** 4(1):1-34, Mar 79 (102 ref.)
Heart rate and blood pressure biofeedback: II. A review and integration of recent theoretical models. Williamson DA, et al. **Biofeedback Self Regul** 4(1):35-50, Mar 79
Voluntary heart rate control: the role of individual differences. Carrol LD. **Biol Psychol** 8(2):137-57, Mar 79
Effects of frontalis EMG feedback on frontalis tension level, cardiac activity and electrodermal activity. Siddle DA, et al. **Biol Psychol** 7(3):169-73, Nov 78
Three experiments on the effects of information frequency and feedback timing on instructed heart rate speeding. Twentyman CT. **Biol Psychol** 8(1):1-29, Feb 79
Clinical applications of biofeedback. Johnston D. **Br J Hosp Med** 20(5):561-6, Nov 78
Biofeedback in the treatment of detrusor instability. Cardozo L, et al. **Br J Urol** 50(4):250-4, Jun 78
Idiopathic bladder instability treated by biofeedback. Cardozo LD, et al. **Br J Urol** 50(7):521-3, Dec 78
Yoga and biofeedback in the management of 'stress' in hypertensive patients. Patel C. **Clin Sci Mol Med** 48 Suppl 2:171s-174s, Jun 75
Biofeedback training for stress diseases. Shealy CN. **Compr Ther** 4(9):46-50, Sep 78
EEG feedback training of epileptic patients: clinical and electroencephalographic analysis. Kuhlman WN. **Electroencephalogr Clin Neurophysiol** 45(6):699-710, Dec 78
EEG operant conditioning for control of epilepsy. Wyler AR, et al. **Epilepsia** 20(3):279-86, Jun 79
Effects of sensorimotor EEG feedback training on seizure susceptibility in the rhesus monkey. Sterman MB, et al. **Exp Neurol** 62(3):735-47, Dec 78
Biofeedback--the light at the end of the tunnel? [editorial] Almy TP, et al. **Gastroenterology** 76(4):874-6, Apr 79
Progress in biofeedback conditioning for fecal incontinence. Cerulli MA, et al. **Gastroenterology** 76(4):742-6, Apr 79
The clinical application of EMG biofeedback therapy for muscle contraction headaches. Tsushima WT, et al. **Hawaii Med J** 37(9):270-1, Sep 78
Clinical applications of biofeedback: a summary of research 1974-1978. Wedding D, et al. **Hawaii Med J** 38(1):9-12, Jan 79 (32 ref.)
T of biofeedback in the treatment of chronic -year study. Diam

Biofeedback patients. H Mar 79
A comparis bruxism. Jul 78
Locus of con rate using **J Pers Ass**
Self-focusing al. **J Pers**
Rest vertica with biof Feldman
Effects persor Half):
New ap with p **J Psyc**
Urodynan sphincte 122(2):20
Biofeedbac observatic 79
From the phenom **JAMA**
Helping h therapy.
Use of ramp control. A 17(2):268-7
A myoelect feedback. S Jan 79
Effect of ar Pinel JP,
Erythrome. **Nurs Clin**
Pain contro traini
Informa

Science Citation Index and Social Science Citation Index

The *Science Citation Index* and the *Social Science Citation Index* list articles published in either the sciences, such as physics, chemistry, and biology, or the social sciences, such as sociology and economics. Parts of psychology are referenced in either or both depending on the area of study. *Science Citation Index* (SCI), as you can see from the example in Box 4.4, lists articles by topic and author. This makes it particularly useful for finding specific types of studies within a general area. For example, when we look under "biofeedback," we see specific areas such as blood pressure, EEG, migraine, temperature biofeedback, and so forth. Next to the topic is the author's name. We then look up the author's name and find a listing that tells the journal in which the article was published.

Box 4.4 Science Citation Index

Science Citation Index is published by the Institute for Scientific Information in Philadelphia. The index is actually composed of three separate indexes. The first is the subject index, which lists articles related to a specific topic. The second is called the source index and lists authors and the articles or books they published during the period covered. The third index is the citation index, which lists articles published during a certain period that reference a particular article. By using this third index, one can determine what work has followed up a specific research publication. Presented here is a portion of a sample page from the subject index of the *Science Citation Index*.

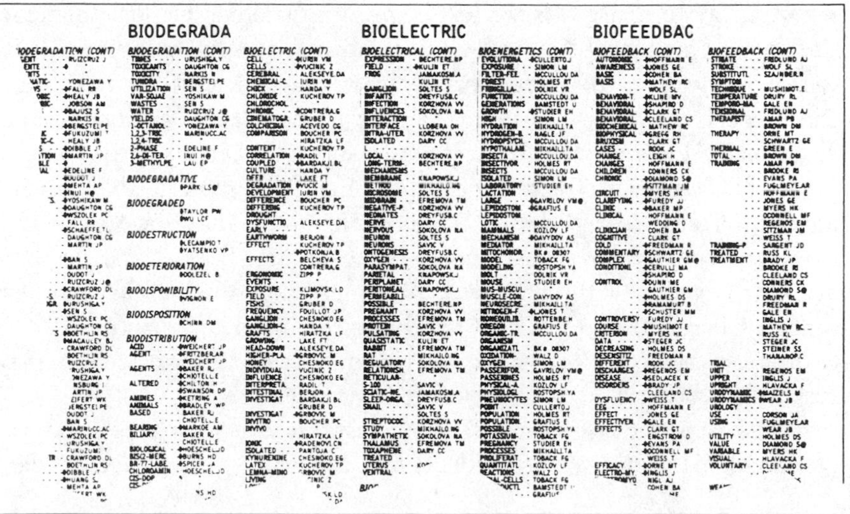
BIODEGRADA

BIOELECTRIC

BIOFEEDBAC

One main advantage of the SCI over other indexes is that it includes in a separate volume a listing of all studies that referenced a particular study, hence the name *Science Citation Index.* This would be particularly useful to a researcher like Dr. Newcombe. As she was beginning to plan her study examining sex and speech types according to the theory of Robin Lakoff, she would want to know whether anyone else had tested this theory. Since, as you will see later, scientists refer in their articles to the research and theories of others, it would be possible to find all the studies that refer to Dr. Lakoff's work. To do this, Dr. Newcombe would look up R. T. Lakoff and note all the articles that referenced her work. Dr. Newcombe could then check these articles to see whether any other scientists had asked the specific question in which she was interested.

We have now discussed developing the hypothesis, including the use of operational definitions, how various scientists have arrived at their ideas for research, and some library resources that you will use as you begin to explore your own ideas. You should be able to consider your own research study. Before moving into the question of experimentation presented in the next chapter, however, we want to expand our discussion of creating testable hypotheses, since many beginning students have difficulty with this.

CREATING TESTABLE RESEARCH HYPOTHESES AND THE PROBLEM OF MEASUREMENT

Making the transition from a general idea to a testable research hypothesis is not always a simple task. Most beginning students present their ideas in the form of a general statement and tend to ask global questions. It is only with considerable work and practice that these generally interesting ideas can be rephrased into a testable hypothesis that clearly spells out a specific relationship between variables. It may even be that many areas of psychology are ignored simply because of the difficulty in making the transition to adequate research hypotheses. Areas such as romantic love, creativity, extrasensory perception, consciousness, and mental illness may be some examples. Because of the nature of the questions, other areas may even be outside the realm of testability, as illustrated by the cartoon on p. 93. Even for the experienced scientist, the transition from a general idea to a specific research hypothesis is a difficult but important process.

One aspect of the transition to a testable research hypothesis is measurement. Measurement considerations underlie the way we develop our

"IT MAY VERY WELL BRING ABOUT IMMORTALITY, BUT IT WILL TAKE FOREVER TO TEST IT."

operational definitions. We touched on this issue when we discussed the work of Dr. Shotland and Dr. Newcombe. At this time we will briefly introduce you to two important aspects of measurement: reliability and validity. For a measurement to be *reliable* means that the measure is consistent. There are many everyday examples of reliable measuring devices; for example, your bathroom scale will give you the same weight no matter how many times you stand on it unless, of course, your weight actually does change between weighings. For a measurement to be *valid* it must be accurate. In the case of the bathroom scale, the reading must accurately reflect your weight in some unit of measurement such as pounds. Now suppose your boyfriend or girlfriend wanted you to lose weight, so he or she set your scale at five pounds overweight. At five pounds overweight, your scale would still be reliable; that is, it would continue to give you and anyone else a *consistent* weight each time you weighed. However, at five pounds overweight, the measurement would not be *valid;* that is, the scale would not reflect your *true* weight. To be valid a measurement must reflect the *true* score within limits. The "within limits" is determined by what we know scientifically about a given construct. Thus, our goal is to use measurements that as much as possible are both true (valid) and consistent (reliable) in our experiments.

Let us say that again. For a measure to be valid, it must *accurately* reflect the construct in question. For a measure to be reliable, it must *consistently* give the same information. To understand this better, consider two clocks, one that was stopped at four o'clock and one that is always five minutes fast. Which is reliable and which is valid? If you say that the fast clock is reliable, you are right. This clock *consistently* gives the same time in relation to the actual time of day. How about validity? Neither clock is totally valid. You could argue that the fast clock was never valid, whereas the stopped clock was accurate twice a day, although that would be of very little use to us.

To return to your psychological experiment, it is your task to choose measurements that are both accurate (validity) and consistent (reliability) in relation to the question you are asking. Yet how do you as a beginning student select methods of measurement that are both reliable and valid for your purposes? You have two alternatives. You can either (1) begin from scratch and demonstrate that your measures are indeed reliable and valid or (2) review the literature and determine what measures have been used by others and adopt them. Since the first option for many areas of study is a difficult and lengthy process requiring highly technical expertise, we recommend that you choose the second option and pattern your measurement devices on those that have been established in the literature. We do not recommend that you do this blindly, however, but that you continue to remember the problems of reliability and validity. For example, even if you are only having a rat press a lever for food, you must still determine what construct lever pressing validly measures. Or, said in the other way, if you were interested in the construct "learning" in animals, you would first ask what would be a good measure of "learning." You would look for a measure with numerous empirical studies to support it, and you might conclude that lever pressing was one such measure. In the final analysis, the task of choosing good measures is yours, although you are greatly aided by previously published studies as well as your own experience in experimentation.

CONCLUSION

It may seem like you have many decisions to make and in a sense you do, but you must also remember that much of the process of doing science is learned through experience. By this we mean that although there are guidelines for how to perform experiments and answer questions through science, many of the procedures that have to be devised are learned through performing experiments.

As you become more familiar with the process of experimentation, you will come to see which considerations of good experimental design are most appropriate in which situations. For now you must mainly rely on understanding the logic of experimentation.

As we pointed out, all experiments begin with an idea or consideration of the world in which we live. This consideration or idea is then formulated in terms of a general statement or question. For example, you may think that schizophrenia is related to diet or that anxiety is related to too much homework, or you might be interested in the factors that produce helping behavior. You might even think that students would be less anxious if they were not given homework. Whatever your idea, you must then translate it into a *specific* research question or hypothesis; that is, you must develop a testable statement that points out what *specific* variables are to be examined and the hypothesized relationship between them. This is when you rely on operational definitions as we discussed previously. If at this point you have clearly stated (1) your independent and dependent variables, (2) how each is measured taking into account reliability and validity, (3) the hypoth-

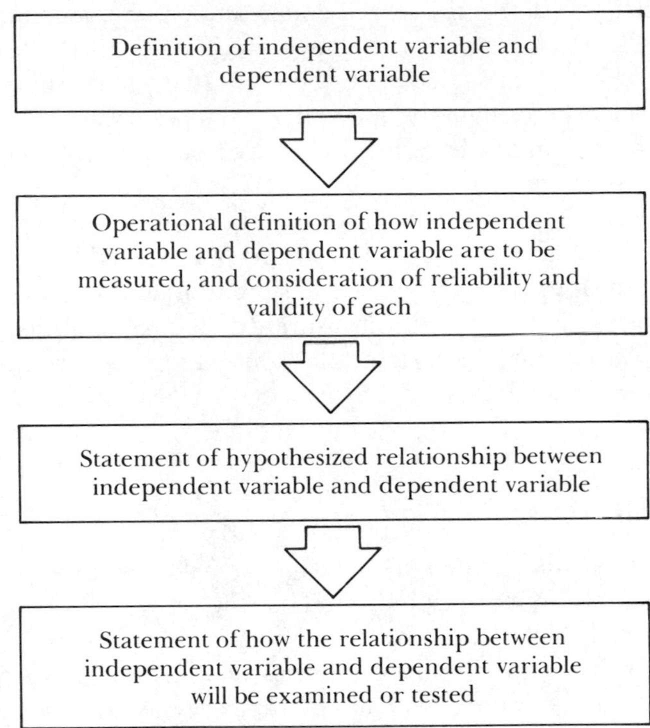

Figure 4.4 Steps required prior to experimentation.

esized relationship between the independent and dependent variables, and (4) how this hypothesized relationship is to be tested, then you have passed one of the major hurdles of performing a scientific experiment (See Figure 4.4). Once you have overcome this hurdle, you are ready to move on and consider the process of experimentation itself.

SUMMARY

This chapter began with the idea that the essence of scientific research is to determine whether or not our ideas about the world are accurate. We then discussed the importance of operational definitions, which are redefinitions of concepts in terms of clearly observable operations that anyone can see and repeat. One major problem with operational definitions is that any given concept may be defined in several possible ways. We suggested that the selection of an operational definition is always arbitrary and that ideally it is safest to use several operational definitions rather than just one.

We reviewed the inductive and deductive methods of reasoning as discussed in Chapter 2, and this led to a discussion of the suggestion that research ideas or hypotheses can be derived from literally any available source. We provided examples to demonstrate the way in which some researchers acquired their specific hypotheses. One particular theory of hypothesis development was presented by Wallas (1926). His theory includes four stages: preparation, incubation, illumination, and verification.

We then discussed the necessary tools required for using the library as a source of information, including the journals: *Psychological Abstracts, Index Medicus,* and the *Science Citation Index* and *Social Science Citation Index*.

This was followed by a description of the problem of measurement as we move from an idea to a testable research hypothesis. Two important aspects of measurement are validity and reliability. One task of the researcher is to choose measures that are both accurate (valid) and consistent (reliable). The chapter concluded with the statement that much of the process of doing science is learned through experience, and with this experience you learn how to move from an idea to a research hypothesis.

CHAPTER FIVE

Testing the Hypothesis: A Conceptual Introduction

INTRODUCTION

Once you have developed your research hypothesis, what do you do next? Most beginning students answer, "I perform an experiment to prove that my hypothesis is correct." It is true that your hypothesis needs to be evaluated in the light of an actual experiment. However, contrary to the manner in which science is sometimes portrayed, the evaluation of a hypothesis is a complex process that takes place on a number of levels. In fact, there is not just one hypothesis, but three separate questions that need to be asked in order to evaluate your original research hypothesis. The first question is related to statistics and asks whether the *numbers* found in an experiment could be due to chance factors alone. The second question is related to alternative explanations for the research findings and asks whether the results of the study could be due to factors other than the independent variable as hypothesized; that is, are there threats to the internal validity of the study? The third question concerns the research hypothesis and asks what support exists for assuming that the independent variable is the cause of the results.

Thus we find ourselves like detectives who sort through one set of clues and then another hoping to determine how a particular situation occurred. What caused this event; who did it? Although the detective always looks to the butler, in research we begin with the curious dilemma that *no one did it;* that is, we ask whether the experimental results as we found them happened not because of a causal factor (the independent variable) but because of chance. Once we determine that chance alone did not produce the results, we are ready to look for causal factors. "If it was not chance, then it was our independent variable," the naive young detective might say. "Not yet," the sage of experience would echo once more. "Let us first look to unknown factors that might be responsible for our experimental outcome." "But how can we know the unknown, Pop?" the number-one son of Charlie Chan always asks on the late show. "Through logic, common sense, and a thorough knowledge of the literature" is the answer.

Let us expand and repeat these considerations. Interpreting the results of an experiment is a three-stage decision process. The first stage does not directly involve our research hypothesis at all! Instead it involves the possibility that chance fluctuations between the performance of our groups may be solely responsible for any differences. The possibility that there are no differences between groups is called the *null hypothesis.* Because chance is always involved in our sampling and observations of the world, the null hypothesis is *always* one possible interpretation of even the most striking differences between our groups that must be evaluated. This means that regardless of how great the differences are between our groups on whatever dependent measure we are using, it is always possible that the results are due to chance fluctuations. Thus, when we make a statement about cause and effect in a psychological experiment, we never state that the independent variable *absolutely* caused the effect on the dependent variable. Rather, we make a probabilistic statement that we can be relatively certain that our results were not due to chance factors alone. It was a realization of the probabilistic nature of experimental outcomes that led to the development of statistical procedures at the beginning of this century. Because of the central importance of chance in modern science, we will have much to say about chance, the null hypothesis, and the importance of statistics. In the meantime, an essential idea to keep in mind is that the initial phase of interpreting the outcome of any experiment is a *statistical decision process.* Thus, when confronted with differences between our groups, we first use statistics to determine the probability that these differences are most likely due to chance (null hypothesis).

Once we have satisfied ourselves that our results are probably not due to chance, we must turn to the second stage and examine another possibility. This is the possibility that our results are due to some systematic but unspecified factor, which we call a *confound.* If indeed our results are due to some factor other than our independent variable, then, as mentioned in

Chapter 1, it is a threat to the internal validity of the experiment. In the fictitious series of breakfast cereal experiments described in Chapter 2, we saw that the weight gain that occurred in the experimental groups was due to the cream, bananas, and sugar and not to the new cereal as the manufacturers had thought. In confounded experiments like this one, the treatment effect is not due to the independent variable as our research hypothesis contended. Instead, the treatment effect is due to one or more overlooked causal factors. Because it is always possible that the internal validity of an experiment is weakened by some unknown factor causing the observed differences, we routinely scrutinize the published experiments of others and our own work for the possibility that some confound occurred. However, even with careful scrutiny we can *never be certain* that some unknown causal factor other than the independent variable is not responsible for the experimental results.

Once we have rejected the null hypothesis and the confound hypothesis as viable interpretations of our results, we can turn to the third consideration. This is the assumption that our results reflect a causal action on the part of the independent variable; that is, there is now a greater probability that our research hypothesis is accurate. At this point we are ready to interpret our data in relation to the research hypothesis. As a digression we want to point out that many people who are not familiar with the process of science tend to view it as consisting of only this third consideration. Most scientists, however, do not speak so much about "proving a hypothesis" as they do about "controlling and seeking alternative explanations." In fact, many research scientists argue that the heart of experimentation lies in ruling out alternative explanations. In this chapter we will emphasize the process of minimizing the likelihood of alternative explanations through a discussion of the null and confound hypotheses. In the next chapter we will emphasize experimental control through a discussion of techniques for controlling, reducing, and eliminating various potential confounds.

Before we continue, let us remind you that throughout this and the next chapter, we will discuss the interpretation of experimental results and experimental design from the standpoint of the *scientist*. We will be presenting the experimental method in its ideal form. Consequently, keep in mind that although internal validity and eventual statistical analysis are important determiners of experimental design, they are by no means the only factors to consider when conducting research. In later chapters we will return to the perspectives of the *subject* and the *witness*. Specifically, we will return to questions of external validity and ecological validity.

Through *external validity* we will examine in more depth the generalizability of research findings. Through *ecological validity* we will focus on research in a broader context as well as the scientist-subject relationship. Finally, we will emphasize value by asking questions of ethics and meaning. Now let us turn to an actual experiment and observe how we evaluate the three possible interpretations of experimental results discussed previously.

THE CONTEXT OF EXPERIMENTATION: AN EXAMPLE

In the early 1970s Bransford and Johnson (1972) performed an experiment to explore some of the factors that influence how we remember and encode what we hear. In particular, they were interested in the role of context in the comprehension and recall of information. Imagine you are a subject in that experiment and you are asked to listen to and later recall the following passage:

> If the balloons popped, the sound wouldn't be able to carry since everything would be too far away from the correct floor. A closed window would also prevent the sound from carrying, since most buildings tend to be well insulated. Since the whole operation depends on a steady flow of electricity, a break in the middle of the wire would also cause problems. Of course, the fellow could shout, but the human voice is not loud enough to carry that far. An additional problem is that a string could break on the instrument. Then there could be no accompaniment to the message. It is clear that the best situation would involve less distance. Then there would be fewer potential problems. With face-to-face contact, the least number of things could go wrong.

After the passage was read, the subjects in the experiment were asked to rate it for comprehensibility; that is, they were asked to rate how well they understood the passage, with a rating of seven meaning it was highly comprehensible. You might try that yourself. If you are like the subjects in the experiment, you would rate the material as incomprehensible. Their actual average rating was 2.3 on the seven-point scale. The next task for the subjects was to recall what they had read. Here they were instructed to write the main ideas that they remembered from the passage. How many ideas did you remember? The subjects in the experiment recalled on the average 3.6 ideas out of a possible 14.

Bransford and Johnson also included a second group of subjects who were shown Figure 5.1 before they heard the passage. As with the no-picture group, the task was to recall as many ideas from the story as possible. If we were to discuss these two groups in terms of the independent variable (the picture), we would say that one group received the complete independent variable and the other group received a zero level of the independent variable. One could also present other levels of the independent variable between the total picture and zero picture. Bransford and Johnson actually did this in their complete experiment, but that is beyond our discussion. After you have seen the picture, go back and read the passage.

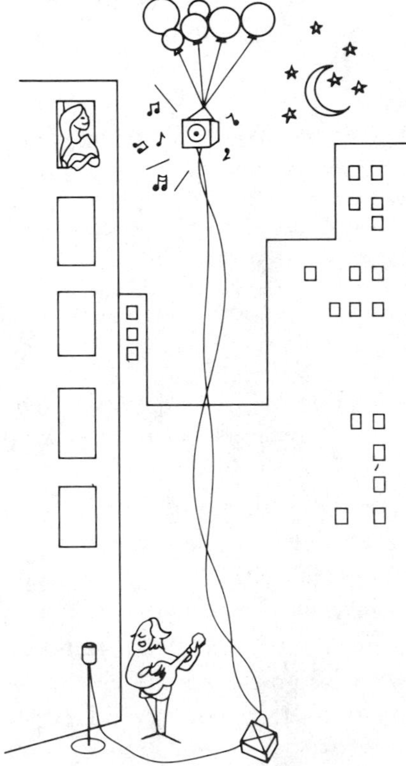

Figure 5.1 Complete context picture for the Bransford and Johnson study.

How would you rate the comprehensibility of the passage now? The subjects in the second experimental group rated comprehensibility more than twice as high as those in the group who did not see the picture (mean rating of 6.1 versus 2.3 on the seven-point scale). This second group also recalled many more ideas than the first group (8 versus 3.6 ideas). Although the Bransford and Johnson experiment is much more complex than we have presented it thus far, we will draw on this simplified version as a means of illustrating the task of evaluating the null, confound, and research hypotheses. We will begin with a discussion of statistical interpretation.

Statistical Interpretation

Philosophers for centuries have told us that everything varies, and in psychology we know this all too well. Some things vary a little; some things vary a lot. Some factors vary systematically; some factors vary by chance. In the process of experimentation we have set the goal of understanding what part of our results may be attributed to *systematic* variation (for example, the influence of the independent variable on the dependent variable) and what part is due to *chance* variation.

Chance variation may also be called *error* variation. Since the words *chance* and *error* have a similar technical meaning in this context, it is important that you understand this meaning. Chance or error variation refers to factors that influence the performance of the subjects in a *nonsystematic* manner. This means that *from the frame of reference of the experiment,* chance variation cannot be ascribed to any given set of factors. This is not to say that we cannot find reasons why any given *individual* subject performed in a certain way. It does say, however, that the reasons given for any one individual cannot be ascribed to the group as a whole. Consider a memory experiment such as that of Bransford and Johnson. One person in the experiment might have performed poorly because he did not sleep well the night before. Another person might have done very well because she had just received some good news from home. Another might have had too much coffee, whereas another was anxious because of a test the next period. Each of these factors would be considered as a chance factor or error factor *from the standpoint of the group* of subjects who took part in the experiment.

When we discuss *systematic variations,* we are referring to those factors that influence one group of subjects as a whole. It is our hope that any systematic variation between groups is due to the influence of our independent variable on the dependent variable, although this may not always be the case. It may happen that some confound systematically influences our data and thus contributes an unintended source of unwanted systematic variation. We will discuss the problem of confounds later in the chapter. Thus far we have suggested that the variation in the scores of subjects in an experiment may be due to three major factors: (1) systematic variation due to our independent variable, (2) systematic variation due to some confound, and (3) nonsystematic variation ascribed to chance factors.

To continue with the Bransford and Johnson example, one group of subjects heard the story without seeing the picture, whereas the other group heard the story after being shown the picture. Once we have collected the results, we are faced with the task of interpretation. In light of the preceding discussion, our overall task both statistically and theoretically is to interpret the results in relation to three possibilities. These are: (1) there are no differences between our groups (null hypothesis); (2) the results were produced by some systematic influence *other than* the independent variable, that is, a confound; and (3) the results were produced in a systematic fashion by the independent variable.

Ignoring the question of confounds for a moment, let us discuss our results in terms of the effects of the independent variable and of chance or error. In the Bransford and Johnson study, we are trying to determine how much influence seeing the picture had on remembering the passage. To answer this question, we begin with what some students feel is a backward approach. We ask the question: What if seeing the picture had no effect on memory? What would the results look like then? We already know the answer theoretically. The two groups would look like each other. Since the groups were presumably chosen to be similar, they would continue to be similar if the independent variable (and confounds) did not influence them.

We can now present this same point in a more technical way. First, let us use a more statistically oriented language—that of the F-ratio. In this case, F stands for Sir Ronald Fisher, the man who developed the statistical technique of analysis of variance. The particular terms we will use in this ratio are *within-groups variance* and *between-groups variance*. In the Bransford and Johnson study, within-groups variance reflects those factors we referred to as chance or error variance. These are factors that influence particular subjects in each group. Factors such as mental alertness, physical health, and present emotional state are expected to have a random or chance effect on the groups as a whole and thus do not contribute to any systematic differences between the two groups *randomly* selected. Factors that systematically influence a group of subjects, such as showing one group the picture before the memory task, are reflected in the between-groups variance. In other words, between-groups variance reflects the difference between the experimental and control groups—that is, the effect of the treatment. Further, we need to say that chance factors also contribute to the total between-groups variance, although when the term is used conceptually we are mainly referring to the effect of systematic variations. Thus, between-groups variance equals the effect of treatment plus error variance, whereas within-groups variance reflects chance or error variance alone.

Consider the relationship of between-groups variance and within-groups variance if the independent variable has no effect in a study. That is, if showing one group the picture has no effect on their remembering the passage, what is the relationship of between-groups variance and within-groups variance? That's right. They are the same. In the form of a ratio,

$$\frac{\text{between-groups variance}}{\text{within-groups variance}} = \frac{\text{treatment effects} + \text{chance variance}}{\text{chance variance}}.$$

If there are no treatment effects, then

$$\frac{\text{between-groups variance}}{\text{within-groups variance}} = \frac{0 + \text{chance variance}}{\text{chance variance}}.$$

Let us ignore confounds for the moment and again assume that the independent variable has no effect on the dependent variable. What would the preceding ratio equal? Before you claim that your great-great-grandmother died of math anxiety, consider the answer from a conceptual point of view. Even if you had to reread the last page, you should realize that if the independent variable has no effect, the ratio will be equal to one. Thus if the independent variable (and confounds) does not systematically influence the results, then

$$\frac{\text{variance between groups}}{\text{variance within groups}} = 1.$$

So what, you might be saying to yourself. Before we discuss why we consider the ratio of between-groups variance to within-groups variance to be important in experimental design and interpretation, take a moment to mathematically examine what factors could cause this ratio to change—that is, become larger. You might also consider how a ratio of one would be involved in addressing our three considerations of (1) chance variation, (2) systematic variation due to confounds, and (3) systematic variation due to the independent variable. Also consider how the null hypothesis is related to the ratio.

Let us begin with the null hypothesis. If the null hypothesis is true (there are no differences between our groups), then the ratio will be equal to or close to one. If, on the other hand, the ratio is equal to a very large number, then we would want to reject the null hypothesis and explore the possibility that there are real differences between our groups. Thus as a general rule we can see that the larger the ratio, the more relatively certain we are that there are real differences between our groups that are not caused by chance alone. We also see that the smaller the ratio, the less certain we can be that the results are not due to chance. Actually, we are never certain that our results are or are not due to chance. Instead we use statistics to help us make a best guess or bet by assigning a probability to our statement that the results are not due to chance alone. That is, we may say that results from our study could have happened by chance only one time out of every hundred. In the published literature you will see this written as $p<.01$. Our ratio is statistically called an *F-ratio,* and you also see this number in published papers as F equals some number—for example, $F=5.8$. If you look on page 264 in Chapter 12 you will see one such example ($F=68.2$, $p<.001$). Thus, in this example we would expect that the particular differences between groups would occur by chance less than 1 time in 1000. As with any bet based on probability, we can be wrong and we do make mistakes. In relation to accepting and rejecting the null hypothesis, we have given our mistakes special names. We call them *Type I* and *Type II* errors, and these are described in Box 5.1.

From our discussion thus far you should have drawn some important conclusions related to the F-ratio. First, the closer the number produced by the ratio is to one, the greater the probability of accepting the null hypothesis. Second, the larger the number produced by the ratio, the greater the chance of rejecting the null hypothesis and assuming that some systematic factor influenced the results. Third, a large F-ratio can be produced mathematically by either *increasing the between-groups variance* or *reducing the within-groups variance*. The practical implication of this is that positive experimental results can be obtained either by having a strong independent variable or by *controlling* the error variance. The presentation of the independent variable may be made stronger by using extreme levels of the independent variable. For example, a zero level of a drug might be given to one group and a high dosage level given to another. Controlling error variance will be discussed in greater detail in the next chapter.

Types of Variation

On a conceptual level we suggested that the variability in an experiment can be divided into three parts: (1) systematic variation due to the independent variable, (2) systematic variation due to confounds, and (3) variation due to chance. Let us repeat these with a slightly different terminology as used by Kerlinger (1973). The first may also be called *primary or controlled systematic variance.* Primary variance is due to the "real" effect of the independent variable (occasionally called the *primary* variable). An-

---

Box 5.1 *Type I and Type II Errors*

Suppose we reject the null hypothesis and assume our results are not simply due to chance. In this case our decision may accurately reflect the world (correct rejection of the null hypothesis) or it may not (incorrect rejection of the null hypothesis). An incorrect rejection of the null hypothesis is referred to as a *Type I error.* A Type I error occurs whenever we incorrectly reject the null hypothesis and the true state is that chance fluctuations are solely responsible for the differences between our groups. Suppose, on the other hand, we accept the null hypothesis and bet that our results are merely due to chance. Our decision may accurately reflect the world (correct acceptance of the null hypothesis) or it may not (incorrect acceptance of the null hypothesis). An incorrect acceptance of the null hypothesis is referred to as a *Type II error.* A Type II error occurs when factors other than chance (for example, the independent variable) are responsible for the differences between our groups and we conclude that they are not.

Null Hypothesis Decision	True State of Affairs: Chance is responsible	True State of Affairs: Chance is not responsible
Accept	Correct acceptance	Type II error (incorrect acceptance)
Reject	Type I error (incorrect rejection)	Correct rejection

---

other aspect of the total variance in any experiment is called *secondary or uncontrolled systematic variance.* Secondary variance is due to other causal variables (secondary variables), which can affect our experiment in either of two ways. They may occur along with the independent variable and thus differentially affect the performance of our two groups. This confounding effect of secondary variables is what we have referred to as *confounds* in our previous discussion. A portion of the remainder of this chapter will focus on this class of secondary variables. Secondary variables can also occur independently of our independent variable, and in this case they tend to have a similar impact on the performance of our two groups of subjects. Secondary variables that fall into this class are often called *extraneous variables.* Typical extraneous variables are time of day, season of the year, color of the room, temperature in the experimental setting, and so forth. These variables could have been controlled by the experimenter but were not. Sometimes they are unknown, and sometimes we realize their existence and decide they are not worth eliminating. Because extraneous variables affect both groups, they can be ignored without influencing the internal validity of our experiments. However, as we shall see, they do contribute to the overall subject variability and thereby affect the acceptance or rejection of the null hypothesis. The third aspect of the total variation in an experiment is called the *error variance.* Error variance refers to those fluctuations in scores that are due solely to chance factors as seen from the standpoint of the group. In psychological research, error variance is generally attributed to *individual* differences in our subjects and can sometimes be rather large.

Table 5.1 summarizes these possible changes and shows how they affect the between- and within-groups variance of the F-ratio.

On a statistical level we must decide whether or not our groups are equal (null hypothesis). There are many kinds of inferential statistics that can be used in a variety of situations. In the final analysis, these statistical manipulations boil down to a consideration of the size of our treatment effect and the amount of subject variation in our experiment. This comparison takes the form of the F-ratio.

As discussed previously, the numerator of this ratio reflects the difference between the scores of the experimental and control groups on the dependent variable. This difference is also referred to as the *treatment effect,* and it is assumed that it is due in part to the independent variable. The difference *between* the experimental and control groups on the dependent measure is reflected in the statistical measure of *between-groups variance.*

The denominator of the F-ratio simply reflects the amount of variabil-

Table 5.1 Effects of Four Types of Changes on Within-Groups and Between-Groups Variance

Type of Change	*Effect on Variance*
1. Random changes in subjects	Increase within-groups variance
2. Systematic changes that influence both groups equally	Increase within-groups variance
3. Systematic changes (not independent variable) that affect groups differently (confounds)	Increase between-groups variance
4. Systematic changes (independent variable) that affect groups differently	Increase between-groups variance

ity on our dependent measure among the subjects in this experiment. Because the subject variability is calculated by determining the amount of variation of our subjects *within* each group, it is sometimes called the *within-groups variance*. If there is a lot of subject variability on the dependent measure within our experimental and control groups, we would say that the within-group variance is high, and as a matter of common sense, we would insist that the treatment effects be quite large before assuming that any treatment effects were due to any cause other than chance. In contrast, if there were only very small individual differences on the dependent measure among the subjects in each group (low within-groups variance), it would be reasonable to consider that smaller differences between the experimental and control groups were not caused by chance.

Thus, our confidence that the treatment effect is not due to chance fluctuations in the performance of the subjects in our two groups is directly related to the size of the treatment effect and inversely related to the variability of scores within our groups.

Once we have made a decision about whether to accept or reject the null hypothesis, we can turn to the second stage of our decision process. If we have accepted the null hypothesis that our groups are equal, we simply interpret our data theoretically to mean that the independent variable did not affect the dependent variable. If, on the other hand, we reject the null hypothesis, we must decide what did produce the results of our experiment. Since the F-ratio cannot tell us whether the systematic variation was due to the independent variable or to a confound, we must logically and conceptually deduce the source of the systematic influence. To do this, we turn first to the question of confounds and then finally to our independent variable. At each stage of this process we are attempting to become more and more certain of whether the independent variable causally affected the dependent variable.

SYSTEMATIC FACTORS NOT RELATED TO THE INDEPENDENT VARIABLE

From our previous consideration of the F-ratio, we have a better understanding of how we conclude that the numbers found in our research were not due to chance. However, this or any other statistic cannot tell us *what* did cause the difference between our groups. Statistics only tell that there is a difference, which is probably not due to chance factors. To determine what caused the differences between our groups, we move to a more conceptual level. To aid us in these decisions, we rely on logic, common sense, and the published literature. Depending on the nature of our research, sometimes we rely on one of these factors more than the others. If we know a lot about an area, then the published literature is a tremendous aid in helping us to interpret the causal factors in our research results. If we know little about an area, however, we must continually rule out alternative hypotheses through the use of logic and common sense. It is only when alternative causal factors have been ruled out that we can conclude that the independent variable did indeed influence our results. Like a court of law, we refrain from implicating the independent variable until we can conclude without a reasonable doubt that the independent variable did it. Although in court the detective always looks to the butler, researchers look to confounds as the most likely suspect.

What is a confound? Almost anything can be a confound. It is something that systematically biases the results of our research. It may be the fact that the day before we ran the experimental group in a social psychology experiment on conformity, there was a television special on how we always do what other people tell us. Or, a confound may be introduced into a weight-reduction experiment by asking one group to lose weight at a time of the year when people eat less and their gastrointestinal system works faster (summer) whereas another group was started at a time when people eat more (winter). A confound may be introduced when one group is made up of more men than women. In one biofeedback study, the control group was instructed by young inexperienced technicians whereas the experimental group was instructed by an older, more experienced physician, and this may have produced a confound in the results. As you consider these and other possible confounds, you quickly realize that some confounds can be prevented or controlled. In the next chapter we will emphasize techniques for controlling systematic bias. Other factors, however, can never be controlled. You cannot control world events, but you can ask whether there is any reason to believe that a particular event that took place inside or outside of the laboratory could have influenced one group differently than another and thus introduced a confound.

THREATS TO INTERNAL VALIDITY

Every confound is a threat to the internal validity of our experiments. As you remember, internal validity asks whether the experimental treatment makes a difference in a specific experimental instance. In order to aid researchers in answering this question, Campbell and Stanley (1963) and more recently Cook and Campbell (1979) presented a list of possible threats to internal validity that must be considered. We present this list for two reasons. First, we want to introduce you to some of the possible confounds that can influence the groups in our experiments differently. Keep in mind that the list does not include every possible confound, because many confounds are related to the specific type of research being performed and thus cannot be listed in a general manner. Second, we want you to begin thinking about ways in which you might control for the effects of these confounds. You already know one way, which is through the use of appropriate control groups. This discussion should help to set up your thinking in preparation for an introduction to experimental design. Let us now turn to several examples of threats to internal validity.

History

History refers to events that take place between measurements in an experiment that are not related to the independent variable. In general, the longer the time between two measurements—a pretest and a posttest for example—the greater the possibility for outside events to influence the situation. In the cereal experiment described in Chapter 2, the availability of other foods made it impossible to know whether the experimental cereal caused the weight gain. Some confounds are subtle and difficult to detect. For example, in a long-term treatment study with psychiatric patients, such factors as new staff or a change of diet can influence the outcome. Cunningham (1979) has shown that the amount of sunshine present during a helping behavior experiment influences the degree to which participants aid an interviewer. Even more subtle confounds may be introduced simply by a person taking part in research. For example, in clinical research studies where individuals come in for the treatment of some specific disorder such as alcoholism or child abuse, it has been noted that once the person is defined as a "patient" under "treatment," his or her family and friends begin to act differently toward the person. Thus it is impossible to know whether any change came about because of the treatment or because of relationships outside the treatment setting.

Maturation

Maturation refers to problems of interpretation resulting from the subject growing older, wiser, stronger, healthier, as well as more tired, more bored, and so forth. The cartoon on p. 113 illustrates this problem. If a scientist is conducting a study that lasts for a period of time, it is imperative that maturational factors be controlled. This is accomplished by the use of a control group. Confounds of this type plague many beginning students because they often have their subjects perform too many tasks over too long a time. The subjects become bored and frustrated, and then the results are due to boredom and not to the independent variable in the study.

Testing

Testing refers to the problems that result from repeated measurement of the same subject. For example, if an individual is given the same math test repeatedly, then both the practice of taking the test and the memory of certain items could influence the results. Another example is when blood pressure is taken once a minute for thirty minutes. With the standard cuff method of measuring blood pressure (like in the physician's office), each inflation and deflation of the cuff results in temporary changes in the tissue of the arm itself. Thus just taking repeated measurements during a short time results in a change in blood pressure readings. Another example of testing as a confound is when subjects are monitored for certain behaviors, and after repeated observations they become sensitive to the behaviors the experimenter is recording.

"OF COURSE I'VE BECOME MORE MATURE SINCE YOU STARTED TREATING ME. YOU'VE BEEN AT IT SINCE I WAS 14 YEARS OLD."

Instrumentation

The problem of instrumentation is related to changes that occur in the measuring device, be it a person or a machine, during the course of an experiment. For example, if you are measuring aggressive behavior in children, you would become more accurate at making ratings as the study continues, and this could influence your results. To avoid this problem, such researchers as Newcombe and Arnkoff (1979) in the study of speech styles discussed in Chapter 3 had more than one rater of the same material and compared the ratings for consistency. If possible it is also important that the ratings for each group be made concurrently so that any improvement in ratings does not systematically influence the groups in the study. Another possible source of confounds is the use of machines. Many individuals believe that machines are always more reliable, but this does not mean that they are always perfect. For example, psychophysiological equipment such as that used to measure heart rate, electrodermal response, or skin temperature may require a certain warm-up time to give accurate results.

Statistical Regression

A simple example of this problem is when subjects are selected because of some score or measurement that turns out to be extreme. On the next testing, the score may return to normal. If this had happened during an experimental treatment, we might conclude that the change in the score was the result of the treatment when in fact it only represented a regression to the mean or average score. Statistical regression thus occurs when extreme scores (very high or very low) change over time (low scores become higher and high scores become lower) without any treatment. A related problem is found in medical, psychotherapy, biofeedback, and drug studies that use individuals who come into a professional's office. Most individuals go to see a professional when a given disorder such as a cold is at its worst. With such disorders, some improvement can be seen over time without any treatment, and thus we may conclude incorrectly that the improvement is related to the treatment alone.

Selection

Selection confounds occur when the subjects in one group differ initially from the subjects in another group. Suppose you were testing a new speed-reading technique. For the experimental group you used people who came to the reading clinic, and these people received the treatment. For the control group you might use students in a psychology course. There are at least three possible problems with this design. First, there could be a difference (in IQ, reading level, achievement, and other factors) in the types of people who come to a reading clinic and those in a psychology class. Second, those who come to the clinic might have a lower reading score initially and be able to improve more statistically than the students who are already reading at their optimal level. Third, the subjects who come to the clinic would probably be more motivated and work harder at learning to read faster no matter what technique was used. This third type of problem must be guarded against in any treatment study (for example, drug, relaxation training, meditation) where the group receiving the treatment seeks the treatment and the control group does not. In each of these cases some characteristics of the subjects might initially constitute important differences in the groups even before the independent variable is introduced. Thus it is best to have the experimental and control groups *both* come from people seeking treatment. In this way the groups are most likely to be similar at the beginning of the experiment.

Mortality

This problem occurs when subjects drop out or refuse to take part in any experiment. The problem is greatest when subjects differentially drop out of one group. For example, suppose you want to measure whether children are more creative after playing with dull toys than with fun toys. You first classify the toys as dull or fun and then establish your measure of creativity. As you run the experiment, some of the children who play with dull toys might leave the experiment or not return for other sessions. Thus after a period of weeks the fun-toy group might be composed of all the subjects who began the experiment whereas the dull-toy group is composed of only half of the original children. If you try to analyze these results, you are faced with the possibility that only a certain type of child remained in the dull-toy group. The dull-toy group would then consist of a different subject population than the fun-toy group, thus making your conclusions invalid.

Selection-Maturation Interaction

This broad category refers to the situation where one group of subjects changes along a given dimension faster than another group. For example, lower- and middle-class children develop cognitive abilities at different rates. If this is not taken into account, the experimenter could ascribe the difference to a specific treatment. Likewise, girls develop verbal abilities before boys; when working with preschool children, this differential development must be taken into account. Another possibility in this broad category is selection-testing interaction. For example, Fry and Greenfield (1980) examined job-related attitudes in a midwestern city. They collected data from 529 policemen and 21 policewomen. Assume that this represented the total police force of the city and that other researchers were also collecting various data from these individuals. One possibility that could occur is that every policewoman was used in every study, whereas only some of the 529 policemen were used in every study. This could cause each policewoman to be more sophisticated and experienced at being a subject in an experiment, whereas it would remain a relatively new experience for any given policeman. Thus experimental results that compared policemen and policewomen in this city could be biased because of the policewomen's greater participation in psychological research. Cook and Campbell (1979) expand this category to include also selection-history and selection-instrumentation interactions.

Diffusion or Imitation of Treatments

This occurs when subjects in an experiment can and do communicate with each other and by this communication reduce the differences between groups. If the difference between the experimental and control groups is that one group has information that the other does not have, then if the subjects communicate with each other, it is possible that this difference may be reduced or even removed completely. Consider what would happen if a subject in the picture condition of the Bransford and Johnson study mentioned to a friend that he was in a psychology experiment and described the experiment and the picture he saw. If the friend was later in the experiment and assigned to the no-picture group, his results would be greatly influenced by the previous knowledge. The sharing of information among subjects is a problem particularly when the subjects are drawn from a group who have daily contact with each other. Dr. Shotland avoided this problem in his simulated attack study by helping the subjects to understand the importance of his research and the necessity that they tell no one of the experiment until the study was completed. This may take place in the debriefing process, which we will discuss in Chapter 11.

SUMMARY

In this chapter we began to examine the process of interpreting the results of our experiment. We suggested three hypotheses that must be considered. First, there is the null hypothesis, which states that there is no difference between the groups in the experiment. Second, the confound hypothesis suggests that the results are produced by some systematic influence *other than* the independent variable—that is, a confound. And third, there is the suggestion that the results are produced in a systematic fashion by the independent variable.

In our discussion of the null hypothesis, we introduced the statistical F-ratio and showed how the rejection or acceptance of the null hypothesis is related to the difference between the groups and the error or chance variation within the groups. It was our goal to help you realize what considerations must go into the design of experimental studies. In particular, we wanted you to begin thinking about questions of experimental control and the possibility of reducing within-groups variance.

After the null hypothesis has been rejected, the question becomes: Are there factors other than the independent variable that could have caused the results? To answer this question, we look to possible confounds or "threats to internal validity" as they are called by Campbell and Stanley. These threats include such possibilities as history, maturation, testing, instrumentation, statistical regression, selection, mortality, interactions, and diffusion of treatments. We will add additional threats as we continue. It was our goal here to help you understand why you would not immediately want to conclude conceptually that your positive results are due to the independent variable.

After ruling out the null hypothesis and the confound hypothesis, we can assume that the results reflect the action of the independent variable. Thus we go back and reexamine our numerical results in light of the assumption that our independent variable is the causal agent. We likewise begin to generalize from our one set of data and consider the implications of our results both for other groups of subjects and for the theoretical implications the data hold. Sometimes we are led to new ideas, which in turn generate new research hypotheses, which can be interpreted with additional experiments.

Figure 5.2 presents a simplified outline of this procedure, which reflects the evolutionary nature of science. The steps are (1) the development of the hypothesis, (2) the translation of this hypothesis into an actual re-

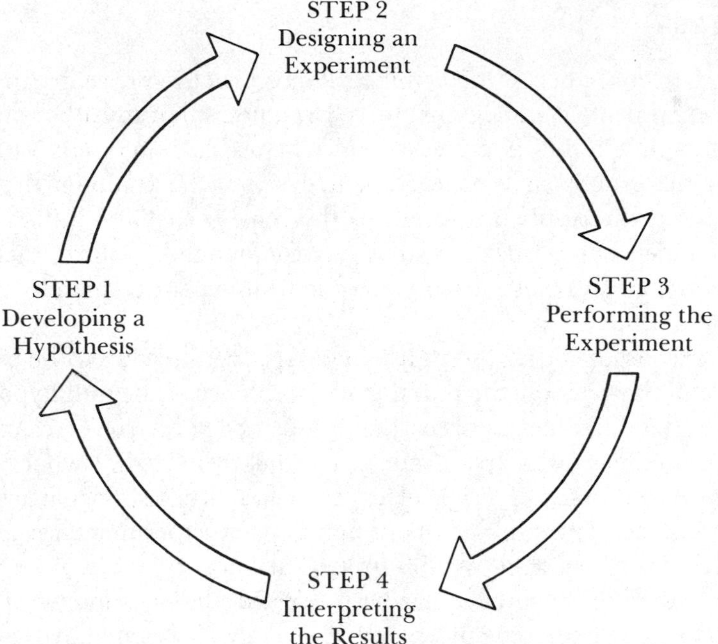

Figure 5.2 Schematic representation of the four major steps in the process of experimentation.

search design, (3) the running of the experiment, and (4) the interpretation of the results. You will notice that there is also an arrow from Step 4 back to Step 1. In this way researchers take the results and interpretations of their studies and create new research studies that refine the previous hypothesis.

Although Figure 5.2 may appear to be circular, it would be better represented by a spiral in which each rotation adds additional information to our knowledge. This is the idea underlying the self-correcting nature of science as discussed in Chapter 1. The overall goal of the process is to help us understand more about what we are studying and to lead us in new directions we could not have discovered by reasoning alone; that is, experimentation gives us an interaction with reality that is not available to reason alone.

CHAPTER SIX

Control: The Keystone of the Experimental Method

INTRODUCTION

In the past chapters we have followed the transformation of an idea into a research hypothesis. We have also begun the process of interpreting experimental results in terms of not one but three separate hypotheses. These hypotheses are (1) the chance hypothesis (the results are caused by chance) and its inverse, the null hypothesis (there are *no* differences between groups); (2) the confound hypothesis (the results are caused by a factor other than the independent variable); and (3) the research hypothesis (the results are caused by the independent variable). We also developed the conceptual thinking underlying the F-ratio and pointed out how this ratio is related to differences between groups in an experiment (between-groups variance) and error or chance variation (within-groups variance). Our ultimate goal in both a conceptual and a practical manner was to understand what influence, if any, the independent variable has on the dependent variable. We want to be certain in our experiments that once we reject the null hypothesis, the differences between our groups are indeed due to the independent variable and not to other factors such as confounds.

In psychological research we have some powerful techniques to help us achieve this aim. Unlike the detective who must always reconstruct events after the fact, the researcher has the advantage of being able to create a new situation in which to test ideas. This would be like the homicide detective being able to bring back to life the dead man and place him in the presence of each suspect until the murder is reenacted. Although such a reenactment of ruling out every possible suspect may lack suspense and not make it in prime time, it does increase the relative certainty of knowing who committed the murder. Increased certainty is a large part of the experimental process. Scientists increase certainty by creating an artificial situation, the experiment, in which important factors can be controlled and manipulated. Through control and manipulation, individual variables may be examined in detail and the influence of one variable on another may be determined with certainty. As a digression we want to point out that since the experiment is an artificial environment created to answer a small number of specific questions, it may not in every case mirror the "real world." In these cases we are often faced with a problem of generalizability and threats to the *external validity* of our research. We will approach these questions in a later chapter. For now we will assume that our research does reflect the real world. In this discussion we will present research in its more ideal form from the standpoint of the scientist, with an emphasis on techniques for reducing threats to the internal validity of an experiment. Throughout the chapter we will emphasize the theme of control in three ways: first, control as related to subject assignment; second, control as related to experimental design and the assurance of internal validity; and third, control as related to the logic of experimentation.

CONTROL ACHIEVED THROUGH SUBJECT ASSIGNMENT AND SUBJECT SELECTION

To illustrate some techniques available for subject assignment, let us begin with a simple illustration of a class designing an experiment. This particular class began with the idea that people can be taught to estimate time more accurately if they are given feedback concerning their performance. From this idea came a formal research hypothesis followed by a discussion of how to conduct the experiment. We pick up the discussion as someone suggests that the experiment simply consist of two groups. One group of subjects will receive verbal feedback on how accurate their estimates of a given time interval are, and the other group will not be given feedback. Thus, we would have two levels of the independent variable—a zero level and a high level. The first question asked is: "How do we go about assigning subjects to groups in this experiment?" It is suggested that someone could contact an equal number of male and female subjects. They could then place the male subjects in one group and the female subjects in the other group. After thinking about this for a moment, the group disagrees. They argue that there might be differences between men and women in the ability to estimate time; that is, perhaps either men are better time estimators than women or women are better time estimators than men, and that this inherent difference might actually create unequal groups before the experiment even begins. Indeed, one person points out that in her recent readings in psychological literature on time estimation she came upon a study indicating that there are sex differences in subjects' ability to estimate time. More specifically, she found that men are more accurate in estimating given intervals of time than women. As it turns out, this student had seen only one part of a larger and somewhat confusing story. Some of the published literature reports sex differences in time estimation and some does not [see Roeckelein (1972) for a more detailed discussion of this literature]. Faced with such ambiguity, the students needed to decide how to control for possible sex differences. Note that the first objection stemmed from common sense, namely that men and women *might* differ in their ability to estimate time. Furthermore, the fact that one student was familiar with experimental evidence that this commonsense idea is correct greatly strengthened this objection. In view of their concern and the evidence supporting their arguments, the group decides not to have all the women in one group and all the men in another group because if they did this, we would never be sure whether the difference between the two groups is due to feedback or to the difference in men's and women's abilities to estimate time. In a very real sense, the experiment would be confounded because they would not know which of the variables—that is, feedback or sex differences between the groups—causes any treatment effects they might observe. Although they might obtain a treatment effect, they could not be sure what the causal factor is.

"Wait a minute!" someone in class yells out. "All of you are getting ahead of yourselves. Even before assigning subjects to groups, we must establish who our subjects are, how many we should use, and only then, how we are going to select them." The question of who are our subjects is, of course, related ultimately to the topic we are studying. If we are interested in time estimation in college students, then college students are the appropriate population. If we decide to use our own college, then we have to ask whether it is in any way different from colleges across the nation. Although this consideration does *not* affect the internal validity of our results, it does influence the generalizability or external validity of our results. The question of how many subjects to use depends in part on the question being asked. We suggest that the literature is the best guide for this consideration. Although using a similar number of subjects as used in other experiments is not infallible (they can be wrong), it is a good guide. For the sake of illustration, the present study was designed with ten subjects (five men and five women) in each group. "We could select our subjects by just calling them on the phone," another student suggests. "That's true, but you may just call your friends and they may not be a representative sample of all college students. Also, you would probably start calling and just keep on calling until you found ten men and ten women. Although we don't know," the student continued, "the set of people you find in their dorm rooms may be different than college students in general. Thus you could select a biased group of subjects related to activities and the amount of time students spend near their phone." Our technique for avoiding this last criticism is to use a procedure known as *random selection* or random sampling. With random selection, every person in the potential subject pool is equally likely to be selected for the study. There are a number of ways this can be accomplished. Box 6.1 illustrates the most common technique—the use of a random number table. Random selection helps to control systematic confounds that could be introduced unknowingly into the subject selection process and to ensure that subjects reflect the population of people we are studying. After the twenty subjects have been randomly selected, the next question is how to assign them to groups.

The group then considers how they can avoid the potential confound created by sex differences in subject assignment to the two groups. One person points out that one way to eliminate this potential confound would be to limit the subjects to one sex. Then, quite correctly, he points out that if they used this *elimination procedure* to remove the potential confound due to sex differences, they would be limiting the generality of the finding tremendously because any new facts they uncover would pertain to only one sex. (This person's concern about the generality of the results is very important and we will return to a more extended discussion of its importance in Chapter 10.) Someone then suggests that they could assign subjects so that an equal number of men and women are in each group. This process of attempting to equate by assigning equal attributes to each group is called a *matching procedure*. In this particular experiment, matching for sex differences consists of simply placing the same number of men and women in each group. In this case, because we know there may be sex differences in time estimation ability, matching provides an important control for not mistaking differences in men's and women's abilities to estimate time with differences caused by our independent variable—verbal feedback—in the accuracy of their estimates.

Before proceeding, it is important to understand exactly how matching

---

Box 6.1 Random Number Table

A random number table is a table of numbers created in such a manner that their occurrence cannot be predicted from a mathematical formula. There are entire books of such numbers that researchers can use for selecting subjects randomly. Look at the random number table in this box. Since there is no order to random number tables, it does not matter whether you read up the page, down the page, across the page, in either direction, or even diagonally. All that matters is that you state beforehand how you will use the table. A simple example would be to use the table to pick out ten subjects from a possible sixty-three for use in the study. First, you might decide that you will use only the last two digits in each number. Second, you might decide you will read the numbers from the bottom to the top of the page. Third, you might decide you will ignore any number greater than 63.

Assume you turned to the page shown in this box. You would begin by closing your eyes and placing your finger on some part of the page, or any other method you wish to use. Once you have your first number (91511), you simply read up the page using only the last two digits. The first ten numbers are as follows—11, 95, 24, 45, 25, 75, 50, 18, 06, 71. Since you cannot use numbers larger than 63, you ignore 95, 75, and 71 and keep reading upward until you find three numbers less than 64. These are 54, 33, and 25. Since 25 occurred twice, you need to pick one final number, which is 05. At this time you could take your list of sixty-three possible subjects and pick subjects who are listed in positions 11, 24, 45, 25, 50, 18, 06, 54, 33, 05. You now have a group of randomly selected subjects.

16631	35006	85900	98275	32388	52390	16815	69298	82732	38480	73817	32523	41961	44437	
96773	20206	42559	78985	05300	22164	24369	54224	35083	19687	11052	91491	60383	19746	
38935	64202	14349	82674	66523	44133	00697	35552	35970	19124	63318	29686	03387	59846	
31624	76384	17403	53363	44167	64486	64758	75366	76554	31601	12614	33072	60332	92325	
78919	19474	23632	27889	47914	02584	37680	20801	72152	39339	34806	08930	85001	87820	
03931	33309	57047	74211	63445	17361	62825	39908	05607	91284	68833	25570	38818	46920	
74426	33278	43972	10119	89917	15665	52872	73823	73144	88662	88970	74492	51805	99378	Last number
09066	00903	20795	95452	92648	45454	09552	88815	16553	51125	79375	97596	16296	66092	
42238	12426	87025	14267	20979	04508	64535	31355	86064	29472	47689	05974	52468	16834	
16153	08002	26504	41744	81959	65642	74240	56302	00033	67107	77510	70625	28725	34191	
21457	40742	29820	96783	29400	21840	15035	34537	33310	06116	95240	15957	16572	06004	
21581	57802	02050	89728	17937	37621	47075	42080	97403	48626	68995	43805	33386	21597	
55612	78095	83197	33732	05810	24813	86902	60397	16489	03264	88525	42786	05269	92532	
44657	66999	99324	51281	84463	60563	79312	93454	68876	25471	93911	25650	12682	73572	
91340	84979	46949	81973	37949	61023	43997	15263	80644	43942	89203	71795	99533	50501	
91227	21199	31935	27022	84067	05462	35216	14486	29891	68607	41867	14951	91696	85065	
50001	38140	66321	19924	72163	09538	12151	06878	91903	18749	34405	56087	82790	70925	
65390	05224	72958	28609	81406	39147	25549	48542	42627	45233	57202	94617	23772	07896	
27504	96131	83944	41575	10573	08619	64482	73923	36152	05184	94142	25299	84387	34925	
37169	94851	39117	89632	00959	16487	65536	49071	39782	17095	02330	74301	00275	48280	
11508	70225	51111	38351	19444	66499	71945	05422	13442	78675	84081	66938	93654	59894	
37449	30362	06694	54690	04052	53115	62757	95348	78662	11163	81651	50245	34971	52924	
46515	70331	85922	3832J	57015	15765	97161	17869	45349	61796	66345	81073	49106	79860	
30986	81223	42416	58353	21532	30502	32305	86482	05174	07901	54339	58861	74818	46942	
63798	64995	46583	09785	44160	78128	83991	42865	92520	83531	80377	35909	81250	54238	
82486	84846	99254	67632	43218	50076	21361	64816	51202	88124	41870	52689	51275	83556	
21885	32906	92431	09060	64297	51674	64126	62570	26123	05155	59194	52799	28225	85762	
60336	98782	07408	53458	13564	59089	26445	29789	85205	41001	12535	12133	14645	23541	
43937	46891	24010	25560	86355	33941	25786	54990	71899	15475	95434	98227	21824	19585	
97656	63175	89303	16275	07100	92063	21942	18611	47348	20203	18534	03862	78095	50136	
03299	01221	05418	38982	55758	92237	26759	86367	21216	98442	08303	56613	91511	75928	First number
79626	06486	03574	17668	07785	76020	79924	25651	83325	88428	85076	72811	22717	50585	
85636	68335	47539	03129	65651	11977	02510	26113	99447	68645	34327	15152	55230	93448	
18039	14367	61337	06177	12143	46609	32989	74014	64708	00533	35398	58408	13261	47908	
08362	15656	60627	36478	65648	16764	53412	09013	07832	41574	17639	82163	60859	75567	

controls for a possible confound due to sex differences. To begin, this procedure *does not eliminate sex differences* as does the elimination procedure, which would limit the experiment to only men or only women. Instead, by placing an equal number of men and women in each group, *we control for any sex differences by distributing them evenly between our experimental and control groups.* In this way, any sex differences in time estimation affect both groups equally and, consequently, no longer differentially affect our experimental and control groups. Thus, matching for sex differences eliminates a potential confound from this experiment. The original experimental design and the revised design are contrasted in Figure 6.1.

One member of the group then suggests that they could ask all twenty subjects to report to the laboratory at 2 P.M. As the subjects arrive, they could simply assign the first five men and five women to the experimental group and the second five men and five women to the control group. After a moment's hesitation, someone points out that one group would be made up of the subjects who arrived on time and the other would include subjects who arrived somewhat later. If there is a relationship between one's ability to get to an experiment on time and the ability to estimate time, another confound would be introduced. Although no one had encountered any pub-

(a) *Original design:*

Experimental (Feedback) all men	*Control (No feedback)* all women
○○○○○○○○○○	△△△△△△△△△△

Note: With this design we wouldn't know if any obtained treatment effects are due to the independent variable (verbal feedback) or sex differences.

(b) *Revised design (Matching for sex differences):*

Experimental (Feedback) ½ men, ½ women	*Control (No feedback)* ½ men, ½ women
○○○○○ △△△△△	○○○○○ △△△△△

Note: Any sex differences in time estimation are distributed evenly across both groups. Thus, we can assume any treatment differences are due to the independent variable (verbal feedback).

Figure 6.1 Original experimental design and revised experimental design.

lished evidence of a relationship between one's ability to get to an experiment on time and ultimate accuracy in estimating time, it is reasonable to suspect that there might well be a correlation. In this case, we would not know whether the ultimate treatment effect is due to the feedback or to the fact that there are a lot of on-time people in one group and not-on-time people in another group. Consequently, it is agreed to control for a possible confound due to the subjects' arrival time as well as sex.

As to exactly how they might do this, one student suggests that they simply alternately assign subjects as they arrive to either the experimental (E) or the control (C) group. With this alternating assignment procedure, subjects would be assigned as follows: ECECECEC . . . . Another disagrees, saying that because E always precedes C, this would create a small but possibly relevant bias. He then suggests assigning subjects the way they used to "choose up" baseball teams in fifth grade: first choice to one team, next two choices to the next team, fourth choice to the first team, and then repeat the sequence until all players are chosen. Although he did not realize it then, he and his fifth-grade teammates had reinvented a commonly used *counterbalancing* procedure. With this particular procedure, subjects would be assigned as follows: ECCE, ECCE, ECCE . . . . Like simple alternation, counterbalancing ensures that each condition (early versus late arrival) appears equally often, and it has the additional advantage that each condition precedes and follows the other condition an equal number of times. In Figure 6.2, this counterbalanced design is contrasted with the previous design, which controlled for sex differences but ignored the potentially confounding influence of arrival time.

By using these matching and counterbalancing procedures, our students arrive at the final experimental design depicted in Figure 6.2. This design is far superior to their original plan to place all men in one group and all women in another because it adequately rules out two potential confounds that may have inadvertently produced unequal groups even before the experiment began. These confounds are: (1) time estimation performance may be different for men and women, and (2) time estimation may be related to a subject's ability to get to an experiment on time. By using matching and counterbalancing, the students feel confident that they have a confound-free design and decide to go ahead with their experiment.

Pause for a moment and think about their final design. Can you think of any other factors that might constitute potential confounds in an experiment designed to determine the effect of verbal feedback on time estimation? Remember, if you suspect that some factor may constitute a potential

(a) *Revised design (which matched for sex differences but ignored arrival time):*

Experimental (Feedback) ½ men, ½ women		*Control (No feedback)* ½ men, ½ women	
○○○○○	△△△△△	○○○○○	△△△△△
1 2 3 4 5	1 2 3 4 5	6 7 8 9 10	6 7 8 9 10

Note: With this design, although we've controlled for sex differences, we still don't know if any eventual treatment differences are due to feedback or to some relationship between one's ability to get to an experiment on time and his ability to estimate time. The numbers under each figure represent the arrival order of each man and woman.

(b) *Final design (matching for sex and counterbalancing for arrival time):*

Experimental (Feedback) ½ men, ½ women		*Control (No feedback)* ½ men, ½ women	
○○○○○	△△△△△	○○○○○	△△△△△
1 4 5 8 9	2 3 6 7 10	2 3 6 7 10	1 4 5 8 9

Note: Both sex differences and arrival time differences are now evenly distributed across our two groups. Because this design balances for both sex and arrival time differences, any experimental effect can be assumed due to the independent variable.

Figure 6.2 Revised experimental design and final experimental design using matching and counterbalancing procedures.

confound, you greatly strengthen your argument if you can find some evidence supporting your concern (as the student did when she cited evidence that men and women differ in their ability to estimate time). In lieu of direct evidence, however, common sense can be a useful tool. For example, it would not surprise us if subjects who could get to an experiment on time were better time estimators, so it is reasonable to control for this factor. In a similar way, our common sense tells us that other factors such as where the subject was born are probably not related to the ability to estimate time; consequently, we would not bother to control for the place of birth of our subjects. As you become increasingly familiar with doing experiments and a research area, you will gain a better feel for what factors are reasonable to control for and what factors can be safely ignored. As we pointed out in Chapter 1, although common sense can be a useful tool, it can sometimes mislead even seasoned researchers. For example, in reaction time experiments, very few researchers bother to control for eye color. Yet one recent study indicates that people with dark eyes have slightly faster reaction times than people with light eyes (Landers, Obermier & Patterson, 1976) Because of such possible confounds, random assignment of subjects to groups is generally the best procedure to follow, as we shall see in the next section of this chapter.

PROCEDURES FOR SUBJECT ASSIGNMENT: MATCHING, COUNTERBALANCING, AND RANDOMIZATION

In the preceding discussion, our students use matching and counterbalancing procedures to ensure that their experiment is not confounded by either sex differences or arrival time differences between their two groups. If either of these variables is permitted to affect our groups differently, a serious confound would result. We would not know whether any difference between our experimental and control groups is due to verbal feedback (independent variable) or to sex or arrival time differences in our groups (confound). To control the impact of these potentially confounding variables, we typically utilize procedures such as matching, counterbalancing, and randomization to distribute their influence between our two groups.

In this section we will discuss each of these procedures for equating groups at the onset of our experiment. Whenever possible we will compare these procedures with each other so that the advantages and disadvantages of each will be evident. In terms of our earlier discussion of subject variability (within-groups variance), notice that when we distribute the impact of these potentially confounding variables between our two groups, we end up *increasing* the amount of subject variability in our experiment! Thus we are often confronted by a choice between a variable influencing a single group (thereby acting as a confound) or having its influence evenly distributed between both groups (thereby serving only to increase subject variability). Given this dilemma, the lesser of two evils is definitely increased subject variability!

Matching consists of assigning subjects to our experimental and control groups so that each group possesses equal attributes of any dimension we wish to equate. Put simply, a design that incorporates matching procedures in subject selection must first evaluate each subject along some relevant dimension and then, on the basis of each subject's score, assign that subject to either the experimental or the control group so that each group possesses an equal amount of the attribute being "matched." Matching groups on the basis of pretest scores can equate groups along any physical or psychological dimension that can be measured: intelligence, anxiety level, racial prejudice, and others. In the time estimation experiment, our students simply placed an equal number of men and women in each group. Another way they might have used matching would have been to equate their groups for the ability to estimate time before the experiment began. (Perhaps you thought of this as you were reading the previous section.) To match the groups for time estimation ability, we would first have to use a pretest or a previous measurement to evaluate each subject's ability to estimate time. Then we would assign subjects so that the two groups are approximately equal in the pretest measure of this attribute. We would then say that the groups are "matched" for their ability to estimate time before the experiment begins.

Matching is most frequently used when we are dealing with a limited number of subjects because we are then most likely to get an uneven distribution of a given attribute if we assign subjects on the basis of chance alone. When matching groups, keep in mind that it is not necessary to match along every possible dimension. Instead it is only necessary to equate our groups along those dimensions that may be related to our subjects' performance on the dependent measure. So, in the time estimation experiment, we would not bother to match for attributes such as body weight, religious background, or intelligence. The only requirements involved in matching are that (1) we already know those attributes of our subjects that, if unevenly distributed between groups, may be confounded with the effect of our independent variables; and (2) our pretest measure of these attributes is adequate.

One disadvantage of matching is that the groups are equated only along the dimension measured by the pretest. For all other attributes we have no assurance that the groups are equal, particularly when dealing with small groups. The danger with this procedure is that if we overlook an attribute that constitutes a potential confound, there is a good chance it will be unevenly distributed between our two groups. This disadvantage can be overcome if we match subjects into pairs and then randomly assign one of each pair to one group and the other to the second group. We will discuss this approach later. A second disadvantage of matching is that it may require that the subjects visit the laboratory twice: once for the measure on which the subjects will be matched (a pretest) and once for the experiment itself. This can be avoided if we match on the basis of available measures such as SAT scores or attributes such as sex or eye color. Thus a pretest is not needed in every situation.

A second procedure used to eliminate potential confounds from experimental designs is *counterbalancing*. To counterbalance the assignment of subjects to experimental and control groups, certain conditions must be met. First, each condition must occur equally often, and second, each condition must precede and follow all other conditions an equal number of times. Thus counterbalancing is a matching procedure with the added restriction that each condition must precede and follow all other conditions an equal number of times. To counterbalance subjects between two groups, we must first rank order all our subjects along the dimension we wish to counterbalance. In the time estimation experiment, our students used counterbalancing to control for the possibility that there may be a relationship between the subject's ability to get to the experiment on time and their ability to estimate time. They simply assigned the first man to arrive to one condition (experimental group), the next two to the other condition (control group), the fourth to the first group, and so on. This generates an ABBA counterbalancing sequence, and they simply repeat it until all male subjects are assigned to a group and then until all female subjects are assigned. Notice that counterbalancing subjects can be done along any physical or psychological dimension once the overall order of scores is known. Thus we could counterbalance our subjects' height, age, intelligence, or emotionality. When considering counterbalancing, keep in mind that more than two factors can be counterbalanced as long as each condition appears equally often and precedes and follows all other conditions an equal number of times. For example, with a counterbalancing procedure, subjects could be assigned to three conditions in the following order: ABCCBA . . . .

Because counterbalancing is a specialized form of matching, its advantages and disadvantages are similar to those described for matching. Like matching, counterbalancing is particularly useful when we are dealing with a limited number of subjects because it eliminates the uneven distribution of conditions that might result from chance or the random assignment of subjects. Similarly one disadvantage of counterbalancing is that the groups are equated only along the dimension measured by the pretest. This means that because it is usually used with small groups, if we overlook an attribute that constitutes a potential confound, there is a good chance it will be unevenly distributed between our two groups.

A third procedure and the most powerful technique we have for eliminating unintended subject assignment confounds from the design of experiments is *randomization*. Randomization simply involves making subject assignments solely on the basis of chance. For example, a simple way to assign subjects randomly to either of two groups is to flip a coin. If the outcome is heads we would assign the first subject to one group, if it is tails we would assign the first subject to the other group. We would continue this process until one group is completely filled and then simply place the remaining subjects in the other group. Another common method of making random assignments is to use a random number table (see Box 6.1). In this case we would use the table to assign each one of our previously selected subjects to groups in the experiment.

Let us take a moment to differentiate two terms that are sometimes confused. These are *random sampling* and *random assignment.* Briefly, random sampling refers to the selection of subjects from a larger population to participate in a piece of research. Random assignment refers to the assignment of selected subjects to groups—for example, experimental and control—in an experiment. Let us now discuss these in more detail.

Random sampling concerns the selection of the entire group of subjects who will participate in an experiment. As we will later emphasize in our discussion of external and ecological validity, when we conduct an experiment we want our conclusions to have relevance for more people than just those who took part in the experiment. One way we ensure this relevance is to have our subjects constitute a representative sample of the entire population in which we are interested. By representative, we mean that our sample is similar to the overall population from which it is taken in all major aspects. For example, if I am interested in the time estimation ability of adult men, I must randomly sample my subjects from the entire adult male population in such a way that all men in the population have an equally likely chance of being selected. I would want to be sure that the local lawyer has just as much chance of being selected as the local garbage collector. In a similar way, I would want to be sure that a given twenty-one-year-old man is just as likely to be selected as the town's only Revolutionary War veteran. The importance of randomly sampling a large population of subjects to obtain the samples we work with in our psychological experiments is crucial to the task of generalizing from the data we obtain in the laboratory back to the entire population. For example, as most of you know, most research done in experimental psychology has involved college sophomores. In a very real sense, our psychology is a psychology of college sophomores and may not generalize to the normal adult population. We will return to this consideration later in this book.

After we have *randomly selected* our subjects from the larger population we are studying, we can *randomly assign* them to our experimental and control groups as a way of equating groups prior to the application of our experimental treatment. The most important advantage of randomly assigning subjects over other procedures for equating groups is that randomization controls for both *known* and *unknown* potentially confounding variables. Unlike the matching and counterbalancing procedures, which attempt to equate our two groups directly on known relevant dimensions, the basic idea behind randomization is to leave the assignment of our subjects to one group or the other solely up to chance. In this way, not only will any *suspected* subject selection biases between our two groups, such as the sex or arrival time or eye color differences, be nullified, but also any other differences, even *unknown* or *unsuspected* differences, will be nullified by randomly distributing them among our two groups. Indeed, it is not an overstatement to say that *randomization randomizes everything*.

As with matching and counterbalancing, it is important to realize that randomization does not remove the differences between the people in our experiment. They are still in our experiment. However, rather than influencing one group as opposed to the other, these subject differences are no longer differentially affecting either group. In this way, randomization provides a powerful tool for control because the impact of both known and unknown potentially confounding assignment biases can be evenly distributed between our experimental and control groups.

CONTROL ACHIEVED THROUGH EXPERIMENTAL DESIGN

As we have emphasized throughout this book, science is a way of asking questions about the world. The quality of the answers we receive is influenced by several factors, one of the most important being the structure we use to reach our answers. In research this structure is determined by our experimental design. Somewhat like a blueprint, the experimental design directs our procedures and gives form to the experiment. In essence, an experimental design is a plan for how a study is to be structured. In an outline form, a design tells us what will be done to whom and when. To be evaluated favorably, a design must perform two related functions. First, it must provide a logical structure that enables us to pinpoint the effects of the independent variable on the dependent variable and thus answer our research questions. Second, it must help us to rule out confounds as an alternative explanation for our findings. In this section we will discuss experimental designs and introduce you to three specific designs that meet these criteria. In the following chapters we will discuss experimental design in greater detail.

A sound design must allow us to logically determine the effect of the independent variable on the dependent variable and to rule out alternative explanations. We informally introduced you to this idea in Chapter 2 with the cereal experiment. As you remember, the cereal company first tried to demonstrate the value of the cereal by giving it to a group of children and then weighing them several months later. If we were to diagram the design of this study, it would be as follows:

Select group of children	Give cereal	Take weight of children

We could also illustrate the design in a more generalized manner as follows:

Group A	Treatment	Measurement

A design such as this would not be much help in pinpointing the effect of the independent variable on the dependent variable, nor would it rule out confounds. As was pointed out in Chapter 2, a stronger design would involve a control group. This design would appear as follows:

Experimental group	Cereal	Measurement
Control group	No cereal	Measurement

Again, we could diagram this in a more generalized manner using T as an abbreviation for treatment and M as an abbreviation for measurement.

Group A	T	M
Group B	T (zero level)	M

This new design helps us to determine the effects of the independent variable. However, does it help us to rule out the various threats to internal validity as presented in the preceding chapter? The answer is no. In particular, we could not rule out the possibility of biased subject selection unless we had randomly assigned subjects to the two groups. To denote this in a design, simply place an R before each group. Campbell and Stanley (1963) refer to this as a posttest-only control group design. The design is diagramed as follows:

R Group A	T	M
R Group B	T (zero level)	M

Look at this design closely and see whether you can remember which study that we have discussed used this design. That's right—the Bransford and Johnson study discussed in Chapter 5 used such a design. In this example, T represents the presentation of the picture and M is the passage-recall measure.

Let us now consider a modification of this design that is similar to the final cereal experiment discussed in Chapter 2. This new design adds a measurement before the treatment. Such measurements are called *pretests,* whereas the measurements after the treatment are called *posttests.* In the terminology of Campbell and Stanley, this design is referred to as a *pretest-posttest control group design.* It is diagramed as follows:

R Group A	M	T	M
R Group B	M	T (zero level)	M

This design would allow us to determine the effects of the independent variable on the dependent variable as well as to control for the threats to internal validity discussed in Chapter 5.

Let us briefly review the threats to internal validity presented by Campbell and Stanley (1963) in relation to the pretest-posttest control group design. History is controlled by the inclusion of a control group, and thus any effects of history on one group would equally affect the other group. Maturation is similarly controlled in that any changes during the course of experimentation would affect both groups equally. Likewise, testing would affect both groups similarly. Notice that when we use the word *controlled,* we use it in the sense of being constant and not just in the sense that we can manipulate some factor. To control a factor in experimentation is the same as holding the effect of that factor constant for all groups throughout a research study. Other threats such as subject selection and statistical regression would be controlled since the groups were randomly assigned in the first place. Mortality or the dropping out of the subjects would likewise not be expected to occur more frequently in one group than the other since the subjects were randomly assigned. Random assignment would also control for the subject-maturation interaction. As you can see, this same design without random assignment would be much weaker.

As a digression it must be noted that although Campbell and Stanley recommend the designs presented in this section as useful in controlling threats to internal validity, they do not mean that the designs are perfect. Confounds such as history can be introduced easily if subjects are not treated consistently throughout a study. Common sense would tell that if you are very nice to one group of subjects and nasty to another group, a confound will be introduced that could affect the results. Likewise in a rating study, if you rate the entire control group before the experimental group, an instrumentation confound may be introduced if your rating ability improves over time. The simple point is that designs serve their function only if used correctly.

A design such as the pretest-posttest control group design has been used by social psychologists as they study the persuasive effects of movies and lectures on the attitudes of individuals. Using this design, they randomly assign subjects to one of two groups. Subjects are then given a questionnaire concerning their attitude toward a certain topic—being politically conservative for example. The experimental group may be shown a movie supporting an extremely conservative position while the control group sees no movie. Following this, each group receives a questionnaire concerning their attitude on conservatism. Using this design, it is possible to measure the amount of attitude change brought about by the movie by comparing the change scores on the pretest and posttest questionnaires of the experimental and control groups.

As researchers used this type of design, it became apparent that the administration of a pretest alone could influence the persuasiveness of a movie or lecture; that is, if someone was asked his or her views on being conservative and was then shown a movie encouraging agreement with an extreme conservative position, the questionnaire alone could reduce the attitude change produced by the movie. To control for this problem, Solomon (1949) suggested the use of a four-group design. Groups 1 and 2 would be the experimental and control groups described previously. Groups 3 and 4 would be like the experimental and control groups except neither group 3 nor group 4 would receive the pretreatment questionnaire. The design could be outlined as follows:

Randomly assigned group 1	Pretest	Treatment	Posttest
Randomly assigned group 2	Pretest		Posttest
Randomly assigned group 3		Treatment	Posttest
Randomly assigned group 4			Posttest

By using the *Solomon four-group design,* researchers are able to determine not only the effects of the treatment but also the interaction of the treatment with whether or not a pretest is given. One can also use this design to determine the effects of maturation and history by comparing the posttest of the fourth group with the pretest of groups 1 and 2.

The three designs presented in this section (posttest only, pretest-posttest, and Solomon four-group) are considered by Campbell and Stanley (1963) to be examples of experimental designs that lead to "true experiments." A true experiment includes at least three characteristics and sometimes a fourth. The first characteristic is that subjects are *randomly assigned* to groups such that a given subject is equally likely to be assigned to any of the groups. As we already mentioned, there are a number of procedures for accomplishing this goal, including the use of a random number table. In certain cases, you may want to match the subjects before they are randomly assigned to groups. A simple procedure after the matching has been done is to flip a coin and allow the heads or tails to determine in which group the first subject of the pair is placed. The second characteristic of a true experiment is that there are at least two levels of the independent variable. One level can, of course, be a zero level as in the Bransford and Johnson study cited earlier; that is, not to present one group with the picture is the same as presenting a zero level of the independent variable. The third characteristic of a true experiment is that it can control for the major threats to internal validity, which we discussed in Chapter 5. Sometimes a fourth characteristic is included, which is of a theoretical nature. Although not agreed upon by all researchers, this characteristic requires that a true experiment compare two alternative theoretical positions. We introduced you to this idea in Box 4.1 with Platt's discussion of strong inference. In this box we used the example of falling weights lending support to either Galileo's theory or the theory of Aristotle. This example illustrates the fourth criterion.

In this section we presented the most ideal cases of experimental design. Specifically, we presented three designs that can lead to true experiments and reduce the threats to internal validity. However, a general point needs to be made, which we will continue to develop throughout this book. This is that research designs are created in response to the needs of researchers as they attempt to answer specific questions and rule out alternative explanations. As such, designs are not sacred in themselves but are valuable only in the manner in which they allow us to make accurate interpretations of experimental results. Thus, an experimental design is never a replacement for an understanding of your research area. With such an understanding, it is important to create useful experimental designs that actually control for the important factors involved. Although true experimental designs aid greatly in our search for understanding, they can never replace logic, common sense, and a thorough knowledge of our research area.

CONTROL AS RELATED TO THE LOGIC OF EXPERIMENTATION

In this section we want to pull together some of the themes related to the logic of experimentation. Let us do this through the simple illustration in Figure 6.3. Imagine an experiment in which subjects are selected and then randomly assigned to one of two groups. It is diagramed as follows:

R	Group A	T	M
R	Group B		M

Let us first turn to Steps 1 and 2 of Figure 6.3. To help us logically determine the effect of the independent variable on the dependent variable, we must first ask whether Group A is equal to Group B before any treatment (independent variable) is introduced. We can assume this to be the case if we have randomly assigned subjects to these two groups. What would the *F*-ratio equal at this point (assuming we had a measure of the dependent variable in each group)? Conceptually the *F*-ratio would equal one. Follow this reasoning for a second. If the two groups are chosen as equal, then we can assume that there are no systematic effects on one group as compared with the other *before* the independent variable is introduced. There should only be variations due to chance. As you remember, between-groups variance is influenced by differences between the groups as well as chance variation. Within-groups variance is influenced mainly by chance variation. Thus,

$$F = \frac{\text{between-groups variance}}{\text{within-groups variance}} = 1 = \frac{\text{treatment effect} + \text{error}}{\text{error}} .$$

If, for some reason, the two groups were unequal at the beginning of the experiment, then the F-ratio would be greater than one *before* the independent variable is ever introduced! In this situation we might find ourselves rejecting the null hypothesis (Group A = Group B) and drawing an inappropriate conclusion. Thus it is imperative that we control subject assignment to groups for the logic of experimentation to be valid. The best method for ensuring that subject groups are equal is through the random assignment of subjects to groups. This is especially true when our design lacks a pretest measure from which our assumption of equal groups can be verified.

Moving to Step 3 of Figure 6.3, we arrive at the introduction of the independent variable. In relation to the logic of experimentation, the main question that we ask here is: Are the different levels of the independent variable the *only* way in which Group A is treated differently from Group B?

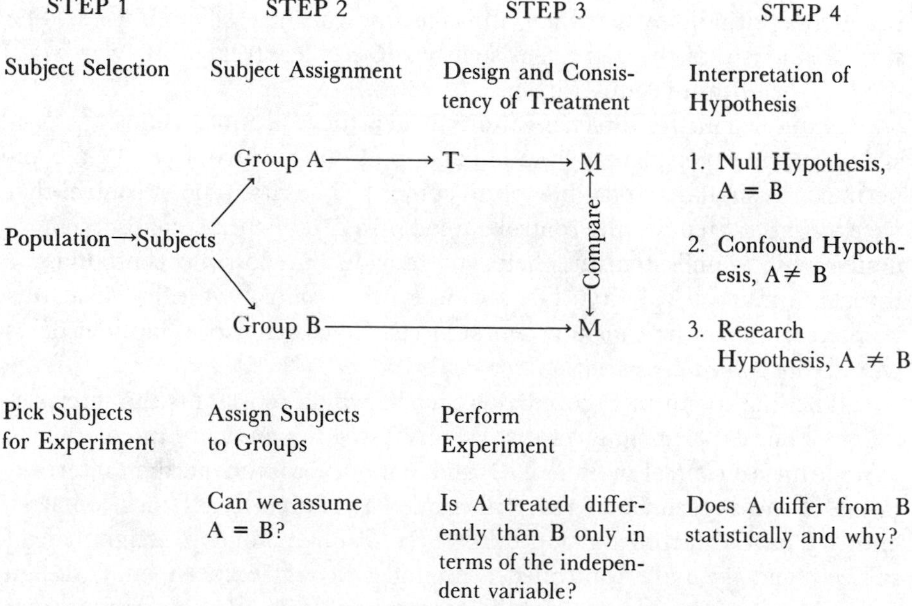

Figure 6.3 Conceptual steps in experimentation.

If the answer is no, then we face a possible confound, which makes interpretation of the data difficult if not impossible. Thus, we must be able to control the experimental situation at Step 3 or else the logic of our experimental design falls apart. Statistics cannot help us at this point since any systematic change in Group A as compared with Group B because of either the independent variable or a confound will increase the between-groups variance and may cause us erroneously to reject the null hypothesis. For the sake of completeness, we want to point out that if an extraneous variable affects *both* Groups A and B, then the within-groups variance is increased, thus making it more difficult to reject the null hypothesis and to see the effect of the independent variable on the dependent variable. For example, if a study with an independent variable that provoked anxiety was performed at the same time college students (both men and women) were being called into the army on short notice, some students (those who could be drafted) might show higher anxiety scores, which would lead to greater variability than normal, making it more difficult to see changes related to the independent variable. As pointed out earlier, the more variability in an experiment, the greater the within-groups variance. On the other hand, if we treat all our subjects the same and every subject is exposed to exactly the same experimental situation, then the within-groups variance is minimized. The simple rule is that the more consistently subjects are treated in every way, the less the within-groups variance.

A simple rule for internal validity is to achieve as much control as possible over the experimental situation and to use this control to make the experiment as similar as possible for all subjects. The first type of control that we exercise at Step 3 is the control gained by a good experimental design. A design with sound structure helps us to rule out possible confounds or threats to internal validity. The second type of control we exercise at this point is consistent treatment of our subjects. Consistency of treatment helps us to reduce *needless* variation.

The final point in Figure 6.3 is Step 4, which represents the interpretation of our experimental results. We discussed this in detail in Chapter 5. If we achieved control in Steps 1, 2, and 3 of our experiment, then interpretation of the experimental results becomes a relatively easy task. That is, once we have controlled group differences through random assignment of subjects and we have controlled confounds through experimental design and minimizing needless variability among subjects, we can assume that our results are due to the independent variable.

SUMMARY

This chapter first discussed the ways in which science investigates possible causal relationships. One way could involve the control and/or manipulation of variables that are suspected of being causally related to the dependent variable. We recommended that you can control potential confounding variables due to unequal groups by appropriate subject assignment procedures; however, there are important problems associated with the assignment of subjects to control and experimental groups. Procedures to avoid these problems include randomization, matching, and counterbalancing. We then discussed the major advantages and problems associated with each method of controlling for subject assignment confounds. We advised that matching and counterbalancing be considered when relatively small numbers of subjects are involved. When there is a larger number of subjects, we recommended randomization because this technique controls for both known and unknown potentially confounding variables and automatically provides for the even distribution of subject differences in both experimental and control groups.

We discussed the importance of sound experimental design in experimental control. A good experimental design should provide a logical structure that will facilitate the identification of the effect of the independent variable on the dependent variable and assist in ruling out confounds as alternative explanations of one outcome. Both the posttest and the pretest/posttest control group designs are "true experimental" designs. Another true experimental design is the Solomon four-group design. This design has the advantage of determining treatment effects as well as treatment by pretest interaction and maturation/history effects. In each of these true experimental designs, subjects are randomly assigned to the conditions, and there should be at least two levels of the independent variable. A third characteristic of the true design involves an ability to control for threats to internal validity. The chapter concluded with the presentation of a sample experimental design following the steps recommended in Figure 6.3.

CHAPTER SEVEN

Applying the Logic of Experimentation: Between-Subjects Designs

INTRODUCTION

In Chapter 6 we emphasized the importance of control in experimentation, and we presented concepts underlying the design of experiments. We introduced you to the idea of the "true experiment" and its advantages in helping us make causal inferences. Specifically, we presented you with the blueprints for three designs that give us a large degree of control over the experimental situation. In this manner, potential confounds are reduced, thus limiting the threats to the internal validity of our experiments. We want to build on that discussion in this chapter. We will show how the potential usefulness of experimental designs can be increased by using more than two levels of the independent variable. We will also introduce you to designs that examine the effects of more than one independent variable on the dependent variable; these are referred to as *factorial designs*.

From the onset of this discussion, it is important that you realize that no design is perfect. Each design has its own strengths and weaknesses in relation to the specific scientific questions being asked. Part of your task as a scientist is to learn which designs are best suited to certain types of questions and how existing designs may be modified to answer future questions. Whenever possible, we will make specific suggestions as to the appropriateness of designs and point out potential problems with certain designs. However, without an exploration of the specific context in which a given design is to be used, it is impossible to fully evaluate the appropriateness of a given design. Some students feel perplexed at this point. Yet part of becoming a mature researcher is seeing that psychological experimentation is more than learning a set of rules and applying them to research. Research in psychology is *work*. It may be fun work, but it is still work, which requires thinking, common sense, and a knowledge of the published literature. It is in this spirit that we suggest you approach the next chapters—not only as an introduction to different types of experimental designs but also as a development of research approaches that you can learn from and modify as needed at a later stage in your career.

BETWEEN-SUBJECTS DESIGN: TERMINOLOGY

Between-subjects designs are a general class of designs in which different subjects are used in each of our groups. To be more precise, these designs involve comparisons *between* different groups of subjects. In the illustrations of research presented thus far in this book, we have emphasized between-subjects designs. For example, the cereal experiment presented in Chapter 2 compared the weight gained by one group of children who ate cereal with that of another group that did not. The "true" experimental designs presented in Chapter 6 are also between-subjects designs. One characteristic of the between-subjects design is that *any given subject* receives *only one level* of the independent variable. Another characteristic is that only one score for each subject is used in the analysis of the results. Although the children in the cereal experiment were weighed more than once (before and after the treatment), the comparison between groups was related to the difference between these two measurements; a single score reflected the amount of weight gained.

The alternative to between-subjects designs is *within-subjects* designs. These designs present different levels of the independent variable to the *same* group of subjects. For example, we could determine the value of feedback in shooting basketballs through a within-subjects design by having you shoot baskets blindfolded (zero level of feedback) and then without the blindfold (high level of feedback). In this case you would receive both levels of the independent variable as well as have more than one measure of the dependent variable. We will examine these designs in much greater detail in the next chapter.

COMPLETELY RANDOMIZED DESIGN

One of the simplest between-subjects designs is the completely randomized design, which is also referred to as the simple randomized design or the simple random subject design. In this type of design, the assignment of subjects is completely randomized between groups. In its simplest form, it is composed of two levels of the independent variable. In Chapter 6 we used the following type of diagram:

R	Group A	T(high level)	M
R	Group B	T(zero level)	M

As you remember from that chapter, Group A received a high level of the independent variable and Group B received a zero level. Let us quickly go through the procedure for using this design. Assume that we have already chosen fifty subjects for our experiment such that twenty-five subjects will be in each of our two groups. The next task is to randomly assign twenty-five subjects to Group A and twenty-five to Group B. As mentioned earlier, this may be accomplished in several ways—for example, with a random number table—with the outcome being that every subject is equally likely to be placed in either Group A or Group B. It is this process of randomization that initially equates our two groups and enables us to ultimately infer causation. The next task prescribed by the design is for Group A to receive a high level of the independent variable and Group B to receive a zero level. The task then is the measurement of the dependent variable for each group. Finally, the dependent variable is compared between the groups, which gives us our treatment effect.

MULTILEVELED COMPLETELY RANDOMIZED DESIGNS

The completely randomized design can also contain more than two levels of the independent variable. Such a design is called a *multileveled completely randomized design* and can be diagramed as follows:

R	Group A	Level 1 T	M
R	Group B	Level 2 T	M
R	Group C	Level 3 T	M
R	Group D	Level 4 T	M

As an example of a completely randomized design with four levels of the independent variable, consider a study of the effects of drinking coffee on flying an airplane. Each group would be given a prescribed number of cups of coffee and then tested in a laboratory equipped with a flight simulator. The number of errors made by each group would serve as the dependent variable. In this hypothetical example, level 4 could equal six cups of coffee, level 3 could equal four cups, level 2 could equal two cups, and level 1 could equal zero cups.

In Chapter 5 we presented the Bransford and Johnson (1972) study in a simple two-group form with one group seeing the entire picture before hearing the passage and the other group seeing no picture. That was an incomplete description of the actual study. In the actual study there were five groups, which would be classified as a multileveled completely randomized design. In addition to the two groups described previously, Bransford and Johnson included three other groups. As you remember, their independent variable was the amount of context (prior knowledge), with the appropriate picture representing total context (Group 1). Group 2 also saw a picture before hearing the passage; however, the picture presented to Group 2 represented only a partial context for the passage, although the individual components were the same as those presented to Group 1 (see Figure 7.1). The third group was presented with a zero level of the independent variable and saw no picture before hearing the passage. There were also a fourth and fifth group that served as controls. Group 4 saw the picture representing the total context but not until *after* the passage had been heard. Group 5 heard the passage twice but did not see the picture. This study is pictorially represented in Figure 7.1.

The most common way to analyze a completely randomized design is to use a single-factor analysis of variance. In this case the null hypothesis would state that every group equals every other group. If we did reject the null hypothesis and found that one or more groups differed significantly from each other, we would then need to apply what are called *post hoc tests* and compare the differences between the groups taken as pairs. In the hypothetical study of the effect of drinking coffee on flying an airplane, we would want to know not only whether the groups as a whole statistically differ from one another, but also which particular groups differ from which other groups. After doing such a post hoc analysis, we might find that six cups of coffee cause different results from no cups of coffee but do not cause any statistical differences compared with two or four cups of coffee. The alternative to using post hoc tests is to plan particular comparisons *before* the study is performed. This is the statistical approach taken by Bransford and Johnson. To be specific, they compared the "context before" condition (Group 1 in Figure 7.1) with each of the four other conditions. For this comparison, they used Dunnett's test, which is beyond the scope of this book.

Group 1

(seeing appropriate picture before hearing passage)

If the balloons popped, the sound wouldn't be able to carry since everything would be too far away from the correct floor. A closed window would also prevent the sound from carrying, since most buildings tend to be well insulated. Since the whole operation depends on a steady flow of electricity, a break in the middle of the wire would also cause problems. Of course, the fellow could shout, but the human voice is not loud enough to carry that far. An additional problem is that a string could break on the instrument. Then there could be no accompaniment to the message. It is clear that the best situation would involve less distance. Then there would be fewer potential problems. With face to face contact, the least number of things could go wrong.

Recall Measure

Group 2

(seeing partial context picture before hearing passage)

If the balloons popped, the sound wouldn't be able to carry since everything would be too far away from the correct floor. A closed window would also prevent the sound from carrying, since most buildings tend to be well insulated. Since the whole operation depends on a steady flow of electricity, a break in the middle of the wire would also cause problems. Of course, the fellow could shout, but the human voice is not loud enough to carry that far. An additional problem is that a string could break on the instrument. Then there could be no accompaniment to the message. It is clear that the best situation would involve less distance. Then there would be fewer potential problems. With face to face contact, the least number of things could go wrong.

Recall Measure

Group 3

(hearing passage

If the balloons popped, the sound wouldn't be able to carry since everything would be too far away from the correct floor. A closed window would also prevent the sound from carrying, since most buildings tend to be well insulated. Since the whole operation depends on a steady flow of electricity, a break in the middle of the wire would also cause problems. Of

Recall Measure

Figure 7.1 Pictorial representation of the Bransford and Johnson study.

without seeing picture)

course, the fellow could shout, but the human voice is not loud enough to carry that far. An additional problem is that a string could break on the instrument. Then there could be no accompaniment to the message. It is clear that the best situation would involve less distance. Then there would be fewer potential problems. With face to face contact, the least number of things could go wrong.

Group 4
(seeing appropriate picture after hearing passage

If the balloons popped, the sound wouldn't be able to carry since everything would be too far away from the correct floor. A closed window would also prevent the sound from carrying, since most buildings tend to be well insulated. Since the whole operation depends on a steady flow of electricity, a break in the middle of the wire would also cause problems. Of course, the fellow could shout, but the human voice is not loud enough to carry that far. An additional problem is that a string could break on the instrument. Then there could be no accompaniment to the message. It is clear that the best situation would involve less distance. Then there would be fewer potential problems. With face to face contact, the least number of things could go wrong.

Recall Measure

Group 5
(hearing passage twice)

If the balloons popped, the sound wouldn't be able to carry since everything would be too far away from the correct floor. A closed window would also prevent the sound from carrying, since most buildings tend to be well insulated. Since the whole operation depends on a steady flow of electricity, a break in the middle of the wire would also cause problems. Of course, the fellow could shout, but the human voice is not loud enough to carry that far. An additional problem is that a string could break on the instrument. Then there could be no accompaniment to the message. It is clear that the best situation would involve less distance. Then there would be fewer potential problems. With face to face contact, the least number of things could go wrong.

If the balloons popped, the sound wouldn't be able to carry since everything would be too far away from the correct floor. A closed window would also prevent the sound from carrying, since most buildings tend to be well insulated. Since the whole operation depends on a steady flow of electricity, a break in the middle of the wire would also cause problems. Of course, the fellow could shout, but the human voice is not loud enough to carry that far. An additional problem is that a string could break on the instrument. Then there could be no accompaniment to the message. It is clear that the best situation would involve less distance. Then there would be fewer potential problems. With face to face contact, the least number of things could go wrong.

Recall Measure

Another illustration of a between-subjects design is from clinical research. Strupp and Hadley (1979) asked how important technical skills are for the therapist in the process of psychotherapy; that is, does a professional psychotherapist learn certain skills or techniques that are required for a successful outcome in psychotherapy? To answer this question, these researchers compared the psychological improvement of clients seeing experienced psychotherapists with that of clients seeing college professors chosen for their ability to form good human relationships. Notice how Strupp and Hadley were attempting to control for the relationship factor in their study. In essence they were asking whether something more than a good relationship is needed for successful psychotherapy to take place. For subjects in the study, they used college students who requested therapy and who scored high on certain scales of a traditional psychological test (the MMPI). Based on traditional diagnostic systems, the subjects were classified as having "neurotic depression" or an "anxiety reaction." The design of the study called for students to be randomly assigned to one of three groups. Group 1 was treated by experienced psychotherapists; Group 2 talked with college professors chosen for their ability to form good relationships; and Group 3 was referred to as a "minimal treatment" group. This third group was told that treatment would be delayed, and thus it served as a no-treatment control during the time the first two groups received therapy. The design of the study was as follows:

R	Group 1	M	T (experienced therapist, therapy skills plus good relationship)	M
R	Group 2	M	T (college professor, good relationship)	M
R	Group 3	M	T (waiting list no treatment)	M

As you can see, this is a multileveled completely randomized design with pretest-posttest measures. In the actual study, a number of dependent variables were used, which included changes in psychological tests and ratings of change by the therapists, students, and outside clinicians, which allowed Strupp and Hadley to assess changes over time. What do you think the results were? Better yet, you should read this study yourself. The complete title is listed in the Bibliography of this book. This study is a good example of how to perform clinical research and illustrates some factors that must be controlled to achieve a scientific understanding of such clinical processes as psychotherapy.

Let us quickly turn to the logic of hypothesis testing as it is related to multileveled between-subjects designs. As with the simple two-level completely randomized experiments presented earlier in the book, we must still answer three questions. First, are the results due to chance? Second, are the results due to a confound? And third, are the results due to the independent variable? The first question is approached through a statistical test of the null hypothesis, which states that no differences exist between the groups. Thus, the null hypothesis for a three-level design states that group 1 = group 2 = group 3. Again we evaluate this through the F-ratio. If the F-ratio is statistically significant, then we know there is a difference between the groups; *however, we do not know which group or groups caused this difference.* To determine whether there is a statistically significant difference between any combination of groups, we must use a post hoc test [these tests are described in most advanced statistics books—for example, Winer (1971)].

After you have rejected the null hypothesis, you turn to the question concerning confounds and utilize the same logic we presented to track down factors that might have played a role in the results. As you can see, if we were not able to assume that our groups were equal before we began the treatment, it would be impossible to conclude what effect, if any, the independent variable had on the dependent variable. Even if you do not read the random number table every night before you go to bed, we hope you have come to understand the extreme importance of the random assignment of subjects to your groups in an experiment. When we are reasonably sure that no significant confounds are present in our study, we can consider our third question concerning causality in relation to the independent variable. If we reject the null hypothesis and rule out confounds, then we may conclude that the independent variable caused our results and theoretically interpret this relationship.

FACTORIAL DESIGN

A survey of published psychological research reported that most research using inferential statistics relied on more complex designs such as factorial designs (Edgington, 1974). The popularity of factorial designs seems related to our acceptance of the fact that there are few, if any, isolated cause-and-effect relationships in psychological processing. Rather, most psychological processes have several causes that *interact* with each other in various ways and cannot be determined from simple experimental designs such as we have discussed thus far. The advantage of factorial designs is that they allow us to examine scientifically the effects of more than one independent variable both individually and collectively on the dependent variable.

An easy way to conceptualize factorial designs is to view them as a composite of a number of simple completely randomized designs such as we have discussed previously. Let us illustrate this point. Consider a completely randomized design to determine the effect of money on memory in psychological experiments. A simple design would be to randomly assign subjects to two groups. Each group would hear the same passage. One group would receive \$1 for every idea remembered and the other group would receive 1¢ for every idea remembered. This would be diagramed as follows:

R	Group 1	T (\$1)	M (recall task)
R	Group 2	T (1¢)	M (recall task)

Now consider a second completely randomized design such as the two-treatment version of Bransford and Johnson's study presented in Chapter 5. We described this study as consisting of a zero level of the independent variable (no picture) and a high level of the independent variable (appropriate context picture). This single-factor experiment can be diagramed as follows:

R	Group 1	T (picture— high context)	M (recall task)
R	Group 2	T (no picture— zero context)	M (recall task)

We could perform these two studies separately; however, then we could not determine the collective effect of both independent variables (money and context) on the dependent variable. This is referred to as the *interaction effect,* but we are getting ahead of ourselves. First, let us see how we might go about combining these two separate studies into one experiment.

An alternative to performing these studies separately would be to combine them into a factorial design. For ease of representation, let us diagram the first experiment in a horizontal fashion as follows:

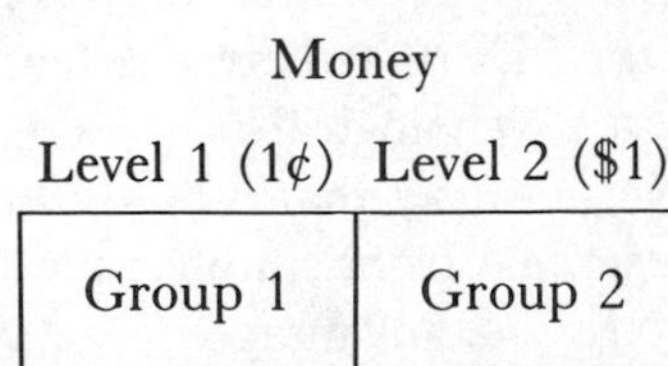

We can likewise diagram the second experiment in a vertical fashion:

Prior Knowledge	Level 1 (no picture)	Group 1
	Level 2 (picture)	Group 2

Now if we simply combine our graphic representations of these two studies, it appears as follows:

		Money Factor	
		Level 1 (1¢)	Level 2 ($1)
Prior Knowledge Factor	Level 1 (no picture)	Group A	Group C
	Level 2 (picture)	Group B	Group D

Notice that with this design we have four *separate* groups, with each subject receiving one level of *each* independent variable. Group A will receive 1¢ for each correct idea recalled and will be given the minimum context or prior knowledge (no picture). Group B will be given 1¢ for each correct idea recalled and will be given the maximum context or prior knowledge (picture). Group C will receive $1 for each idea recalled and minimum context (no picture). Group D will receive $1 for each idea recalled and maximum context (picture).

This type of design is referred to as a *2 × 2 design* (read "two by two"). In this notation 2 × 2 refers to the fact that there are two levels of one independent variable and two levels of another. The independent variables are also referred to as *factors*. If, instead, we had a design involving six levels of factor A and two levels of factor B, then it would be called a 6 × 2 factorial design. Similarly, a design that consisted of two levels of factor A, three levels of factor B, and four levels of factor C would be called a 2 × 3 × 4 factorial design.

The treatment differences (between levels of a given factor) in a factorial design are referred to as *main effects*. Thus it is possible to determine

A general representation of a 2 × 2 design:

		Factor A Level 1 A_1	Factor A Level 2 A_2
Factor B	Level 1 B_1	A_1B_1	A_2B_1
	Level 2 B_2	A_1B_2	A_2B_2

A general representation of a 3 × 3 factorial design:

		Factor A A_1 Level 1	A_2 Level 2	A_3 Level 3
Factor B	Level 1 B_1	A_1B_1	A_2B_1	A_3B_1
	Level 2 B_2	A_1B_2	A_2B_2	A_3B_2
	Level 3 B_3	A_1B_3	A_2B_3	A_3B_3

Figure 7.2 This figure is a schematic representation of 2 x 2, 3 x 3, and 2 x 3 x 2 (opposite page) factorial designs. Note that the total number of treatment conditions in each design can be obtained by multiplying the number of levels of each factor together.

A general representation of a 2 × 3 × 2 design:

Factor C

Level 1 C_1

		Factor A A_1	Factor A A_2
Factor B	B_1	$A_1B_1C_1$	$A_2B_1C_1$
	B_2	$A_1B_2C_1$	$A_2B_2C_1$
	B_3	$A_1B_3C_1$	$A_2B_3C_1$

Level 2 C_2

		Factor A A_1	Factor A A_2
Factor B	B_1	$A_1B_1C_2$	$A_2B_1C_2$
	B_2	$A_1B_2C_2$	$A_2B_2C_2$
	B_3	$A_1B_3C_2$	$A_2B_3C_2$

A 2 × 3 × 2 design can also be diagramed as follows:

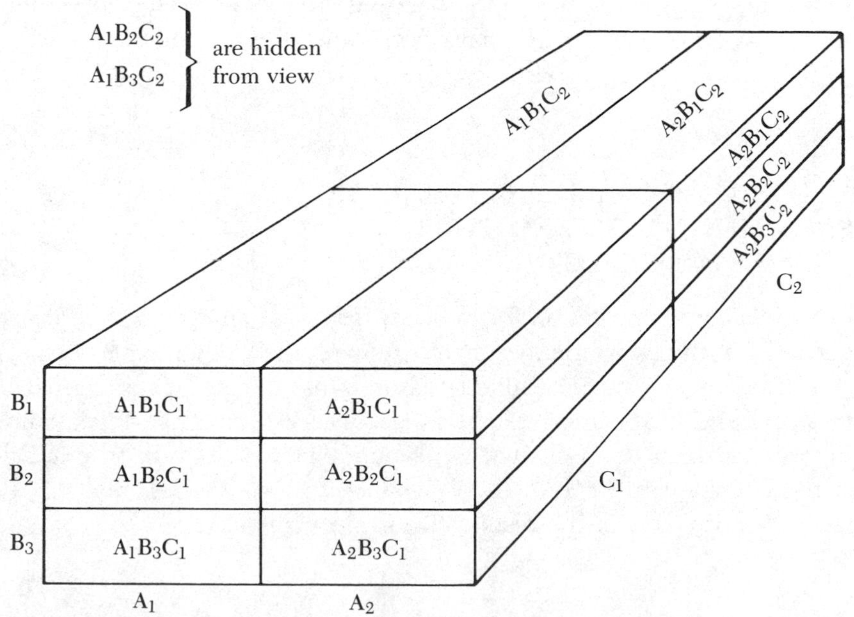

the main effect for each factor. In our previous example, this would be equivalent to performing two single-factor experiments; one would compare the amounts of money given for recall and one would compare the levels of pictorial context. However, in factorial designs the independent variables may combine in various ways in their effects on the dependent variable. Such a combined effect is referred to as an *interaction effect.* Interaction effects cannot be determined by performing separate single-factor studies and thus are unique to factorial designs.

What is an interaction effect? An interaction effect is the result of two independent variables combining to produce a result different from that produced by either variable alone. To give you an extreme example, we know that combining moderate levels of barbiturates and alcohol leads to severe illness and sometimes death, whereas moderate levels of either drug alone do not. Thus it is only in combination that the interaction effect is produced. This is only one type of interaction. We will present additional possible interaction effects later in this chapter.

Before we leave the question of terminology, let us look at schematic diagrams of three different factorial designs (see Figure 7.2 on pp. 150–151). The blocks in the diagram are called *cells.* Notice that the individual cells are labeled according to the level of each independent variable that affects the cell. For example, the group of subjects that receive level 1 of factor A and level 2 of factor B is labeled A_1B_2. Remember that in between-subjects designs, which we are discussing here, each cell represents a different group of subjects that have been randomly assigned to the cells.

FACTORIAL DESIGNS: THE LOGIC OF EXPERIMENTATION AND THE INTERACTION EFFECT

The logic of experimentation for factorial designs is similar to that already described for single-factor experiments. As with these other experiments, in factorial designs we must be able to assume that our groups are equal before any of the treatments are presented. Once we can make this assumption, we may turn to an evaluation of our hypotheses. As with other designs, we will seek the role of (1) chance, (2) confounds, and (3) the independent variable in the results of our experiment.

Because a factorial design involves the simultaneous evaluation of two or more factors and their interactions, the evaluation process is more involved than in a single-factor design. For example, in a factorial design there is not one but many null hypotheses. There is a null hypothesis for each factor of our design. As in a simple design, this null hypothesis states that every level of a factor is equal to every other level. In our 2 × 2 example, one null hypothesis would state that level 1 of factor A is the same as level 2 of factor A. A second null hypothesis would state that level 1 of factor B is the same as level 2 of factor B. A third null hypothesis is also required. This null hypothesis states that there are no interaction effects. It is theoretically possible for any combination of these three null hypotheses in a 2 × 2 design to be accepted or rejected. Once we have made this determination, we can then continue to look for confounds and eventually conclude what effects, if any, the independent variables have on the dependent variable. With more than one independent variable, the logic of searching for confounds is similar to that of the single-factor study, although the complexity is increased.

Let us continue to illustrate factorial designs and their evaluation with a hypothetical experiment. In this experiment we want to study two factors and their effects on the learning ability of old mice. The dependent variable will be the number of errors in running a maze. One factor is whether the mice live in an "enriched" environment with other mice and many "playthings" or live alone in a standard laboratory cage. The second factor concerns the feeding schedule of these old mice. More specifically, we want to determine whether unlimited access to food and water (called an *ad lib* schedule) affects these old mice differently than a feeding of enough food once a day to maintain normal body weight. In our tentative design we have designated the living environment as factor A (with A_1 = enriched, A_2 = standard) and the feeding schedule as factor B (with B_1 = ad lib, B_2 = once a day). Consequently, in this design there are four possible combinations of the two independent variables: A_1B_1, A_2B_1, A_1B_2, and A_2B_2. This particular design is represented by the matrix in Figure 7.3. Each cell of the matrix contains one of the four possible combinations of our two independent variables.

In actually executing such a factorial design, we would first obtain, say, forty mice to participate in our experiment. Our subjects would then be randomly assigned to any one of these four possible combinations of independent variables until there was an equal number of subjects in each cell

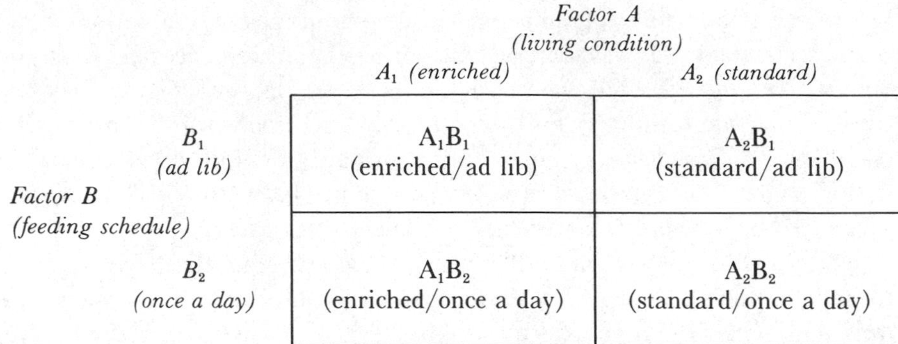

Figure 7.3 This matrix shows the four possible combinations of each of the two levels of a 2 x 2 factorial random subject design. Notice that each cell contains one of the four possible combinations of our two independent variables (living condition and feeding schedule).

of the matrix. This hypothetical experiment is depicted in Figure 7.4. Next, the subjects in the upper left-hand cell would receive the first level of independent variables A and B (A_1B_1 = enriched housing/ad lib feeding). Consequently, their performance on our dependent measure (the number of errors in running a maze) would reflect a combined effect of enriched housing and ad lib feeding. Subjects in the upper right-hand cell of the matrix would receive the second level of independent variable A and the first level of independent variable B (A_2B_1 = standard housing/ad lib feeding). Their performance would reflect the influence of standard housing and ad lib feeding. The same holds for the combinations A_1B_2 (enriched housing/fed once a day) and A_2B_2 (standard housing/fed once a day).

In analyzing the outcome of any factorial design, we are interested in two major questions. First, *do either of our independent variables produce a statistically significant treatment effect?* As mentioned earlier, in a factorial design we call the treatment effect of each independent variable the *main effect* of that variable. In the preceding experiment we have two main effects: type of housing and type of feeding schedule. To determine the extent of the main effect of each independent variable, we compare the different levels of each of our two independent variables. We calculate the performance on our dependent measure for each row and column of our matrix.

For example, Table 7.1 shows hypothetical data from forty old mice

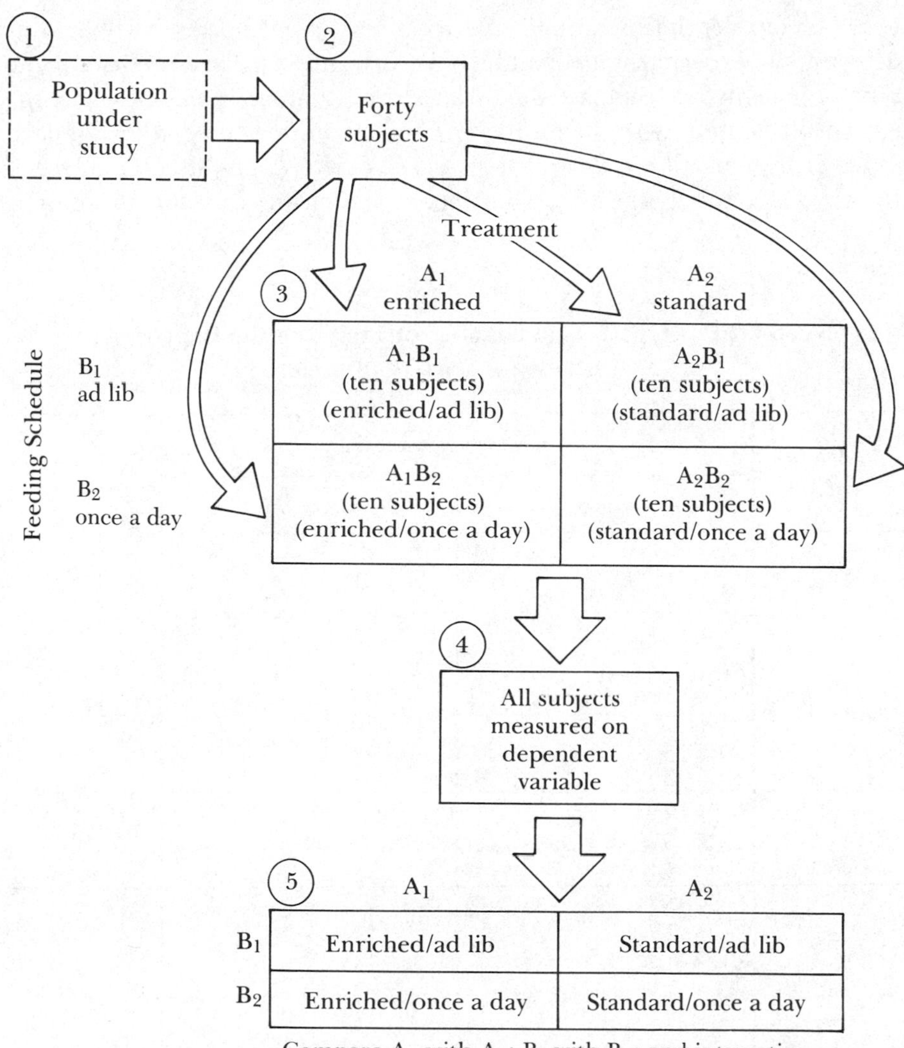

Figure 7.4 This is a schematic representation of the five steps involved in a factorial random subject design involving two levels of each of two independent variables. (1) The entire group of forty mice is obtained from a commercial animal supplier. (2) These forty mice are randomly assigned to four groups of ten each. (3) Each group is exposed to the appropriate level of each factor. (4) All subjects are measured on our dependent variable. (5) We determine whether the interaction effect and the main effect are statistically significant.

tested on our dependent variable following a six-month period of living under our two experimental conditions. To determine the main effect of the type of housing, we compare the mean score for all animals housed in the enriched condition with the mean score for all animals housed in standard cages (10 versus 18 errors in Table 7.1). To determine the main effect of the type of feeding schedule, we compare the mean score for all animals

Table 7.1 Hypothetical Number of Errors on the Dependent Variable for Forty Old Mice

Feeding Schedule	*Type of Housing*				*Row Mean*
	Enriched		*Standard*		
Ad lib	6 4 8 5 7 7 5 6 4 8	$\bar{x} = 6$	21 23 22 22 24 20 20 24 22 22	$\bar{x} = 22$	14
Once a Day	13 15 15 13 18 16 10 12 14 14	$\bar{x} = 14$	14 14 13 15 12 16 14 14 15 13	$\bar{x} = 14$	14
Column Mean	10		18		

who were fed ad lib with the mean score for all animals who were fed once a day (14 versus 14 errors in Table 7.1). From just glancing at these data, it appears that the type of housing had a definite effect on the final performance of the old mice on our dependent variable, whereas the type of feeding schedule apparently did not result in differences in performance. These data must be subjected to appropriate statistical tests before drawing any final conclusions regarding the null hypotheses.

The second question we want to ask with a factorial design is: *As our two independent variables occur together, do they influence each other or do they remain relatively independent of one another?* The extent to which the impact of one independent variable varies as a function of the level of the other independent variable in the experiment is referred to as the *interaction effect*. The manner in which we assess interaction effects involves determining whether the difference between the means of the levels of one independent variable varies as a function of the levels of the other independent variable.

Consider the hypothetical data shown in Table 7.1 for the forty mice tested on the learning task. As we pointed out, animals housed in the enriched environment learned the maze with fewer errors than animals housed in standard cages. In contrast, the type of feeding schedule *did not* have an effect on overall maze performance (14 versus 14 errors). Although there was no overall difference in the mean number of errors for the mice on ad lib versus once a day feeding schedules, the performance of these mice was quite different depending on whether they lived in enriched or standard cages. More specifically, the animals fed once a day all performed about average regardless of housing (14 versus 14 errors). In contrast, the mean performance of the ad lib animals ranged from very good (only 6 errors) for the mice that lived in enriched housing to very poor (22 errors) for the mice that lived alone in standard cages. Thus performance on the learning task showed a strong interaction effect. In this particular case, the ad lib animals were differentially affected by the type of housing, whereas animals fed once a day were uniformly affected by their living conditions.

Let us now turn to an example of an interaction from the research literature. This interaction occurred in an experiment dealing with intimacy that was summarized by Rubin (1974). In this experiment, Rubin and Hill wanted to know what effect the amount of perceived freedom or spontaneity has on either high or low levels of intimate behavior. To answer this question, they conducted a laboratory experiment involving written exchanges of self-disclosure statements between dating couples. In other words, the study relates to how you would respond if your boyfriend or girlfriend sent you a message (either very intimate or not very intimate) if you believed that the experimenter told him or her to write the message versus how you would respond if you believed that your boyfriend or girlfriend sent the message spontaneously. As you might predict, the return message (your message back to your boyfriend or girlfriend) was related both to the level of intimacy of the first message and to whether or not the person believed that the boyfriend or girlfriend had produced the message spontaneously or under direction of the experimenter. See if you can draw a graph to illustrate this interaction generating your own numbers.

When you interpret the results of a factorial experiment, you *always interpret the interaction effects first.* If you think about this for a moment, you will realize that if there is an interaction effect, then the main effects cannot be discussed without a qualifier. This is difficult for some people to understand. However, if you consider the example of the barbiturates and alcohol, you can quickly see that an interaction effect makes it impossible to discuss the effects of either drug alone without qualifying the statement to include the interaction. That is, you can say that moderate drinking does not immediately lead to illness if you include the qualifier that this is true only when barbiturates are not also taken in moderate amounts, and vice versa. To give you another example, if you look at the data in Table 7.1, you can see that it would be inaccurate to conclude that type of housing is an important independent variable without qualifying the statement to say that this is true only if the feeding schedule is ad lib. Thus, the interaction effect must be interpreted before the main effects so that any necessary qualifiers can be added to the main effects.

Let us pause for a moment and examine the form of an analysis of variance summary table that we might see when reading experiments using factorial designs (see Table 7.2). For our present purposes, we are only interested that you know how to read such a table, and it is not necessary that you understand the calculational procedures. In the first column we see listed the sources of the variance. In a simple experiment such as the cereal experiment described in Chapter 2, there would be two entries in this column. The first would be for the treatment variance due to eating cereal (between-groups variance) and the second would be for the error variance (within-groups variance). In factorial experiments, this column would list the treatment variance due to each independent variable and the interactions. The next column lists the degrees of freedom (df) as we discussed in

Table 7.2 Analysis of Variance *F*-Table for the Mouse Study

Source of Variance	*df*	*SS*	*MS*	F	p
Housing (factor A)	1	640	640	245.21	.001
Feeding (factor B)	1	0	0	0	ns
A × B (interaction)	1	640	640	245.21	.001
Error (within-groups variance)	36	94	2.61		

Chapter 3. The third column lists the sum of squares (SS). The fourth column lists the mean square (MS). *Mean square* is what we call a variance when it comes from the statistic analysis of variance. The fifth column depicts the *F*-ratio, which, as we discussed, is the between-groups variance divided by the within-groups variance (error variance). In a factorial design, you must evaluate the treatment effect for each independent variable and for the interactions involved. Thus, you will have an *F*-ratio for each main effect and interaction. The error term (within-groups variance) remains the same for each *F*-ratio. Often there is an additional column listing the probability (p). It is based on this probability that we either accept or reject the null hypothesis.

Table 7.2 is the analysis of variance *F*-table for the mouse study presented earlier in this chapter. Based on this table, we would reject the null hypothesis for factor A (housing) and for the A × B interaction (the interaction of housing and feeding schedule). We would not reject the null hypothesis for factor B (feeding). It is rare in actual practice that we obtain an *F*-ratio of less than one, although it is possible in actual calculations as was the case for factor B (housing).

After the null hypotheses have been evaluated for the interaction of A × B, the main effect of factor A, and the main effect of factor B, then conceptually one turns to the role of confounds and the independent variable in causing the results. By the way, to make your life interesting, there is a possible confound in the mouse study we just presented. See if you can find it.

Because factorial designs are frequently used in the published reports you will be reading, it will be helpful for you to have some idea of how the main effects and interaction effects are actually manifested in data. With this goal in mind, the next section describes a hypothetical series of eight factorial experimental outcomes. In each case the outcome is depicted in two ways: numerically and graphically. If you are not yet accustomed to dealing with factorial designs, proceed slowly. Allow yourself several careful readings to get a feel for the main effects and interaction effects.

EIGHT POSSIBLE OUTCOMES OF 2 × 2 FACTORIAL EXPERIMENTS SHOWING DIFFERENT COMBINATIONS OF SIGNIFICANT AND NONSIGNIFICANT MAIN EFFECTS AND INTERACTIONS

The purpose of this section is to attempt to clarify the idea of both main effects and interactions in factorial designs. To achieve this goal, we will work directly with specific examples. In each of the examples, a different hypothetical outcome will be described in which either the main effects or the interaction effects may be assumed to be statistically significant.

The first example is Figure A, in which the same results are shown in two different ways: first numerically and then pictorially. In the left-hand portion of this figure is a matrix. The numbers inside the box represent the outcomes for each of the four groups in a hypothetical experiment. For example, the group that received treatment combination A_1B_1 is represented in the upper left-hand cell of the matrix, the group that received condition A_1B_2 in the lower left-hand cell, the group that received A_2B_1 in the upper right-hand cell, and the group that received A_2B_2 in the lower right-hand cell of the matrix. The numbers to the right of the box represent the mean for condition B_1 and the mean for condition B_2, and the numbers below the box represent the means for conditions A_1 and A_2, respectively. In the right-

Figure A

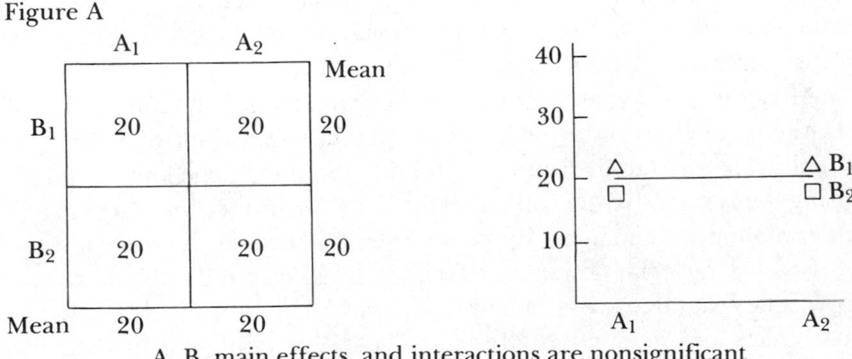

A, B, main effects, and interactions are nonsignificant

hand portion of the figure, the outcome is represented pictorially in graph form. The *x*-axis of this graph—that is, the horizontal axis—indicates groups A_1 and A_2. The *y*-axis, or vertical axis, of the graph gives the values 10, 20, 30, and so on. In this first example, the outcomes for the four groups are 20, 20, 20, and 20, so obviously there was no main effect and no interaction effect. This same outcome is pictorially represented to the right of Figure A. Those subjects who received treatment combination A_1B_1 responded with a dependent variable measure of 20, and this outcome is represented by the triangle above A_1 on the *x*-axis. In a similar way, the outcome of group A_2B_1 is represented by a triangle above A_2 on the *x*-axis. The line connecting these points is intended to highlight the total effect of the first level of condition B. The outcomes for groups A_1B_2 and A_2B_2 are represented by squares above A_1 and A_2 on the *x*-axis and are joined by lines to show the total effect of the second level of condition B. In this figure, the results are the same for all groups. Neither the main effects nor the interaction effects are statistically significant. In the right-hand portion, this is indicated by the line representing condition B_1 and the line representing B_2 falling directly on top of one another. This shows that there is no difference between the main effects of B_1 and B_2. The fact that A_1 and A_2 are both equal to 20 is shown by the corresponding points falling at the 20 on the *y*-axis, so in this case nothing is significant.

Figure B shows a hypothetical condition in which the main effect of A is statistically significant, while the main effect of B and the interaction between A and B are insignificant. In the left-hand portion, the mean for condition B_1 and the mean for condition B_2 are both 30; that is, there is no difference between these two levels of factor B. In contrast, the mean effect of

Figure B

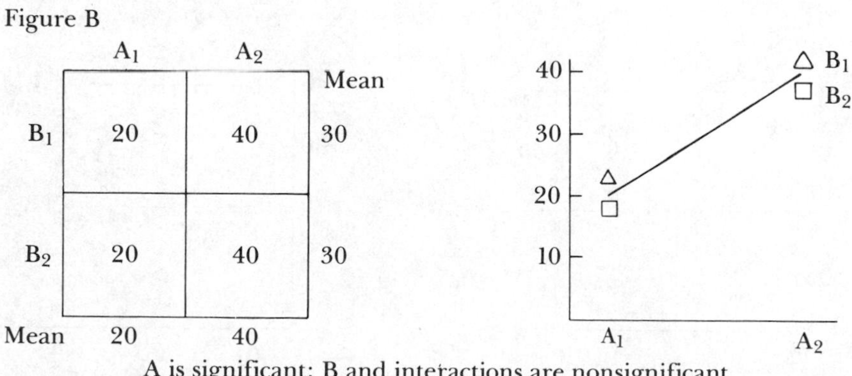

A is significant; B and interactions are nonsignificant

A_1 is 20 and the mean effect of A_2 is 40. Looking at the figure at the right, we see this graphically. The fact that there is no difference between B_1 and B_2 is represented by the two lines overlapping. Furthermore, the fact that the midpoint of each line corresponds to a value of 30 on the *y*-axis reflects that 30 is the mean for both levels of condition B. In contrast, the values for A_1 and A_2 are quite different, which accounts for the slope in the lines between 20 and 40 along the *y*-axis. In this case, then, the main effect of A is significant, whereas the main effect of B and the interaction effect are insignificant.

Example C shows a case in which the main effect of B is significant and the main effect of A and the interaction effect are insignificant. There is a large difference between the values of B_1 and B_2 across conditions A_1 and A_2. The mean value of B_1 is 40. The mean value of B_2 is 20. The values of A_1 and A_2 across both conditions of B are the same—namely 30. In the right-hand portion, these same results are graphically depicted. Two parallel lines occur at 20 and 40 along the *y*-axis. Note also that there is no difference in the mean values of A. The average of both levels is 30.

Figure D shows a hypothetical example in which the interaction effect is significant and neither A nor B is statistically significant. In this case, the means of levels A_1, A_2, B_1, and B_2 are exactly the same—namely 30. This means that A_1 and A_2 and B_1 and B_2 are not statistically different from one another. Thus, the main effects of A and B are both insignificant. On the other hand, notice that the effect of B_1 in the presence of A_1 is 40, whereas the effect of B_1 in the presence of A_2 is 20. For B_2, exactly the opposite occurs; that is, for B_2 in the presence of A_1, the value is 20, whereas in the presence of A_2, the value of B_2 is 40. Although the mean of each group is the same, the actual value of both levels of B is highly dependent on which

Figure C

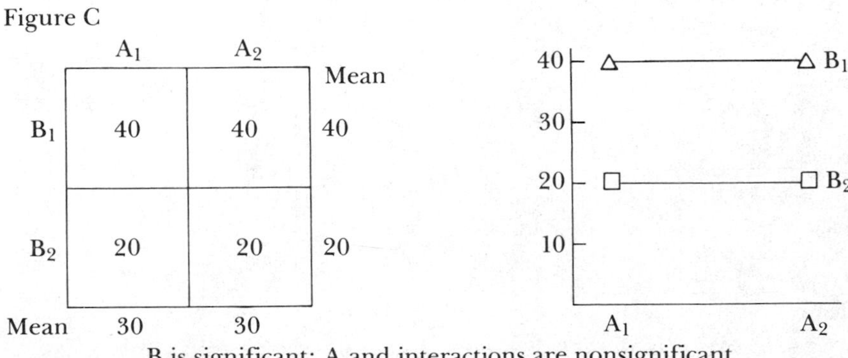

B is significant; A and interactions are nonsignificant

level of A is involved. This is what we mean by a strong interaction effect. The same thing is shown in the right-hand portion of the figure. In this case, the line for B_1 slopes downward as you move from A_1 to A_2. In contrast, the line for B_2 slopes upward as you move from A_1 to A_2, and this illustrates that B_2 is larger in the presence of A_2 so that the effect of B_1 and B_2 varies with whether it occurs in the presence of A_1 or A_2. Again, this is exactly what we mean by a significant interaction.

Before proceeding, note for a moment that in Figures A, B, and C, the lines representing B_1 and B_2 are parallel. In Figure A they are parallel and superimposed in the horizontal direction. In Figure B they are parallel and superimposed in an inclined direction. In Figure C they are not superimposed but are parallel in the horizontal direction. In each case, the interaction is insignificant. In Figure D, however, when the interaction is statistically significant, the lines are not parallel. Indeed, a useful rule of thumb is that whenever the outcome of a factorial experiment involves nonparallel lines, you are probably dealing with a significant interaction effect. This same sort of result can be seen in several of the following examples.

In the next case (Figure E), an example is shown in which the main effect of A and the interaction effect are statistically significant, but the main effect of B is insignificant. The means for the two levels of A are 30 and 10, and the means for the two levels of B are 20 and 20. There is also an interaction effect illustrated by the fact that B_1 in the presence of A_1 and A_2 is markedly different from B_2 in the presence of A_1 and A_2. In one case there is no decrease, and in the other case there is a decrease. The same outcome is depicted in the right-hand portion of the figure. Note that B_2 is the same whether in the presence of A_1 or A_2, whereas the effect of B_1 varies considerably depending on whether it is occurring in the presence of A_1 or

Figure D

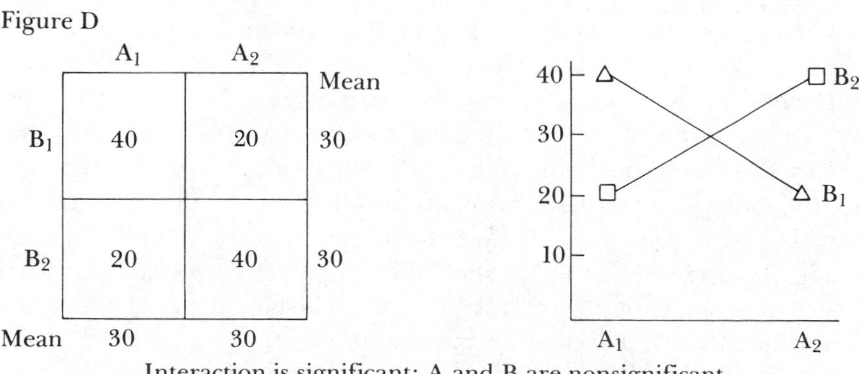

	A_1	A_2	Mean
B_1	40	20	30
B_2	20	40	30
Mean	30	30	

Interaction is significant; A and B are nonsignificant

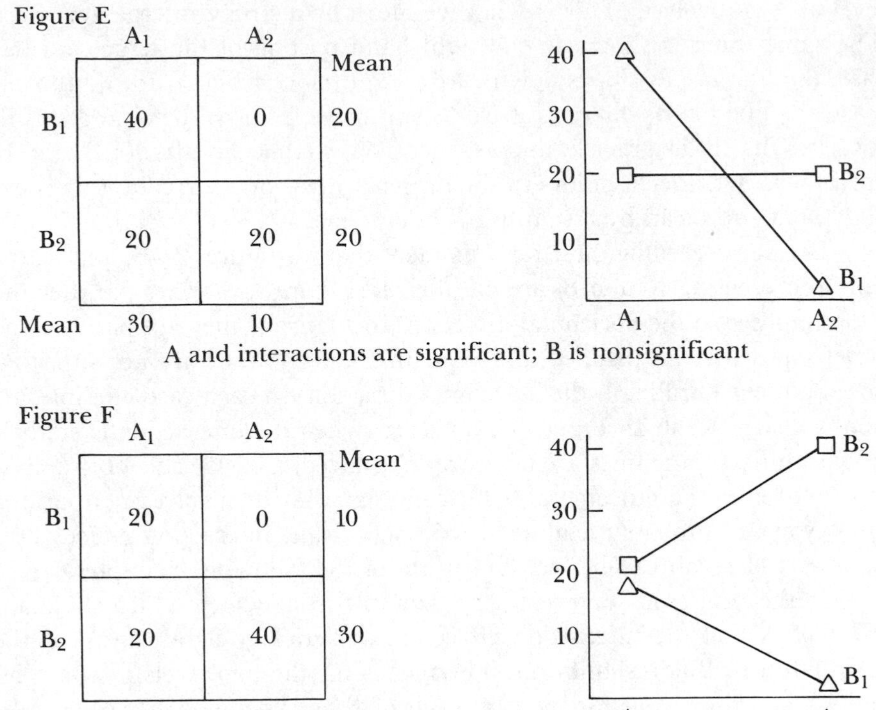

A and interactions are significant; B is nonsignificant

B and interactions are significant; A is nonsignificant

A_2. Note also that the lines are not parallel, which, as mentioned above, is a clue that perhaps we are dealing with a significant interaction effect. Remember, interaction simply means that the various levels of the independent variable are not affecting one another in the same way.

Figure F shows a case in which B and the interaction effect are significant and A is not. The means for B_1 and B_2 are 10 and 30; the means for A_1 and A_2 are 20 and 20. In the right-hand portion of the figure, the data are represented by two lines divergent from one another. Note that once again the two lines are not parallel, thus suggesting a possible interaction effect.

In Figure G, the main effects of A and B are statistically significant and the interaction effect is not significant. The mean differences between levels B_1 and B_2 are 10 and 30, and the means for levels A_1 and A_2 are also 10 and 30. In the right-hand portion of this figure, this outcome is depicted as two parallel lines rising from left to right. The fact that the lines are parallel demonstrates the lack of an interaction effect.

In Figure H, an outcome is shown in which all main effects and the

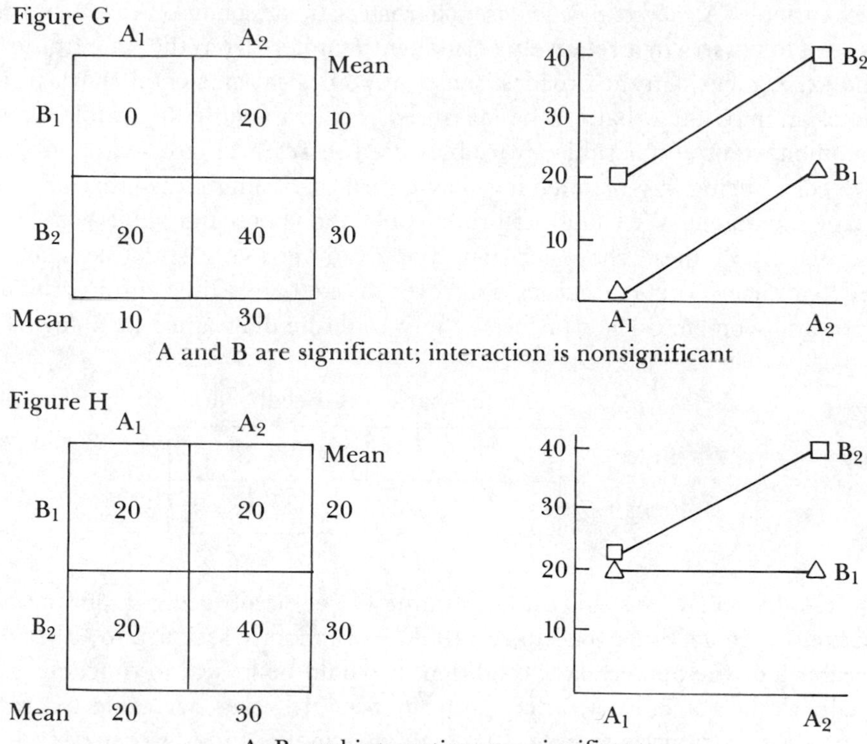

A and B are significant; interaction is nonsignificant

A, B, and interactions are significant

interaction effects are significant. The means for B_1 and B_2 are 20 and 30, respectively. The means for A_1 and A_2 are also 20 and 30, respectively. In the right-hand portion of the figure, we see two nonparallel lines; B_1 is the horizontal line representing the scores 20 and 20, and B_2 is a rising line from 20 to 40. The fact that at A_2 the effect of B_1 and B_2 is quite different from the effect of B_1 and B_2 at A_1 is consistent with the idea that we are working with a statistically significant interaction.

THE INTERPRETATION OF SUBJECT VARIABLES WITH FACTORIAL DESIGNS

In this section we want to add a warning based on the type of research in which some students try to use factorial designs. For the logic of experimentation to work best, it is necessary that you are able to randomly assign subjects to groups such that any subject may be placed in any cell of the factorial design. This is not possible if one of the factors in the design is a subject variable. A *subject variable* is a characteristic or condition that a subject is seen to possess in a relatively permanent manner (from the time frame of the experiment). In the broadest sense, any physical or mental characteristic of an individual that can be measured is called a subject variable. Some common examples of subject variables used in research are sex of subject, eye color, being shy or outgoing, having cancer, being schizophrenic, and being intelligent. We could perform a study and choose our subjects according to any of these characteristics. For example, we might ask whether feedback concerning accuracy improves basketball scores differently for men and women. Such a factorial study could be diagramed as follows:

	No feedback	Feedback
Males		
Females		

A design such as this could examine the effect of feedback on making basketball shots. Since the subjects could be randomly assigned to either the feedback or the nonfeedback condition, it would be logical to conclude that feedback did (or did not) affect performance. However, we could not randomly assign subjects to either the male or female condition, since sex is a subject characteristic. Thus if we found differences between men and women, it would not be logical to conclude that the differences were due to sex. For example, men and women may have had different amounts of practice with basketball before the study. As an exercise you might note other possible confounds that could account for differential results between men and women in such a study.

The point we want to make is that when we cannot randomly assign subjects to groups, it is very difficult to control for the previous history of subjects. Thus, the logic of our conclusions becomes weakened and causality is impossible to specify. With this word of caution, we must also point out that the study of subject variables forms a very important part of psychology. For example, many studies in psychology are devoted to the differences between schizophrenics and normals, or males and females, or high-anxiety and low-anxiety subjects, or even children and adults. In such comparisons, the logic of experimentation is considerably weakened and additional control measures are required for a meaningful interpretation of the results. We will return to this point in Chapter 8.

ADVANTAGES OF FACTORIAL DESIGNS

Before concluding this discussion of factorial designs, it will be useful to point out several strengths of factorial designs. One major strength we have already seen is that we can simultaneously examine more than one hypothesis or potential causal factor. This is very important because human behavior is frequently influenced by more than one factor. A second advantage is that because factorial experiments simultaneously evaluate each factor, they are much more economical in terms of the number of subjects and total experimenter effort than studying each factor separately. For example, suppose we wanted to investigate two independent variables, each of which has two factors (see Figure 7.5). Furthermore, suppose we wanted twenty subjects to experience each condition. If we used two separate completely randomized designs a total of eighty subjects would be required, whereas if we used a single 2 × 2 factorial design only forty subjects would be required. The third and perhaps most important advantage of factorial designs is that we can see how the various causal factors influence one another by examining the extent of interactions between the different levels of the factors.

SUMMARY

One of the first points made in this chapter is that no design is perfect. Each design has particular strengths and weaknesses. This chapter focused on between-subjects designs, in which each subject receives only one level of the independent variable and only one score per subject is used in the analysis of the results. One of the most elementary forms of this design is the completely randomized design. We described the use of several levels of the single independent variable with this design.

We discussed the factorial design, the most popular design in psychology. The factorial design permits us to assess the effects of more than one independent variable on our dependent variable simultaneously and to study any interactions that take place between these variables. One way of conceptualizing factorial designs is to consider them as a composite of several simple completely randomized designs. The terminology specific to factorial designs includes *factors, main effects, interaction effects,* and *cells*. We presented an example of a factorial design and reviewed at length the steps from the first stage of obtaining subjects, to random assignment, exposure to various levels of the independent variable, measurement of the dependent

A. Two completely randomized design experiments:

	Experiment I (money)		Experiment II (prior knowledge)	
	Level 1 (1¢) 20 subjects	Level 2 ($1) 20 subjects	Level 1 (no picture) 20 subjects	Level 2 (picture) 20 subjects
Total number of subjects for each experiment	40		40	
Overall total	80			

B. One 2 × 2 factorial design experiment:

		Money: Level 1 (1¢)	Money: Level 2 ($1)	Total subjects across factor A
Prior Knowledge	Level 1 (no picture)	10	10	20
	Level 2 (picture)	10	10	20
	Total subjects across factor B	20	20	
	Overall total	40		

Figure 7.5 This figure shows a comparison of subject requirements for (A) two completely randomized experiments and (B) a single 2 x 2 factorial design experiment. Note that the factorial design experiment requires half as many subjects.

variable, and the statistical determination of main effects and interaction effects. In interpreting the results of factorial designs, we stressed the importance of always explaining the interaction effects first.

We then described an *F*-table. We gave a hypothetical series of eight factorial experimental outcomes and depicted them both numerically and graphically.

We addressed the issue of subject variables within the context of factorial designs and made the point that the lack of random assignment of subjects to groups may make the previous history of subjects very difficult to control. In conclusion, we stressed three major advantages of factorial designs: (1) the simultaneous examination of more than one potential causal factor, (2) economic savings in the number of subjects and total experimenter effort, and (3) the observation of interactions between different levels of factors.

CHAPTER EIGHT

Extending the Logic of Experimentation: Within-Subjects and Matched-Subjects Approaches

INTRODUCTION

From the onset of our discussion of experimental design in Chapter 5, we have stressed two themes. First, we stressed the logical necessity of beginning our experiments with groups that can be assumed to be equal. Second, we stressed the statistical importance of reducing variation, especially the within-groups variation (error variance) component of the F-ratio. In relation to the need for beginning our experiment with equal groups, we suggested that the random assignment of subjects is one of the best techniques for ensuring that no systematic differences are present at the onset of our experiment. In Chapters 6 and 7 we also discussed a number of experimental designs with their logic based on the random assignment of subjects to groups. However, as we shall see in this chapter, there are times when random assignment alone may not be the most appropriate approach to subject assignment.

In this chapter we will discuss two other approaches to experimental design that do not use random assignment alone. The first section of this chapter will be devoted to *within-subjects designs* in which the same subject is used in different experimental conditions. The second section will discuss what are referred to as *matched-subjects designs*. We will discuss how matching can be used both as a control procedure and as an experimental procedure for analyzing differences between groups. As in the previous chapters, we will stress the need for beginning our experiment with equal groups and the importance of reducing the within-groups variance component in the F-ratio. Although the overall logic of experimentation presented in this chapter is similar to that discussed previously, the specific techniques for achieving these goals are slightly different.

WITHIN-SUBJECTS DESIGNS

In previous chapters we discussed designs that compared the performance of one group of subjects with the performance of a different group of subjects. These designs were referred to as *between subjects designs*. In *within-subjects designs*, each subject receives every treatment; that is, every subject serves in every group and receives all levels of the independent variable. In these designs, performance on the dependent variable is compared following different treatments on the *same* set of subjects. Let us now quickly illustrate the same experiment performed as both a between-subjects experiment and a within-subjects experiment.

In a simple between-subjects experiment, an experimenter can determine the role of immediate feedback in shooting basketballs by having one group shoot baskets blindfolded (zero level of feedback) and another group shoot without a blindfold (high level of feedback). This is diagramed as follows:

R	Group 1	T(feedback)	M(number of shots made)
R	Group 2	F(zero level of feedback)	M(number of shots made)

If we further identify individual subjects, this same between-subjects experiment appears as follows:

R	Group 1	Subject 1 Subject 2 Subject 3 Subject 4 Subject 5	T(feedback)	M(number of shots made)
R	Group 2	Subject 6 Subject 7 Subject 8 Subject 9 Subject 10	T(zero level of feedback)	M(number of shots made)

We can perform this same study as a within-subjects design in which each subject is exposed to both levels of the independent variable; that is, every subject in the study shoots baskets both with and without a blindfold. We can diagram such a study in a fashion similar to the previous two-group study except that we just list the *same* five subjects in the no-feedback condition, and thus the total experiment is composed of only five subjects.

Group 1	Subject 1 Subject 2 Subject 3 Subject 4 Subject 5	T(feedback)	M(number of shots made)
Group 2	Subject 1 Subject 2 Subject 3 Subject 4 Subject 5	T(zero level of feedback)	M(number of shots made)

For simplicity we usually list the subjects only once in a within-subjects design, as follows:

	Factor A	
	Level 1 (zero feedback)	Level 2 (feedback)
Subject 1		
Subject 2		
Subject 3		
Subject 4		
Subject 5		

In terms of our two goals—equating groups before the presentation of the independent variable and reducing within-groups variance—the within-subjects designs accomplish both. Since the same subjects are used in each group, we can be certain that before any treatment has been presented, the groups are exactly the same. A within-subjects design also increases the sensitivity of a study by decreasing the within-groups variance (error variance). The logic behind this last statement is that we would expect someone's behavior in a series of different conditions to be more similar than the behavior of various individuals in different conditions. Statistically, the error variance term of the F-ratio for a within-subjects design is smaller than that of a comparable between-subjects design. This means that smaller treatment differences are required for the rejection of the null hypothesis.

Let us now illustrate a within-subjects design with an actual experiment.

An Illustration of Within-Subjects Research

The 727 airplane was introduced in the fall of 1965. Although pilots liked the airplane and the early test flights were good, within a year there were four accidents involving the plane (Kraft, 1978). The first accident involved a 727 flying into Chicago from the Northeast. This plane began an approach from 22,000 feet and continued to descend until it literally flew into Lake Michigan some 19 miles from the shore. The second accident occurred as a 727 flew into the Cincinnati area from the East. To make the landing, the plane had to fly over the river at night and land on a built-up runway. Unfortunately, the plane attempted to land some 12 feet below the level of the runway. The third accident happened as a 727 approached Salt Lake City from the South. From the airplane, the lights of Salt Lake City could be seen past the runway and to the right. In front of the runway it was dark. This airplane also attempted to land short of the runway. The fourth accident occurred as a 727 attempted to land in Tokyo. It was a clear night so the pilot decided to use the flight rules for visual landings (VFR) rather than for instrument landings (IFR). The pilot began the descent over Tokyo Bay with the lights of the city visible. The descent was abruptly halted when the plane hit the water of Tokyo Bay 6½ miles east of the runway.

What happened? Assume that you are a psychologist called to help determine what caused the accidents. How would you go about this? First, you need to rule out mechanical problems with the airplanes, especially the altimeters (meters that indicate altitude). After other experts eliminate mechanical problems as a cause, you might look to the manner in which the planes were being flown by the pilots. You might also look for any pattern of events present at each of the accidents. The clues so far available to you are: (1) all accidents happened at night, (2) the pilots were all operating under visual rather than instrument flight rules, (3) the instruments did not appear to be malfunctioning, and (4) each approach required pilots to fly over dark areas with lights in the distance.

Conrad Kraft, a researcher for the Boeing Company, reports that from this information it was hypothesized that the problem was a miscalculation of space perception on the part of the pilots. This hypothesis suggested that the pilots saw the equivalent of a visual illusion, which resulted in their misjudging the location of the ground. Analysis of the accidents also suggested that for various reasons—for example, looking for another airplane—the pilots had been distracted from their instruments. In the factorial language presented in the preceding chapter, we would guess that the plane crashes were the result of an interaction effect; that is, they were caused by a visual illusion but only when the pilots were distracted from the instruments. To determine whether this was the case, we could perform a simple 2 × 2 design with one level of factor A being the necessary conditions for the visual illusion (clear night, no lights before the runway, and lights in the distance) and the second level being a zero level of these conditions. The first level of factor B would be pilot distraction from instruments and the second level would be a zero level of distraction. We could schematically represent this factorial design as follows:

		Conditions Necessary for Visual Illusion	
		Presence A_1	Absence A_2
Distraction from Instruments	Presence B_1		
	Absence B_2		

The dependent variable in such a factorial design would be the amount of landing error. Since simulators can be programmed to behave the same as actual flying, this entire study could be performed in the laboratory, which would both save money and control for environmental factors such as wind speed and pressure level. Using a *between-subjects design*, we would randomly assign pilots to one of the four possible conditions (A_1B_1, A_1B_2, A_2B_1, A_2B_2). We could then conduct the study and determine any interaction or main effects.

Let us think about the realities of this situation for a moment and see whether a *between-subjects design* is really the best alternative. One factor we must consider is the subject population. In this example we are interested in a rather special population—pilots who fly 727 airplanes. Thus it seems somewhat wasteful, in terms of both time and money, to bring a large number of subjects to the laboratory just to make one landing in the simulator. We would more likely want to collect as much data as possible from the pilots. A second consideration is to make the experimental and control groups as similar as possible. Are there any factors that we do *not* want to vary systematically between our groups? Experience with night flying in general, or with the 727 aircraft in particular, might be one such factor. One solution to both considerations would be to use a *within-subjects* design. This would answer our first consideration by having each pilot serve in every condition. It would address our second consideration by allowing each pilot to serve as his or her own control. Allowing each pilot to serve as a subject in each of the groups would automatically equate the groups for such factors as total flying time and knowledge of the 727 airplane. We can schematically represent such a within-subjects design exactly as we would a between-subjects design *except* that each cell is composed of the same subjects.

Advantages and Disadvantages of Within-Subjects Designs

There are several advantages to within-subjects designs that have been previously mentioned. To begin, because the same subjects serve in each group, this experimental procedure ensures that all groups are equal on every factor at the beginning of the experiment.

An additional benefit derived from using a within-subjects design is that the total number of subjects can be reduced dramatically. For example, in the simulator study just described, rather than using twelve subjects per cell (4 cells times 12 subjects = 48 total subjects) in a between-subjects design, we could use a total of twelve in the entire experiment by performing a within-subjects design. The advantages in terms of the number of subjects become even greater as the complexity of the design increases (for example, a $2 \times 3 \times 2$ design).

Another advantage to within-subjects designs is that they are statistically more sensitive to changes in the treatment effect. Why is this so? The reason is that most of the error variance in psychological studies results from differences between individuals who take part in the study. Within-subjects studies reduce this source of variance by using the same subject in every condition. Because of this, in the F-ratio a smaller within-subjects variance term is used. This term is derived by taking the within-subjects variance as it would be found in a between-subjects design and subtracting an estimate of how consistent subjects are over the different treatment conditions. This means that the F-ratio for within-subjects designs is more *sensitive* to changes in the treatments; that is, given the *same* treatment difference, we would be more likely to reject the null hypothesis with a within-subjects design than with a between-subjects design.

Before you throw out the last chapter and center your research career around within-subjects designs, let us consider some of their disadvantages. Remember, experimental designs are plans for helping us to answer research questions, and some questions cannot be appropriately answered by a within-subjects design. For example, if a treatment has any lasting effects on the subjects, then a within-subjects design is inappropriate. To illustrate this point, consider the outcome of the Bransford and Johnson study as a within-subjects design. Each subject would both be shown the picture and not be shown the picture. Clearly, seeing the picture would have a carry-over or residual effect when they were asked to remember the passage in the no-picture condition. Clinical treatment studies such as the Strupp and Hadley psychotherapy study or a drug treatment study would also be difficult to interpret with a within-subjects design.

Another disadvantage of within-subjects designs is that they are extremely sensitive to time-related effects. To illustrate this, consider a simple learning study in which the independent variable is the complexity of the material learned. The subjects could be given different sets of materials to learn, each differing in the level of complexity from easy to hard. If the material is presented in this order, can you see any confound that would make interpretation difficult? One possible confound might be fatigue; that is, by the time the subjects reach the difficult material, they may be tired. The results would then be due not only to the independent variable (complexity) but also to being tired (a confound). Another confound that could give us the opposite results is practice; that is, each time the subjects perform the experimental tasks, they may become better through practice. The effects brought about through continued repetition of the tasks, whether they are increases or decreases, are referred to as *practice effects*.

In many cases, order and time can be controlled (not eliminated) through such procedures as *counterbalancing*. Counterbalancing assures that every possible sequence appears at each presentation of the treatment. For example, we could counterbalance the complexity learning study mentioned above so that in the first presentation of the independent variable the first subject would receive the easy level, the second the medium level, and the third the hard level (assuming there are three levels). In the second presentation the first subject would receive the medium level, the second subject the hard level, and the third subject the easy level. The third presentation would have the first subject receive the hard level, the second the easy, and the third the medium, and so forth. This is illustrated as follows:

Subject 1	easy	medium	hard
Subject 2	medium	hard	easy
Subject 3	hard	easy	medium
Subject 4	easy	hard	medium
Subject 5	hard	medium	easy
Subject 6	medium	easy	hard

This would control for such time-related effects as improved performance through practice or decreased performance through fatigue or boredom. Counterbalancing will not control for a *differential order* effect, however, such as would be the case if the Bransford and Johnson study was presented as a within-subjects experiment; that is, if one particular order differentially affects the results, then counterbalancing will not control for this confound. For example, to present the picture condition before the no-picture condition in the Bransford and Johnson study would affect the results differently than presenting the no-picture condition first. This type of confound cannot be controlled through counterbalancing.

Repeated Measures

One common application of within-subjects designs uses repeated measures as one factor in a factorial design. This design is useful in studying psychological processes that occur over time. For example, this design is widely used in studying human and animal learning processes. We might have levels of problem difficulty as one factor (easy versus difficult problems), and the other factor might be the number of trials (the repeated measure factor). The dependent variable in such a study could be the number of problems solved correctly. This design would tell us whether there are differences in the number of problems solved over repeated trials—that is, whether the two levels of difficulty are mastered at different rates. In this case we use repeated measures to study the process of learning or practice effects directly. At other times we use a repeated measures design as a control technique to ensure that learning or practice effects are not present in our study.

MIXED DESIGNS

Probably the most common design used in psychological research combines a between-subjects design with a within-subjects design. Designs that include both within and between components are referred to as *mixed designs*. For example, assume we want to perform a biofeedback experiment to determine the effect of feedback on our ability to control heart rate. One factor is the amount of feedback—either total or partial feedback. Should we use a between-subjects or a within-subjects design? If one can learn the ability to control heart rate, there could be a carryover effect or a transfer of training from one condition to the other, especially if a subject learned to control heart rate with total feedback first. This suggests that it would be better to use a between-subjects design and to assign subjects randomly to two groups—one that receives total feedback and one that receives partial feedback. We might also want to look at the effects of this training over a period of days. Thus our second factor would be a repeated measures component consisting of the number of days. Such an experiment is diagramed as follows:

			Within Factor, Days							
			Day 1	2	3	4	5	6	7	8
Between Factor, Feedback	Total Feedback	Subject 1								
		2								
		3								
		4								
		5								
	Partial Feedback	Subject 6								
		7								
		8								
		9								
		10								

The within factor in a mixed design is not limited to a temporal factor such as days or trials, although this is one of the more common choices.

The statistical analysis of mixed designs is complicated because they use different error terms in the F-ratio. The error variance for the between comparison (level of feedback in our example) is computed differently from that of the within comparison (days in our example). Although a discussion of these statistical procedures is beyond this presentation, the logic of the *F*-ratio remains the same and you must still interpret the role of the independent variable and rule out the role of chance and confounds in the results.

MATCHED-SUBJECTS PROCEDURES

In this section we will examine matching as a procedure for accomplishing the goals of equating groups in an experiment and of reducing the within-groups variance (error variance). To help us in this discussion, we build upon the logic of the within-subjects design. As you remember, within-subjects experiments equate groups by using the same subject in every treatment condition. Likewise, by using the same subjects in each group, the within-groups variance is reduced since a given individual will perform more consistently in different situations than different individuals will perform in different situations. What if, rather than using the same subjects, we use subjects who are very similar in different groups? By this procedure we could reap some of the advantages of within-subjects designs and simultaneously take advantage of the random assignment of subjects which is possible with a between-subjects design. Our first task would be to find subjects who are very much alike. We might use twins, for example, whom we would expect to perform more similarly on a variety of tasks than strangers since they are more alike physiologically. If we randomly assign one twin to the experimental group and the other twin to the control group, we should be able to equate our groups at the beginning of the experiment as well as reduce within-groups variance (error variance). However, since we cannot use twins in every study we perform, an alternative is to *match* subjects. If we pair subjects along some factor and then randomly assign one subject to each of two groups, we can likewise assume our groups are equal at the beginning of the experiment as well as reduce within-group variance (error variance).

In terms of error variance, by this method we create a type of design that is between within-subjects designs and between-subjects designs. We would not have as much error variance as in a between-subjects design or as little as in a within-subjects design. Obviously, the characteristics we use to match our groups of subjects are of central importance to this design.

In the broadest sense, any physical or mental characteristic of an individual that can be measured may be used for matching. Thus, characteristics such as height, weight, intelligence, anxiety level, achievement motivation, hair color, and emotional sensitivity are all subject characteristics that can be measured. Consequently, they are all potential subject variables on which matching can be based. Is there a criterion for choosing the subject variable on which the subjects will be matched? Yes. For a matching procedure to work, there must be a high correlation between the variable used for matching and the dependent variable. If the subjects are matched on a factor that does not correlate with the dependent variable, then the within-groups variance will be no smaller than the variance obtained by random selection alone, and the amount of effort required for matching will have been wasted.

Matching can be used in one of two major ways. First, it can be used as a control procedure. We introduced you to this idea in Chapter 6 in the time estimation experiment. Since there were reported differences between men and women in their ability to estimate time, it was suggested that these differences might be controlled for by assigning an equal number of men and women to each group. In this way the groups were matched by sex. However, we did not analyze the sex factor in that example. If we had analyzed the sex factor, we would have illustrated the second use of matching—that of an experimental procedure. We will discuss this use in more detail as we introduce you to matching as an experimental procedure in this chapter. Although it would be technically correct to refer to this second use of matching only as an experimental design as contrasted with a control procedure, few researchers follow this procedure.

Matching as a Control Procedure

When we know that a particular subject variable or characteristic has a high correlation with the dependent variable, equal groups may be obtained by matching along this characteristic. The task of actually forming matched groups of subjects consists of two major steps. First, pairs of subjects are matched on some measure that is correlated with performance on the dependent variable. Second, each member of the pair is randomly assigned to either the experimental or the control group. Such a design can be schematically represented as follows:

MR	Group 1	T	M
MR	Group 2	T (zero level)	M

Notice that we placed an M before the R to denote that the subjects were matched before they were randomly assigned to groups. In essence, we have a completely randomized design.

As you remember from Chapter 6, in the time estimation experiment we matched subjects according to sex and then randomly assigned subjects to groups such that there was an equal number of each sex in each group. In this study, matching took place according to sex—a nominal scale of measurement.

Let us look at another example of matching as a control procedure. In this illustration the matching takes place along an ordinal scale of measurement. Suppose we are interested in neurochemical changes that result from prolonged periods of sensory deprivation. For a number of reasons we decide to use monkeys. Since monkeys are difficult to obtain, we decide to use as few subjects as possible. To control for potential bias in the groups, we might decide to match along a dimension that is highly correlated with our dependent variable—a certain amino acid in the brain, for example. The overall procedure is presented in Figure 8.1. We begin by performing a blood chemistry analysis of our monkeys and then rank order them on the basis of this analysis. After we complete the initial rank ordering, we pair the animals (for a two-group study) according to the rankings. We begin with the two animals that have the highest rankings and then go to the next two and so on. We then randomly assign one member of each pair to one group and the other to the second group and proceed with the experiment.

Matching as an Experimental Procedure

In the previous examples of matching as a control procedure, subjects are matched according to some factor (subject variable) but the factor itself is not analyzed. It is possible to analyze the matching factor, however. When the matching factor is analyzed, the resulting procedure is traditionally referred to as a *randomized block design*. The term *block* in this case refers back to the development of the design by Sir Ronald Fisher when he studied agricultural procedures on different blocks of land. Let us now discuss how the matching factor can be described and used experimentally. To begin, let us again schematically represent a randomized design in which matching is used as a control factor. Take the time estimation study, for ex-

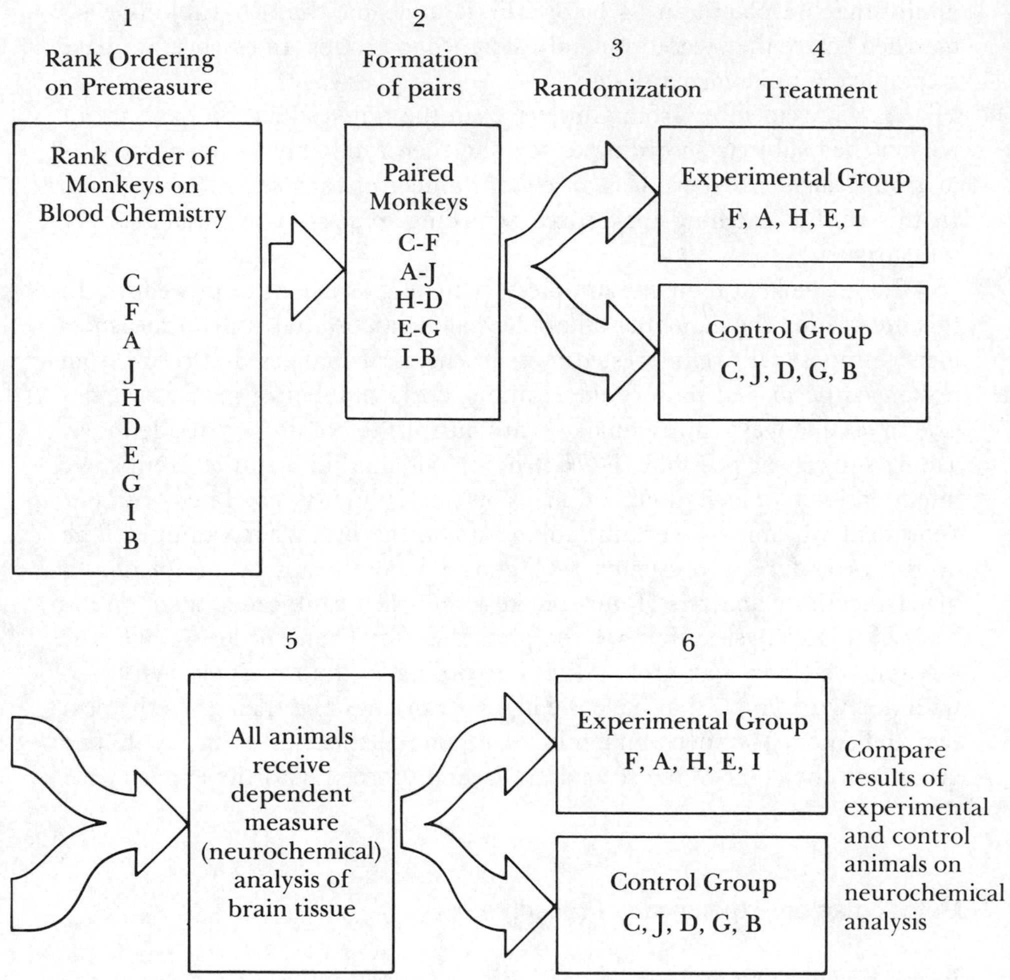

Figure 8.1 This figure schematically represents the six major steps in a matched-subjects design used to study changes in brain chemistry resulting from prolonged sensory deprivation. (1) Rank order all subjects on the aspects of blood chemistry that are known to be correlated with brain neurochemistry. (2) Form pairs of subjects on the basis of order in the initial ranking. (3) Randomly assign one member of each pair to the experimental group and one member to the control group. (4) Conduct the experimental treatments. (5) Conduct neurochemical analyses. (6) Compare the results for the experimental and control animals. Note that except for our ranking and matching procedures, the design is similar to the completely randomized designs discussed earlier.

ample, in which an equal number of men and women are placed in each group. We might diagram such a design as follows:

MR	Group 1 (males and females)	T	M
MR	Group 2 (males and females)	T (zero level)	M

We could further break down this design as:

Group 1	Males	T	M
Group 1	Females	T	M
Group 2	Males	T (zero level)	M
Group 2	Females	T (zero level)	M

At this point it is possible to convert this experiment into a two-factor factorial design and to analyze the factor of sex. Such a factorial design is diagramed as follows:

		Factor A	
		Level 1	Level 2 (zero level)
Factor B, Sex	Males		
	Females		

As we have discussed, we can now analyze for the main effect of Factor A, the main effect of Factor B, and the interaction of A × B. It must be remembered that the factor according to which the subjects are classified is not a factor on which the subjects were randomly selected, and it must be interpreted with caution. If there is a significant main effect for this factor, we may be able to conclude that there is a relationship between this factor and the dependent variable, but we cannot conclude that the relationship is a *causal* one. However, this does not mean that we want to ignore the classification factor. Especially if there is an interaction between the classification variable and the treatment variable, there is much information to be gained. Such an interaction will tell us to what groups and under what conditions the findings of a particular study may be generalized. For example, in a study of the effects of feedback on performance, Ray, Katahn, and Snyder (1971) divided subjects into high- and low-anxiety groups and then randomly assigned them to either a high-feedback condition (feedback on the number correct after each study trial) or a low-feedback condition (feedback only after a series of study trials). It was found in this study that there was no difference between anxiety groups when feedback was given at the end of a series of trials, but there was a difference when feedback was given at the end of each trial. With feedback after each trial, the low-anxiety group increased the number of items learned more than the high-anxiety group. Such an interaction may be valuable in generalizing from this particular study to other studies concerning the role of feedback in learning.

In addition to the knowledge gained from the interaction effect, we have discussed two other advantages acquired through the prior matching of subjects to groups. The first is ensuring that the groups in a study are equal before the introduction of the treatment. This equating of groups is especially valuable for those situations in which we have only a limited number of subjects yet we cannot use a within-subjects design. The second advantage of matching subjects is that it reduces the within-groups variance (error variance) and thus makes our design more sensitive to treatments than a comparable between-subjects design. However, this is possible only when the matching factor has a high correlation with the dependent variable.

Before we leave this section, let us briefly introduce you to some terminology concerning what has traditionally been referred to as the randomized block design. Glass and Stanley (1970) suggest that we reserve the term *blocking* for cases in which the matching takes place on a nominal scale factor such as sex. They also suggest that the use of twins be likewise considered a nominal scale factor. When the matching uses ordinal measurements such as ranking, Glass and Stanley suggest that the term *stratifying* be used. An experiment that ranks subjects into high, medium, and low socioeconomic classes is one example of a stratifying variable. When interval or ratio scales are used, then Glass and Stanley suggest that the term *leveling* be used. Some common examples are dividing subjects according to intelligence levels (high, medium, and low), anxiety levels, or depression levels. It must be remembered that although the groups are developed in terms of subject variables—the members of each of the blocks, strata, or levels—it is still necessary to randomly assign subjects to treatment conditions.

SUMMARY

The first part of this chapter described within-subjects designs in which each subject experiences all levels of the independent variable. Performances on the dependent variable following different treatments with the same set of subjects are then compared. This contrasts with between-subjects designs, in which different groups of subjects are used. We stressed the two goals of equating groups before presenting the independent variable and reducing within-group variance. In a within-subjects design, error variance is reduced because the same individual's behavior across conditions is expected to be more similar than the behavior of different individuals across conditions. Therefore, smaller treatment differences are required for the rejection of the null hypothesis. Following an example of a within-subjects design, we discussed some advantages and disadvantages of these designs.

We then described repeated measure factorial designs and mixed designs. These designs actually combine between- and within-subjects designs.

We discussed the procedure of matching subjects, this time in the context of a compromise between within-subjects designs and between-subjects designs. The subject characteristics selected as matching variables must be highly correlated with the dependent variable for the matching procedure to be of value. When matching is used as a control procedure, subjects are matched and then randomly assigned to groups. When it is used as an experimental procedure, the same two things occur, plus the matching factor is analyzed for statistical significance. The matched factor must be interpreted with caution because the subjects were not randomly selected.

Matching used as an experimental procedure has traditionally been referred to as a randomized block design. In closing, we identified some of the terminology used with randomized block designs, such as *blocking, stratifying,* and *leveling.*

CHAPTER NINE

The Ecology of the Experiment: The Scientist and Subject in Relation to Their Environment

INTRODUCTION

In this chapter we want to move beyond our consideration of specific designs to a discussion of the context in which psychological research takes place. By *context,* we mean not only the particular laboratory or setting where the research is conducted but also the worlds in which scientists and subjects live outside of the experiment. To accomplish this, we will recall some of our initial discussions related to performing a science of behavior and experience. In our earlier discussion, we suggested that science can be viewed from three separate perspectives: that of the scientist, the subject, and the witness.

In the previous chapters we emphasized the role of the scientist and the manner in which he or she interacts with the subject matter of psychology through research. As you have learned, it is the scientist who plays an active role in science by the type of questions he or she asks, the methods by which these questions are answered, and the types of answers that are ultimately acceptable. We were particularly interested in helping you as a scientist to learn to make accurate statements through experimental procedures. In doing this, we were talking to you from the perspective of the scientist.

We are equally interested in helping you make valid statements from a broader perspective. Not only will we discuss methods for performing more valid experiments as seen from the perspective of the scientist, but we will also give you a clearer picture of how the humanness of both the scientist and the subject influences the actual conduct of the experiment. If these factors are not taken into consideration, both the internal and external validity of an experiment may be severely threatened. To facilitate conveying these issues, we will now shift our perspective to include that of the witness, who observes the interplay between the scientist and the subject.

We realize that for some individuals the perspective of the witness is frustrating, since it reminds us of aspects of science that are beyond our control as methodologists and contradicts the picture of science as completely objective. However, as a careful reading of history will show, science has never been and probably never will be completely objective. Science is, as we have tried to show you throughout this book, a means for helping us as people to explore, passionately at times, the world in which we live and to come to some understanding of this world. In our better moments, science may offer us a means of transcending some of our limitations as humans. Yet most often science faithfully reflects our humanness and thus our limitations as well. It is the viewpoint of the witness that, through an observation of the interactions of the scientist and the subject, helps us to understand the value and relevance as well as the limitations of any new information that our research produces.

In this chapter we will look at how some of these limitations affect science from the perspective of the witness. As scientists we can control for some limitations; for others we can only accept them for what they are—limitations. In this vein, we will consider the psychological worlds of the scientist and of the subject and how these might influence either collectively or separately the outcome of psychological research.

The consideration of subject-scientist interactions is so important that some researchers believe all human experimentation is really a social event that should be viewed from a broad perspective (Petrinovich, 1979). This focus is important both for the broad perspective it gives us of psychological research and as a means of understanding and perhaps even eliminating potential biases that either purposefully or accidentally enter into the process of research. To study the relationship among the scientist, the subject, and the experimental environment, we will refer by analogy to the science of ecology.

ECOLOGY

Ecology, a term coined more than 100 years ago, is defined as the scientific study of the relationship of living organisms with each other and their environment (Miller, 1975). Most students are familiar with the word *ecology* as it is applied to the relationship between humans and their environment. For example, we may find by following the food chain that if certain chemicals are used to kill weeds on a farmer's field, the same chemicals might later appear in the breast milk that mothers feed their babies. In the 1970s it was shown that when an atomic explosion took place in China, the fallout could be found in the milk consumed by the people in Philadelphia. We have also seen that decreases in the population of one type of animal, the lion for example, have led to increases in another animal such as the deer. The general lesson we have learned from the study of ecology is that all parts of nature are closely interconnected and that it is impossible to make environmental changes without affecting the entire system, at least to some extent.

In the same way that we can discuss the ecology of nature by looking at the interrelationships between humans and their environment, we can discuss the ecology of the psychological experiment and examine the relationships among the scientist, the subject, and the experimental situation. By using the word *ecology,* we emphasize that there are ongoing dynamic interactions among the scientist, subject, and context that must be considered before a complete understanding of experimental psychology is possible. Without this complete understanding of the ecological aspects of the scientific context, our conclusions and theoretical ideas may be invalid. From this perspective, we can introduce the concept of *ecological validity.*

Ecological validity asks the question: Has the full impact of the important relationships among the scientist, the subject, and the context been fully considered in evaluating a given piece of research? As we will see in this chapter, this includes the relationship of the scientist and the subject to each other, to the particular research being conducted, as well as to the greater context of the society in which each lives and works. The motivation of the witness, somewhat like that of a consumer protection agency, is not to suggest that no scientific study can ever be acceptable, but rather to offer considerations and at times outright warnings concerning the ecological validity of science. Just as no consumer product or service has been developed that will give perfect results each time, there will never be the perfect scientific experiment. Remember, our goal in science is not to perform a perfect experiment but *to use science to ask questions and to increase our understanding of a given phenomenon.* When used in an appropriate manner, science is one of the most powerful tools we have. When used out of context or in a haphazard manner, it is important that considerations and even warning labels be prominently attached. Let us now turn to some of the considerations to be made when assessing *ecological validity*.

EXPERIMENTER FACTORS

One initial warning in the acceptance and generalizability of research is the possibility of scientist or *experimenter effects*. To examine experimenter effects is to ask what portion of the results of an experiment can be said to be *caused* by the attitudes or behavior of the experimenter. In this section we will discuss two types of experimenter effects: (1) those due to biased data collection by the experimenter and (2) those stemming from the experimenter somehow biasing the subject's performance.

Biased Data Collection

One very real potential source of experimenter bias in the actual collection of data stems from the fact that we are all different and two experimenters may actually see the world differently. In his history of psychology, Boring (1950) tells of an incident in the late 1700s and early 1800s that points up the importance of experimenter variability in scientific research. The story goes that an astronomer, Maskelyne, dismissed his assistant Kinnebrook because the assistant timed the passing of stars almost a second later than Maskelyne. The method of noting star movement in those days was to observe a clock and then, listening to its ticking, count the ticks to record the time a star crosses wires in the telescope. In reading of this event some twenty years later, another astronomer named Bessel began to compare his own observations with others. Bessel found that different observers using the same method differ by a constant amount. In this case, however, Bessel did not fire his assistants. Rather he became one of the first researchers to point to the great effect that inherent differences in experimenters can have on the data we record.

The constant error in the observations of different scientists is what we call the *personal equation* in psychology. The personal equation suggests that because of one's physiological and psychological makeup, there are differences, yet consistent differences, in the way we as experimenters observe the world. And these unique experimenter differences form a very real source of experimenter bias. Because of this, it is a common procedure in an observational or rating experiment for two or more independent observers to be used. To check for inconsistent observations, the observations of these observers are then correlated and this correlation is referred to as *inter-rater reliability*. The higher the correlation between the ratings of two independent observers, the less the ratings represent inconsistent subjective factors of the raters.

In addition to these inherent differences between experimenters in the way they perceive and respond to the world, there is a whole level of personality that may create a source of experimenter bias. Remember, scientists are human and at times their desire to see their hypothesis supported exceeds their honest viewing of the world as it is. In most cases this temporary reversal of priorities exerts itself in an unconscious or unintentional manner. For example, psychologists who have carefully studied other scientists doing research have learned that if an experimenter makes an error recording a single piece of data, that error is most likely to be in support of the research hypothesis (Rosenthal, 1979). In addition there are other, more subtle ways a scientist can influence the outcome of an experiment. For example, any unintended variations from the experimental plan tend to favor the hypothesis; the decision about whether to accept or discard a subject's data tends to be influenced by whether or not the performance supported the hypothesis; and the use of inappropriate statistical techniques such as unplanned ad hoc analyses may be misleading. As it turns out, this confusion of priorities is by no means limited to modern researchers. In fact, Barber (1976) has suggested that some of our more famous scientists including Newton, Dalton, and Mendel may have presented their data as being more precise than was possible during the time in which they lived. There is also the alternative possibility that some of these scientists' assistants, like college students performing an experiment for which the answer is "known," may have "helped" the data to fit the predicted theory in order to please the person for whom they worked.

In the first half of the nineteenth century, a new and exciting field was emerging which represented what intelligence testing is today. The field was called *craniometry,* and one of the leading figures in this field in America was Samuel George Morton, a well-known physician and scientist (Gould, 1978). The basic premise behind craniometry was that there existed a relationship between brain size and intelligence and that measurements of the skull would correlate with brain size. Although today we know that there is little relationship between brain size and intelligence in humans, at that time it was part of the accepted beliefs. Millions of people are said to have had their head measured in hopes of learning about their abilities. Morton extended this work by studying the skulls of individuals from various races and countries. He then measured the quantity of BBs that the skull would hold and used this as a measure of intelligence. Before you decide this was a crazy man, you should realize that when he died, the *New York Daily Tribune* proclaimed that "probably no scientific man in America enjoyed a higher reputation among scholars throughout the world than Dr. Morton" (Gould, 1978). Much of his reputation was based on the fact that he actually made objective scientific measurements much in the tradition of modern-day empiricism. One of his major conclusions was that there is a difference in intelligence among the races of the world and that within races one can also find intelligence differences. For example, Morton described the English and Germans as more intelligent than Jewish people and Jewish people as more intelligent than Hindus. In terms of races, whites were seen at the top of the intelligence ladder, with Indians in the middle and blacks on the bottom. Recently Stephen Gould, a scholar interested in the history of science, reexamined Morton's data and the methods by which he came to his conclusions. Gould found that Morton had "unconsciously" selected his samples such that the head size of the Indians would appear smaller and that of the Caucasians larger. Morton also made two errors in his mathematical computations; both favored the view of Caucasian supremacy, which was in vogue at that time.

There are, however, other cases in which scientists did more than unconsciously or consciously "push" the data in the direction of their hypotheses; there are cases of outright fraud. Two representative examples are the studies of Sir Cyril Burt and Walter Levy. Burt was interested in demonstrating that intelligence is the result of genetic factors. One method of testing an idea such as this is to examine the intelligence of monozygotic twins. Monozygotic twins are twins in which both individuals develop from the same egg and thus are genetically identical. As you can imagine, if twins who are genetically identical but have had different environmental influences have similar IQs, then it can be concluded that heredity as opposed to environment is most responsible. (These same types of studies are used for determining the genetic component of disorders including schizophrenia.) Recently two findings of Burt have come to light. The first is that when his data were reexamined, the results of his studies presented an almost impossible occurrence. The occurrence was that the correlation between the intelligence of monozygotic twins reared apart was .771 in the first sample of sets of twins, .771 in the second sample, and .771 in the third sample. As Burt found more and more twins who could be used in his study, he performed other correlations (how closely the IQs of the twins were similar), and whether the correlation was done using 21, 30, or 51 pairs of twins, the results were always .771. It is extremely unlikely that the correlations in all three studies would be exactly the same; most scientists familiar with his work assume his data were misreported to support his theory [for a discussion of this case, see Hearnshaw (1979)].

The second case is that of Walter Levy. Levy performed research in parapsychology. Specifically, Levy was observed to alter data to support his previous research. After this came to light, Levy resigned and admitted that he had "fudged" the data. Barber (1976) not only discusses these cases but points out that in a number of studies, college students who have been asked to run laboratory experiments have been shown to fudge data or to alter the instructions or procedure of the experiment. Whether these students wanted to get a good grade or were in a hurry to finish their midterm exam is not known, but it is important to understand that scientists are people and may inadvertently or purposely alter their data in a biased manner.

More recently, the journal *Science* reported a case that resulted in the resignation of two scientists from two separate major medical centers and the retraction of eleven research reports from the scientific literature (Broad, 1980). The story began with a researcher submitting her paper to a scientific journal for publication. In the journal review process, which we will discuss in Chapter 12, another scientist saw the paper and made a copy of it. During the next month the second scientist wrote a paper which included passages from the first scientist's paper without reference to her. By chance, in the review process for this second paper, the first scientist saw the paper and realized that it included passages from her own work. She then wrote to the journal and to the dean of the medical school where the other scientist worked and accused the other scientist of plagiarism. At first, according to *Science*, the dean felt that the scientist at the medical school had acted improperly in copying from the work of another but that, since the copying was not related to the actual data collection, it did not call into question the research itself. However, further investigation revealed that the original research had never been completely performed and that the results had been fabricated. In the process of the investigation, another scientist was implicated and the results from eleven published papers were called into question.

What we have been calling experimenter bias not only can affect the actual data the experimenter records, but it can also exert a strong influence on the theoretical interpretation of our findings. As with any human beings, scientists may consciously or unconsciously choose to view their own and other scientists' results from a biased position that supports their earlier viewpoint. Although few people would consider this type of behavior as fraud, it is important to be aware of the possibility when evaluating published theories and review papers or even just reading the discussion sections of published papers.

Biased Interactions with Subjects

To understand one way an experimenter might unintentionally bias the interactions with subjects, consider yourself a subject in an experiment in which the scientist is testing the hypothesis that more college men than women dream about violating social taboos. Imagine what type of person (male or female, attractive or unattractive, old or young) you would be most willing to tell your uncommon dreams. Imagine what type of person you would be least likely to tell your dreams. As you realize that you react differently to different people in your life, you can also see how subjects in a psychological experiment might react differently to different experimenters. To some experimenters subjects would be withholding, and to others they would talk freely. Such experimenter characteristics as sex, attractiveness, dress, race, and age are known to influence many types of psychological experimentation and should be considered when evaluating a set of studies.

Once the experimenter begins to interact with subjects in the actual experiment, additional factors are likely to influence the research. For example, consider your first experiment in which you ask people to serve as subjects. Did you feel anxious? Did you feel ill at ease that you were imposing on these people? Did you want one group to respond differently than another? Most experimenters do want their experimental groups to be different from their control groups. It is only natural, but it is also a source of bias if the experimenter communicates to the subjects that they are to respond in a certain manner or if the experimenter treats one group differently than another.

Let us now consider two examples of this process. As you know, it is possible to breed animals for certain characteristics such as color, temperament, and predisposition for specific diseases. In this first study, students were given rats to train in running a maze. Half the students were told that they had received rats specially bred for being "maze bright" and the other half were told that they were given "maze dull" animals. In reality, all the animals were bred the same and randomly assigned to the two groups of student experimenters. At the end of the study, the authors report that rats that were trained and tested by experimenters expecting brighter behavior showed statistically significant superior learning when compared with the rats run by the experimenters expecting dull behavior (Rosenthal & Fode, 1963). A second study showed the same findings with other experimenters and animals, this time using a Skinner box (Rosenthal & Lawson, 1964). Rosenthal and Rubin (1978) have recently reviewed 345 studies of interpersonal expectancy, and it is now apparent that scientists, like people everywhere, have expectations and that these expectations influence the outcomes of their studies. Although we all like to think of ourselves as objective in our research, it is important to realize that our passionate commitment to our own hypotheses leads us to give special attention to our own expectations about the outcome of our research. In this way we create self-fulfilling prophesies; that is, we expect something to happen and we look for confirmation of our expectation.

In this section we discussed two major sources of experimenter bias: biased data collection by scientists, and effects related to biases conveyed by interactions between the experimenter and the subject. Although research has described various possible sources of experimenter bias, this issue is very complex and our understanding of these sources of bias is far from complete. Consequently, it is difficult to say exactly how various situations bring forth bias. Thus, it becomes the task of the scientist when designing a new study and the witness when evaluating research to ask whether there are situations in which experimenter bias might have influenced either the treatment of subjects or the collection of the data. Perhaps the best way we can minimize this problem is to remind ourselves that the only way we will ever understand human behavior and experience is to examine it in its complexity, which includes the manner in which scientists and subjects interact with one another.

Some Ways to Avoid Experimenter Bias

There are a number of possible procedures that can help to reduce experimenter bias. As suggested, one of the most common is to use several different experimenters and even to include this as a factor in the study. Maher (1978) has suggested that it may be necessary, especially in clinical psychology research, to expose the subjects to a number of different experimenters and experimental situations. This is based on Brunswik's notion that we should sample not only from subject populations but from a number of stimulus situations (Brunswik, 1947). By this Brunswik means that not only should the psychological phenomena under study be presented to a representative sample of subjects, but that they should also be presented in a representative sample of situations.

Another procedure to reduce experimenter bias is to keep the person who is interacting with the subject "blind" to the hypothesis and the particular groups with which he or she is working. For example, blind studies are frequently used in drug research where behavioral ratings are made after a certain drug is administered. In this type of study, the raters are not told which subjects received what drugs or even if they received a drug at all. In this way the experimenter's expectation cannot be conveyed to the subjects nor can it affect the manner in which the data are recorded. For more recommendations for improving research, see Box 9.1.

The most useful way to begin eliminating experimenter bias from your own experiments is consciously to intend to see the experiment from varying perspectives. We are always in a stronger position if we accept that we all are human and make mistakes. After all, at one time we all believed the world was flat. The important point for science is not that we were wrong but that we were willing to change.

SUBJECT FACTORS

Another potential source of misinterpretation is subject factors. Subject factors or bias refer to the fact that the subjects are not behaving *in the way we expect them to behave*. Some of these factors come about because we have not really considered how a particular subject might experience our experiment. In a nutshell, subject factors boil down to the realization that subjects are human. In some cases they are highly motivated to please the experimenter. In other cases they may actually try to figure out the experiment and behave in a way that will support or even sabotage the experiment. In many psychology departments, introductory students serve as subjects to get extra points on their final grade. Scientists working in these settings will be quick to tell you that near the end of the term, when students are working under increased pressure, subject bias can become a real problem. At exam time, the available subjects may be hassled, anxious, tired, and generally negative toward participating in research. From a broader ecological perspective, it is clear that such a subject has little motivation to be part of a psychological experiment. Thus, it is the task of the scientist to consider how the subject experiences the experiment and to look for personal and social factors that might bias the results of an experiment.

One classic example of an initially overlooked factor was in an experiment conducted in the 1930s. The experiment took place at the Hawthorne plant of Western Electric and was designed to determine how factors such as lighting and working hours affect productivity. The subjects were a group of women who worked at the plant and they were asked to work un-

---

Box 9.1 *Recommendations for Research*

In an attempt to improve psychological research, Theodore X. Barber (1976) has suggested thirteen changes that need to be made in the way research is performed. Presented below is a summary of these changes.

1. Based on Kuhn's analysis of the importance of paradigms, researchers need to be aware of their underlying assumptions and to state these explicitly when possible.
2. There would be less bias if the person who plans the study (the investigator) is not the same person who analyzes the data.
3. There would be less bias if the person who plans the study (the investigator) is not the same person who actually performs the study (the experimenter).
4. Researchers should be pilot subjects in their own experiments to understand the actual experience of experimentation as encountered by the subjects.
5. Investigators (those who plan studies) should specify *exactly* what the experimenters (those who run the studies) should and should not do and when.
6. Pilot studies carried out by experimenters should be run and carefully supervised by investigators to ensure correct and rehearsed procedures before the actual experimental phase begins.
7. Researchers should be trained in the complexity of data analysis and the manner in which different types of analyses may lead to different conclusions.
8. Students should be taught more the value of good research methods in answering questions and less the importance of finding significant results.
9. Teachers in beginning experimental courses should emphasize the importance of following research procedures to the letter and honestly recording the data.
10. When investigators use experimenters to run the experiment, the investigators should monitor carefully to see that the procedures are being followed.
11. Investigators should use multiple experimenters who vary in personal attributes to collect the data.
12. Whenever possible, experiments should be performed "blind," and if possible the experimenter giving the treatment should be different from the experimenter recording the results.
13. One should not rely on any one study for the answer but seek replications performed by different experimenters in different locations. For the beginning student, a replication of a previous experiment should be encouraged and rewarded as a worthwhile activity.

---

der varying conditions. The productivity of these women was compared with general productivity. When the data were analyzed, a strange finding emerged. No matter what the experimental condition was, the productivity of these women increased. It even increased under a condition in which the lighting in the experimental condition was not as good as that in the actual plant. What conclusion would you draw from these studies? From an experimental design standpoint it was difficult to understand the data until the experimenters examined how they had treated these women. The answer they came up with was that the women in the experiment had been given special attention just by being in an experiment. These women were able to consider themselves as *special* and this was reflected in the work they performed. Today the Hawthorne effect remains a warning to experimenters that giving attention and considering oneself special may produce either directly or indirectly results much stronger than those of the experimental independent variables. This is not to suggest that you treat the subjects of your experiments in a cold, impersonal manner, but you should take into account the way that the subjects experience your experiment. The easiest way to do this is simply to ask a few people to be a subject in your study and then discuss how they felt and how they reacted to your study.

Another type of subject bias took place during the Depression and involved a group of dental students who were paid to be subjects. The study had been designed to examine a new type of toothpaste and its effects on bacterial concentration and tooth decay. Consequently subjects with high bacterial concentrations were sought to participate. To qualify for the study and earn some needed money, the students ate candy bars to increase bacterial concentration. Once the study was over and the subjects were paid, they quit eating candy and thus the bacterial count decreased. The experimenters did not realize the subjects had been eating candy bars, and in the follow-up reports they believed the decrease in bacterial concentration was due to the new experimental toothpaste (Simon, 1978). This story points out that in psychology we are dealing with human beings whose behavior may be motivated by any number of factors, many of which we do not even suspect. The overall ecology of the dental study helps to stress that the subjects were reacting not only to the demands of the experimental environment by using the new toothpaste but also to the demands of a larger environment, in this case an economic one.

In the psychological experiment, the witness reminds us that it is not enough to watch the behavior of human beings as one would watch material objects. Although people may *just* react to the experiment as designed, their reaction may involve many factors we are not aware of. It is the delightful complexity of ourselves and others that makes psychological research both difficult and exciting. Psychological scientists have had to learn that subjects are not passive robots; they are active, creative people with definite motives. It is impossible for any experimenter to know exactly which aspects of the study the subject is responding to and what his motives are. For example, when a subject takes part in a psychological experiment, it is impossible to predict (regardless of the design of the study) whether the subject will react to the experimenter as someone to make contact with, as someone to talk to, as a neutral person just doing his job, or as a person who is keeping the subject away from some important work such as studying for an exam.

Because the subject is an active, creative, complex human being, it is not surprising that the subject may decide not to follow the instructions of the experiment but to second-guess the experimenter and act in a certain manner. Consider an experiment in which the subject is shown erotic films and then a physiological measure such as pulse rate is taken. In reality the subjects might find the films boring, but because they like the experimenter and want to help her, they decide to think about someone that does make them feel erotic and thus give the experimenter results. Unfortunately, of course, the results have nothing to do with the research as it was designed. Let us now examine three possible ways a subject might respond. If the experimenter asks a subject to watch an erotic film, the subject might (1) just watch the film and react "naturally," (2) react out of humanness more to the experimenter than to the film, or (3) consciously construct what he thinks the experiment is about and respond to the thought rather than to the film. Restated in broad terms, we are saying that subjects may react to themselves, to the experimenter, or to the experimental situation. What makes the interpretation of scientific research even more difficult is that these three possibilities may be brought forth systematically and thus bias the results in any number of complex ways. For example, in the erotic film example, we might find a *sex by experimenter* interaction in which men react differently than women to a female experimenter. As we shall see in the next section, subjects may react differently not only to the experimenter but also to the experimental situation itself. In the next section we will consider two important phenomena: the placebo effect and the demand characteristic. These two processes point out the importance of having a broad ecological understanding of the relationship among the scientist, the subject, and the experimental situation.

PLACEBO FACTORS

One potential problem is the influence of placebo effects in the experiment. Imagine you have just picked up your newspaper and there is a story that says "Scientists have found a new cure for headache." As you continue to read the story, you are told of a technique called *biofeedback* in which physiological changes from a person's body are fed back to the person, and it is because of this feedback that headaches are being cured. Now, as a consumer of scientific research, how would you go about evaluating this story? First, you might use common sense and note that it seems reasonable that as one learns to relax there should be a decrease in muscle tension and, in turn, the number of headaches that are thought to be related to tension should also decrease. Second, you might check the experimental design to see whether the study included a baseline condition in which the number of headaches per person was recorded before biofeedback was administered. You might at this point, especially if you have headaches yourself, be ready to run out to the local biofeedback practitioner and sign up. Even if the biofeedback treatment worked for you as it did for the people in the study, it still would not have been demonstrated scientifically that biofeedback was the ingredient that caused your headache to decrease. Both the consumer and the scientist would need to consider one important factor, and that is the *placebo factor.*

The term *placebo* comes from the Latin verb "to please." The phenomenon is such that some people will show physiological changes just by the mere suggestion that a change will take place. For example, considering a number of studies that have attempted to treat tension headaches with a variety of procedures, it has been shown that 60% of the people will report signs of improvement when given only placebo treatments such as a pill containing nothing but sugar or other inert ingredients (Hass, Fink & Hartfelder, 1963).

The placebo phenomenon is so strong with some individuals that a placebo operation (opening up the chest but not performing a heart operation) has been shown to give similar recovery rates for persons with angina pectoris (pains in the chest) as an actual coronary bypass operation (see pp. 250–251). To control for the placebo effect in research, various procedures have been used. One is to use a control group that receives either no treatment or a treatment previously shown to be ineffective for the particular disorder under study. A more powerful control is to use a *double blind experiment.* In a double blind experiment the experimental group is divided into two groups. One group is given the actual treatment and the other is given a treatment exactly like the experimental treatment but without the active ingredient. For example, in a study of medication, the placebo group would receive a medicine that looks and tastes like the experimental one but does not contain the medication being tested. Neither the placebo nor the experimental medicine group would know which medications they were receiving, and in this way these subjects are said to be "blind." The double blind part of the procedure is that the physicians or nurses giving the medication are also "blind" to which medication is experimental or placebo. A more sophisticated version of this design would allow for the placebo and experimental subjects to be switched systematically during the study, and thus the same subject would receive at times the active treatment and at times the placebo treatment.

DEMAND CHARACTERISTICS

A phenomenon similar to the placebo effect is demand characteristics in psychological research. Demand characteristics occur when a subject's response is influenced more by the research setting than the independent variable. For example, when testing the effect of marijuana on behavior or the effects of hypnosis, most subjects have some idea of how they "should" act and they may respond in this manner. This may include actual faking on the part of the subject.

One study of hypnosis that attempted to control for demand characteristics was reported by Martin Orne (Orne, 1969; Orne & Evans, 1966). The purpose of the study was to find out what would happen if the hypnotist left the room after deep hypnosis had been induced. This particular experiment had theoretical importance because one theory of hypnosis suggested that the subjects would return to their normal state of awareness rapidly and another predicted that it would take some time; that is, the study was designed to see which of the two theories more accurately reflected reality. In the study a group of hypnotic subjects was compared with a control group that was asked to simulate hypnosis and act as if they were hypnotized. Orne and Evans referred to their control group as a *quasi-control,* since the control group was being used more to check out the experimental conditions than to directly compare with the experimental group.

The experimenters wanted to design a study in which the hypnotist left the room in an apparently accidental manner in order to avoid breaking

"IT WAS MORE OF A '<u>TRIPLE-BLIND</u>' TEST. THE PATIENTS DIDN'T KNOW WHICH ONES WERE GETTING THE REAL DRUG, THE DOCTORS DIDN'T KNOW, AND, I'M AFRAID, <u>NOBODY</u> KNEW."

the implicit agreement that the hypnotist will remain with and take care of the hypnotized subject. To accomplish this end, the experimenters staged a power failure. During the second of two sessions, after the experimental subjects were hypnotized and tapping their foot to imagined music, a tape recorder in the room stopped and a desk light went off. The experimenter then said that a fuse had blown and left the room. The findings of the study were apparently clear. The quasi-control group continued to act as if hypnotized until the experimenter returned some thirty minutes later. The experimental subjects, on the other hand, brought themselves out from the hypnotic trance. However, this required varying amounts of time and, once out from under the trance, they appeared somewhat confused. During the postexperimental interviews it appeared that the quasi-control subjects believed that the power failure was not real but only contrived. The experimental group, on the other hand, did not seem to suspect the deception. Since the control subjects were aware of the deception, it was difficult to conclude anything directly from the study. The experimenters then considered ways to make the power failure seem more real. They first reexamined the experimental situation and realized that although the tape recorder and the desk lamp had gone off, the room lights as well as a small polygraph continued to be on. Also, the room with the one-way mirror suggested to subjects that they were being observed, which they were.

A new study was then designed. This study also used an experimental and quasi-control group, but the room had changed. There was no one-way mirror, and when the "power failure" occurred, all the equipment as well as the lights in the room went off. The experimenter was blind as to which was the real hypnotic group and which was the simulated one. Under the new conditions the results for the experimental group were the same. However, the quasi-control groups showed just the opposite results. As soon as the experimenter left the room, the great majority of these subjects stopped simulating and acted as if they were not being observed. Orne and Evans concluded from the second study that the power failure was considered real and that their experimental manipulation was meaningful. Without a control for demand characteristics, an experimenter might have concluded that the theories were correct when in fact the results were due to the subjects acting as they believed they should.

When evaluating research, it is important to consider the role of placebo factors and demand characteristics. It is also important for the researcher to check through such techniques as the quasi-control group and the acceptability of the experimental manipulations. *It is not enough to assume that the subjects in an experiment believe what is being said and accept rationales as true; this needs to be checked out, especially in any study where deception is used!*

CULTURAL AND SOCIAL BIAS

You may think it strange to suggest that the society and environment in which you live could cause significant bias in scientific research. Yet this is certainly the case. The most common manner in which scientific research is influenced is through a shared *paradigm* (Kuhn, 1970). A paradigm is an accepted world view, which may include ideas about the value of what one is doing as well as specific assumptions about how the world is. Before the time of Columbus, map makers drew flat maps because they had never assumed the world to be other than flat. It is important to realize that because a paradigm shapes the way in which you see the world, when it changes, everything seems to change. There have been a number of paradigm changes in science that have altered the manner in which we see the world. One of the first was the change from seeing the earth as the center of the universe to seeing it as just another planet. Once the earth became just another planet, it could be considered as other planets and a new scientific cosmology became possible, as did a new idea about the place of humans in the universe. In psychology we have seen changes in scientific viewpoints that have allowed for research never considered possible. For example, at one time it was considered impossible for an animal to either learn language or use it to communicate. Today, there are a number of research projects in which chimpanzees are being taught to communicate through either a computer or sign language, thus opening an entire new field of research which a few years ago was considered impossible. Likewise, we are gaining a new view of both very young and old people that suggests they are capable of far greater potential than we had previously assumed. We are now beginning to realize that children immediately after birth can interact with their external environment, which includes a recognition of faces. Not only our children but also we are beginning to be seen in a new light. As recently as the 1960s it was assumed that an individual's autonomic nervous system (cardiac functioning, stomach activity, smooth muscles, and glands) was beyond any type of conscious control. However, once that assumption was challenged, entire new fields such as biofeedback developed. The point to be made is that we introduce a bias into our scientific research by letting the believed limitations of our time restrict the scope of our vision. Consequently, we never consider certain aspects of behavior that lie beyond our limited view. Every scientist and society hold limited views of the world. That is not the point; the point is to realize that this is the case.

SUMMARY

In this chapter we used the term *ecological validity* to stress the importance of relationships among the subject, the scientist, and the experimental environment in interpreting the outcome of our research. We emphasized that the goal of science is not to perform perfect experiments but rather to ask questions and increase our understanding of relevant phenomena.

We turned our attention to how we might bias our data collection or our interactions with subjects. We provided examples of ways in which researchers may unintentionally, or even fraudulently, make experimental errors that favor an outcome supporting the specific hypothesis advanced. We also examined how aspects of the experimenter, such as attractiveness, sex, dress, race, and age, can influence many types of experiments. We described how our expectations can become an important potentially confounding variable. This threat of experimenter bias can be minimized by techniques such as computing inter-rater reliability coefficients and using multiple experimenters or "blind" experimenters. We then turned to how subjects may bias our experiments, and we discussed factors such as their desire to please the experimenter by providing data that support the hypothesis or conversely to intentionally sabotage the experiment. The classic Hawthorne experiment was presented as an example of such a problem in experimental psychology.

Two important phenomena in experimentation are known as the placebo effect and demand characteristics. We recommended the double blind experiment as a powerful control method to deal with the placebo effect. The example stressing the importance of demand characteristics (Orne & Evans, 1966) pointed out that this problem is especially important in any study where deception is involved. We briefly described cultural and social biases and the research recommendations outlined by Barber (1976).

CHAPTER TEN

Quasi-Experimental, Single-Subject, and Naturalistic Observation Designs

INTRODUCTION

In the preceding chapters we emphasized that one major goal of science is the study of causal relationships. At the present time the experimental designs outlined in Chapters 7 and 8 are the most powerful tools we have for determining causal relationships. The great usefulness of these designs stems from the fact that we have maximum control over both the independent variable and various potential secondary variables that may confound our experiment. Consequently, with experimental designs we have the greatest confidence that our dependent variables truly reflect the effect of our independent variables. In particular the designs help us to conclude that we have not made a logical error in attributing causal relationships, and they are said to possess a high degree of *internal validity*.

To be sure, sound experimental control and the resulting high degree of internal validity are extremely desirable features in any experiment we might design. Yet, as important as it is that our designs be internally valid, it is equally important that they reflect other issues as well. For example, one important issue is the generality of our research findings. Can the results of an experiment be generalized beyond our particular laboratory setting to ongoing life situations? As you may remember, *external validity* refers to the generalizability of an experimental outcome. When Campbell and Stanley (1963) first used the term *external validity,* they were asking to what other groups, settings, treatment variables, and measurement variables this experimental outcome could be generalized.

Today many scientists and nonscientists are insisting that research findings also have direct relevance to the everyday psychological issues that affect us all. This growing concern for the applicability of our research findings to the life situations we all face influences our research efforts in two ways. First, the theoretical questions and hypotheses we generate increasingly deal with complex, relevant psychological issues and processes. Second, our research subjects and settings increasingly reflect real-life situations.

One method for increasing the generality and relevance of our research is to move the research from the laboratory to the setting where the phenomenon we are studying naturally occurs. For example, you could not study the effect of some unplanned event such as an inner-city riot or an earthquake, or the impact of some federal intervention program such as the Head Start program of the 1960s, in a laboratory. If we are studying the effect of anxiety on final-examination performance, a possible natural setting would be the actual final examination session of a college course. If, however, our theoretical issue deals with interpersonal relationships between strangers in a large city, then the natural setting is the streets of that city.

One effect of extending our research inquiries out of the laboratory and into more natural settings is that we may not be able to exercise control over important aspects of the experiment that are easily controlled in the laboratory. In some cases we are unable to manipulate the levels of the independent variable; in others we cannot adequately eliminate potentially confounding variables; and in most we cannot randomly assign subjects to groups.

Let us consider one striking anecdote told to us by the developmental psychologist, Dale Harris. When Professor Harris was teaching at the University of Minnesota, one student decided to perform an experiment that used elderly individuals in retirement homes around Minneapolis. To make his study a true experiment, this student collected the names of all the residents of the homes and began randomly sampling subjects so that each resident had an equal chance of being selected for the study. However, the time required to complete this sampling process correlated with an event that was unforeseen by the student. During the time in which random sampling was taking place, 12% of the subjects in the retirement homes died! This points up the importance and necessity of reducing tight experimental controls when the phenomenon under study occurs in a changing environment. Additional examples of this problem are studies performed in a changing work environment or clinical studies performed in hospitals and clinics where both patients and staff change frequently. These changes prevent tight experimental controls if the study is to be completed.

Other naturally occurring phenomena also defy true experimental control. For example, suppose we were interested in studying the effect of a natural disaster such as an earthquake on the desirability of living in a given area. To begin with, there is no way we could control the onset or the site of the quake. Nor could we randomly assign subjects to "quaked" and "unquaked" groups. Furthermore, when dealing with the people affected, it would be difficult to eliminate other factors that may have coincided with the quake itself. Some of these influences may have been positive, such as the generous support of friends and neighbors, which the victims never expected. Perhaps others were more negative, such as the irresponsible behavior of looters or inept civil authorities. Consequently, whenever we attempt to increase the external validity of our inquiries by studying phenomena in real-life situations, we run a strong risk of decreasing the internal validity of these same experiments.

In most cases the internal validity of our research is jeopardized or even decreased as we move from the laboratory to more natural settings. Yet, at the same time, the overall applicability and relevance of our research may be increased greatly and, in turn, may enhance the value of our work even further. Thus we are always faced with a trade-off between (1) precision and direct control over experimental design and (2) desire for as much generalizability and relevance to life situations as possible. The process of conducting *sound* and *relevant* research involves a balance between our concern for both *internal* and *external* validity.

In this chapter we will examine three general classes of empirical research designs that offer alternative approaches to research. With the first group of designs we lack sufficient control over the variable under study and over potentially confounding variables to make meaningful comparisons between groups, and thus we are unable to make definite statements about cause and effect. Consequently, we rely instead on *logically* discounting alternative interpretations of our data. To emphasize that these designs are less rigorous and not as useful in demonstrating causal relationships, many researchers call them *quasi-experimental designs*. Furthermore, because these designs are often used to evaluate the impact of some variable on an ongoing process, they are also referred to as evaluation research designs. As we shall see, there are many ways in which quasi-experimental designs approximate true experimental designs. Yet these designs are not true experimental designs. This means that when using these designs we cannot be so confident about causal statements as we are with true experimental designs. Nevertheless, *they are extremely useful in uncovering potential causal relationships in complex psychological phenomena that occur in natural settings*. Consequently, because of our growing interest in studying psychological processes outside the laboratory, these designs can play an important role in our early study of many complex psychological phenomena that occur in natural settings. In a similar fashion these designs are useful in showing where a relationship does not exist and thus reducing the necessity for performing more highly controlled designs. For example, if a new form of psychotherapy is shown not to work in quasi-experimental situations where a variety of placebo and suggestibility factors would help its effectiveness, it would be difficult to argue that the therapy would work better under highly controlled situations.

The second class of designs that we will consider is *single-subject designs*. These research designs offer an alternative to group designs for examining psychological processing. Single-subject designs are particularly useful when the subject population is limited. For example, when one wants to study a rare disorder, it would be difficult if not impossible to obtain enough subjects for a group design. Even when adequate numbers of subjects are available, some researchers (Sidman, 1960) have argued that single-subject research offers more control and may be preferable to group studies for particular types of research questions.

The final class of designs that we will examine is *naturalistic observation techniques* (also called field research designs). These designs are not focused on discovering causal relationships. Instead they provide a powerful tool for describing an ongoing process in its natural setting.

QUASI-EXPERIMENTAL DESIGNS

Time Series Design

A time series design is a within-subjects design; that is, the performance of a single group of subjects is measured *both* before and after the experimental treatment. This particular design is useful when we are interested in the effects of an event that has happened to all members of the population we are studying. For example, suppose you decide to become a college guidance counselor, and after obtaining your Ph.D. you take a job at a small college. One day you are talking to your friend who is the women's gymnastics coach and she mentions that her gymnasts perform very well in practice and during warmups but seem to "fall apart" during actual competition. As a psychologist you know that certain relaxation training and simple concentration exercises have been shown to improve test performance in other test situations. You mention this to the coach and she immediately asks you to try these relaxation exercises with the team. You agree, and for the next week you spend time working with each athlete during daily practice. The entire team enjoys the exercises and feels that they are helping. To evaluate the effectiveness of these relaxation procedures more objectively, you decide to simply compare the final score for the team's next meet with the score for their previous meet.

This particular design, which involves comparing a single pretest measure (total score on first meet) with a single posttest measure (total score on second meet), is called a *single-group, pretest-posttest design*. During their next meet, their composure was much improved and their overall score was better than in the previous meet. Because the coach kept a record of each woman's apparent composure during each performance, it was also possible to rate each woman's composure for these two meets. Hypothetical team results of skills performance and composure are shown in Figure 10.1. As you can see, both the total score and the coach's estimate of composure increased markedly following the relaxation and concentration exercises. Before accepting this conclusion, however, we should keep in mind that because we have utilized only a single pretest and posttest measure, we have no idea how much fluctuation would normally occur between any two

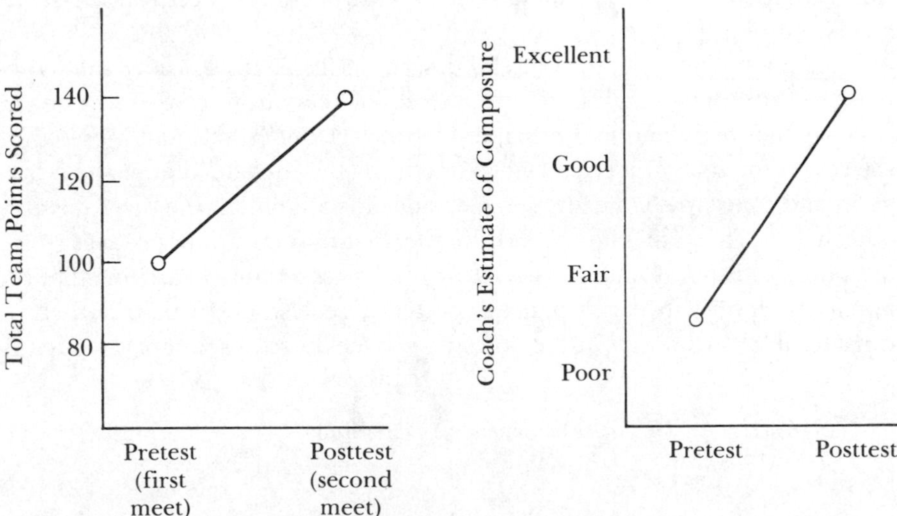

Figure 10.1 These are the hypothetical results of a single-group, pretest-posttest design studying the effects of relaxation and concentration exercises on the total points scored by a women's gymnastics team and the coach's estimate of the gymnasts' composure.

meets. In other words, perhaps the sharp increase in the score or the composure ratings shift is independent of the relaxation exercises. This lack of knowledge concerning the normal amount of fluctuation between any two measures is a very serious weakness of this single-group, pretest-posttest design.

Interrupted Time Series Design

One way to minimize this weakness is to use an *interrupted time series design*. This design involves making several pretest and several posttest measurements. The basic idea behind this type of design is that the additional pretest and posttest scores give us a better estimate of the normal amount of fluctuation from test to test or in this case from gymnastics meet to meet. Once we know the amount of normal fluctuation, we can better interpret the impact of the phenomenon we are studying. Figure 10.2 is a schematic representation of this design. As a point of notation, the interrupted time series design is also referred to as an A-B-A design, where A represents baseline measurements and B represents the treatment manipulation. The A-B-A notation is most often seen in behavioral journals, with B being a specific intervention such as praise for an increase in some target behavior (for example, completing homework or making more positive self-statements).

As an example of a time series design, let us again consider the hypothetical experiment dealing with the effect of relaxation procedures on the performance of gymnasts. In this case a time series design could incorporate the scores for several meets prior to and after the introduction of the relaxation and concentration exercises. Consider for a moment the three possible outcomes depicted in Figure 10.3. In part A the pretest and posttest scores are fairly constant. Consequently, it would be reasonable to assume that the apparent change in performance reflected a real shift. In part B there is considerable fluctuation in the outcome of weekly scores, and consequently

Pretests	Phenomenon under Study	Posttests
O_1 , O_2 , O_3 , O_4	X	O_5 , O_6 , O_7 , O_8

Figure 10.2 In this figure, O represents each observation or test score, and X represents the occurrence of the phenomenon under study. Note that the phenomenon under study, X, interrupts the periodic measurement on our group of subjects. (After Campbell & Stanley, 1963.)

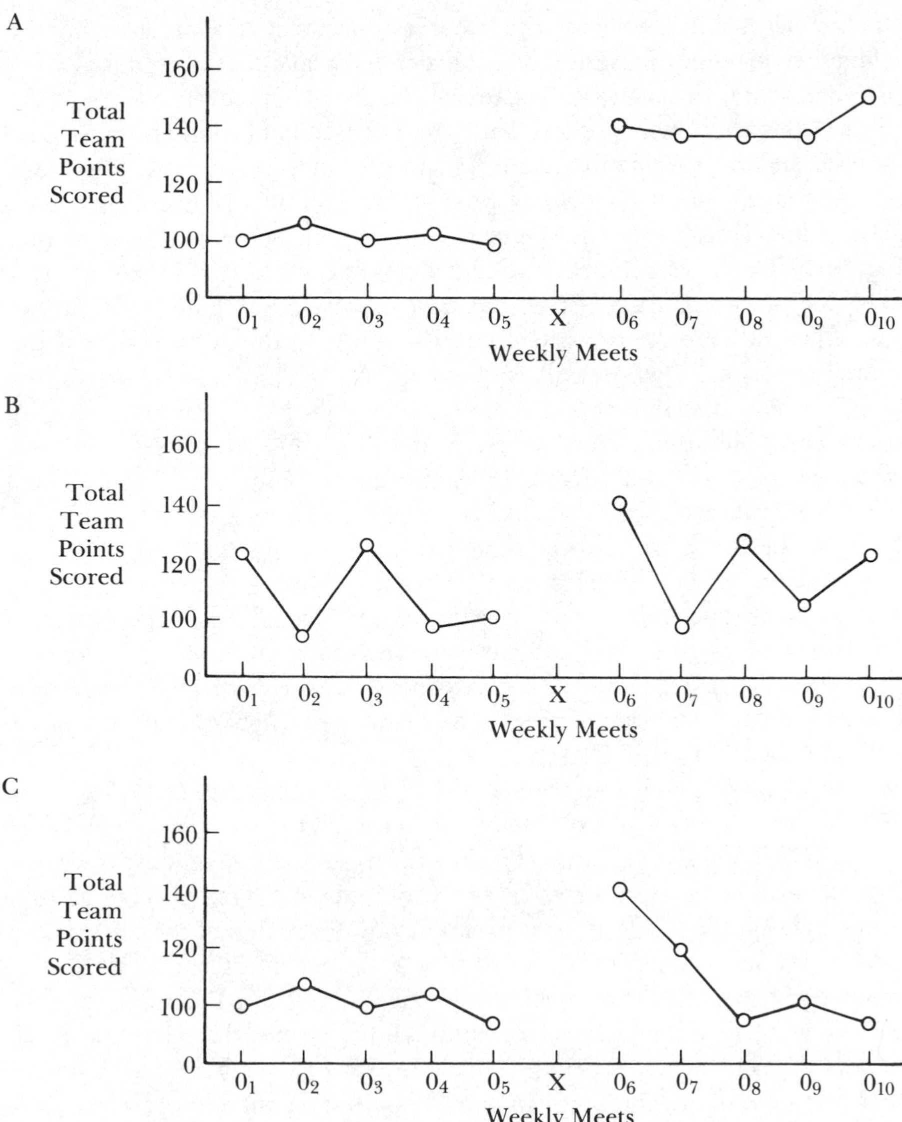

Figure 10.3 This figure shows the hypothetical outcomes of an interrupted time series design examining the effects of relaxation and concentration exercises on the total points scored by a women's gymnastics team in ten weekly meets. X marks the point at which the exercises were introduced. Part A shows an outcome in which the pretest and posttest scores are fairly constant. Part B shows an outcome characterized by much variability in weekly scores. Part C shows what might be a transient effect superimposed on a relatively constant background.

our best bet is that the sharp increase in performance after introducing the relaxation procedures is simply chance fluctuation that would have occurred anyway. In each case we gain confidence in our interpretation of the effect of the phenomenon under study by being able to compare its impact with normally occurring fluctuations of weekly meet scores. It is important to note that an *interrupted time series design* can also provide some estimate of how long-lasting the influence of the phenomenon is. For example, Figure 10.3A shows a hypothetical outcome that would lead us to suspect a fairly long-lasting impact of the relaxation procedures. Figure 10.3C shows a hypothetical outcome consistent with the idea that the performance of the gymnasts was only temporarily improved.

Although the interrupted time series design is a great improvement over the simple pretest-posttest design, it still leaves us far short of a clear statement of cause and effect. For example, if Figure 10.3A represented your data, you could certainly feel confident that a real shift in team performance occurred at about the time you introduced your relaxation procedures. However, any number of other events might be contributing to this unusually abrupt shift in team performance. Perhaps the increased care and attention given to each athlete were responsible and not the exercises themselves, or maybe some campus event that occurred about that time caused the shift, or perhaps there was even a television special on women gymnasts bound for the Olympics.

Ideally, we could control for many of these alternative interpretations by including a control group of some sort. However, because *all* members of the population under study have been exposed to the relaxation procedure, it is impossible to select a second group of women gymnasts to serve as a control group. This, of course, is an important limitation of the interrupted time series design, and it must be kept in mind when interpreting the outcome. As it turns out, it is sometimes possible to redefine the population we are studying to utilize control subjects who were not directly exposed to whatever phenomenon is being studied. In this case we might see whether there was a shift in the performance of the men gymnasts or in the performance of women gymnasts from a nearby college. This expanded form of the interrupted time series design is called a multiple time series design.

Multiple Time Series Design

A *multiple time series design* attempts to rule out some potential alternative interpretations by including a control group that does not receive the experimental treatment. Because of this second group of subjects, the multiple

	Pretests	Phenomenon under Study	Posttests
Experimental group	O_1, O_2, O_3, O_4, O_5	X	$O_6, O_7, O_8, O_9, O_{10}$
Control group	O_1, O_2, O_3, O_4, O_5		$O_6, O_7, O_8, O_9, O_{10}$

Figure 10.4 Multiple time series design. In the figure, O represents each periodic observation or test score; X represents the occurrence of the phenomenon under study. Note that the phenomenon under study, X, interrupts the periodic measurements of our experimental group but not of our control group. (After Campbell & Stanley, 1963.)

time series design is not a within-subjects design, like the interrupted time series design, but rather is a between-subjects design. A multiple time series design is schematically represented in Figure 10.4.

In our study of the effectiveness of relaxation procedures on the performance of women gymnasts, it might be helpful to utilize a control group of women gymnasts from a neighboring college. We could use their total weekly team scores as control data. To the extent that these subjects are similar to our original subjects in any relevant subject variables and are living under similar social and environmental influences, we can assume that these two groups are equal for factors other than the experience of the relaxation training itself. Figure 10.5 shows two sets of hypothetical data for each team. In Figure 10.5A the hypothetical scores from Figure 10.3C for the gymnasts who received the relaxation are shown along with the total team score for the women gymnasts from the neighboring college who did not receive the special training. The abrupt difference between the two teams in the two meets following the special training is certainly consistent with the idea that the relaxation procedures had a definite, although transient, influence on the overall performance of the woman gymnasts. Before accepting this conclusion, however, keep in mind that we may have overlooked some social or environmental influence that affected our experimental group and not our control group. For example, it is quite possible that some local campus event or even some independent event among the team members at about the same time influenced their "team spirit" and consequently their performance. This latter interpretation is *always* a real possibility when using the multiple time series design to study complex phenomena in their natural settings.

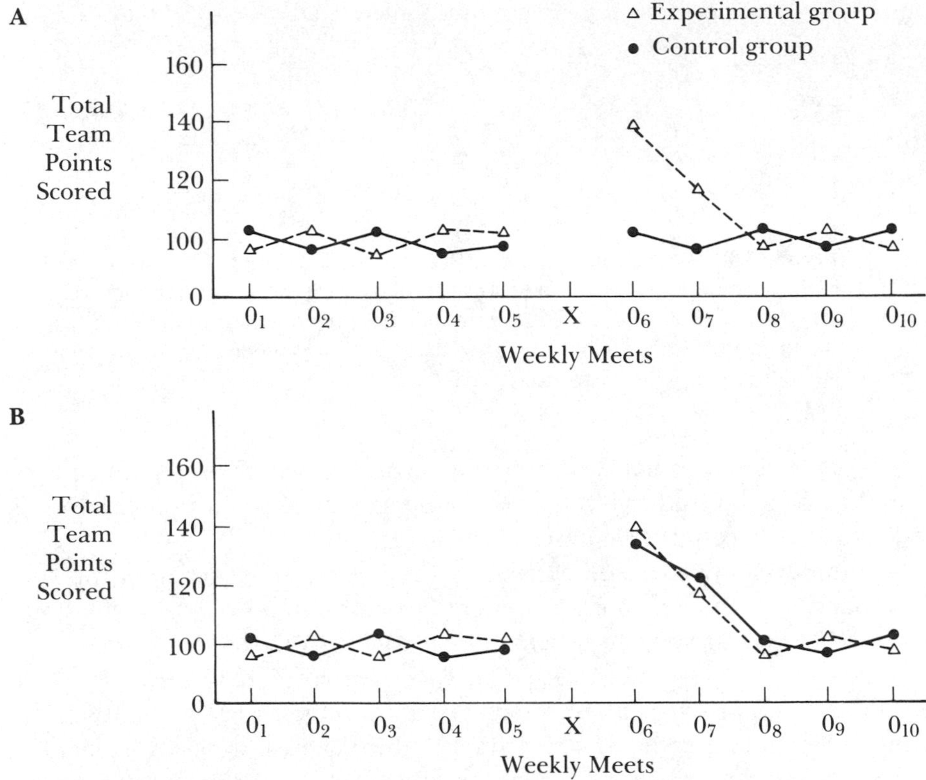

Figure 10.5 In this figure, two sets of hypothetical data are shown for a multiple time series design used to study the effect of relaxation training on the weekly performance of women gymnasts. The dotted line represents weekly total team scores for the gymnasts who received the relaxation training. The solid line represents weekly scores for the gymnastics team from a neighboring college that did not receive the relaxation training.

In Figure 10.5B the hypothetical weekly scores for the two teams show a sharp increase following relaxation training. Because the gymnasts from the neighboring college did not receive the relaxation training, it is likely that some factor other than the relaxation training is responsible for this improvement. One possibility is that both teams were affected by some common event. Can you think of any common events that could account for this parallel performance?

It should be increasingly evident that the interpretation of quasi-experimental designs is a tricky business and that there is *always* a real danger that unknown variables may be contributing to the performance differences between our experimental and control groups. This adds to the difficulty of deciding which of several possible interpretations of our final outcome best reflects the true causal factor. In many cases we will never know which interpretation is correct!

Nonequivalent Before-After Design

A *nonequivalent before-after design* is used when we want to make comparisons between two groups that we strongly suspect may differ in important ways even before the experiment begins. Because the two groups in this design are initially unequal, there is an unusually high risk of ultimately confusing these initial differences with the effects of the independent variable. Consequently, in this design we avoid simply comparing both groups on a single dependent measure. Instead, each group is first given a pretest and then a posttest, and finally we compare the amount of change in test scores for the experimental and control groups. Thus, by comparing difference scores rather than single dependent measures, we attempt to control more directly for the fact that we are dealing with initially unequal groups. So in a real sense each group's pretest score serves as a sort of baseline from which we estimate the amount of change from pretest to posttest. Then we compare the magnitude of change for each group by comparing difference scores. This design is schematically represented in Figure 10.6.

The nonequivalent before-after design is widely used in educational research where we are frequently interested in comparing different schools,

	Pretreatment Measure	Treatment	Posttreatment Measure	Difference
Experimental group	O_1	X	O_2	$O_1 - O_2$
Control group	O_1		O_2	$O_1 - O_2$

Figure 10.6 Example of a nonequivalent before-after design. In this figure, O_1 and O_2 represent the pre- and posttreatment dependent measures for each group, respectively; X represents the treatment or independent variable. Note that for this design, group comparisons are made between the difference scores for each group rather than directly between posttreatment scores. (After Campbell & Stanley, 1963.)

classes, or programs. As an example, let's assume you have just completed your Ph.D. and have taken a job teaching psychology at the college level. One bright spring day your department head asks if you would be willing to develop a new course in human sexuality and, if so, you could teach a morning and afternoon section of it next fall. Having never taught a course on sexuality before, you would like to know whether a lecture or discussion format would be most effective in influencing student attitudes toward human sexuality. Because you will teach two sections, you could begin to answer this question by teaching the morning session with a discussion format and the afternoon session with a lecture format. Then at the end of the term, you could give an attitude questionnaire to each section and directly compare their scores. Because teaching is still a new experience for you, you decide to ask one of the senior professors what she thinks about your idea. To your surprise, she points out that students who voluntarily schedule 8:00 A.M. classes are very different from those who take 4:00 P.M. classes. Consequently, she warns that a direct comparison of attitudes at the end of the term may reflect these initial subject differences as well as the effects of your discussion and lecture formats. Impressed by her comments, your initial impulse might be simply to assign students randomly to each class as you would do in any experiment you were conducting in our laboratory. In this case, however, you are not in the laboratory, and because your students voluntarily select which section of your course they will enroll in, you have no control over the assignment of subjects. Consequently, you cannot control for these potentially confounding subject differences by randomly assigning subjects to each group.

At this point, while on the verge of abandoning the whole idea and avoiding such applied questions, you recall that quasi-experimental designs can often be used in real-life situations where experimental designs cannot. In this particular case, your major problem is that you strongly suspect that the two groups will be very different at the onset of the experiment. Therefore, you decide to use the nonequivalent before-after design, which was developed for situations in which we cannot randomly assign subjects to groups and are faced with having to compare groups that may differ from the onset of the experiment. The final design you might arrive at is depicted in Figure 10.7.

Ex Post Facto Design

In the designs we have discussed thus far, the experimenter planned a study that would take place in the future. The *ex post facto design* attempts to use

	Pretreatment	Treatment	Posttreatment	Difference
Experimental group	Attitude questionnaire	Discussion	Attitude questionnaire	Pretest−posttest score
Control group	Attitude questionnaire	Lecture	Attitude questionnaire	Pretest−posttest score

Figure 10.7 Example of a nonequivalent before-after design.

empirical procedures for suggesting causal relationships from events that have occurred in the past. Some researchers see this procedure as important for suggesting how a significant event in the past (for example, growing up under Hitler or television watching) might have influenced people. Schnelle and Lee (1974) used an ex post facto time series analysis when they studied the manner in which transferring "problem" prisoners to another prison affected the number of offenses committed by the prisoners who were not transferred. From prison records, these authors created an ex post facto A-B-A design, with B being the transfer of problem prisoners and A being the measurement of offenses by the prisoners not transferred. As with other quasi-experimental designs, such studies as this can say *whether* a change took place, but it is impossible to state *why* the change took place.

Other uses of the ex post facto design are found in studies of educational techniques, disease, and psychopathology. For example, Barthell and Holmes (1968) studied the number of listed activities of students in a high school yearbook to determine whether there were differential rates of high school activity between schizophrenics and nonschizophrenics identified later in life. Since the study took place "after the fact," these researchers had to determine a possible control group also after the fact. For their control group they chose students whose pictures appeared next to the schizophrenics in the yearbooks. In one sense you are working backward in the ex post facto procedure since you know the outcome and wish to determine the antecedents of this outcome. Thus, one of the important questions is: Did you select the correct measure (high school activity in the preceding example) to compare the two groups? This, of course, is an unanswerable question and for this reason the procedure is a very weak form of inference.

Let us consider another example of ex post facto research that points up some additional interpretation problems. You might be interested in people who have a particular disease. If you have a theory that nutrition is important, you might study what healthy and diseased people ate for breakfast. You might then find that the people with the particular disease did not eat breakfast. You could then conclude that eating breakfasts helps one to stay healthy, right? Wrong! Eating may or may not have been the causal factor in the disease, but you cannot know from ex post facto designs. The same results may have been brought about because the people with the disease did not feel good when they woke up in the morning and thus chose not to eat breakfast. Thus, subjects may have been self-selected on the treatment variable and in this way invalidate your conclusion that the treatment variable affected the groups. In a true experiment, this objection would have been avoided since you would have selected the subjects and assigned them to groups.

Although ex post facto designs are one of the weakest forms of inference, Kerlinger (1973) suggests that these designs can be used to good advantage in a particular case. This particular case involves testing alternative hypotheses. His ideas are based on those of Chamberlin (1890/1965) and Platt (1964; see Box 4.1). Using ex post facto procedures, one can examine *alternative dependent* variables. For example, retrospectively, cigarette smoking might be shown to be associated with more lung cancer than brain tumors. Although the research still cannot make causal statements, testing alternatives can lead to a greater understanding of the phenomenon under study.

SINGLE-SUBJECT DESIGNS

In general there are two types of *single-subject designs;* one is primarily descriptive and the other is more experimental in its intent. When our primary goal is to provide a detailed description of an individual, the *case study* design is useful. In contrast, when our primary goal is to begin to focus on a particular aspect of an individual's behavior that may be influenced by some external factor, single-subject designs such as the *reversal* and *multiple baseline designs* may be used.

Case Study Design

Historically the case study is one of the most widely used methods for studying individual subjects. Indeed for years it has been the primary method for studying phenomena in clinical medicine and clinical psychology. Typically a case study is a brief narrative description of an individual or some aspect of an individual that brings together relevant aspects of the patient's history and present situation. The information that makes up the case study may come from a variety of sources, including the patient's recollection of events, information from friends or relatives, public records, and others.

In one sense we all use case study techniques when we go to a professional complaining of a pain somewhere in our body. The professional then diagnoses the problem and prescribes some form of therapy. After some time, we then return and give the professional feedback concerning whether or not the pain decreased. Since both physical pain such as headaches and psychological distress such as feeling lost or without purpose cannot be seen from behavior alone, the case study technique represents onc of the oldest techniques of medical and psychological description. While case studies based solely on the reports of subjects or patients are open to all the problems of self-report such as selective forgetting, the desire to show ourselves in a positive light, and outright deception, there are times in which this can be a useful technique.

For example, Gottmann (1973) suggests that systematic case study observation offers therapists a means of obtaining information concerning specific interventions in therapy during an ongoing series of sessions. As a digression, it should be pointed out that the case study may offer the best type of information when the goal is to note the change of a single individual and the average change of all patients or subjects would give an incorrect picture of change. To illustrate this point, consider a treatment that produced a beneficial change in half the patients and an equally negative change in the other half. If group means or averages were calculated, one might erroneously conclude that the treatment had no effect on patients. Thus in some cases it is more accurate to record a number of systematic single case studies than to record group data. This is true not only for studies of pathology but also for studies of potential. For example, Maslow (1970) used the case study technique to study exceptional people whom he considered to be self-actualizing individuals. Likewise developmental psychologists dating back to the last century have kept records of the development of their own children (Bolgar, 1965). In the case of Piaget, these observations led to his later theories.

In addition to this use of the case study method to provide a general description, there is a second, somewhat more specific use of the case study design. In this instance a case study is a narrative that summarizes an *experimenter's* direct observations of a subject's behavior after some sort of treatment has been performed. This design is represented in Figure 10.8 (sometimes called the one-shot case study). In some instances the case study

	Treatment	Response
Single subject	X	O

Figure 10.8 In this figure, the X refers to the treatment given to a single subject, and the O refers to whatever observations the experimenter makes.

can be a useful tool in research. The observations may suggest new hypotheses, demonstrate rare phenomena, or even show exceptions to established facts. However, in terms of good design, the case study is very weak; like the single-group, pretest-posttest design, we simply have no assurance that the observations would not be exactly the same without the treatment. Because of the lack of control procedures, we can say absolutely nothing about causal factors and run a high risk of confusing any number of confounding variables with our treatment. In spite of these disadvantages, in some clinical areas the case study design can provide valuable initial descriptions of

Box 10.1 A Patient with Bilateral Temporal Lobe Damage

In 1957 Scoville and Milner first described a thirty-one-year-old male patient (H.M.) who underwent bilateral temporal lobe surgery in 1953. The lesions involved the removal of the tissue on the medial surface of both temporal lobes, including large portions of the hippocampi. The purpose of the operation was to relieve very frequent and severe epileptic seizures, which were unrelieved by anticonvulsant medication. (Dr. Scoville was encouraged to attempt this procedure because he had strong reason to believe that some abnormality of this region was responsible for the seizures and because evidence involving nonhuman primates indicated no behavioral abnormalities following removal of this area.) Although the surgical procedure strikingly reduced the number of epileptic seizures, the operation had an unanticipated and awful consequence: The patient was unable to either learn or remember any new material!

Prior to surgery H.M. was a motor-winder who was unable to work because of his epileptic seizures. After surgery he was pleasant and easygoing, as he had been prior to surgery. His measured IQ actually rose from 104 to 119 (presumably it was depressed prior to surgery by the epileptic abnormality). However, H.M. exhibited striking memory deficits for events both before and after surgery. For example, except for Dr. Scoville, whom he had known for many years prior to surgery, he was completely unable to recognize members of the hospital staff; he could not even learn his way to the bathroom. He was unable to remember the death of a close uncle, even though he was repeatedly reminded and became genuinely upset every time he was informed.

new phenomena, which can then be carefully studied with more rigorous experimental methods. One area where the case study method has proved useful is in neuroscience. For example, Scoville and Milner (1957) published a case study describing the effect of removal of the hippocampal region of the brain from a thirty-five-year-old patient (see Box 10.1). In spite of the weakness of case study designs, this particular case study provided much new information about hippocampal function in humans. Some of these findings have been verified with more rigorous designs in nonhuman primates.

Reversal Design

As you might imagine, there are times when we want more than a simple description of the relevant behaviors of our single subject. Ideally we want to be able to begin to point toward causal relationships. However, with single-subject designs, control groups and randomization are obviously impos-

---

As the years passed, his ability to remember events has remained severely impaired. H.M. was unable to remember his new house address even after living there for six years. He could not recognize neighbors and when left alone would invite strangers into his house thinking they were friends whom he had forgotten. He was able to perform simple jobs such as mowing the lawn, but could not remember where to find the lawnmower or that he had used it the previous day. He read newspapers over and over, forgetting that he had already read them. He spent many hours resolving the same jigsaw puzzle without any sign of learning it. His memory deficit is paralleled by a total lack of appreciation for the passage of time. His deficit in registering new material has remained severe even many years later (Milner, 1966).

In addition to many informal observations such as these, over the years H.M. and his mother have faithfully cooperated with a number of psychologists in the United States and Canada who have carefully examined the nature of his unfortunate deficit. Taken together, their findings provide a wealth of information about human temporal lobe function. Yet this case obviously raises moral issues which Dr. Scoville (1968) stresses:

> This one case, so carefully studied, has demonstrated to many the grave danger of bilateral resection of the medial parts of the temporal lobes when the hippocampus is included in the removal. Even at this late date, however, scientific publications continue to propose the removal of the hippocampus bilaterally for relief of behavioral disorders, intractable pain, and other reasons; such proposals no longer seem justifiable in view of the profound anterograde amnesia which results.

---

sible, so the task of controlling for extraneous variables is difficult. We have pointed out that when more rigorous means of experimental control are not possible, we can sometimes logically render alternative hypotheses unlikely. The reversal designs rely primarily on the use of logic to gain at least some control. The rationale behind this design is simple: If a subject behaves one way as a given treatment is presented, then behaves quite differently when it is removed, and finally behaves in the original manner when the treatment is presented a second time, it is reasonable to suspect that this fluctuation in the subject's behavior is due to the treatment. It is extremely hard to even imagine how an extraneous variable might vary in an exactly parallel manner to producc a similar fluctuation in the subject's behavior.

Reversal designs may use any number of reversals. For example a design that measures a subject's behavior before, during, and after a treatment is called an ABA design. During the before and after conditions, here designated the A conditions, baseline behavior is monitored in the absence of the treatment condition. During the B phase of the design, the subject's behavior is monitored during the treatment conditions. An ABAB reversal design is depicted in Figure 10.9.

In considering the reversal design, it is important to keep in mind that we are using the phenomenon of reversibility of some behavior in the presence or absence of the treatment condition to indicate that these behaviors may be causally related. One limitation with the reversal design is that it will only work when we are studying the effect of treatment conditions on behaviors that quickly return to baseline levels once the treatment is over. Obviously, the influence of all treatments is not this transient. When we are dealing with treatments that result in more permanent shifts in behavior, this particular design cannot be used to suggest causal relationships. In-

	A Baseline	B Treatment X	A Baseline	B Treatment X
Single subject	O_1	O_2	O_3	O_4

Figure 10.9 This figure represents an ABAB single-subject reversal design. X refers to the administration of the independent variable on observations 2 and 4; O refers to the behavioral observations made on the subject. Note that O_1 and O_3 reflect the occurrence of the dependent variable in the absence of the treatment condition, and O_2 and O_4 reflect the measure of the dependent variable in the presence of the treatment condition.

stead, when we are interested in studying the longer-lasting effects of various independent variables on single subjects, one solution is to use a multiple baseline design.

Multiple Baseline Design

Like the reversal designs just discussed, the multiple baseline, single-subject design relies primarily on logic to gain at least some degree of experimental control. With the multiple baseline design we monitor several behaviors of a single subject simultaneously. Once baseline levels are established for each behavior, we then apply our treatment to one of these behaviors. The likelihood of a causal relation is inferred from the fact that of the several monitored behaviors, *only* the behavior exposed to the experimental treatment changes while all nontreated behaviors remain unchanged. Once this first behavioral shift is noted, the treatment is then applied to the next behavior and so on. The idea behind this design is that it is very unlikely that each of the baseline behaviors would successively shift as each behavior received the treatment. Consequently in the multiple baseline design it is the successive shifting of baseline levels as the treatment is applied that serves as the basis for suspecting a causal relationship. Unlike the reversal designs, which work only for behaviors that are readily reversible, multiple baseline designs can be used for behaviors that are permanently changed by the experimental treatment. A schematic representation of a multiple baseline, single-subject design is depicted in Figure 10.10.

Concerning the limitations of the multiple baseline design, it is important to keep in mind that each behavior being monitored and successively

Several	A	Baseline	*Treatment*	Baseline	Baseline	Baseline
behaviors	B	Baseline	Baseline	*Treatment*	Baseline	Baseline
of a single	C	Baseline	Baseline	Baseline	*Treatment*	Baseline
subject	D	Baseline	Baseline	Baseline	Baseline	*Treatment*

Figure 10.10 This figure shows a schematic representation of a multiple baseline design. In this design several behaviors (A, B, C, and D) are simultaneously monitored. Whatever treatment condition being used is then successively applied to each of these behaviors. The continuation of baseline measures after treatment is sometimes omitted. Note that evidence suggestive of a causal relationship would consist of a successive shift in baseline activity as each successive behavior receives the treatment condition.

receiving the treatment conditions must be relatively *independent* of the others. That is, the behaviors we are monitoring must not be so highly interrelated that a change in one behavior results in parallel changes in other behaviors even though the subjects did not receive the treatment conditions. If the behaviors under investigation were interdependent, then the successive unfolding of baseline shifts due to the successive application of our treatment condition would be destroyed and this design would lose much of its usefulness. For example, Kazdin (1973) notes that this design may be of limited value in studying inappropriate classroom behaviors because many of these behaviors are interrelated and any treatment that is effective for one behavior is likely to influence other behaviors as well. Although the interrelatedness of these behaviors may eventually facilitate whatever intervention program is implemented, the fact that several of these behaviors may simultaneously be altered by the treatment of any one negates the usefulness of the multiple baseline design in studying these interrelated classroom behaviors.

NATURALISTIC OBSERVATIONS

In the first two chapters we stressed that our basic scientific methods are direct extensions of ways we normally learn about and interact with the world. In many ways the method of naturalistic observation derives from what may be our most primitive way of learning about the world—simply paying attention and observing what happens. The method of naturalistic observation, sometimes called *field studies*, is particularly useful in the early stages of investigating a phenomenon. In this case we usually know very little about the phenomenon and can benefit tremendously from a detailed description of the process we are studying. Natural scientists have made use of this technique for many years. Initially they focused on simply classifying and describing a wide variety of plant and animal life on our planet. More recently they have used this technique to study animal behavior. Perhaps the greatest single application of this technique was Darwin's five-year voyage on the HMS *Beagle* during which he compiled countless detailed descriptions of plant and animal life over a wide part of the world. As he observed and recorded his observations, ideas about how this great abundance of plant and animal life developed came to him. It was these ideas that he later synthesized to form the foundation of our modern theory of organic evolution. Darwin's early work stressed two functions of naturalistic observation. First, it allows us to compile a mass of descriptive knowledge about a phenomenon. Then, as we become more familiar with it, we may get insight about general patterns or lawful relationships in the phenomenon.

Moving into the present century, we encounter the naturalistic methods of such men as Lorenz and Tinbergen (Lehner, 1979). Initial research may be composed of simply recording in a descriptive manner the behavior that is observed. From these initial observations, new hypotheses and theories may be developed and further explored through observation. In one such study of the herringgull, Tinbergen observed young chicks obtain food from their parent's bill. He was particularly impressed by how fast the young chick could learn to peck the parent's bill and wondered how they could distinguish it from other objects in their environment.

At this point Tinbergen returned to the literature and discovered two conditions that would bring forth the pecking. The first was that a red object must be placed in front of the young bird, and the second was that the red object be kept low to the ground. Using simple quasi-experimental designs, it was shown that the bird would peck at many objects that were both red and low to the ground, including cherries and even the red soles of bathing shoes. This understanding then led Tinbergen into more experimental studies using carved birds as stimuli. This work also led to some beginning hypotheses concerning the sensory apparatus of these birds.

As we have followed this particular work of Tinbergen, we have seen him move from naturalistic observation to more experimental studies. This refinement of ideas is a natural process in which scientists begin with a broad perspective and then focus on a more narrow experimental question. It is equally important to continue to return to the broad perspective of naturalistic observation to add validity to the experimental findings. Both Tinbergen (1972) and Lorenz (1973) have argued that for the study of animal behavior, it is necessary to create a balance between naturalistic and experimental methods as the key to good research.

As we begin to use naturalistic methods to study ourselves, the scientist is faced with greater complexity in terms of both subject matter and the scientist's own role in what is being observed. In some cases the observer may choose to remain undetected or can just blend into the background. Krantz (1979) used this approach when he observed obese and nonobese individuals eating with others in a university cafeteria. In other situations the scientist may find it more useful to become a participant in the situation under study. One classic example of scientists as participants in a naturalistic study is that of D. L. Rosenhan (1973), entitled "On Being Sane in Insane Places."

Rosenhan's research focused on the manner in which mental hospital staffs distinguish sane individuals from insane ones and the types of experiences that patients in these hospitals face. In this study eight sane individuals gained admission to twelve different hospitals across the country. These individuals, or *pseudopatients* as they might be called, called the hospital and reported that they heard voices. Initial interviews were established for admission and, except for the initial complaint of voices and giving a false name and occupation, all other information given was correct. Once admitted to the hospital, the pseudopatients ceased to simulate any symptoms of pathology and followed instructions from the staff as required. Surprising as it may seem, in none of the hospitals were the researchers treated in any other way than as "insane" patients, and their true identities were never realized. This was true even though most of the researchers took notes openly and attempted to have "normal" conversations with the staff. In the published report, Rosenhan discusses his observations and the subjective experiences of powerlessness and depersonalization that the research had on the researchers themselves. This report is extremely interesting reading and points up the role of the scientist as investigative reporter using the methods of naturalistic observation.

Concerns While Making Naturalistic Observations

Although naturalistic methods do not draw causal connections, questions of validity are still important. In these designs we also want to know whether our observations are valid and whether there are reasons why our observations may not be accurate. In this section we will go through the steps involved in naturalistic observation and consider possible problems in each step.

Data Collection One problem any observer faces is that if the subjects realize they are being observed, they may behave differently than if they are not being observed. When a subject's behavior is influenced by the mere presence of the observer, it is called *reactive behavior*. Reactive behaviors tell us what people are like when they know they are being observed. They tell us nothing about behavior under normal circumstances. To keep our observations free from reactive behaviors, we attempt to avoid interfering in any way with the process we are studying by concealing our identity as researchers. These undetected observations, which are called *unobtrusive observations*, greatly facilitate the task of interpreting observations [see Webb et al. (1966) for an excellent discussion of unobtrusive measures]. Researchers attempt to make unobtrusive observations in a variety of ways. In some cases they attempt to conduct their observations without being seen by the subject. Some use one-way mirrors; some use hidden closed-circuit televisions. In some cases ethologists and comparative psychologists have surgically implanted tiny radio transmitters in wandering animals such as wild wolves to study their natural migratory patterns. Obviously this procedure would avoid any reactive behaviors of the wolves such as would occur if they were being tracked across the Arctic by a howling dog sled or a noisy helicopter.

As we mentioned in Chapter 2, simply observing can be difficult. Part of the difficulty is that we do not usually observe for prolonged periods of time without somehow interfering with the process. Our natural tendency is to jump in and influence the process. Try, for example, simply listening to a friend with a minimum of interference other than an occasional supportive statement. Another reason it is difficult to observe accurately is that we are influenced by *selective perception;* that is, the observations of untrained observers are markedly influenced by what they expect to see. Obviously, the extent to which our observations are restricted by our selective perceptions has a great impact on the accuracy of our observations. Fortunately it is possible to teach observers to observe more accurately. One common first step is simply to emphasize the dangers of selective perception. Once we realize that what we expect to see acts as a filtering device, we have come a long way toward seeing things as they are. The use of additional observers can also be a good way to increase the accuracy of observations, particularly if their expectations or selective perceptions are different from our own. One common problem particularly for new observers may be boredom. Remember, when you feel bored you are observing boredom and not the phenomenon you are supposed to be observing. So use boredom as a warning sign that you are not focusing on the observation. A useful technique for ensuring a minimum of selective perceptions and boredom is to pretend every few seconds that you have never before witnessed the setting you are observing. In this way you are constantly looking at the scene with a fresh perspective or with a beginner's mind. With this attitude you are constantly reopening yourself to any subtle changes or surprises.

The process of recording observations is equally crucial. Careful, immediately recorded, legible notes are of great value. If you cannot record your observations as they occur, then take sketchy notes and, after the observation session is over, use these highlights to assist recalling as much detail as you can. Obviously mechanical devices such as video tape and cassette recorders can be useful aids. Remember, though, that these devices are limited; they capture only a portion of what is going on. And although they may involve miles of tape, they will never have a single theoretical insight.

Data Analysis The task of processing and analyzing field study data may initially seem monumental. Typically much data are redundant, so the task of analyzing them is usually not so involved as it initially appears. A good place to begin is to review all your data several times so you get the whole picture of what happened. Next it may be helpful to describe the major patterns of behavior. This initial emphasis on common or invariant behavior is helpful because it provides a baseline of the relevant behavior. Once these primary behavior patterns are outlined, it may be profitable to examine instances of atypical behavior. For example, if you are observing the play behavior of a group of children, ask: Are there a small number who prefer not to play? What do they do instead? Sometimes you will find situations in which no clear patterns of behavior emerge. In these cases it is useful to develop a complete behavioral taxonomy or an organized listing of the behaviors involved along with the relative frequency of each behavior.

Once the major results become apparent, you will have an excellent basis for evaluating any theoretical ideas you may have recorded while directly observing your subjects. You may find that ideas that initially seemed very fruitful simply do not reflect the major patterns of your overall empirical observations. Any incorrect notions can easily be disregarded and replaced by your empirical findings. As you process and analyze your data, you may get insights about possible causal factors that may underlie the natural behaviors you are observing. These can be added to any you thought of while observing your subjects and later evaluated for possible study with formal experimental designs. In some cases you may decide that a simple intervention in a future field setting may provide useful clues to possible cause-and-effect relationships. If you decide to explore cause-and-effect issues in your field setting, keep in mind that you will no longer be using the method of naturalistic observation. Instead you will most likely be using one of the quasi-experimental designs discussed in the early part of this chapter. As we mentioned, this is precisely what quasi-experimental designs were developed to do!

To Conceal or Not to Conceal; To Participate or Not to Participate Before concluding our discussion of naturalistic observation research, there are two issues every observer must face. Both stem from the fact that in actual practice the basic method we just outlined sometimes needs to be modified to fit the realities of the situation we are attempting to study. The first concerns whether or not to conceal our identity as researchers; the second concerns whether we actually participate in the social process we are observing.

In our previous discussion, we emphasized the importance of unobtrusive observation techniques as a means of minimizing the likelihood of reactive behaviors contaminating our observations. Sometimes, however, the phenomenon we are studying is such that there is simply no reasonable way to collect data without being seen. In these cases we can best observe the process we are studying by concealing our identity as researchers and becoming actively involved in the process we are studying. For example, Randal Alfred (1976) posed as a member of the Church of Satan for several years while he studied the sociological and psychological aspects of its members. No one knew he was conducting research until he revealed his true purpose to their leader and requested permission to publish a summary of what he had learned.

Other researchers make no attempt to conceal themselves while collecting data. Anthropologists living among and observing people from other cultures typically do not attempt to conceal themselves. In her study of adolescents in Samoa, Margaret Mead (1928) made no attempt to conceal her identity from her subjects. Mead found that Samoan adolescents do not experience the extent of psychological problems seen among adolescents in the United States. And, furthermore, she suggested that their more open attitudes toward sexual behavior may underlie this difference.

The decision about whether or not to be an active participant in the process we are observing will also depend on the phenomenon we are studying. In the cases of ethologists such as Lorenz and Tinbergen and anthropologists such as Margaret Mead, data are usually collected without the researcher becoming part of the process under study. In contrast, Alfred's valuable contribution was based on his active participation in the process he was observing. Obviously, there is always a danger that the researcher's participation may unintentionally alter the process being observed. On the positive side, participation enables the researcher to experience the process personally. And this introspective data can provide a fruitful source of subjective data and new ideas about underlying psychological processes.

The task of deciding whether to remain concealed or reveal your identity depends to a large extent on whether you are observing highly reactive behaviors. If you suspect that the behavior of your subjects will be different if they know they are being observed, then use some sort of concealed observation strategy. In a similar way, if you suspect that there is much to be gained by personally experiencing the process you are studying *and* if you feel the overall process would not be significantly influenced by your participation, then you might consider participating directly in the process you are studying.

Strengths and Weaknesses of Naturalistic Observation

Before proceeding it may be helpful to mention briefly some strengths and weaknesses of the method of naturalistic observation. One advantage is that it attempts to describe behavior as it naturally occurs in real-life settings. This emphasis on observing how things naturally occur enables us to begin our study of a new process with an accurate description of naturally occurring relevant behaviors. As our observations unfold, new ideas about possible causal relationships or the possible survival value of the behavior we are observing may occur to us. Another advantage to naturalistic observation is that it studies behavioral processes as they unfold over a period of time. This emphasis on observing sequences of behavior provides an important temporal dimension to studying human behavior. This consideration of the flow of ongoing behavior constitutes a valuable complement to experimental and quasi-experimental designs, which focus instead on discovering causal factors that may be influencing behavior at a given time.

As with any human activity, there are also weaknesses or disadvantages that we must be aware of when using naturalistic observation. Generally this method tends to be qualitative and to rely more on the subjective judgment of the observer than do other research methods. Consequently the problem of *selective perception* can pose a serious threat to the validity of our data. If we study a single instance of a process very extensively, we create a potential problem concerning the representativeness of our sample. Unless we also examine other instances of the same phenomenon, we run the risk of making inappropriate generalizations and this would constitute a serious threat to the external validity of our observations. One final point to keep in mind is that naturalistic observations do not provide information about causal relationships. Of course, this is not really a weakness any more than Beethoven is weak compared with Bach. Instead it reminds us that no single technique answers all our questions. We will return to this point later. In the meantime keep in mind that science is a fluid yet pragmatic process, which makes use of a variety of techniques and approaches to answer our questions about reality.

SUMMARY

In recent years there has been an increasing interest in studying ongoing psychological processes in natural settings. This has resulted in an increase in the number of experiments conducted outside the laboratory setting. These inquiries focus on phenomena that cannot be studied in the laboratory, and they typically involve experimental designs that are less rigorous than true experimental designs. Thus, as we attempt to improve the external validity and relevance of our research, we often decrease the internal validity of these experiments.

We discussed two types of designs that are used in natural settings where true experimental designs are not feasible. These are quasi-experimental and naturalistic observation designs. We began by discussing several types of quasi-experimental designs: *time series designs* (comparing pretest and posttest scores for a single group of subjects), *interrupted time series designs* (involving several pretest and posttest measurements), *multiple time series designs* (including a control group that does not receive the independent variable), *nonequivalent before-after designs* (attempting to deal with initially unequal groups), and finally *ex post facto designs* (using empirical procedures for suggesting relationships from events that occurred in the past). The major problem with each of these designs is not in determining when changes occur, but rather in discerning the reason(s) why changes occurred. We then turned our attention to single-subject designs such as the *case study, reversal,* and *multiple baseline designs.* Case studies are primarily descriptive, whereas reversal and multiple baseline designs are experimental and offer an alternative to large group studies.

We presented the method of naturalistic observation as an alternative that is especially useful in the early stages of investigating a given phenomenon, particularly one that unfolds over a period of time. We discussed some of the concerns involved with this method. They include reactive behavior, unobstrusive measures, selective perception, problems with data analysis, and the decisions as to whether or not to conceal one's identity as a researcher, and whether or not to actually participate in the social process being observed.

CHAPTER ELEVEN

Ethics

INTRODUCTION

In Chapter 9 we discussed the ecology of an experiment. We assumed the viewpoint of the witness and focused on two issues. One issue dealt with the relevance of our research and the other with subject-scientist interactions. Among other things we pointed out that subject-scientist interactions are complex and that these interactions can influence our results in unexpected and sometimes even biased ways. Our concern with subject-scientist interactions focused on the validity of our scientific findings. That is, we examined the subject-scientist interaction hoping that through a fuller understanding of their psychological interaction we could better understand some limitations of the process of experimentation when studying human behavior and experience. Through a clearer understanding of their interactions, we hoped to point out potential confounds and ways to eliminate them so we could eventually increase both the internal and external validity of our conclusions.

In this chapter we will shift our focus. We will again examine the subject-scientist relationship from the viewpoint of the witness, yet we will do so from a new perspective. We will shift our concern from how their interaction influences the scientific validity of our research to the important issue of human ethics. Remember, an experiment is just another form of human interaction. Consequently the witness must also view subject-scientist interactions as if they were interactions between any two people. In making this shift, we move from the world of observation and theory to the world of human values; consequently, we can no longer use the same criteria for making decisions as we did in the world of science. The new criteria will be based on human values. Yet how do we make value judgments? Upon what criterion do we base our ethical behaviors? The study of ethics offers us one answer to these questions.

Ethics is the study of proper action. Ethics examines relationships between human beings and poses suggestions or principles as to how we should treat each other. The ultimate decision in ethical questions resides in judgments of value. Most individuals have either explicitly or implicitly formulated or adopted statements that reflect their values and give direction to their actions. Some of these statements or principles may be based on a religious tradition. One example of this is the golden rule, which states that you should do unto others as you would have them do unto you. Other principles may have a philosophical bias for determining action, such as "Kant's imperative." Immanuel Kant, an eighteenth-century philosopher, suggested that one should "act as to treat humanity, either yourself or others, always as an end also and never as a means only." Although rules of action may be useful in the abstract, problems often arise when one begins to apply these principles to concrete situations. In this chapter we want to look at one particular concrete situation—the scientific experiment—and attempt to determine some guidelines for making ethical decisions within this context.

Before we begin, there are three points we need to make clear. First, although most research scientists are concerned about ethics, actual ethical problems are minimal in most psychological experimentation. As we shall point out, there are exceptions to this and it is the exceptions that require careful consideration. Second, ethical decisions are somewhat regulated in our society by both the federal government and professional societies such as the American Psychological Association. In this chapter we will present their recommended guidelines and procedures. And third, although there are guidelines, there are no hard and fast rules for every situation. *Whether in the role of a scientist or a subject, you, as a human being, must ultimately decide how you will act and then assume responsibility for that action!*

ETHICAL CONSIDERATION OF PSYCHOLOGICAL EXPERIMENTATION

Ethical consideration of psychological experimentation has at its heart the idea that subjects participating in psychological research should not be harmed or negatively transformed in a way that would result in a lower level of any aspect of human functioning. Additionally, ethical considerations must point up the scientist's right to know and to seek answers to questions; that is, it would also be considered unethical to prevent a scientist from seeking knowledge without consideration of his or her rights. Thus, we begin with the rights of the scientist to know and pursue knowledge and the rights of the subject to protection from undue harm.

In most cases, the scientist has a question that he or she wants to ask and the subject is willing to help. In some cases, the subject learns something about himself or psychology from the experience and is glad to have participated. In psychophysiological experiments, for example, subjects often report that they enjoy seeing their brain wave activity (electroencephalogram—EEG) or heart rate (electrocardiogram—EKG) written out by a polygraph and are willing to participate in research for these types of experiences. Other subjects, like some travelers to a foreign country, enter the world of experimentation and leave it again without ever realizing the underlying structure of the place they have been. Although ignorant of the underlying structure, they still leave with the *experience* of the event and may become changed by it. If these experiences were always pleasant and any changes in the subject always positive, subjects would gladly participate in experiments and scientists would face few ethical questions.

However, at times the scientist may wish to answer a question that requires that the subject experience either psychological or physiological discomfort. These situations raise a number of questions or issues, including: What are the responsibilities of the scientist toward the subject? What are the rights of the subject? Are there guidelines for reconciling conflicts between the rights of the subjects for pursuing happiness and the rights of the scientists for pursuing knowledge? What type of relationship or dialogue would be most productive for helping the scientist and the subject to fulfill their needs and desires? These are the questions we will approach in this chapter.

THE RIGHTS OF THE SCIENTIST AND THE SUBJECT

In our society, individuals have rights to search for that activity or substance that is of importance to them. The Bill of Rights to the Constitution includes the individual's right to "life, liberty, and the pursuit of happiness." We begin with the idea that individuals, whether they later be called scientists or subjects, have the right to pursue those activities that are im-

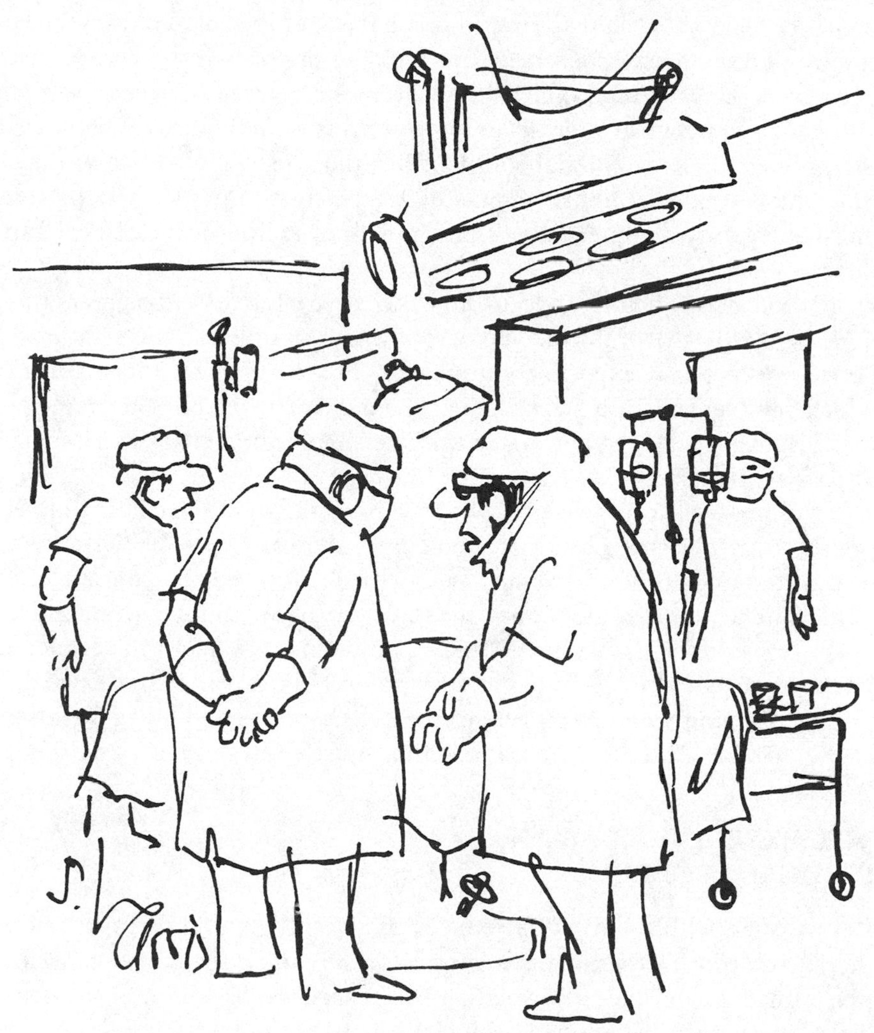

"WE'LL ONLY DO 72% OF IT, SINCE IT'S BEEN REPORTED THAT 28% OF ALL SURGERY IS UNNECESSARY."

portant to them. There are, however, activities that may infringe on the rights of others. These activities range from the extreme case of murder, which reduces your right to life, to less harmful types of activities such as creating noise outside your bedroom window or throwing a cream pie at you across the cafeteria. When there becomes a conflict between my rights and your rights, we are forced to find a means of arriving at a solution to the problem. The traditional solutions are those of ethics and law; that is, individuals seek to establish some ethical principle to guide their behavior and society may adopt these ethical guidelines in the form of legal sanctions.

What does all this have to do with psychological experimentation? This is exactly the problem. We do not know completely the relationship between ethics and experimentation, nor do we agree on the manner in which involvement in a scientific experiment infringes on someone's personal rights. Yet this is not to say that we should just ignore the issue and hope it will go away.

Science itself can give us few answers to the question of ethical relationships since science has focused on observation and theory. Thus, we are forced to look outside of science. In this book we used the concept of the witness to help us gain this broad perspective. In this chapter we will imagine ourselves to be the witnesses and examine in more detail the ethical relationship between the scientist and the subject. To accomplish this goal, let us now examine some specific experimental situations and bring forth some of the possible ethical considerations that must be examined.

THE EXPERIMENT AS AN ETHICAL PROBLEM

Let us begin with the most extreme cases of conflictual experimentation—the Nazi medical experiments during World War II. In several concentration camps during the war, such as Ravensbrueck, Dachau, and Buchenwald, prisoners were injected with virus or bacteria and then administered drugs to determine their effectiveness. Although "medical facts" were gained from these experiments, the world as a witness judged these experiments to be unethical and criminal. During the trials of these scientist-physicians held at Nuremberg, it was determined that they themselves were guilty of crimes; seven of them were later hanged and eight received long prison sentences. From these trials a code of medical experimentation was adopted as a guideline for future research with human subjects.

What was unethical about the experiments at the German concentration camps? Was it that human beings were given a virus? The answer to this question would be *no,* since almost all our current techniques of preventive medicine such as the development of the polio vaccine required that it be tested on human beings at a late phase of its development. Was it unethical to gain scientific knowledge of medical procedures? The answer again would be *no,* for our society requires that new drugs and treatments be scientifically tested. What were these German physicians convicted of at the trials at Nuremburg? The answer is they were tried for conducting experiments without the *consent* of their subjects. One of the first principles of research is that the subjects must consent to being part of the experiment. Not only is it required that subjects agree to be a part of an experimental procedure, but they must also be informed of what the experiment is about and what the potential risks are. Thus, major ingredients that the witness looks for in the dialogue between the scientist and the subject are *voluntary participation* and *informed consent.*

INGREDIENTS OF THE INITIAL SCIENTIST-SUBJECT DIALOGUE

In the initial dialogue between the scientist and the subject, the scientist must ask the subject to be a part of the experiment. This is the principle of *voluntary participation.* In essence, this principle suggests that a subject should participate in an experiment of her or his own choice. Additionally, this principle suggests that a subject should be free to leave an experiment at any time whether or not the experiment has been completed.

There are a number of issues involved with the concept of voluntary participation. For example, is it ethical to use prisoners in an experiment? That is, is it really possible for a captive audience to say no without fear of reprisal? One answer to this problem has been to reward subjects by reducing their sentence for participation in research. Yet it has been argued that if a prisoner "agrees" to be in an experiment because he is seeking a lesser sentence, then this agreement would not really be a "free" decision but a form of duress. In the same vein, it has been argued that giving a college student extra credit (points toward the final grade) for participation in psychological experimentation is unethical. What do you think? As you think about this issue, you will become entangled in the question of whether anyone can ever make a "free" decision and, if so, under what circumstances. As you might have already realized, this question becomes even more complicated for someone interested in developmental psychology, which requires research with children, or for someone interested in psychopathology, which requires research with mental patients.

Assuming for a moment that someone can freely agree to participate in research, what information must the scientist give the subject so that he or she can make a sound judgment and consent to be in the experiment? It is suggested that the scientist in the initial dialogue must inform the subject as to what will be required of her or him during the study. The scientist must also inform the subject as to any potential harm that may come from participation. Thus, the subject must be given complete information upon which to make a judgment. This is the principle of *informed consent.* As you can imagine, informed consent also raises a number of issues as to how much information about an experiment is enough. Can you ever tell subjects enough so that they could understand the study? It has been suggested that *informed* consent may not be the same as *educated* consent and that subjects can never really be given enough information. What do you think? Additional problems are raised when the research involves some form of deception, such as when a new drug is being tested against a placebo to determine its effectiveness. Although there are many problems being debated in relation to informed consent, the working procedure at this time is for the scientist to tell the subject as fully as possible without jeopardizing the value of the experiment what will be required of him and any possible risks he might be taking by participating in the experimentation. From the principles of voluntary participation and informed consent, one can see that it is the initial task of the scientist to discuss the experimental procedure fully with the subject, and to remind the subject that he is a human being who does not give his rights away just because he is taking part in a psychological experiment.

THE RIGHTS OF THE SUBJECT AND THE RESPONSIBILITY OF THE EXPERIMENTER

In our society a subject is considered to have the same rights during an experiment as she has outside of the experimental situation. What are these rights? One major one is the *right to privacy.* What is meant by this right? Most of us at first think of people as having the right to spend time by themselves or with others of their choosing without being disturbed. This is the external manifestation of the right to privacy. But there is also an internal or intrapersonal manifestation of this right (see Raebhausen & Brim, 1967). This is the right to have private thoughts or, as it is sometimes called, a private personality. This means that the thoughts and feelings of a subject should not be made public without the subject's consent. It further suggests that a conversation between a subject and a scientist should be considered as a private and not a public event. But how, you may ask, can the scientist ever report her or his findings? There are two considerations that are part of the scientist's responsibility to the subject. The first is *confidentiality* and the second is *anonymity*. The principle of confidentiality requires that the scientist not release data of a personal nature to other scientists or groups without the subject's consent. The second and related principle of anonymity is the situation in which the personal identity of a given subject and his or her data are kept separately. The easiest way to accomplish this is not to request names in the first place; however, there are times when this may be impossible. Another alternative is to use code numbers that protect the identity of the subject, and to destroy the names of subjects once the data analysis has been completed.

WHAT IS HARMFUL TO A SUBJECT?

As suggested, it is the right of a subject not to be harmed. But what is harm? In most psychological research, physical pain and harm present no problems since either they are absent completely or the subject is fully informed of the particular stimulus, such as a loud noise or placing one's hand in cold water to measure physiological responsiveness, that will be used. However, the question of psychological harm presents a much larger issue that will continue to be debated for years to come. Is it harmful to show a subject something true but negative about himself? Is it harmful to create situations in which a subject feels negative emotions such as fear or anger? Is it harmful to make a subject feel like a failure in order to determine how this affects her performance? These are the types of questions that are presently being asked and debated. As a beginning scientist, where do you go for help? There are two major sources; the first is the APA guidelines on ethics and the second is the human subjects committee in the institution in which you study or work.

THE AMERICAN PSYCHOLOGICAL ASSOCIATION ETHICAL GUIDELINES

Because it may be unclear and confusing to determine how to resolve conflicts between the scientist's right to know and the right of the subject not to be harmed psychologically from participating in an experiment, the American Psychological Association has developed a set of guidelines to help individual scientists determine some of their responsibilities toward subjects and the manner in which the scientist-subject dialogue should be conducted. The guidelines were developed by the American Psychological Association after much consideration by the members of the association and subsequent revisions. Detailed ethical guidelines including cases were published in 1973 and may be ordered from the American Psychological Association (122 17th Street, Washington, D.C. 20036) by requesting *Ethical Principles in the Conduct of Research with Human Participants.* Let us now examine these principles.

Principle 1: *In planning a study the investigator has the personal responsibility to make a careful evaluation of its ethical acceptability, taking into account these Principles for research with human beings. To the extent that this appraisal, weighing scientific and humane values, suggests a deviation from any Principle, the investigator incurs an increasingly serious obligation to seek ethical advice and to observe more stringent safeguards to protect the rights of the human research participant.*

Principle 2: *Responsibility for the establishment and maintenance of acceptable ethical practice in research always remains with the individual investigator. The investigator is also responsible for the ethical treatment of research participants by collaborators, assistants, students, and employees, all of whom, however, incur parallel obligations.*

Principle 3: *Ethical practice requires the investigator to inform the participant of all features of the research that reasonably might be expected to influence willingness to participate and to explain all other aspects of the research about which the participant inquires. Failure to make full disclosure gives added emphasis to the investigator's responsibility to protect the welfare and dignity of the research participant.*

Principle 4: *Openness and honesty are essential characteristics of the relationship between investigator and research participant. When the methodological requirements of a study necessitate concealment or deception, the investigator is required to ensure the participant's understanding of the reasons for* *this action and to restore the quality of the relationship with the investigator.*

Principle 5: *Ethical research practice requires the investigator to respect the individual's freedom to decline to participate in research or to discontinue participation at any time. The obligation to protect this freedom requires special vigilance when the investigator is in a position of power over the participant. The decision to limit this freedom increases the investigator's responsibility to protect the participant's dignity and welfare.*

Principle 6: *Ethically acceptable research begins with the establishment of a clear and fair agreement between the investigator and the research participant that clarifies the responsibilities of each. The investigator has the obligation to honor all promises and commitments included in that agreement.*

Principle 7: *The ethical investigator protects participants from physical and mental discomfort, harm, and danger. If the risk of such consequences exists, the investigator is required to inform the participant of that fact, secure consent before proceeding, and take all possible measures to minimize distress. A research procedure may not be used if it is likely to cause serious and lasting harm to participants.*

Principle 8: *After the data are collected, ethical practice requires the investigator to provide the participant with a full clarification of the nature of the study and to remove any misconceptions that may have arisen. Where scientific or humane values justify delaying or withholding information, the investigator acquires a special responsibility to assure that there are no damaging consequences for the participant.*

Principle 9: *Where research procedures may result in undesirable consequences for the participant, the investigator has the responsibility to detect and remove or correct these consequences, including, where relevant, long-term aftereffects.*

Principle 10: *Information obtained about the research participants during the course of an investigation is confidential. When the possibility exists that others may obtain access to such informa-*

> *tion, ethical research practice requires that this possibility, together with the plans for protecting confidentiality, be explained to the participants as a part of the procedure for obtaining informed consent.*

As stated, APA principles should not be considered as laws which a scientist follows and thereby hands over the problems of ethics to another group. Rather, these principles may be considered as *guidelines that direct one's thinking when ethical matters are considered.* In fact, the first and second principles emphasize that the responsibility of research is always with the individual scientist, and it is the scientist who must make decisions as to how to respond to the ethical considerations of an experiment. The APA guidelines do suggest, however, that when an individual scientist does deviate from these principles, she or he should seek advice from other professionals in the field.

INTERNAL REVIEW COMMITTEES

In recent years it has been not only suggested but also required by the Department of Health and Human Services that each scientist (whose institution receives federal funds) seek a review of the ethical considerations of research with human subjects whether or not there is a deviation from APA guidelines. This type of review is required not only of psychological research but of any type of research with human subjects. The committee that reviews the research is made up of individuals who work at the same university, hospital school, or other institution with the scientist as well as members of the community where the institution is located.

The main task of the human subjects review committee is to determine whether the subject is adequately protected in terms of both welfare and rights. One major question that the committee asks is: Are there any risks, physical, psychological, or social, that could come about as a result of participating in a given piece of research? As you can imagine, almost everything we do each day involves varying degrees of risk, and thus the committee attempts to determine when a given risk is unreasonable or might have a long-term effect on a person. For example, asking subjects to run a mile, to give a small sample of their blood, to have their heart rate measured, or to discuss their own childhood or sexual preference involves some *risks* in the way the term is used by most internal review committees. However, the committee may decide that these risks are not sufficient to prevent a study from being performed in light of the information that would be gained.

Thus, a second major question that a human subjects review committee asks is: Are the risks to the subjects outweighed by the potential benefits to them or by the estimated importance to society of the knowledge to be gained? Once the committee has determined that the answer to this question is yes, a third question is asked: Has the experimenter allowed the subjects to determine freely whether or not they will participate in the experiment through informed consent?

Before we continue, it should be pointed out that not everyone agrees with the principle of informed consent or at least not with the current interpretations of it. For example, in one study using a traditional verbal conditioning paradigm, it was shown that giving the subjects a complete description of the experiment resulted in the subjects not demonstrating conditioning (Resnick & Schwartz, 1973). A complete description actually eliminated the very phenomenon they were studying. These authors also reported that, although the informed subjects took part in the study, they did so in a more uncooperative manner. Another argument against fully informed consent is presented in Box 11.1, in which Loftus and Fries argue that fully informed consent may actually be more harmful than helpful. What do you think? Another consequence of adopting a strict definition of informed consent is that it becomes almost impossible to perform research that involves deception—that is, research in which the subject is not told the complete purpose of an experiment. Let us now examine deception studies and some of the ethical questions involved.

DECEPTION STUDIES

A deception study is any study in which the subject is deceived about the true purpose of the experiment or experimental procedures. For example, if an experimenter wished to examine the effects of anxiety on performance in college students, the scientist might create an anxiety-provoking situation followed by a performance measure. One method used to create anxiety in college students is to administer a so-called IQ test that cannot be completed in the allotted time with the statement that most college students who later go to graduate school have no trouble finishing this test. Another type of deception often used in medical research is the placebo treatment. For example, subjects are given a pill made up of sugar or other inactive ingredients and told that it will cause certain physiological changes such as reducing the number of headaches they have been experiencing. Since it is impossible to obtain informed consent in deception research, is it unethical to perform this research?

This is not an easy question to answer and the professionals in the field presently fall into two camps. The first group suggests that any deception is unethical and thus no deception research is possible, while the second group argues that certain types of deception research are necessary. The second group further argues that given appropriate safeguards, deception research is the only way to answer certain questions. We will not attempt to determine which group is ethically correct but will present some important questions raised by deception research and ways in which some

---

Box 11.1 Informed Consent May Be Hazardous to Your Health

The following was an editorial in *Science*, the journal of the American Association for the Advancement of Science. In this editorial the authors suggest that informed consent may actually harm the subject in some cases. Read the editorial and see what you think (Loftus & Fries, 1979).

> Before human subjects are enrolled in experimental studies, a variety of preliminary rituals are now required. These include an explanation of the nature of the experimental procedure and a specific elaboration of possible adverse reactions. The subjects, in turn, can either withdraw from the experiment or give their "informed consent." These rituals are said to increase the subjects' understanding of the procedures but, perhaps more important, they came into existence because of a strong belief in the fundamental principle that human beings have the right to determine what will be done to their minds and bodies.
>
> Some, on the other hand, consider that the purpose of informed consent is not protection of subjects, but rather protection of investigators and sponsoring institutions from lawsuits based on the charge of subject deception should a misadventure result. But lawsuits arise in any case; subjects simply claim that they did not understand the rituals. It is reasonable, then, to ask whether the putative beneficiary, the subject, might be harmed rather than helped by the current informed consent procedure.
>
> A considerable body of psychological evidence indicates that humans are highly suggestible. Information has been found to change people's attitudes, to change their moods and feelings, and even to make them believe they have experienced events that never in fact occurred. This alone would lead one to suspect that adverse reactions might result from information given during an informed consent discussion.
>
> An examination of the medical evidence demonstrates that there is also a dark side to the placebo effect. Not only can positive therapeutic effects be achieved by suggestion, but negative side effects and complications can similarly result. For example, among subjects who

---

of these questions have been answered. To do this, we will present three deception studies in further detail.

Obedience-to-Authority Research

One of the classic deception research studies is Stanley Milgram's obedience-to-authority study (Milgram, 1963, 1977). Using as a background such authority situations as the Old Testament story of God (the authority)

---

participated in a drug study after the usual informed consent procedure, many of those given an injection of a placebo reported physiologically unlikely symptoms such as dizziness, nausea, vomiting, and even mental depression. One subject given the placebo reported that these effects were so strong that they caused an automobile accident. Many other studies provide similar data indicating that to a variable but often scarifying degree, explicit suggestion of possible adverse effects causes subjects to experience these effects. Recent hypotheses that heart attack may follow coronary spasm indicate physiological mechanisms by which explicit suggestions, and the stress that may be produced by them, might prove fatal. Thus, the possible consequences of suggested symptoms range from minor annoyance to, in extreme cases, death.

If protection of the subject is the reason for obtaining informed consent, the possibility of iatrogenic harm to the subject as a direct result of the consent ritual must be considered. This clear cost must be weighed against the potential benefit of giving some people an increased sense of freedom of choice about the use of their bodies. The current legalistic devices, which are designed in part to limit subject recourse, intensify rather than solve a dilemma.

The features of informed consent procedures that do protect subjects should be retained. Experimental procedures should be reviewed by peers and public representatives. A statement to the subject describing the procedure and the general level of risk is reasonable. But detailed information should be reserved for those who request it. Specific slight risks, particularly those resulting from common procedures, should not be routinely disclosed to all subjects. And when a specific risk is disclosed, it should be discussed in the context of placebo effects in general, why they occur and how to guard against them. A growing literature indicates that just as knowledge of possible symptoms can cause those symptoms, so can knowledge of placebo effects be used to defend against those effects. A move in this direction may ensure that a subject will not be at greater risk from self-appointed guardians than from the experiment itself.

---

commanding Abraham to kill his son, and the situation of war where one person (the authority) tells another to go out and kill (the enemy), Milgram asked the question: Under what conditions would one person (who is not the authority) harm another and how is this related to authority? To examine this question in a concrete situation, Milgram chose the setting of a psychological experiment. He sought to determine whether subjects would harm other subjects on the authority of the experimenter.

The subjects in this experiment were individuals who varied in age and occupation. The general procedure was to have a subject come into the laboratory for a "learning experiment." The subject meets the experimenter and another "subject," who is really an associate of the experimenter. It is explained to the subject that little is known about the effects of punishment on memory and that in the experiment one subject will be the learner and one will be the teacher. A rigged drawing is held in which the associate of the experimenter draws the role of learner and the naive subject draws the role of teacher. Following this, the learner is taken to another room and strapped into a chair with what appear to be shock electrodes.

The naive subject is told that it is her or his job to teach the learner a series of words and to administer a shock as punishment whenever the learner makes a mistake. The subject is further instructed to increase the shock with each error made by moving a switch on the control box. The control box along with voltage levels has such verbal labels as "Danger: Severe shock" at the higher levels.

Once the experiment begins, the learner begins to make mistakes and the subject, following the instructions of the experimenter, administers shocks. However, as the voltage levels are increased, the subject begins to hear moans coming from the learner. With more increases in voltage, the learner cries about the pain and later refuses to answer any more questions. The experimenter tells the subject to treat any nonresponse as a wrong answer and to administer additional shocks. At the point at which the subject refuses to administer additional shocks, the experiment is concluded. The measure on the shock machine is used as a means of determining the subject's willingness to obey authority even in the face of pressure from the learner not to inflict pain. As presented thus far, would you consider this experiment ethical? Why or why not?

As you might imagine, objections have been raised to this research. One of the first objections to Milgram's work concerned whether or not the subjects were protected in the experiment. In specific, Baumrind (1964) refers to the Milgram study as a case in which the subjects were not treated with respect but rather were manipulated and experienced the discomfort of emotional disturbance.

Milgram responds by suggesting that the emotional distress experienced by the subjects was unexpected. He reports from conversations with colleagues and psychiatrists that they all expected that most subjects would terminate the experiment at an early stage by refusing to give shocks once the learner began to complain. Although Milgram agrees that once a number of subjects had been run he could have terminated the experiment, he decided that "momentary excitement is not the same as harm." Thus Milgram chose to continue the experiment.

Once the experiment had been concluded, it would have been unethical to allow an individual subject to leave the experimental situation without a true understanding of what had taken place. This process is referred to as *debriefing*. In the debriefing procedure, the experimenter, in accord with APA principle 8, removes any misconceptions and offers a full discussion of the experiment. Although the ethical principles had not been fully developed when Milgram ran his experiment, he appears to have followed this principle as follows: First, the subjects were all told the nature of the hoax and that the learner never received any electric shock. Second, each subject had a "friendly reconciliation" with the learner and an opportunity to discuss the experiment. Third, subjects were assured that their behavior was normal and that the tension or emotion they felt was also felt by other subjects.

As required by APA principle 9, Milgram also conducted follow-up evaluations. Once the entire study was completed, all the subjects received a report of the experiment. According to Milgram, the subjects' behavior in this follow-up report was treated in a dignified manner. Additionally, all subjects received a questionnaire that allowed them to express their thoughts and feelings concerning their participation in the experiment. As a matter of interest, Milgram reports that 84% of the subjects were glad to have participated in the experiment, 15% were neutral, and 1.3% expressed negative feelings about their participation. In addition, 80% of the subjects believed that this type of research should be carried out and 74% said they had learned something of personal importance from their participation in the experiment. As a further check for possible long-term consequences of the experiment, a psychiatrist interviewed selected subjects seeking any negative long-term effects of the experiment, which he reports not finding.

As you can see, it is not easy to follow APA principles 8 and 9 when it comes to deception research since it requires as much, if not more, work to follow up the subjects as it did to run the original experiment. However, when there is a possibility of long-term harm, either psychological or physical, it is necessary that this type of follow-up be carried out.

It's Not a Crime the Way I See It

When reading newspaper reports of the break-in at the Watergate as told by the press and by the Nixon administration, some felt they were hearing the reports of two different events. West, Gunn, and Chernicky (1975) pointed out the manner in which the differing reports fit into current theory in social psychology. As suggested by the theory of Jones and Nisbett (1971), those involved in Watergate tended to focus on environmental determinants of behavior, such as thinking break-ins were necessary because of the violent nature of the radical left. Members of the press, on the other hand, were observers and tended to explain the break-in in terms of the characteristics of the participants. Other events in history have also shown this trend according to West, Gunn, and Chernicky. For example, those involved in the Nazi armies claimed that they had to follow orders or they would have been shot. Whereas those in the army used situational cues, those who tried these individuals for war crimes saw the problem in terms of the character of the individuals. Likewise, if you remember the story of Kitty Genovese from Chapter 4, you may have thought to yourself something like, why didn't anyone help, or what was wrong with those people? You, as an outside observer, were reacting to the characteristics of the people involved, whereas the people involved seem to have been reacting to the situational characteristics.

Although the three cases of Watergate, Nazi soldiers, and Kitty Genovese lend support to the theory of Jones and Nisbett, a scientist would still like to see the theory tested in a laboratory situation. West, Gunn, and Chernicky set about to do this. They reasoned that if situational factors were important variables in the Watergate crime, then a significant percentage of individuals would agree to break the law if the situational pressure was high. Likewise others, when being told of the "crime," would attribute the event to the person involved and not to the situation. These authors designed the following experiment.

In a field study, subjects were led to believe that they could participate in an illegal burglary. To determine the role of situational variables, rationales for the burglary varied across groups. The first rationale stated that the crime was being sponsored by a government agency. The second rationale offered the subjects in that group a large amount of money for committing the crime. The third rationale offered immunity from prosecution for committing the crime. The fourth rationale served as a control for compliance and offered no money or immunity from prosecution. The last group was designed to give the researchers some indication of how frequently subjects would agree to be part of a crime and thus could be used to assess the demand characteristics of the experiment itself.

A second experiment was performed with another group of subjects who were given booklets describing in detail one of the four conditions from the field experiment. These subjects were asked to estimate how many people out of 100 would agree to participate in the burglary as described by one of the four conditions. They were also asked whether they would participate and were given the opportunity to describe some characteristics of a person who would or would not participate. Based on the theory of Jones and Nisbett (1971), it was predicted that those who participated in the field experiment would attribute their actions to the situational cues, whereas those in the second experiment would focus on the characteristics of the person who agreed or disagreed to be part of the crime.

Imagine yourself in the field study. You do not know you are part of a study. You are approached as you go about your business by someone you know to be a local private investigator. He says to you that he has "a project you might be interested in" and suggests that you meet him at his home or a local restaurant. When you meet the private investigator at the restaurant, he has another person with him and elaborates plans of the burglary of a local advertising firm. The break-in is then explained to you in terms of one of the four rationales presented above. How would you respond? Do you feel your ethics have been violated thus far? Why or why not?

As you might imagine, some professionals believed this study violated the APA ethical principles (Cook, 1975). Cook suggested that the ethical issues should be considered for two major reasons. First, the study has the potential for negative effects on subjects that go beyond the violation of personal moral standards. And second, because the study paralleled the Watergate scandal, it would receive wide publicity.

The authors of the study responded to the concerns of Cook by describing the procedures they included to protect the subjects. First, the field study was carried out in such a manner that the subjects could not leave the experiment feeling that they had become involved in an illegal activity. The subjects in the study were debriefed as to the real nature of the meeting and the concerns of the experimenters for having to use deception. Cook points out, and the authors agree, that the subjects should go away from the experiment feeling that their participation aided in gaining new knowledge and that the experimenters were concerned for the welfare of the subjects at all times. Second, the authors point out that the "experimental" meeting was not forced on any subject but took place only after an initial agreement to meet at another location. Third, alternative experimental procedures that did not involve deception were considered and rejected. For example, a study in which people role-played the situation might have been used. However, since the study was to determine the difference between observing and actually participating in the situation, alternative designs were rejected. Fourth, a lawyer-psychologist served as a consultant during the planning and implementation of the field study to protect the rights of the subjects and the experimenters. Also the state's attorney's office found the procedure to be legally acceptable. How would you discuss this study and the ethics involved?

Bypassing the Bypass

Let us examine one other study that required deception. It raised a number of interesting issues, particularly the question of when the information gained is important enough to violate normal ethical standards. This particular study deals with medical research—a heart operation for the treatment of angina (Cobb et al., 1959). However, the same questions raised by this study are also applicable to studies dealing with the evaluation of new psychotherapy techniques, techniques in biofeedback, and procedures of behavioral medicine, just to name a few. It should be pointed out that this study was reported more than twenty years ago; with the adoption of human subjects review committees, such a study would probably not be permitted today.

In the study, seventeen patients with angina pectoris attributed to coronary artery disease were invited to participate in an experimental evaluation of an operation to relieve the angina (pains in the chest). The patients knew that they were part of an experimental evaluation of the operation, but they did not know the nature of the evaluation. Furthermore, most patients knew from the popular press that the operation was considered to be a new and exciting treatment for angina. It should also be pointed out that the angina was such that it limited the activities of the patients, with the majority of them reported to be unemployed.

Once the patient was in the operating room and the anesthesia had been given, the surgeon opened an envelope that told him to which experimental group the patient belonged. For half the patients the operation was carried out as usual; that is, there was a ligation of the internal mammary artery. In the other half of the patients, the chest was cut open and the artery of the heart was found, as in the normal procedure, but the artery was not cut and tied in the usual manner. Rather, the cardiac system was left untouched and the patient's chest closed. Both groups of patients were cared for normally without the attending physicians knowing to which group each belonged. Would you consider this experiment a violation of ethics?

Most people would consider it unethical to operate on another human being without his or her consent as to the nature of the operation. However, let us look at the results of the study. During the first six months following the operation, the same number of patients in both the experimental (ligation) and the control (skin incision only) groups showed "significant subjective improvement." Just opening and closing the chest was shown to be associated with the same improvement rate as actually performing the operation. Positive changes were also noted in electrocardiograph (EKG) evaluations. For example, one patient who before the operation showed irregular heart-wave patterns on an EKG during exercise showed no irregularities after the operation. Surprising as it may seem, this patient was in the control group.

We are now faced with some very difficult questions. For example, how can we go about testing the value of new therapeutic procedures, whether they be surgical or psychotherapeutic, without violating the ethics of the individual? Are there times in which we might consider it ethical to deceive an individual so that knowledge about a procedure might be gained? That is, are there times in which the savings in terms of both patient distress and economic resources justify less than full disclosure? Would you want to "debrief" the patients who received the skin incision only if they were reporting a significant improvement in their disorder? What do you think about this type of research?

DEBRIEFING—WHEN IS ENOUGH ENOUGH?

Whether or not deception is used in an experiment, an experiment does not end without a completion of the dialogue between the scientist and the subject begun at the start of the experiment. Some researchers call this concluding dialogue *debriefing*. It is the goal of this dialogue to ensure that subjects leave the laboratory with at least as much self-esteem and as little anxiety as when they came to the experiment (Kelman, 1968). Thus, it is suggested that the debriefing process consist of two major aspects. The first is a time for the subjects to tell the experimenter how they felt about being part of the experiment. This not only will be good feedback for the experimenter but will also allow the subjects to express any self-doubt about their performance and to deal with thoughts and feelings that arose during the experiment. The second aspect of debriefing is that it allows the experimenter to explain the study to the subjects in greater detail. It is often difficult for the experimenter to determine how much information should be conveyed to the subjects. For example, the design of the study might be too complex to describe in detail. Or, when children are used as subjects, it might be difficult to convey what was being asked to the child, and the experiment might rely on the parents to help with this task. In the case of deception research, Carlsmith, Ellsworth, and Aronson (1976) suggest that just telling the truth is not enough and may even be more harmful than no explanation at all. These authors suggest that the scientist include a discussion of why deception was necessary and the experimenter's regret for using deception. Furthermore, it is suggested that one lead the subjects to see that the experiment was designed to deceive *anyone* and that it is normal to feel foolish or silly because they were taken in by the deception. These authors also suggest that the subjects be given the opportunity to develop and express their own reactions to deception research in general and to the present experiment in particular.

THE SUBJECT AS COLLEAGUE

Throughout the discussion of ethics it has been suggested that the experimenter value the subjects and respect their rights. A useful metaphor is to consider the subject as a colleague; that is, the subject is best seen as someone who helps with an experiment. As with any colleague, you as a scientist would discuss with the subject what you were interested in doing and the manner in which you would go about doing it. Once the experiment was completed, you would likewise discuss with your colleague and subject the results of the study. This not only would allow for the subject to learn more about the experimentation but would also allow you as scientist to understand the subject's *experience* of the experiment and thus aid in your interpretation of the results. Although more difficult, this same model could be used when performing deception research. For example, if one were using college students in a deception study, Campbell suggests that the student might be told at the beginning of the term that some of the research being performed that term involved some deception. The general nature of the whys and hows of deception studies could be discussed at this time, and the potential subject could be allowed to see the importance of this type of research, whether it be of the placebo type or more straightforward deception. Those students who did not wish ever to participate in a deception study could so indicate in some private manner and then be excluded from future studies of that type. In summary, what is being suggested is that the subject be treated as one treats a colleague; the subject is treated as someone who is valued and respected for the information he or she can offer. Using this approach, many ethical questions of psychological research will remain in the background and arise in only rare and special circumstances.

SUMMARY

In this chapter we addressed the issue of human values in our science of behavior and experience. We stressed the importance of scientists and subjects being the ultimate judges as to how each will act and assume responsibility for that action. We discussed the right of the scientist to use science to study our world, as well as the right of the subject to be protected from undue harm. Informed consent and voluntary participation are the major issues in the scientist-subject interaction. Every subject has the right to privacy in our society, and in experimental situations this requires the scientist to maintain the subject's confidentiality and anonymity.

We then discussed exactly what is harmful to a subject and pointed out the role played by the APA ethical guidelines as well as the local human subjects committee. We subsequently examined the ten principles set forth by the APA and reviewed the functions of human subjects committees. We reviewed three specific deception studies in some detail. Debriefing is also important, and we suggested that it be a routine part of all experimentation. We recommended considering the subject as a colleague assisting in our research and, therefore, as someone of value to be respected for his or her humanity and for any insights he or she may offer.

CHAPTER TWELVE

Sharing the Results

INTRODUCTION

In the preceding chapters we traced the unfolding of an experiment from its initial conception through the analysis of the results. Once the final outcome is known, we can integrate this new fact into our understanding of whatever particular phenomenon we are studying and in this way slowly expand our understanding of the world. One important responsibility of the scientist in this process is to communicate new facts to other scientists and, equally important, to nonscientists. In this way not only do we expand our own understanding but we also share our findings with others so that they too may integrate our new findings into their understanding of the world. The idea that science is a shared activity is by no means new. Indeed more than 2,000 years ago Aristotle emphasized that science had two parts: inquiry and argument. *Inquiry* for us includes the actual experiments or observations that generate the new facts. *Argument* includes our responsibility to communicate our findings in either oral or written form.

The particular manner in which we choose to communicate our findings is directed by the audience with whom we wish to communicate. In psychology there are generally two types of audiences to whom we direct our communication. In the majority of instances we are addressing other scientists who are studying related phenomena and might be interested in our findings. The availability of our findings frequently means that other scientists need not repeat our work and can move on to studying a new aspect of the same phenomenon. In addition to making our findings available to other researchers, we have a responsibility to convey the essential direction of our findings and their ethical and moral implications to nonscientists as well. This second responsibility is particularly relevant to psychologists whose findings may have direct bearing on how we relate to one another, interact with our children, and understand ourselves. In this chapter we will describe how scientists communicate with each other by describing how a formal scientific paper is written.

COMMUNICATION WITH OTHER SCIENTISTS: THE SCIENTIFIC ARTICLE

There are many ways we can share our findings with other scientists. In some cases new facts are shared in informal conversations with colleague-friends over something to drink at the local hangout. In other cases new material is presented orally at scientific meetings or perhaps an entire book is written describing a lengthy series of experiments. In most cases, however, formal communication between scientists takes the form of published journal articles. Consequently we will now describe the process of writing a scientific article and the steps by which an article is accepted for publication and published.

Preparing Your Article

In simple terms a scientific article is the story of an experiment. This narrative begins with a description of what is already known about the particular phenomenon being studied and a clear statement of the purpose of the experiment. The narrative then describes the manner in which the experiment was performed and the results of the experiment. Finally, the results are interpreted in relation to themselves (are there any confounds or interpretation problems?) and then in relation to what we already know about the phenomenon under study. To facilitate this communication process, a specific format or outline for scientific papers has been developed. Briefly, scientific articles are divided into five parts: (1) abstract, (2) introduction, (3) method, (4) results, and (5) discussion. Detailed descriptions of what should be covered in each section and other guides to writing style are presented in the American Psychological Association *Publication Manual* (1974) (available from APA, 1200 17th Street, N.W., Washington, D.C. 20036). An addition to the APA manual was published in 1977 including guidelines for the nonsexist use of language in APA journals. We believe that these are important points to consider and thus we have reproduced this addition in Appendix A. It is important that you become familiar with both format and language style since these are used by scientific journals around the world. Once you are familiar with them, you will find it easier to read articles and to locate information quickly in those you are just skimming. Furthermore, you will undoubtedly use the APA format as a model in preparing your own proposals or papers. Because of the widespread use of the APA format, we will now briefly describe what makes up each of the five parts of a scientific article.

Abstract Most scientific papers open with a brief 100–175-word *abstract* or summary of the entire article. The purpose of this abstract is to give an overall description of the experiment so that the readers can quickly decide whether they want to take the time to read the entire paper. In this way we avoid reading halfway through an article before we realize it is not the sort of experiment we thought it was simply from reading the title. With this purpose in mind, the typical abstract provides a very brief, clear statement of purpose, methodology, and results of the experiment. It is written in a concise manner yet describes the essential features of your article. To give you an idea of how an abstract is organized, the following "abstract" was taken from an article appearing in the *Journal of Consulting and Clinical Psychology* (Gaul, Craighead & Mahoney, 1975).

> A comparison was made of the eating behaviors of obese and nonobese subjects in a naturalistic setting. It was found that obese subjects took more bites, performed fewer chews per bite, and spent less time chewing than did nonobese subjects. The clinical implications of these data are discussed.

Introduction The *introduction* of a scientific paper is designed to provide background information about the phenomenon you are studying and to help the reader understand how you arrived at your hypothesis and the experiment you eventually performed. A typical introduction begins with a simple sentence or two explaining the nature of the research problem in broad terms. It then describes what we already know about the phenomenon being studied. As this narrative unfolds, *relevant* facts and theoretical speculations are described. Once this background information has been presented and the reader knows the present status of the research area, the introduction concludes with a clear statement of purpose, which may include the particular hypothesis being evaluated. For example, when Dr. Shotland (Shotland & Straw, 1976) wrote an article describing his research on bystander behavior discussed in Chapter 4, he began his article like this:

> From time to time newspapers report that bystanders have witnessed an attack by a man on a woman without adequately helping the victim.

Shotland continues by describing some current theories that attempt to explain why bystanders do not help. Since the theories were derived from the reports of actual events and after-the-fact reports of witnesses, Shotland sought to test empirically certain aspects of these theories. He concludes his introduction section with a statement of purpose and hypothesis.

> The set of experiments we describe explores the implications and effects of a perceived relationship between a victim and her attacker on helping behavior. Specifically, the hypothesis for Experiment 1 was: If bystanders perceive a relationship between a woman and her attacker, they will be less likely to intervene than if the victim and attacker are perceived as strangers.

Likewise, Dr. Newcombe (Newcombe & Arnkoff, 1979) began her research report on speech styles and the sex of the speaker with the sentence: "Our impressions of other people are derived from many sources: What they say, what they do, what others think of them, and so on." She then continues the introduction by discussing some important research that has been performed in this area and helps the reader to understand why she performed this particular study. The introduction concludes with a statement of why the study was performed. In this particular study the purpose was stated as follows:

> In these initial experiments, the concern was to evaluate the effects, if any, of a variable over which people have some control (speech style) as compared to the effects of a set of variables over many of which they have less or no control (the pitch of their voice, their sex).

Thus, the general formulation of an introduction is to begin with a broad conception of the problem followed by a discussion of previous research related to this topic and then to end with a specific statement of the hypothesis or purpose of the study. Notice that as an introduction unfolds there is a progression from a general topic to a specific purpose. So you might think of an introduction as the simple story of relevant published experiments, which led us from our general topic of interest to our specific purpose or hypothesis.

Introductions may be brief, as we shall see in the following example. Following is the introduction from the study on eating rate and obesity (Gaul, Craighead & Mahoney, 1975). Note again how the last part of the introduction presents the purpose or hypothesis of the study.

INTRODUCTION

In their recent review Stunkard and Mahoney (in press) concluded that behavior modification techniques have demonstrated considerable effectiveness in the treatment of obesity. Many of these techniques were based in part on the behavioral analysis of eating patterns first presented by Ferster, Nurnberger, and Levitt (1962).

An implicit assumption of many behavior modification programs has been that eating patterns differ for obese and nonobese people. Specifically, it has been presumed that overweight individuals eat faster and take fewer bites (cf. Stuart & Davis, 1972). However, virtually no empirical data regarding that assumption have been presented. The purpose of the present study was to determine if obese people consume their food more rapidly than nonobese people, and if consummatory behaviors (chewing and drinking) differ for two groups.

The following example of an introduction is from an exploratory study by Kenneth Ravizza (1977) examining the subjective experience of athletes during sporting events. Again you will see how the author first describes the focus of his study in relation to previous research. He helps the reader to understand how this specific research is both different from and similar to other studies and then concludes with a statement of purpose. Since the research is an exploratory study into an unknown area, the purpose is presented not in the form of a hypothesis but in the form of the goals of the study.

INTRODUCTION

The traditional emphasis of research on sports has been to develop techniques to improve physical performance. One result of this emphasis is that the major focus in sport research has been on motor performance. In contrast, the subjective experience of the athlete has been minimized (Kleinman, 1973; Park, 1973). One explanation for this emphasis on motor performance is that athletes' subjective experiences

> are difficult to measure and to study scientifically. Some progress has been made in studying nonpathological, yet extraordinary, psychological experience (Laski, 1961; Maslow, 1968). The limited research dealing with this aspect of sport reveals that participation provides the athlete with a wide domain of subjective experiences (Leonard, 1975; Metheny, 1968; Slusher, 1967; Thomas, 1972). Some of these studies have focused on specific aspects of the subjective experience of the athlete (Beisser, 1967; Csikszentmihalyi, 1975; Gallwey, 1974; Murphy, 1972, 1973; Ravizza, 1973).
>
> The purpose of the present investigation is twofold: first, to use the interview technique to ascertain the personal experiences of athletes; and second, to achieve a general characterization of at least one subjective aspect in sport, those experiences involved in an athlete's "greatest moment" while participating in sport.

Method The third section of a scientific paper is called the *method* section and consists of a detailed description of how the experiment was conducted. The goal of this section is to provide enough detail so another researcher could conduct an exact replication of your experiment. Additionally, the procedural details provided in the method section allow the reader to visualize exactly how you conducted your experiment. In this way a careful reader may spot design problems that escaped your attention. The method section is generally divided into three parts (subjects, apparatus, and procedure). Typically, the method section begins with a description of the subjects in the study; that is, were they males or females, college students or patients in a hospital, and so forth. It is important to include the number of subjects who took part in the experiment as well as the manner in which they were recruited. In studies in which a control group was used, how was it selected? Two examples of how subjects might be described are given below. The first is from Harris and Ray (1977).

> SUBJECTS. The subjects were 32 students (13 males, 19 females) enrolled in introductory psychology. The subjects were told that they were to keep a dream log for a period of six weeks, and that their dreams would be kept confidential. Participation in the study was voluntary.

The next example of a subjects section comes from the clinical literature and was published in the *Journal of Consulting and Clinical Psychology* (Giannetti, Johnson, Klingler, and Williams, 1978). Notice that this description tells both how subjects were selected and important characteristics of the groups (age and IQ).

SUBJECTS. The sample was composed of male veterans who were evaluated at the time of application for treatment at the Psychiatric Assessment Unit of the Salt Lake City Veterans Hospital. Subject selection was limited to those veterans who completed the experimental evaluation and testing with 48 hours of referral. In addition, all subjects whose MMPI had more than 30 missing items or had an F-K dissimulation index (Gough, 1950) greater than 14 were eliminated. This resulted in a sample of 572 subjects classified into seven psychotic groups (n = 218), three sociopathic groups (n = 208), three neurotic groups (n = 88) and one "no mental illness" group (n = 58). The mean age for the sample was 37.7 years (SD = 12.4). The mean IQ from the Shipley-Hartford (Paulson & Lin, 1970) was 103.4 (SD = 12.7).

Following the description of the subjects used in the experiment, there is a statement of the experimental situation and any equipment or apparatus that might have been used. In physiological studies, psychophysiological studies, and biofeedback studies, this would include a statement of the instrumentation settings that were used in the study.

The final part of the method section is a statement of the procedure utilized in the study. In describing the manner in which the study was conducted, it is important to include everything that the subject was told or was led to believe. Since the experiment is a social situation, it is also important to include some statement of the manner in which the experimenter treated the subject as well as the important social characteristics of each of the experimenters such as sex, race, and so forth. When your design calls for dividing subjects into various groups, it is necessary to describe how group assignment was determined (random, matching, and so on). It is also necessary to describe how you operationally defined your independent and dependent variables and how your various groups were tested. For example, if you used a subject variable such as anxiety, you would want to include the mean scores and standard deviations on whatever anxiety scale you used in assigning subjects to either low- or high-anxiety conditions. It should also be stated whether the experimenter who actually tested the subjects knew to which group a given subject belonged. If there is a scoring procedure, was this performed blind? For example, in a study that examined the content of dreams of anxious and nonanxious individuals, did the dream rater know whether a given dream belonged to a high- or low-anxiety subject? To give you an idea of how a method section is written, consider the following section from the obesity study by Gaul, Craighead, and Mahoney (1975). In this example, the subjects and procedure sections describe how the study on the eating rates of obese and nonobese subjects was measured.

METHOD

SUBJECTS. One hundred subjects were chosen for observation at an eating establishment that specializes in the sale of hamburgers, french fried potatoes, and soft drinks. One criterion for subject selection was that he purchase all three items and only those items. Additionally, for a subject to be included he had to sip his drink through a straw (which nearly all people did). Finally, the subject had to be between the ages of 18 and 35 in the opinion of two trained observers. As each potential subject purchased his food, the two observers independently categorized them on age and obesity. The first 50 males (25 obese, 25 nonobese) to meet joint agreement criteria were included in the study.

PROCEDURE. The consummatory behaviors of each subject were unobtrusively recorded by two trained observers. Any subject who indicated awareness of being observed was excluded from the study. Observations were made, one subject at the time, in order of subjects' appearance until the requisite number (n = 25) for each cell was obtained.

Beginning with the subject's first bite or sip of drink, frequency counts were taken by both observers for five minutes. Data were obtained for the following dependent measures: number of bites taken during the five minutes (three french fries were considered equal to one bite of hamburger), number of chews per bite, total number of seconds (of possible 300) spent chewing, and total number of sips of soft drink.

In some psychology experiments, it is necessary to have an extended methods section so that other scientists understand exactly what happened to a subject during the experiment and how particular behaviors were measured. This is particularly true in social psychology experiments in which any type of deception is used. The method section in deception studies includes not only the methodology but also the safeguards such as debriefing and follow-up measures that were involved in the study. The following is one example (Shotland and Straw, 1976).

METHOD

The first procedure attempted was similar to the one used by Borofsky et al. (1971) in which a male attacked a female during a psychodrama. The fight was actually videotaped and played for each subject, who was told he or she had been arbitrarily selected to act in the next psychodrama pairing of the three participants and was asked to leave the other two participants (the confederates) so as not to inhibit them and to watch their psychodrama on television in the next room. This procedure proved unworkable as approximately 40% of the subjects thought the fight was staged.

A second procedure was needed that was more believable. The local police department was made aware of the impending experiment and their advice was sought. Three of the first author's colleagues in the Department of Psychology were asked to review the procedure for ethical considerations.

SUBJECTS. The subjects were 51 male and female students who participated in order to receive course credit for either an introductory psychology or Man-Environment Relations course during the summer of 1974 at The Pennsylvania State University.

PROCEDURE. Two couples with theatrical training were recruited through the cooperation of a faculty member in the Drama Department. One couple (Team 1) consisted of a man who was 1.70 m, 63.50 kg (5 feet 7 inches, 140 pounds) with brown hair conventionally cut, paired with a woman who was 1.57 m, 49.90 kg (5 feet 2 inches, 110 pounds) with shoulder-length black hair. The second couple (Team 2) consisted of a man who was 1.85 m, 90.72 kg (6 feet 1 inch, 200 pounds) with light brown hair conventionally cut, paired with a 1.70 m, 54.43 kg (5 feet 7 inches, 120 pounds) woman with long blonde hair. All of the college-age actors wore the usual jeans and shirts.

Each couple worked on alternate nights with subjects being randomly assigned to conditions, the only provision being that the conditions contained an equal number of male and female subjects. The subject came to take part in a study of attitudes in which he or she expected to answer a questionnaire and be interviewed. The subject arrived at the appointed room and found a note explaining that the experimenter would arrive later to interview him or her and asking that the subject begin filling out the questionnaire. On the table with the questionnaires were what appeared to be a university phone with a standard sticker giving emergency telephone numbers, including the police. The telephone was not functioning and was rigged to provide a dial tone when it was appropriate, and to record any telephone number that the subject might try to call.

Other rooms on the floor had apparent activity in them. From the room across the hall emanated the sound of a computer printer, and in the room next to the experimental room a radio played.

After the subject entered the room 5 minutes passed, during which time the subject proceeded to fill out the questionnaire. The confederates, on a different floor of the building, received a signal by walkie-talkie and took the elevator to the proper floor. Before the doors opened, a loud verbal argument could be heard. The woman was accused by the man of picking up a dollar she claimed to have dropped. After approximately 15 sec of heated discussion, the man physically attacked the woman, violently shaking her while she struggled, resisting and screaming. The screams were loud piercing shrieks, interspersed with pleas to "get away from me." Along with the shrieks one of two conditions was introduced and then repeated several times. In the stranger condition the woman screamed, "I don't know you," and in the married condition, "I don't know why I ever married you." From the first designation of the condition the physical fight lasted a maximum of 45 sec, with the entire incident not lasting more than a minute.

The fight was immediately terminated with the attacker fleeing at any attempt by the subject to intervene. If no one intervened, the fight was terminated by a third confederate (male), who came out of a nearby room and demanded in a loud voice that the attacker stop beating up the woman. The attacker then ran away while the false intervener consoled the woman. Every effort was made to keep a direct intervener away from the actors to insure their safety. Two confederates were placed in concealed locations between the actors and the subject, one to falsely intervene, the other to inform the subject it was an experiment, if necessary.

A subject was considered an intervener if he or she called the police on our phone, asked a person in the computer room to help stop the fight, shouted at the attacker to stop, or acted to intervene directly. The fight was staged 15.85–16.15 m (52–53 feet) away from the room containing the subject. If the subject came down the hall toward the fight some 9.14 m (30 feet) and did not turn into an intersecting hallway, he or she was counted as intervening.

The subjects were interviewed immediately following the experiment and fully debriefed by the first author, who spent up to 45 minutes with each subject. The interviews were unstructured except for several standard questions. First, the subjects were asked to describe what they had seen. If they did not adequately describe the experimental condition to which they were assigned, they were asked: (a) What was the relationship between the two people fighting? (b) How do you know? Subjects were asked (c) What caused the fight? and (d) Did you think it was a rape? They were then asked to describe their thoughts and behavior in the sequence in which they had occurred while witnessing the fight. After the debriefing each subject was specifically asked: (e) Do you think we have done any harm to you by having you go through that experience? and (f) Do you think that the potential results and implications of the research are worth the experience you went through? Each subject was urged to call the first author if he or she wished to discuss any aspect of the experiment in the future.

Results The fourth part of a research article is the *results* section. The chief purpose of this section is simply to state the outcome of the experiment and then indicate whether or not the outcome was statistically significant. For example, a results section might begin with the statement that the experimental and control groups did or did not differ significantly in terms of whatever dependent variable was measured. Following this general statement, the actual group scores may be presented and then the manner in which the results were analyzed is briefly described. Quite frequently the results section also contains a figure or table that aids the reader in visualizing the major outcome of the experiment.

Any hypothesis presented in the introduction should have the corresponding results presented in the results section. Although there are no hard and fast rules concerning discussion and reference to other studies in the results section, references to other studies are usually saved for the discussion section. The following example is from the eating study presented previously in which two observers watched obese and nonobese people eat to see whether there were differences in their eating behaviors.

RESULTS

Interobserver agreement was calculated by dividing the number of ratings for which both observers agreed by the number of agreements plus disagreements and multiplying the quotient by 100. Interobserver agreement was 100% for all measures except number of chews per bite, where the average interobserver agreement was 92% (range = 87%–100%).

The means and standard deviations for all the dependent measures are presented in Table 1. The data represent averages between observers for all measures.

All data were submitted to 2 × 2 (Obesity × Sex) analyses of variance. The main effect for obesity was significant for number of bites taken ($F = 68.2$, df = 1/96, $p < .001$), number of chews per bite ($F = 126.8$, df = 1/96, $p < .001$), and for total amount of time spent chewing ($F = 70.1$, df = 1/96, $p < .001$).

Obese subjects took more bites ($M = 16.94$) than nonobese subjects ($M = 12.66$), performed fewer chews per bite (M obese = 9.24, M nonobese = 18.60), spent less time chewing (M obese = 104.26, M nonobese = 157.54).

There was a significant main effect for sex ($F = 5.8$, df = 1/96, $p < .018$) and a significant Sex × Obesity interaction effect ($F = 3.7$, df = 1/9), $p < .056$) for total number of sips taken. Males ($M = 7.72$) took a greater total of sips than did females ($M = 6.92$); however, this was primarily the result of obese males ($M = 8.00$) who took a significantly greater number of sips than did the obese female subjects ($M = 6.56$).

Discussion The final section is called the *discussion*. In general the discussion is a three-part process. In the first section you simply report the chief finding of the present experiment. Next, you point out any limitations

"I THINK YOU SHOULD BE MORE EXPLICIT HERE IN STEP TWO."

or potential confounds that may affect your interpretation of the results and restate the results in light of these limitations. Quite frequently this second step is omitted for fear that the article will not be accepted for publication. We believe this is an essential step in any discussion, however, and encourage you to make it a part of your scientific papers from the very beginning. In the final part of the discussion, you directly relate the results of your experiment to other published experiments on the same topic and describe how the present experiment expands our understanding of the phenomenon we are studying.

DISCUSSION

The foregoing results suggest several clinically relevant implications for the behavioral treatment of obesity. To begin with, it does appear that there are differences in the eating styles of obese and nonobese individuals. Obese subjects in the present study spent less time chewing than nonobese subjects and took more bites during the five-minute observation period. This latter finding corroborates the notion that overweight individuals are often rapid eaters (Ferster et al., 1962). Therapeutic strategies aimed at reducing eating pace may therefore be effective. However, the fact that obese subjects took more bites than nonobese subjects is at least partially contradictory to the popular recommendation that overweight individuals increase the number of bites they take (Stuart & Davis, 1972). Unless this increase is accompanied by a slowing of the eating pace, countertherapeutic results might ensue.

The dramatic difference between groups on the mastication variable also deserves comment. Although relatively little therapeutic attention has been paid to this dimension, it seems possible that increased mastication may facilitate weight reduction. This speculation is consistent with recent findings on the role of food texture and mastication in satiety (Balagura, 1973).

The strategy of counting bites (Stuart & David, 1972) may be contraindicated unless obese clients are given specific standards and eating behavior guidelines to pursue. At an intuitive level, the overweight person may interpret this self-monitoring task as suggesting that he should take fewer bites. Were this to result, he might inadvertently develop the maladaptive pattern of rapid, large (but few) bites. A laboratory study subsequent to the one described in this article asked obese and nonobese individuals to eat a standardized meal in a laboratory setting. Within the next three days the subjects were asked to count the bites they took while consuming the same standardized meal. Extensive intersubject variability was encountered. Self-monitoring did not have any systematic effect on eating pace for either group of individuals. A noteworthy finding, however, was that obese subjects were significantly less accurate in their self-monitoring than nonobese subjects ($U_2 = 4.5$, $n_1 = 6$, $n_2 = 7$, $p < .05$).

One final comment has to do with the assumption that obese individuals will lose weight if they adopt the eating styles of normal persons (Stunkard & Mahoney, in press). While there is strong evidence that modifying *what* people eat (calorically) can result in weight loss, the data on modifying *how* they eat are less conclusive. Further inquiries need to evaluate the relationship between these variables.

In attempting to grasp the fundamental differences among these sections, one rule of thumb is that the method and results sections must be written in an exact manner. The method section must be detailed enough to permit another scientist to perform an exact replication of your experiment; the results section must be an accurate statement of what actually happened in your experiment. In a sense, because these sections are a statement of how you performed your experiment and what your results were, they are a simple record of your experiment and can be expected always to be an accurate description of what happened. In contrast, the discussion is in fact a statement of what you think your finding means for our understanding of the phenomenon you are studying. Although your finding will last forever, your interpretation of your actual data may vary considerably as your understanding of the phenomenon grows with each successive experiment.

Once you have finished writing the five major sections of the article, all that remain are to find a title for your paper and to list your references. The title of your paper is very important because, like the abstract, it describes the nature of your experiment. Consequently many titles are written so that they describe the nature of the independent and dependent variables. For example, in 1958 Silverstine and Klee published an article in the *American Medical Association Archives of Neurology and Psychiatry* entitled: "Effects of lysergic acid diethylamide (LSD-25) on intellectual functions." The title of this paper tells us the independent variable (lysergic acid) and the dependent variables (some measure of intellectual function). Finally, the title, author, and reference information for every study you can cite in your paper are listed on a separate page at the end of the paper.

In Appendix B, the Gaul, Craighead, and Mahoney article on eating behavior is presented in its entirety as it was published in the journal. For additional help with preparing papers in APA format, we have included a typed copy of this article showing the proper spacing, headings, and so forth in Appendix C. This shows both the format a student might use to submit a research paper to a class and the manner in which it *must* be submitted for publication in an APA and other journals. As you may have noticed, the five major parts of this study—the abstract, introduction, method, results, and discussion—along with the title and references are presented in their entirety. Also, if you look at the conclusion of the reference section, you can see the date in which the journal received the article.

Now that you know the sections required for writing an article, we can turn to the next step—submitting the article for publication. Before we do this we want to remind you that the submitting of proposals for research may also follow lines similar to the APA format. In a proposal, of course, you would not have actual data. Your results section would describe how your data would be quantified and which specific statistical tests you would use. Likewise the discussion section could discuss possible outcomes and what these might mean scientifically. To aid you in the preparation of proposals, we have included a checklist for preparing a research proposal in Box 12.1 (Holt, 1965).

Box 12.1 Preparing a Research Proposal

For some students, there is less emphasis on the writing of formal research papers for publication and more emphasis on the development of sound research proposals. In the development of proposals, there are many conceptual as well as "down to earth" questions that must be considered. In this process a checklist is helpful. The following checklist was developed by Robert Holt. Students who have particular problems with developing a research project will find Dr. Holt's clear-cut advice helpful and should consult his original article (Holt, 1965).

Checklist of Questions to Be Asked About a Research Proposal

1. What is the problem?
   a. Is it clearly stated?
   b. Is it focused enough to facilitate efficient work (i.e., are hypotheses directly testable)?
2. What are the underlying objectives?
   a. Is the problem clearly related to the objectives?
3. What is the significance of the proposed research?
   a. How does it tie in with theory?
   b. What are its implications for application?
4. Has the relevant literature been adequately surveyed?
   a. Is the research adequately related to other people's work on the same or similar topics?
5. Are the concepts and variables adequately defined (theoretically and operationally)?
6. Is the design adequate?
   a. Does it meet formal standards for consistency, power, and efficiency?
   b. Is it appropriate to the problem and the objectives?
   c. Will negative results be meaningful?

Publishing Your Article

Now that we have discussed the basic form of a research article, let us talk about the process of submitting an article for publication. One of the first questions that a scientist asks is: Who or what portion of the scientific community do I want to read my article? For example, suppose someone has performed a study that examines the EEG (electrical activity of the brain) changes in humans over a period of years and how this correlates with education and psychological development. Depending on the particular hypothesis of the study and its focus, the final article might be sent to a journal that reports physiological research, such as *Psychophysiology, EEG and Clinical Neurology,* or *Neuropsychologia,* or a journal emphasizing developmental processes, such as *Developmental Psychology,* or even a journal that discusses educational development. Each of these journals is read by a

---

   d. Are possibly misleading and confounding variables controlled?
   e. How are the independent and dependent variables measured or specified?
7. What instruments or techniques will be used to gather data?
   a. Are the reliabilities and validities of these techniques well established?
8. Is the sampling of subjects adequately planned for?
   a. Is the population (to which generalizations are to be aimed) specified?
   b. Is there a specific and acceptable method of drawing a sample from this population?
9. Is the sampling of objects (or situations) adequately planned for?
   a. To what population of objects (situations) will generalizations be aimed?
   b. Is there a specific and acceptable method of drawing a sample from this population?
10. What is the setting in which data will be gathered?
    a. Is it feasible and practical to carry out the research plan in this setting?
    b. Is the cooperation of the necessary persons obtainable?
11. How are the data to be analyzed?
    a. What techniques of "data reduction" are contemplated?
    b. Are methods specified for analyzing data qualitatively?
    c. Are methods specified for analyzing data quantitatively?
12. In the light of available resources, how feasible is the design?
    a. What compromises must be made in translating an idealized research design into a practical research design?
    b. What limitations or generalizations will result?
    c. What will be needed in terms of time, money, personnel, and facilities?

different group of scientists, and thus publishing an article in one journal will give you a different audience than publishing in another. To help the potential author, most journals include a statement at the beginning as to the type of articles they accept. If your study is a replication and continuation of some of the articles cited in your introduction, probably the same journal that published the other studies would be interested in your work. Once you have decided upon an audience and a journal, it is a good procedure to look through recent issues of the journal to see whether the particular style that is used deviates from the APA recommendation. For example, journals may differ in the reference and results sections. Thus, the particular form of reference citation must be checked carefully, as well as the manner in which statistical significance is reported.

Once you have written the article following the guidelines in the front of the journal, you send the number of copies requested to the editor of the journal and wait. Some journals give information concerning publishing your article very quickly and others take many months. To understand why there is a delay before your article is accepted or rejected, let us examine what happens when an article is received by the editor of a journal. In most cases the editor is a scientist employed by a university or research laboratory who has agreed to be editor for a few years. To begin with, the editor has another job on which he or she spends considerable time. The day-to-day processes of the journal are generally performed by a paid assistant. Once the manuscript is received by the editor, the editor usually chooses two scientists who are studying phenomena similar to yours and asks them to recommend whether the article should be accepted for publication. The process of review by other scientists is referred to as the *peer review system*. Each reviewer reads your article and evaluates it as to the clarity of presentation, the logic of the experiment, the appropriateness of the data analysis utilized, and the meaningfulness of the discussion section. This is similar to the type of feedback your professors give you concerning research reports and proposals. In this chapter we will present in more detail some exact evaluative criteria that are used for research evaluation.

After a reviewer has read and evaluated an article, she or he writes a review, which is sent back to the editor. Usually these reviews are a couple of pages long and are designed to give feedback to the author. In some cases the reviewers point out limitations of the experiment itself or of the way the article is written. Frequently specific suggestions are made to improve your paper. And in each case a general recommendation is made as to whether the article should be published or not. The editor takes these reviews and then makes a final decision about whether to publish the paper and then informs the author of the decision. Sometimes the reviewers differ as to the quality of the article and the editor must make a decision. Other times the reviewers suggest publication only if the author agrees to rewrite or reanalyze part of the study. Thus, after some wait, you receive the reviews and the editor's disposition as to publication of your article. Even if the editor agrees to publish your article as it stands, there is still another wait for the article to come into print. This delay is referred to as the *publication lag.* This lag is generally brought about because a journal accepts many good articles and is able to publish only a few of them in any given issue. The publication lag may range from a month or two to almost a year and a half.

WHAT MAKES A GOOD ARTICLE?

One question beginning students ask is: What criterion do editors and reviewers keep in mind as they are reviewing papers for publication? Obviously the answer is important because it should provide you with an idea of what senior scientists consider both good research and a well-written experiment. In August 1978 Brendan Maher, the editor of the *Journal of Consulting and Clinical Psychology,* reported that four out of every five articles submitted to the journal are rejected. Because most of these are rejected for methodological reasons, Maher produced a set of guidelines (reproduced below) that may be used not only by reviewers but also by writers and readers of scientific articles. Some of these guidelines, such as the ones related to factor analysis, you may come to understand after learning more advanced statistical techniques in more advanced courses.

A Reader's, Writer's, and Reviewer's Guide to Assessing Research Reports in Clinical Psychology

Brendan A. Maher
Harvard University

The Editors of the *Journal of Consulting and Clinical Psychology* who served between 1974 and 1978 have seen some 3,500 manuscripts in the area of consulting and clinical psychology. Working with this number of manuscripts has made it possible to formulate a set of general guidelines that may be helpful in the assessment of research reports. Originally developed by and for journal reviewers, the guidelines are necessarily skeletal and summary and omit many methodological concerns. They do, however, address the methodological concerns that have proved to be significant in a substantial number of cases. In response to a number of requests, the guidelines are being made available here.

Topic Content

1. Is the article appropriate to this journal? Does it fall within the boundaries mandated in the masthead description?

Style

1. Does the manuscript conform to APA style in its major aspects?

Introduction

1. Is the introduction as brief as possible given the topic of the article?
2. Are all of the citations correct and necessary, or is there padding? Are important citations missing? Has the author been careful to cite prior reports contrary to the current hypothesis?
3. Is there an explicit hypothesis?
4. Has the *origin* of the hypothesis been made explicit?
5. Was the hypothesis *correctly* derived from the theory that has been cited? Are other, contrary hypotheses compatible with the same theory?
6. Is there an explicit rationale for the selection of measures, and was it derived logically from the hypothesis?

Method

1. Is the method so described that replication is possible without further information?
2. Subjects: Were they sampled randomly from the population to which the results will be generalized?
3. Under what circumstances was informed consent obtained?
4. Are there probable biases in sampling (e.g., volunteers, high refusal rates, institution population atypical for the country at large, etc.)?
5. What was the "set" given to subjects? Was there deception? Was there control for experimenter influence and expectancy effects?
6. How were subjects debriefed?
7. Were subjects (patients) led to believe that they were receiving "treatment"?
8. Were there special variables affecting the subjects, such as medication, fatigue, and threat that were not part of the experimental manipulation? In clinical samples, was "organicity" measured and/or eliminated?
9. Controls: Were there appropriate control groups? What was being controlled for?

10. When more than one measure was used, was the order counterbalanced? If so, were order effects actually analyzed statistically?
11. Was there a control task(s) to confirm specificity of results?
12. Measures: For both dependent and independent variable measures—was validity and reliability established and reported? When a measure is tailor-made for a study, this is very important. When validities and reliabilities are already available in the literature, it is less important.
13. Is there adequate description of tasks, materials, apparatus, and so forth?
14. Is there discriminant validity of the measures?
15. Are distributions of scores on measures typical of scores that have been reported for similar samples in previous literature?
16. Are measures free from biases such as
    a. Social desirability?
    b. Yeasaying and naysaying?
    c. Correlations with general responsivity?
    d. Verbal ability, intelligence?
17. If measures are scored by observers using categories or codes, what is the interrater reliability?
18. Was administration and scoring of the measures done blind?
19. If short versions, foreign-language translations, and so forth, of common measures are used, has the validity and reliability of these been established?
20. In correlational designs, do the two measures have theoretical and/or methodological independence?

Representative Design

1. When the stimulus is a human (e.g., in clinical judgments of clients of differing race, sex, etc.), is there a *sample* of stimuli (e.g., more than one client of each race or each sex)?
2. When only one stimulus or a few human stimuli were used, was an adequate explanation of the failure to sample given?

Statistics

1. Were the statistics used with appropriate assumptions fulfilled by the data (e.g., normalcy of distributions for parametric techniques)? Where necessary, have scores been transformed appropriately?
2. Were tests of significance properly used and reported? For example, did the author use the p value of a correlation to justify conclusions when the actual size of the correlation suggests little common variance between two measures?
3. Have statistical significance levels been accompanied by an analysis of practical significance levels?
4. Has the author considered the effects of a limited range of scores, and so forth, in using correlations?

5. Is the basic statistical strategy that of a "fishing expedition"; that is, if many comparisons are made, were the obtained significance levels predicted in advance? Consider the number of significance levels as a function of the total number of comparisons made.

Factor Analytic Statistics

1. Have the correlation and factor matrices been made available to the reviewers and to the readers through the National Auxiliary Publications Service or other methods?
2. Is it stated what was used for communalities and is the choice appropriate? Ones in the diagonals are especially undesirable when items are correlated as the variables.
3. Is the method of termination of factor extraction stated, and is it appropriate in this case?
4. Is the method of factor rotation stated, and is it appropriate in this case?
5. If items are used as variables, what are the proportions of yes and no responses for each variable?
6. Is the sample size given, and is it adequate?
7. Are there evidences of distortion in the final solution, such as singlet factors, excessively high communalities, obliqueness when an orthogonal solution is used, linearly dependent variables, or too many complex variables?
8. Are artificial factors evident because of inclusion of variables in the analysis that are alternate forms of each other?

Figures and Tables

1. Are the figures and tables (a) necessary and (b) self-explanatory? Large tables of nonsignificant differences, for example, should be eliminated if the few obtained significances can be reported in a sentence or two in the text. Could several tables be combined into a smaller number?
2. Are the axes of figures identified clearly?
3. Do graphs correspond logically to the textual argument of the article? (E.g., if the text states that a certain technique leads to an *increment* of mental health and the accompanying graph shows a *decline* in symptoms, the point is not as clear to the reader as it would be if the text or the graph were amended to achieve visual and verbal congruence.)

Discussion and Conclusion

1. Is the discussion properly confined to the findings or is it digressive, including new post hoc speculations?
2. Has the author explicitly considered and discussed viable alternative explanations of the findings?

3. Have nonsignificant trends in the data been promoted to "findings"?
4. Are the limits of the generalizations possible from the data made clear? Has the author identified his/her own methodological difficulties in the study?
5. Has the author "accepted" the null hypothesis?
6. Has the author considered the possible methodological bases for discrepancies between the results reported and other findings in the literature?

Requests for reprints should be sent to Brendan A. Maher, Department of Psychology and Social Relations, Harvard University, Cambridge, Massachusetts 02138.

SUMMARY

In this chapter we first reviewed the traditional manner in which research results are communicated to our fellow scientists. We discussed the five major parts of scientific articles in detail, and we gave examples of each. The abstract is a brief 100–175-word summary of the article. Next comes the introduction, which is designed (1) to review what is already known about the phenomenon being studied, (2) to explain the reasons why we are performing the experiment, and (3) to outline our hypotheses. The method section consists of a detailed description of what we have done so that another scientist could precisely replicate our experiment. The results section describes the outcome of an experiment and states whether or not our findings are statistically significant. The final section is called the discussion and it contains an interpretation of our outcome in light of any limitations or confounds in our experiment. The discussion addresses the scientific significance of our findings and relates them to previously published research.

We then discussed the process of submitting an article for publication, such as selecting an appropriate journal and subjecting the article to editorial review. We presented a set of guidelines (Maher, 1978) detailing the specific types of questions editors, reviewers, and authors should consider in determining the suitability of any article submitted for publication. Finally, we offered some basic questions for beginning students relating to the development of specific research proposals (Holt, 1965).

CHAPTER THIRTEEN

Beyond Method

INTRODUCTION

Throughout this book we have sought to teach you more than just methods. This stems from our conviction that the process of science is *more* than the simple application of the scientific method to the study of human behavior and experience. In this chapter we want to move beyond the specific application of particular designs, as important as these approaches are, and to focus on some of the broad themes we have presented throughout this book. To emphasize this point we have entitled this final chapter "Beyond Method." Before beginning this task, let us first review schematically the approaches to research we have presented thus far.

In the preceding chapters we said a great deal about contemporary research methods used to study human behavior and experience. Now we will simply attempt to bring them together in a single schematic representation. To facilitate viewing them together, let's consider three continua (see Figure 13.1). The first continuum refers to the extent to which we directly intervene in the phenomenon we are studying. At one extreme is the experimental method. This is an active method, which involves studying causal relationships by directly manipulating an independent variable and observing its effect on the dependent variable. Typically experimenters are interested in causal factors at a given point in time. At the other extreme is the method of naturalistic observation. This is typically a passive method, which attempts to describe an ongoing process as it unfolds over time.

It is important to realize that something is gained and something lost

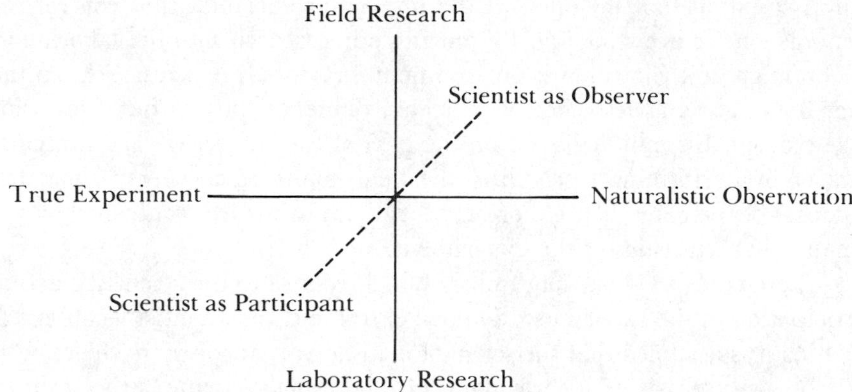

Figure 13.1 Three-dimensional illustration of research approaches.

whenever we adopt either of these methods. When we use naturalistic observation, we find ourselves unable to point out causal relationships. Likewise it is impossible to produce changes in the subjects we study; we must wait until new behaviors and experiences "spontaneously" appear. The experimental methods give us the advantage of increased control and thus the ability to infer causal relationships between events. However, *we have to know what we are looking for to use this method successfully.* As soon as we choose a dependent variable, certain information is excluded. In general the information that is excluded is what *we do not know to begin with.* For example, how many of us consider the weather (temperature, pressure, humidity) when we design experiments? We *assume* that weather is not an important factor. But some migraine sufferers, for example, report an increase of episodes before storms.

We would like to suggest using both the experimental method and naturalistic observation simultaneously. When conducting a true experiment, we are interested not only in the dependent variable that is being collected but also in watching the total experiment. Likewise, when observing subjects in naturalistic research, we consider what variables might be related and what variables might affect others. Thus, as one is developing ideas concerning a topic, there is a continuous interplay between naturalistic and experimental methods. This is true in terms of both research and the development of ideas.

The second dimension involves the research setting: laboratory versus field research. Laboratory research refers to our desire to create an experimental situation that includes all the important variables that control the phenomenon we are studying. By moving our research into the laboratory, we obtain greater control over environmental factors. Field research, on the other hand, gives us less control over environmental factors but allows for more ecologically valid behavior on the part of the subject we are studying. That is, by performing research in the field, many researchers believe the responses of the subjects are more "natural" and thus less controlled by the demand characteristics of the experiment.

There is also a third continuum, which relates to the scientist's actual participation in the experiment. On one extreme is the scientist as observer, in which it is assumed that the scientist is in no way involved in the experiment but only passively records data. On the other extreme is the scientist as participant, in which the scientist is actually part of the study. There is no hard and fast rule that suggests whether scientist as observer or scientist as participant gives the greatest objectivity. It depends on the questions being asked. If you were studying the social psychology of a motorcycle gang, then more accurate information might be obtained by being part of the group rather than being seen as an outsider. However, if you wanted to see how individuals react to a motorcycle gang driving through their town, then it might be better to be an observer so that you could see the reaction of the town both during and after the gang moved through.

As you look at the continua in Figure 13.1, you can see that you as a scientist have available a variety of methods and approaches to understand the question you are studying. No one approach or method is superior in itself. Methods are useful only in relation to a particular question being asked. To help illustrate this point, let us now divide the three-dimensional illustration of research approaches in Figure 13.1 into the two-dimensional ones in Figure 13.2. As an exercise, try to determine in which quadrant particular research studies discussed throughout this book should be placed.

Depending on the particular topics you study and the particular questions you ask, you are led to one of the methods presented in Figure 13.1 to study it. This brings us to the second aspect of science that we want to address—the questions we study.

BEGINNING WITH A QUESTION

As we have stressed throughout our discussion, the process of science is more than the mere application of method. In fact, much of the important work of learning to be a scientist lies in the realm of remembering how to

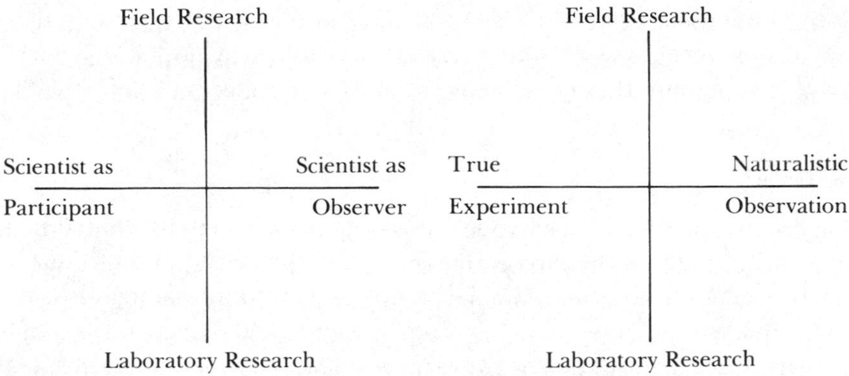

Figure 13.2 Two-dimensional illustrations of research approaches.

ask questions. We said *remembering* rather than *learning* because we wanted to remind you that doing science is not some special activity that sets us apart from humanity but rather an activity that stems from it. To emphasize this in the beginning of this book, we used the metaphor of the scientist being a child out to discover the world. Part of your task on the way to becoming a scientist is to recapture that childlike perspective—to remember how to find the wonder and excitement of asking questions. Once you become fascinated with a process or phenomenon, then you naturally consider it, explore it, and begin to ask questions about it.

Excitement and wonder are not enough, however. Just as the child grows up and matures, the scientist moves beyond the initial excitement of a question and begins to formulate a systematic approach concerning how the question might be answered. This usually means not just one experiment but a series of directed research studies referred to as a *research program* (see Box 13.1). In formulating such an approach, the scientist draws upon both the previous work of others and his or her own independent ideas. We will discuss the scientist's reliance on others and himself or herself in greater detail later in this chapter. For now we only want to emphasize that being excited about an idea or research question is an important beginning, but it is only the beginning. Then comes hard work.

LIMITATIONS TO FINDING ANSWERS

The scientist finds many obstacles within the hard work of research that may limit the types of questions that can be asked. Three of the most important limitations are (1) the tools we have available to us, (2) our shared view of the world, and (3) our personal psychological limitations such as fear of making mistakes or being rejected by our colleagues and friends.

Our Tools

Many of the questions we may wish to ask in science may be limited by the particular techniques that are available to us in the period in which we live. This is true of physical tools and technologies as well as methodological sophistication. In the same way that the telescope and the microscope allowed scientists to see a world that was previously unknown, recent electronic developments such as the computer and the physiological amplifier allow us to study new worlds of human behavior and experience previously beyond our limits. With new tools come new methodological advances. However, it is possible to fall in love with a particular tool or research technique, be it methodological, statistical, or a piece of apparatus. This often results in a person trying to make all human behavior and experience conform to one tool. There is an old saying that if you give a child *only* a hammer, he or

---

Box 13.1 Philosophy of Science: Imre Lakatos

Imre Lakatos advocated that the important advances in science are made through the adherence to *research programs.* By saying this, Lakatos means that science is more than following trial-and-error hypotheses. A research program is the examination of a number of major and minor hypotheses concerning a topic. Some examples of research programs according to Lakatos are Newton's theory of gravity, Einstein's relativity theory, and the theories of Freud.

An important point according to Lakatos is whether the research program is progressive or degenerating. How do you tell the difference? The main characteristic of a *progressive* research program is that *it predicts novel facts.* Thus a progressive program leads to the discovery of new facts, whereas according to Lakatos a *degenerating* program only reinterprets *known* facts in light of that theory. By this he means that a degenerating research program only explains the results of already existing experiments, whereas a progressive research program leads one into new directions and predicts new facts. In this way, Lakatos advocates that science changes not by sudden revolutions, as Kuhn suggested, but through the replacement of degenerating research programs with progressive ones.

For more information on Lakatos, see Lakatos (1978) and Eysenck (1976).

---

she will treat everything as if it is a nail. This, of course, is not the fault of the hammer but of the child's view of how a hammer should be used. The same is true for the scientist's view of the purpose of research tools; this leads us to our second point.

Our Shared View of the World

One of the greatest problems for a scientist interested in discovering new truths is related to our view of the world. Some writers refer to these views as "tacit" or "metaphysical" as well as "unconscious." The real point to be made is that we all have some assumptions that guide and direct our behavior, such as "people are evil," "man is an aggressive animal," "all behavior is learned," and "all behavior is innate." Even the law of parsimony (the best explanation in science is the least complicated), which has guided research in science, is itself an untested metaphysical assumption. Having assumptions is not the problem; the real problem, as the biologist David Bohm suggests, is when an individual confuses the assumptions themselves with directly observed facts (Bohm, 1969). Take a very common example of this problem we engage in each day. In the morning we "see" the "sunrise" and at night we "see" the "sunset." But of course the sun neither rises nor sets; it is rather we who are turning in space and move into sight of the sun and out of sight of the sun. Once we have pointed it out to you, you will say, yes, of course, and may even actually "see" the next "sunrise" or "sunset" differently.

Looking at scientific examples, it is possible to point out that historically we once all believed that the world was flat and that heavy bodies would reach the ground faster than lighter ones. A more recent example was the belief that organs innervated by the autonomic nervous system (the heart, stomach, and certain glands) was beyond self-regulation. Pioneer work by Neal Miller (1969) and others is beginning to show this assumption to be incorrect. This work has led to the development of new fields such as biofeedback and behavioral medicine. Another example that is presently of great interest is the cognitive processes of nonhumans. Such questions as *Can an ape create a sentence or do primates have self-awareness?* have become hotly debated topics among scientists. There has also been a renewed interest in the so-called mind-brain question and the study of consciousness. This has included such traditional questions as how we think as well as less studied questions relating to ESP and Eastern approaches to development. Along with this has been an explanation concerning new approaches to studying human functioning. Much traditional scientific research and thought have been directed at so-called normal behavior and the pathological exception as exemplified by neurosis and psychosis. One area yet to be systematically explored is that of human potential. Questions of potential ask what a person can do in the *best of cases*. In relation to this question, researchers are exploring creativity, musical and artistic abilities, genius, and even what makes excellent scientists. In science we have a number of approaches available, yet what we study is largely a personal decision shaped by our shared conceptions and personal perceptions. Even the question of why we study what we do is approachable from a scientific perspective.

Psychological Limitations

One topic of interest to cognitive psychologists has been emotional blocks toward learning (Bransford, 1979). Included within these blocks are fear of performing poorly, looking stupid in the eyes of others, and feeling foolish. Some authors (Maslow, 1971; Horner, 1972) have even suggested that some of us fear success. In all fairness, if the subjects in our learning experiments and other studies display these fears, then we must entertain the possibility that we as scientists possess these same fears. Thus one major limitation to new discovery is our own fear of what the discovery might mean for us personally.

Some scientists have begun to record their psychological processing as they perform the work of science and thus give us valuable insight into some of our psychological limitations. One famous example is John Watson's book *The Double Helix* (1968). This book records not only the scientific search for the structure of DNA but also the psychological jealousies and ego-motivated strivings that surrounded this search and something of the manner in which these influenced science. In a formal study, Ian Mitroff has studied scientists and their psychological reaction to science. In particular, he has examined how moon scientists have reacted to new data and rock specimens when these are in conflict with their own theories. Mitroff has also examined how scientists psychologically relate to their families and their work as well as how they express their own emotions (Mitroff, 1974; Mitroff & Fitzgerald, 1977). Mitroff and Fitzgerald end their report by agreeing with Maslow's conclusion that science can serve as a defense and as a way of avoiding life or it can serve as a means of increasing psychological health (Maslow, 1966). Likewise Mahoney (1976) has attempted to examine our myths of the scientist and to replace them with a more accurate picture of science as performed by real people who, like everyone, have real emotions and limitations.

SCIENCE AS A COMPLEX HUMAN PROCESS

In this section we want to make more explicit some of the themes we have presented throughout this book. Many of these themes have emphasized that science is a complex human process involving (1) a deep commitment to experience the world as it is regardless of our preconceived notions or hypotheses about its nature; (2) a strong concern for both the scientist and the subject, which involves both ethical and moral issues; and (3) a profound desire to better understand the many issues and problems that confront us and our world. Thus, we are saying that science concerns itself with truth, value, and relevance.

In 1890, T. C. Chamberlin, a scientist and president of the University of Wisconsin, published a paper in the journal *Science* (Chamberlin, 1890/reprinted 1965) in which he addressed many of the issues we have been indirectly concerned with in this book. In particular he discussed the means for transcending our own preconceptions and pet theories to arrive at a more accurate picture of reality. Chamberlin began his article by suggesting that there are two fundamental approaches to learning about the world. The first consists of "attempting to follow by close imitation the processes of previous thinkers, or to acquire by memorizing the results of their investigations." By this, Chamberlin means that you learn science by copying the experiments of previously successful scientists and you come to learn the methods that they used. This type of study has comprised the majority of the material in this book. As a beginning student in science, it is your first task to be able to replicate the successful approaches of others, and to do this you must know the accepted methods of study. We outlined many of these approaches in Figures 13.1 and 13.2. The second approach for Chamberlin is referred to as "primary or creative study." He describes this approach as follows:

> In it the effort is to think independently, or at least individually, in the endeavor to discover new truth, or to make new combinations of truth, or at least to develop an individualized aggregation of truth. The endeavor is to think for one's self, whether the thinking lies wholly in the fields of previous thought or not. It is not necessary to this habit of study that the subject-material be new; but the process of thought and

> its results must be individual and independent, not the mere following of previous lines of thought ending in predetermined results (Chamberlin, 1890/1965, p. 754).

One clear example in the history of science of someone following this approach is Einstein. In the early 1900s physicists relied on either Newton's theory or Maxwell's equations to help them understand the world. Einstein chose neither approach but began with what he considered a "thought experiment." He imagined a person riding on a streetcar moving away from a town clock. What would happen, Einstein thought, if the car traveled at the speed of light? Think about this for a moment. Since the light reflected from the clock would be traveling at the speed of light and the person in the car was also traveling at the speed of light, the light reflecting from the clock would be traveling at the same speed as the person perceiving the clock. Thus the person would always be "seeing" the same time—time would have stopped. If one could likewise imagine the person in the car going faster than the speed of light, he would actually be going faster than the light reflected from the clock. In this situation he would see the clock going backward. These thought experiments made Einstein see the world in a new and independent way that he himself was unsure of. Since these thought experiments made predictions that Einstein did not initially believe, he turned to other fields, namely philosophy, to consider his predictions. The result was a realization on Einstein's part that our concept of time comes out of the unconscious. That is to say, our concept of time is not something absolute but rather an unconscious conclusion of our mind based on the input of sensory information. We had always *assumed* time to be an absolute. The real absolute, as Einstein was soon to suggest, was not time but the speed of light. Later experimentation supported this conclusion.

Not only does the example of Einstein help us to understand Chamberlin's second or creative approach to science, but it is also a good illustration of the scientist's willingness to work through a problem logically and to consider surprising outcomes, even when the outcomes go against personal or traditional conceptions of the world.

Chamberlin suggests that a scientist's desire to see the world from a particular perspective can be transcended through a method he refers to as "multiple working hypotheses." For Chamberlin this method can be applied both to one's thinking and to one's research. (In Box 4.1 we presented Platt's interpretation of this method in relation to research.) The method is simply that one considers a family of hypotheses, each leading to different conclusions or interpretations. By considering two or more alternative hypotheses, we are most often able to advance to more sophisticated questions. For example, in the early history of psychology, some scientists argued that all behavior was innate, and they were able to find support for this theory. Other scientists suggested that all behavior was environmentally determined, and they found support for this theory. Today, by considering both theories, it has been possible to move beyond either and to study how environmental and innate factors interact to produce the particular behavior under study. Of course, here again we do not want to consider just one hypothesis but rather a family of hypotheses that compete with each other and offer alternative views of reality. Chamberlin suggests that the method of multiple working hypotheses can be applied not only to hypotheses but also to methods themselves. We will demonstrate this application later in the chapter. In conclusion, by adopting the method of multiple working hypotheses, Chamberlin suggests that one will not accidentally place one's motivation in the demonstration that a pet theory is true but rather will search for truth itself. The second theme we have emphasized in this book is the role of value in science. We will now turn to this issue.

VALUE IN SCIENCE

As we suggested, the domain of value is separate from the domain of science. However, this is not to say there is no overlap between the domains. Consider Figure 13.3. In this illustration the domain of science represents a world in which we test hypotheses and create theory. The domain of value

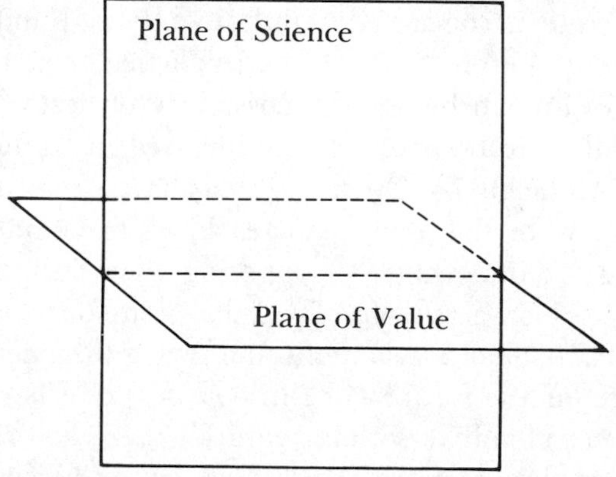

Figure 13.3 Interception of the planes of science and value.

cuts across the domain of science and thus influences science. The question of ethical research and moral concern for the scientist and the subject is one clear example of the manner in which the world of value influences science. It should be remembered that although we are influenced in science by value, we in no way test the validity of our ethical and moral values; that is, every scientist brings with him or her specific values that remain unexamined in the process of science. However, based on our common human heritage and collective statements such as the American Psychological Association ethical principles, there is often little actual difference between scientists in terms of ethical values.

As important as ethics are, there are other values that individuals bring to the scientific enterprise. Like ethics these values are untestable from the standpoint of science, but they often enter into the choice of research questions as well as the interpretation of information. For example, many atomic scientists have been committed to the peaceful use of atomic energy, and some of these individuals have refused to work on projects that could lead to weapons of war. Other scientists, on the other hand, have felt that a strong defense system is necessary for maintaining their values, and these individuals have engaged in scientific searches that could lead to better weapons of war. Likewise, in the behavioral sciences, some scientists suggest that behavior modification techniques offer an important means of rehabilitating prisoners, whereas others see these techniques as a denial of freedom and refuse to support such efforts.

Beyond the question of applying scientific knowledge to technological advances, individual scientists also hold personal values not directly connected with their scientific work. For example, Jonas Salk, the developer of the Salk polio vaccine, is concerned with humanity and understanding how we shape our own evolution (Salk, 1973). In particular he has stressed how our own ego gives human beings the possibility of destroying our species unless we are willing to become actively involved in trying to understand the value judgments facing us. Other scientists have stressed the importance of unconditional love or the nonviolent teachings of Gandhi. Einstein, for example, stressed the importance of opposing war. Still others have pursued music or poetry on a personal level. Newton spent much of his time reading the biblical book of Revelations and trying to understand its meaning and relevance for the future. The important point is that the scientist never has been an individual without values—there is no such thing as a completely dispassionate scientist! *Science cannot be performed in a value-free state.* In relation to this point, the historian of science J. Bronowski

(1965) has argued "that the practice of science compels the practitioner to form for himself a fundamental set of universal values."

RELEVANCE

The third theme we suggested was that scientists as a group possess a desire to better understand the world in which we all live as well as the organisms (including ourselves) who live in it. For many scientists this desire has manifested itself in a cry for relevance. Some scientists have directed their research toward broad ecological concerns. Others have focused their explorations on understanding both physical and mental pathologies. Still others have attempted to explore new areas that hold promise for the future development of humans as a species. In recent years there have been increasing efforts not only to understand psychological pathologies but also to develop and evaluate new methods of treatments. Such work as B. F. Skinner's early attempts to help neurotic and psychotic individuals through the application of learning theory techniques is one example. Another is Neal Miller's attempt to apply learning principles to the modification of physiological disorders through biofeedback. Other psychologists have attempted to move beyond normal and pathological processing and ask: What is an individual's potential? Abraham Maslow (1970) has tried to study individuals who are living up to their abilities. He calls these individuals "self-actualized" and has begun initial descriptive explorations into their behavior and experience. Other researchers point out that since we study lessened states of awareness such as sleep and coma, why not also study hyperaware states or altered states of consciousness? Charles Tart is a psychologist interested in this question. In an article in *Science*, Tart (1972) suggested that we need to develop a state-specific science. By this he means that scientific methods and approaches that are appropriate to one state of consciousness (such as sleep) may not be appropriate to the study of other states of consciousness (such as drug experiences or states of ecstasy). Thus each state of consciousness may require different scientific approaches.

Not only does the question of relevance address broad concerns, but it also leads us in evaluating specific research efforts. One case in point is the need to distinguish *scientifically significant* results from results that are *statistically significant*. When researchers compare experimental and control groups in an experiment, it is possible to find statistically significant differences suggesting that the variations were not the result of chance. *However the differences themselves, even if statistically significant, may be so small as to have no significant scientific meaning.* Let us look at a simple example to illustrate this point. Assume you developed a new technique for lowering blood pressure through relaxation. After months of testing, you might find that your technique did indeed result in statistically significant differences between experimental and control groups. However, upon close examination, you might discover that members of the experimental group reduced their blood pressure only 2–4 mm Hg and still showed blood pressures in the hypertensive range. Your results, although statistically significant, would not be clinically significant and thus could not be presented as a treatment for high blood pressure. In the same way, it is possible to achieve statistical differences in science that are not of such a magnitude as to be considered scientifically significant.

SCIENCE AS A MEANS OF TRANSCENDENCE

In the previous sections we suggested that scientists are influenced by truth, by values, and by relevance. Thus, science is and always has been something beyond mere methods. We approached these influences from the standpoint of the scientist! However, science can serve another function besides the growth of knowledge. It can aid us in our own growth and development both as individuals and as a society. We are suggesting that one value of science is its ability to aid us in transcending our personal and collective limitations. In the process of science we commit ourselves to the search for truth over and above our personal beliefs. To begin a search for understanding carries with it the commitment to accept the answers that we find and to share these answers with others (see Box 13.2). In this manner scientific knowledge represents a superior knowledge—a knowledge that remains constantly open to question and revision.

We want to be sure you understand the point being made. Scientific knowledge represents superior knowledge not in the sense that it is correct but in the sense that it is open to question, to rebuttal, and to change. Without the willingness to reconsider, to reexamine, and to reevaluate knowledge, that knowledge, however valuable at the moment in which it is presented, becomes dogma and lacks the life to lead us to an increasing understanding of the world in which we live.

As Karl Popper (1959, 1972), G. Spencer Brown (1972), Thomas Kuhn (1970), and others have shown us, we must consider that every theory is inadequate and will one day be refuted. This should cause not despair but hope, however—the hope that through science we can reduce the amount of ignorance we collectively hold. With each new theory we can ad-

"ALTHOUGH HUMANS MAKE SOUNDS WITH THEIR MOUTHS AND OCCASIONALLY LOOK AT EACH OTHER, THERE IS NO SOLID EVIDENCE THAT THEY ACTUALLY COMMUNICATE WITH EACH OTHER."

vance, we give ourselves the opportunity to understand the world in a new way. Each new approach and theory is somewhat like a pair of glasses that shapes our perspective and gives a certain focus to what we view. With a particular pair of glasses we are able to view our world and to draw a map of what we see. As useful as this process is for science, it is equally important that we remember there is a difference between the map and the reality that the map represents. Herein lie both the hope and the limitation of science. The hope is that through science we can reduce the amount of ignorance that we collectively hold and produce maps useful for our times. The limitation is that we can forget that there is a difference and confuse the map we have drawn with the reality in which we live.

To remind you that there is a distinction between the world in which we live and the manner in which we describe it scientifically, we introduced three separate perspectives in this book: the perspectives of the scientist, the subject, and the witness. At this time we can reunite these perspectives and remind ourselves that they are not separate but actually highly interrelated. As single beings incorporating these perspectives, we can begin to understand our world not from a single level but from a multifaceted perspective. It is through the interplay of these three aspects that science comes alive. Just as we suggested at the beginning of this book that to understand life we must experience it, we likewise suggest now that to know science we

---

Box 13.2 Lewis Thomas on the Nature of Science

It is hard to predict how science is going to turn out, and if it is really good science it is impossible to predict. This is in the nature of the enterprise. If the things to be found are actually new, they are by definition unknown in advance, and there is no way of telling in advance where a really new line of inquiry will lead. You cannot make choices in this matter, selecting things you think you're going to like and shutting off the lines that make for discomfort. You either have science or you don't, and if you have it you are obliged to accept the surprising and disturbing pieces of information, even the overwhelming and upheaving ones, along with the neat and promptly useful bits. It is like that.

The only solid piece of scientific truth about which I feel totally confident is that we are profoundly ignorant about nature. Indeed, I regard this as the major discovery of the past hundred years of biology. It is, in its way, an illuminating piece of news. It would have amazed the brightest minds of the eighteenth-century Enlightenment to be told by any of us how little we know, and how bewildering seems the way ahead. It is this sudden confrontation with the depth and scope of ignorance that represents the most significant contribution of twentieth-

must fully perceive these three aspects: the scientist, the subject, and the witness within ourselves.

It is also important that we reexamine the domains of exploration as presented in Chapter 1. Consider the matrix in Figure 13.4, which represents one way of studying ourselves and others. On one side of the matrix are the categories "I" and "You" and across the top the categories "Experience" and "Behavior." Throughout the brief history of scientific psychology we have focused our energy on the fourth cell—the study of external behavior—although the beginning of psychology included an emphasis on the first cell—personal experience. As the science of psychology developed, the early work directed at the first cell was ignored or discarded often in the name of being scientific. Psychology almost became a battleground for those who were interested in behavior to fight those who were interested in experience. Today this has begun to change, and we are seeing a new group of scientists coming forth who are interested in the study of both behavior *and* experience, not only in others but also in themselves. Thus, whereas we had been actively attempting to reduce the specific cells in the matrix we were studying, we are now beginning to include topics and approaches from all the cells.

For example, some scientists have recently used the naturalistic approach for the study of the behavior of others and modified this to study

---

century science to the human intellect. We are, at last, facing up to it. In earlier times, we either pretended to understand how things worked or ignored the problem, or simply made up stories to fill the gaps. Now that we have begun exploring in earnest, doing serious science, we are getting glimpses of how huge the questions are, and how far from being answered. Because of this, these are hard times for the human intellect, and it is no wonder that we are depressed. It is not so bad being ignorant if you are totally ignorant; the hard thing is knowing in some detail the reality of ignorance, the worst spots and here and there the not-so-bad spots, but no true light at the end of any tunnel nor even any tunnels that can yet be trusted. Hard times, indeed.

But we are making a beginning, and there ought to be some satisfaction, even exhilaration, in that. The method works. There are probably no questions we can think up that can't be answered, sooner or later, including even the matter of consciousness. To be sure, there may well be questions we can't think up, ever, and therefore limits to the reach of human intellect which we will never know about, but that is another matter. Within our limits, we should be able to work our way through to all our answers, if we keep at it long enough, and pay attention.

From Thomas (1979, pp. 73–74).

	Experience	Behavior (appearance)
"I"	How do I study my own experiences? 1	How do I study my own behavior? 3
"You"	How do I study your experiences? 2	How do I study your behavior? 4

Figure 13.4 Four fields of knowing.

their own experience during meditation and psychotherapy (Walsh, 1976, 1977, 1978; Evans & Robinson, 1978). They have used naturalistic observation, an approach associated with cell 4 (the study of others' behavior), to study their own experience (cell 1). Premack and Woodruff (1978) have begun to use experimental methods to approach cell 2 with primates. They are asking whether an ape can infer your mental state from watching your behavior; that is, what is the ape's experience of your experience? In a similar way, Wicklund (1979) has sought to determine the relationship between cell 1 and cell 3—how I experience myself and appear to others. He reports that the person who experiences himself or herself as he or she appears to others acts in a more consistent manner and is able to give more accurate self-reports.

As you can imagine, we are just beginning to explore the behavior and experience we have available to us, and there are many gaps in our knowledge that need to be completed. We hope that you have come to see that the topics we study in psychology are complex and defy single-minded approaches. It should be clear that the study of any cell of the matrix, although an important and useful beginning, can never give us a complete and total picture of psychological functioning. As a beginning student, it is your job to understand the traditional methods and approaches and be able to replicate important work. However, it is also your job to look to the future to a fuller understanding of behavior and experience.

SUMMARY

We began this final chapter with a review of the basic research strategies discussed in the preceding chapters. We reiterated our conviction that the key to good science is to answer a relevant question by appealing to our direct experience of the world. We emphasized the ways in which our attempts at science are limited. These limitations involve the nature of our scientific and technological tools, our shared philosophical view of the world, and our personal shortcomings and biases.

In an attempt to explicate some of the themes presented throughout this book, we stressed science as the search for truth, value, and relevance. With respect to the first of these themes, we emphasized the suggestions made by Chamberlin (1890/1965), which dealt with methodology. We discussed the importance of human values in science and stressed that science cannot be performed in a value-free state and that there is no such thing as a dispassionate scientist. We pointed out that the issue of relevance plays an increasingly important role in our contemporary science of behavior and experience. This growing interest in relevance encourages researchers to focus on new questions, such as better understanding psychopathology and moving beyond the study of normal and pathological processing to ask what is an individual's potential.

We drew a distinction between results that are statistically significant and those that are scientifically significant. We proceeded to discuss an alternative function of science involving our psychological unfolding as individuals and as a species.

In conclusion, we hope that a science of behavior and experience will play a role in helping us to better understand all aspects of human behavior and experience. At the same time, we must see the limitations of our science; at best it is only one way of viewing the world that should not be confused with a total and complete picture of our world.

APPENDIX A

Guidelines for Nonsexist Language in APA Journals

The *Publication Manual* of American Psychological Association (1974, p. 28) suggests that journal authors "be aware of the current move to avoid generic use of male nouns and pronouns when content refers to both sexes . . . [and] avoid overuse of the pronoun *he* when *she* or *they* is equally appropriate." The first change sheet to the *Publication Manual* (1975, p. 2) says: "For some specific suggestions on how to avoid such language, see 'Guidelines for Nonsexist Use of Language,' which was prepared by the APA Task Force on Issues of Sexual Bias in Graduate Education and published in the June 1975 *American Psychologist* (pp. 682–684)." Those guidelines, while helpful, are not specific to journal articles.

This second change sheet states the policy on sexist language in APA journals, offers some general principles for journal authors to consider, and suggests some ways to avoid sexist language.

To obtain single copies of this change sheet, send a stamped, self-addressed envelope to Publication Manual, Change Sheet 2, American Psychological Association, 1200 Seventeenth Street, N.W., Washington, D.C. 20036.

POLICY STATEMENT

APA as a publisher accepts journal authors' word choices unless those choices are inaccurate, unclear, or ungrammatical. However, because APA as an organization is committed to both science and the fair treatment of individuals and groups, authors of journal articles are expected to avoid writing in a manner that reinforces questionable attitudes and assumptions about people and sex roles.

Language that reinforces sexism can spring from subtle errors in research design, inaccurate interpretation, or imprecise word choices. Faulty logic in design, for example, may lead an investigator to report sex differences when the stimulus materials and measures used give one sex an unwarranted advantage over the other. Or, in interpretation, an investigator may make unwarranted generalizations about all people from data about one sex. Imprecise word choices, which occur frequently in journal writing, may be interpreted as biased, discriminatory, or demeaning even if they are not intended to be.

Advice on research design and interpretation is beyond the scope of the APA *Publication Manual.* However, in the spirit of the guidelines on writing style in Chapter 2, the following guidelines on nonsexist language are intended to help authors recognize and change instances where word choices may be inaccurate, misleading, or discriminatory.

GUIDELINES

Sexism in journal writing may be classified into two categories that are conceptually different: problems of *designation* and problems of *evaluation.*

Problems of designation

An author must use care in choosing words to ensure accuracy, clarity, and freedom from bias. In the case of sexism, long-established cultural practice can exert a powerful insidious influence over even the most conscientious author. Nouns, pronouns, and adjectives that designate persons can be chosen to eliminate, or at least to minimize, the possibility of ambiguity in sex identity or sex role. In the following examples, problems of designation are divided into two subcategories: *ambiguity of referent,* where it is unclear whether the author means one or both sexes, and *stereotyping,* where the writing conveys unsupported or biased connotations about sex roles and identity.

Problems of evaluation

By definition, scientific writing should be free of implied or irrelevant evaluation of the sexes. Difficulties may derive from the habitual use of clichés, or familiar expressions, such as "man and wife." The use of *man and wife* together implies differences in the freedom and activities of each, and evaluation of roles can occur. Thus, *husband and wife* are parallel, *man and wife* are not. In the examples that follow, problems of evaluation, like problems of designation, are divided into *ambiguity of referent* and *stereotyping*.

I. Problems of Designation

Examples of common usage	*Consider meaning. An alternative may be better.*	*Comment*
	A. AMBIGUITY OF REFERENT	
1. The *client* is usually the best judge of the value of *his* counseling.	The *client* is usually the best judge of the value of counseling.	*His* deleted.
	Clients are usually the best judges of the value of the counseling they receive.	Changed to plural.
	The best judge of the value of counseling is usually *the client*.	Rephrased.
2. *Man's search* for knowledge has led *him* into ways of learning that bear examination.	*The search* for knowledge has led *us* into ways of learning that bear examination.	Rephrased, using first person.
	People have continually sought knowledge. The search has led them, etc. . . .	Rewritten in two sentences.
3. man, mankind	people, humanity, human beings, humankind, human species	In this group of examples, a variety of terms may be substituted.
man's achievements	human achievements, achievements of the human species	
the average man	the average person, people in general	
man a project	staff a project, hire personnel, employ staff	

Examples of common usage	*Consider meaning. An alternative may be better.*	*Comment*
manpower	work force, personnel, workers	
Department of Manpower	(No alternative.)	Official titles should not be changed.
4. The use of experiments in psychology presupposes the mechanistic nature of *man*.	The use of experiments in psychology presupposes the mechanistic nature of the *human being*.	Noun substituted.
5. This interference phenomenon, called learned helplessness, has been demonstrated in rats, cats, fish, dogs, monkeys, and *men*.	This interference phenomenon, called learned helplessness, has been demonstrated in rats, cats, fish, dogs, monkeys, and *humans*.	Noun substituted.
6. Issues raised were whether the lack of cardiac responsivity in the premature *infant* is secondary to *his* heightened level of autonomic arousal . . .	. . . responsivity in the premature *infant* is secondary to *the* heightened level . . .	*His* changed to *the*.
	. . . responsivity in premature *infants* is secondary to *their* heightened levels . . .	Rewritten in plural.
7. First the *individual* becomes aroused by violations of *his* personal space, and then *he* attributes the cause of this arousal to other people in *his* environment.	First *we* become aroused by violations of *our* personal space, and then *we* attribute the cause of this arousal to other people in *the* environment.	Pronouns substituted, *he* and *his* omitted.
8. Much has been written about the effect that a *child's* position among *his* siblings has on *his* intellectual development.	Much has been written about the relationship between sibling position and intellectual development in *children*.	Rewritten, plural introduced.

Examples of common usage	*Consider meaning. An alternative may be better.*	*Comment*
9. Subjects were 16 girls and 16 boys. Each *child* was to place a car on *his* board so that two cars and boards looked alike.	Each child was to place a car on *his* or *her* board so that two cars and boards looked alike.	Changed *his* to *his or her;* however, use sparingly to avoid monotonous repetition. *Her or his* may also be used, but it sounds awkward. In either case, keep pronoun order consistent to avoid ambiguity.
10. Each person's alertness was measured by the difference between *his* obtained relaxation score and *his* obtained arousal score.	Each person's alertness was measured by the difference between *the* obtained relaxation and arousal scores.	*His* deleted, plural introduced.
11. The client's husband *lets* her teach part-time.	The client's husband *"lets"* her teach part-time. The husband says he *"lets"* the client teach part-time. The client *says her husband "lets"* her teach part-time.	Punctuation added to clarify location of the bias, that is, with husband and wife, not with author. If necessary, rewrite to clarify as allegation. See Example 24 below.
	B. STEREOTYPING	
12. males, females	men, women, boys, girls, adults, children, adolescents	Specific nouns reduce possibility of stereotypic bias and often clarify discussion. Use *male* and *female* as adjectives where appropriate and relevant (female experimenter, male subject). Avoid unparallel usages such as 10 *men* and 16 *females.*

Examples of common usage	*Consider meaning. An alternative may be better.*	*Comment*
13. Research scientists often neglect their *wives* and *children.*	Research scientists often neglect their *families.*	Alternative wording acknowledges that women as well as men are research scientists.
14. When a *test developer or test user* fails to satisfy these requirements, *he* should . . .	When *test developers or test users* fail to satisfy these requirements, *they* should . . .	Same as Example 13.
15. the psychologist . . . *he*	psychologists . . . *they;* the psychologist . . . *she*	Be specific or change to plural if discussing women as well as men.
the therapist . . . *he*	therapists . . . *they;* the therapist . . . *she*	
the nurse . . . *she*	nurses . . . *they;* nurse . . . *he*	
the teacher . . . *she*	teachers . . . *they;* teacher . . . *he*	
16. woman doctor, lady lawyer, male nurse	doctor, physician, lawyer, nurse	Specify sex if it is a variable or if sex designation is necessary to the discussion ("13 female doctors and 22 male doctors").
17. mothering	parenting, nurturing (or specify exact behavior)	Noun substituted.
18. chairman (of an academic department)	Use *chairperson* or *chair* if it is known that the institution has established either form as an official title. Otherwise use *chairman.*	*Department head* may be appropriate, but the term is not synonymous with *chairman* and *chairperson* at all institutions.
chairman (presiding officer of a committee or meeting)	chairperson, moderator, discussion leader	In parliamentary usage *chairman* is the official term. Alternatives are acceptable in most writing.

Examples of common usage	*Consider meaning. An alternative may be better.*	*Comment*
19. Only *freshmen* were eligible for the project. All the students had matriculated for three years, but the majority were still *freshmen.*	(No alternative if academic standing is meant.)	*First-year student* is often an acceptable alternative to *freshman,* but in these cases, *freshmen* is used for accuracy.
20. foreman, policeman, stewardess, mailman	supervisor, police officer, flight attendant, postal worker or letter carrier	Noun substituted.

II. Problems of Evaluation

A. AMBIGUITY OF REFERENT

21. The authors acknowledge the assistance of *Mrs. John Smith.*	The authors acknowledge the assistance of *Jane Smith.*	Use given names in author acknowledgments. When forms of address are used in text, use the appropriate form: Mr., Mrs., Miss, or Ms.
22. men and women, sons and daughters, boys and girls, husbands and wives	women and men, daughters and sons, girls and boys, wives and husbands	Vary the order if content does not require traditional order.

B. STEREOTYPING

23. men and girls	men and women, women and men	Use parallel terms. Of course, use *men and girls* if that is literally what is meant.
24. The client's husband lets her teach part-time.	The client teaches part-time.	The author of this example intended to communicate the working status of the woman but inadvertently revealed a stereotype about husband-wife relationships; see Example 11 above.

Examples of common usage	*Consider meaning. An alternative may be better.*	*Comment*
25. ambitious men and aggressive women	ambitious women and men or ambitious people aggressive men and women or aggressive people	Some adjectives, depending on whether the person described is a man or a woman, connote bias. The examples illustrate some common usages that may not always convey exact meaning, especially when paired, as in column 1.
cautious men and timid women	cautious women and men, cautious people timid men and women or timid people	
26. The boys chose typically male toys.	The boys chose (specify)	Being specific reduces possibility of stereotypic bias.
The client's behavior was typically female.	The client's behavior was (specify)	
27. woman driver	driver	If specifying sex is necessary, use *female driver.*
28. The *girls* in the office greeted all clients.	secretaries, office assistants	Noun substituted.
29. coed	female student	Noun substituted.
30. women's lib, women's libber	women's movement, feminist, supporter of women's movement	Noun substituted.
31. Subjects were 16 men and 4 women. *The women were housewives.*	The men were (specify) and the women were (specify).	Describe women and men in parallel terms. *Housewife* indicates sex, marital status, and occupation, and excludes men. *Homemaker* indicates occupation, and includes men.

A FINAL WORD

Attempting to introduce nonsexist language at the cost of awkwardness, obscurity, or euphemistic phrasing does not improve scientific communication. An author should make clear that both sexes are under discussion when they are and should indicate sex when only one sex is discussed. Under no circumstances should an author hide sex identity in an attempt to be unbiased, if knowledge of sex may be important to the reader.

Any endeavor to change the language is an awesome task at best. Some aspects of our language that may be considered sexist are firmly embedded in our culture, and we presently have no acceptable substitutes. In English, the use of third-person singular pronouns is one example: the generic use of *he* is misleading, *it* is inaccurate, *one* conveys a different meaning, and *he or she* can become an annoying repetition. Nevertheless, with some rephrasing and careful attention to meaning, even the generic *he* can be avoided most of the time. The result of such efforts is accurate, unbiased communication, the purpose of these guidelines.

SUGGESTED READING

APA Task Force on Issues of Sexual Bias in Graduate Education. Guidelines for nonsexist use of language. *American Psychologist,* 1975, *30,* 682–684.

Burr, E., Dunn, S., & Farquhar, N. *Guidelines for equal treatment of the sexes in social studies textbooks.* Los Angeles: Westside Women's Committee, 1973. (Available from Westside Women's Committee, P.O. Box 24D20, Los Angeles, California 90024.)

DeBoard, D., Fisher, A. M., Moran, M. C., & Zawodny, L. *Guidelines to promote the awareness of human potential.* Philadelphia, Pa.: Lippincott, undated.

Harper & Row. *Harper & Row guidelines on equal treatment of the sexes in textbooks.* New York: Author, 1976.

Henley, N., & Thorne, B. *She said/he said: An annotated bibliography of sex differences in language, speech, and nonverbal communication.* Pittsburgh, Pa.: Know, 1975. (Available from Know, Inc., P.O. Box 86031, Pittsburgh, Pennsylvania 15221.)

Holt, Rinehart & Winston (College Department). *The treatment of sex roles and minorities.* New York: Author, 1976.

Lakoff, R. *Language and woman's place.* New York: Harper & Row, 1975.

Lerner, H. E. Girls, ladies, or women? The unconscious dynamics of language choice. *Comprehensive Psychiatry,* 1976, *17,* 295–299.

McGraw-Hill. *Guidelines for equal treatment of the sexes in McGraw-Hill Book Company publications.* New York: Author, undated.

Miller, C., & Swift, K. *Words and women.* Garden City, N.Y.: Anchor Press/Doubleday, 1976.

Prentice-Hall. *Prentice-Hall author's guide* (5th ed.). Englewood Cliffs, N.J.: Author, 1975.

Random House. *Guidelines for multiethnic/nonsexist survey.* New York: Author, 1975.

Scott, Foresman. *Guidelines for improving the image of women in textbooks.* Glenview, Ill.: Author, 1974.

John Wiley & Sons. *Wiley guidelines on sexism in language.* New York: Author, 1977.

This change sheet was prepared by the APA Publication Manual Task Force. Members of the task force are Charles N. Cofer (Chairperson), Robert S. Daniel, Frances Y. Dunham, and Walter I. Heimer. Ellen Kimmel served as liaison from the Committee on Women in Psychology, and Anita De-Vivo as APA staff liaison. This material may be reproduced in whole or in part without permission, provided that acknowledgment is made to the American Psychological Association.

APPENDIX B

Printed Article

Journal of Consulting and Clinical Psychology
1975, Vol. 43, No. 2, 123-125

Relationship Between Eating Rates and Obesity

Donna J. Gaul, W. Edward Craighead, and Michael J. Mahoney
Pennsylvania State University

A comparison was made of the eating behaviors of obese and nonobese subjects in a naturalistic setting. It was found that obese subjects took more bites, performed fewer chews per bite, and spent less time chewing than did nonobese subjects. The clinical implications of these data are discussed.

In their recent review Stunkard and Mahoney (in press) concluded that behavior modification techniques have demonstrated considerable effectiveness in the treatment of obesity. Many of these techniques were based in part on the behavioral analysis of eating patterns first presented by Ferster, Nurnberger, and Levitt (1962).

An implicit assumption of many behavior modification programs has been that eating patterns differ for obese and nonobese people. Specifically, it has been presumed that overweight individuals eat faster and take fewer bites (cf. Stuart & Davis, 1972). However, virtually no empirical data regarding that assumption have been presented. The purpose of the present study was to determine if obese people consume their food more rapidly than nonobese people, and if consummatory behaviors (chewing and drinking) differ for the two groups.

Method

Subjects

One hundred subjects were chosen for observation at an eating establishment that specializes in the sale of hamburgers, french fried potatoes, and soft drinks. One criterion for subject selection was that he purchase all three items and only those items. Additionally, for a subject to be included he had to sip his drink through a straw (which nearly all people did). Finally, the subject had to be between the ages of 18 and 35 in the opinion of two trained observers. As each potential subject purchased his food, the two observers independently categorized them on age and obesity. The first 50 males (25 obese, 25 nonobese) and first 50 females (25 obese, 25 nonobese) to meet joint agreement criteria were included in the study.

Requests for reprints should be sent to W. Edward Craighead, Department of Psychology, 512 Moore Building, Pennsylvania State University, University Park, Pennsylvania 16802.

Procedure

The consummatory behaviors of each subject were unobtrusively recorded by two trained observers. Any subject who indicated awareness of being observed was excluded from the study. Observations were made, one subject at the time, in order of subjects' appearance until the requisite number ($n = 25$) for each cell was obtained.

Beginning with the subject's first bite or sip of drink, frequency counts were taken by both observers for five minutes. Data were obtained for the following dependent measures: number of bites taken during the five minutes (three french fries were considered equal to one bite of hamburger), number of chews per bite, total number of seconds (of possible 300) spent chewing, and total number of sips of soft drink.

Results

Interobserver agreement was calculated by dividing the number of ratings for which both observers agreed by the number of agreements plus disagreements and multiplying the quotient by 100. Interobserver agreement was 100% for all measures except number of chews per bite where the average interobserver agreement was 92% (range = 87%–100%).

The means and standard deviations for all the dependent measures are presented in Table 1. The data represent averages between observers for all measures.

All data were submitted to 2 × 2 (Obesity × Sex) analyses of variance. The main effect for obesity was significant for number of bites taken ($F = 63.2$, $df = 1/96$, $p < .001$), number of chews per bite ($F = 126.8$, $df = 1/96$, $p < .001$), and for total amount of time spent chewing ($F = 70.1$, $df = 1/96$, $p < .001$).

TABLE 1

MEANS AND STANDARD DEVIATIONS FOR ALL DEPENDENT MEASURES FOR ALL GROUPS

Condition	Obese		Nonobese	
	Males	Females	Males	Females
No. bites				
M	17.04	16.84	13.00	12.32
SD	2.68	3.26	2.20	2.51
No. of chews per bite				
M	9.76	9.20	21.36	18.84
SD	3.23	3.03	11.51	4.72
Time spent chewing (in seconds)				
M	104.44	104.08	161.60	153.48
SD	23.01	35.42	33.41	33.89
No. sips				
M	8.00	6.56	7.44	7.28
SD	1.29	2.02	1.36	1.84

Obese subjects took more bites ($M = 16.94$) than nonobese subjects ($M = 12.66$), performed fewer chews per bite (M obese = 9.24, M nonobese = 18.60), spent less time chewing (M obese = 104.26, M nonobese = 157.54).

There was a significant main effect for sex ($F = 5.8$, $df = 1/96$, $p < .018$) and a significant Sex × Obesity interaction effect ($F = 3.7$, $df = 1/96$, $p < .056$) for total number of sips taken. Males ($M = 7.72$) took a greater total of sips than did females ($M = 6.92$); however, this was primarily the result of obese males ($M = 8.00$) who took a significantly greater number of sips than did the obese female subjects ($M = 6.56$).

DISCUSSION

The foregoing results suggest several clinically relevant implications for the behavioral treatment of obesity. To begin with, it does appear that there are differences in the eating styles of obese and nonobese individuals. Obese subjects in the present study spent less time chewing than nonobese subjects and took more bites during the five-minute observation period. This latter finding corroborates the notion that overweight individuals are often rapid eaters (Ferster et al., 1962). Therapeutic strategies aimed at reducing eating pace may therefore be effective. However, the fact that obese subjects took more bites than nonobese subjects is at least partially contradictory to the popular recommendation that overweight individuals *increase* the number of bites they take (Stuart & Davis, 1972). Unless this increase is accompanied by a slowing of the eating pace, countertherapeutic results might ensue.

The dramatic difference between groups on the mastication variable also deserves comment. Although relatively little therapeutic attention has been paid to this dimension, it seems possible that increased mastication may facilitate weight reduction. This speculation is consistent with recent findings on the role of food texture and mastication in satiety (Balagura, 1973).

The strategy of counting bites (Stuart & Davis, 1972) may be contraindicated unless obese clients are given specific standards and eating behavior guidelines to pursue. At an intuitive level, the overweight person might interpret this self-monitoring task as suggesting that he should take fewer bites. Were this to result, he might inadvertently develop the maladaptive pattern of rapid, large (but few) bites. A laboratory study subsequent to the one described in this article asked obese and nonobese individuals to eat a standardized meal in a laboratory setting. Within the next three days the subjects were asked to count the bites they took while consuming the same standardized meal. Extensive intersubject variability was encountered. Self-monitoring did not have any systematic effect on eating pace for either group of individuals. A noteworthy finding, however, was that obese subjects were significantly less accurate in their self-monitoring than nonobese subjects ($U_2 = 4.5$, $n_1 = 6$, $n_2 = 7$, $p < .05$).

One final comment has to do with the assumption that obese individuals will lose weight if they adopt the eating styles of normal persons (Stunkard & Mahoney, in press). While there is strong evidence that modifying *what* people eat (calorically) can result in weight loss, the data on modifying *how* they

eat are less conclusive. Further inquiries need to evaluate the relationship between these variables.

REFERENCES

Balagura, S. *Hunger: A biopsychological analysis.* New York: Basic Books, 1973.

Ferster, C. B., Nurnberger, J. I., & Levitt, E. B. The control of eating. *Journal of Mathetics*, 1962, 1, 87–109.

Stuart, R. B., & Davis, B. *Slim chance in a fat world.* Champaign, Ill.: Research Press, 1972.

Stunkard, A. J., & Mahoney, M. J. Behavioral treatment of the eating disorders. In H. Leitenberg (Ed.), *Handbook of behavior modification.* New York: Appleton-Century-Crofts, in press.

(Received May 23, 1974)

APPENDIX C

Article Manuscript

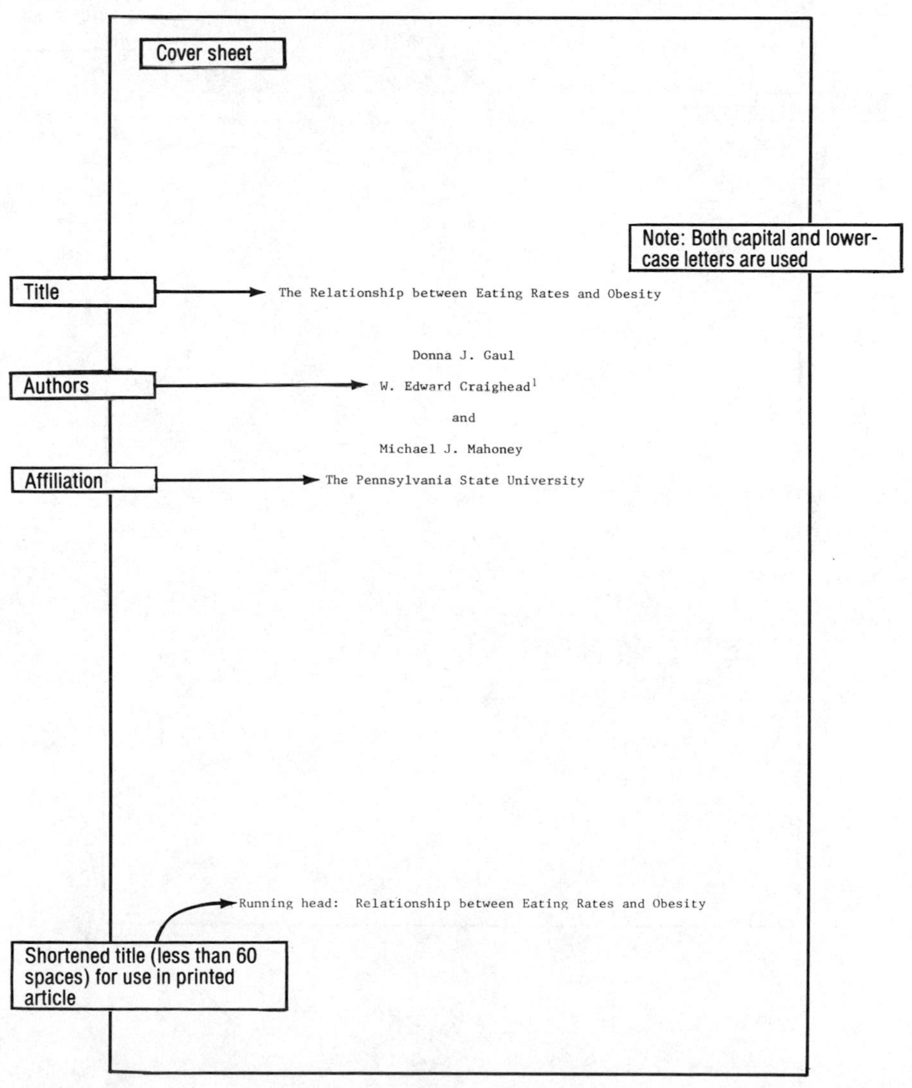

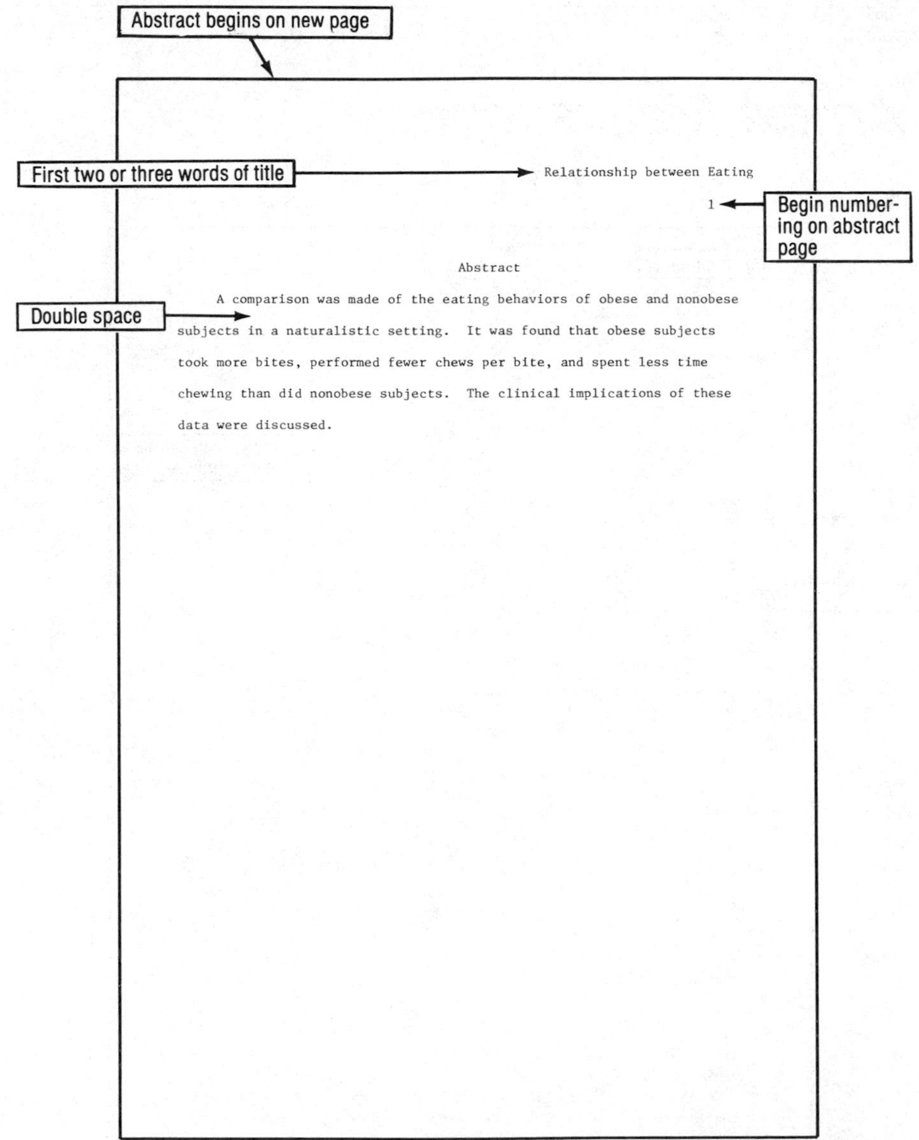
Abstract begins on new page
First two or three words of title
Relationship between Eating
1
Begin numbering on abstract page
Abstract
Double space
A comparison was made of the eating behaviors of obese and nonobese subjects in a naturalistic setting. It was found that obese subjects took more bites, performed fewer chews per bite, and spent less time chewing than did nonobese subjects. The clinical implications of these data were discussed.

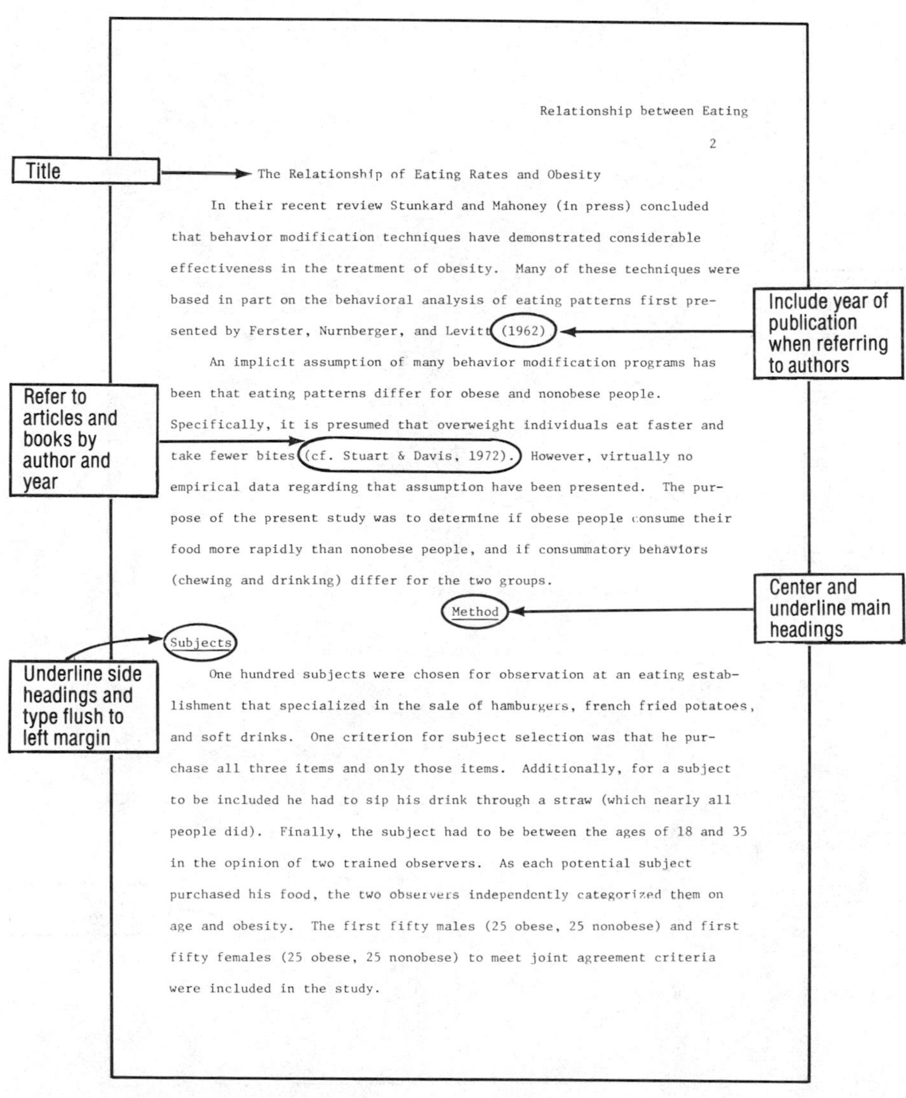
Relationship between Eating

2

The Relationship of Eating Rates and Obesity

In their recent review Stunkard and Mahoney (in press) concluded that behavior modification techniques have demonstrated considerable effectiveness in the treatment of obesity. Many of these techniques were based in part on the behavioral analysis of eating patterns first presented by Ferster, Nurnberger, and Levitt (1962).

An implicit assumption of many behavior modification programs has been that eating patterns differ for obese and nonobese people. Specifically, it is presumed that overweight individuals eat faster and take fewer bites (cf. Stuart & Davis, 1972). However, virtually no empirical data regarding that assumption have been presented. The purpose of the present study was to determine if obese people consume their food more rapidly than nonobese people, and if consummatory behaviors (chewing and drinking) differ for the two groups.

Method

Subjects

One hundred subjects were chosen for observation at an eating establishment that specialized in the sale of hamburgers, french fried potatoes, and soft drinks. One criterion for subject selection was that he purchase all three items and only those items. Additionally, for a subject to be included he had to sip his drink through a straw (which nearly all people did). Finally, the subject had to be between the ages of 18 and 35 in the opinion of two trained observers. As each potential subject purchased his food, the two observers independently categorized them on age and obesity. The first fifty males (25 obese, 25 nonobese) and first fifty females (25 obese, 25 nonobese) to meet joint agreement criteria were included in the study.

Note: Research is described in the past tense

Procedure

The consummatory behaviors of each subject were unobtrusively recorded by two trained observers. Any subject who indicated awareness of being observed was excluded from the study. Observations were made, one subject at the time, in order of subjects' appearance until the requisite number ($\underline{n}$ = 25) for each cell was obtained.

Underline statistical symbols

Beginning with the subject's first bite or sip of drink, frequency counts were taken by both observers for five minutes. Data were obtained for the following dependent measures: number of bites taken during the five minutes (three french fries were considered equal to one bite of hamburger), number of chews per bite, total number of seconds (of possible 300) spent chewing, and total number of sips of soft drink.

Results

Interobserver agreement was calculated by dividing the number of ratings for which both observers agreed by the number of agreements plus disagreements and multiplying the quotient by 100. Interobserver agreement was 100% for all measures except number of chews per bite where the average interobserver agreement was 92% (range = 87%-100%).

The means and standard deviations for all the dependent measures are presented in Table 1. The data represent averages between observers for all measures.

Indicate position of each table or figure

Insert Table 1 about here

Include name of statistic

All data were submitted to 2 × 2 (obesity by sex) analyses of variance. The main effect for obesity was significant for number of bites

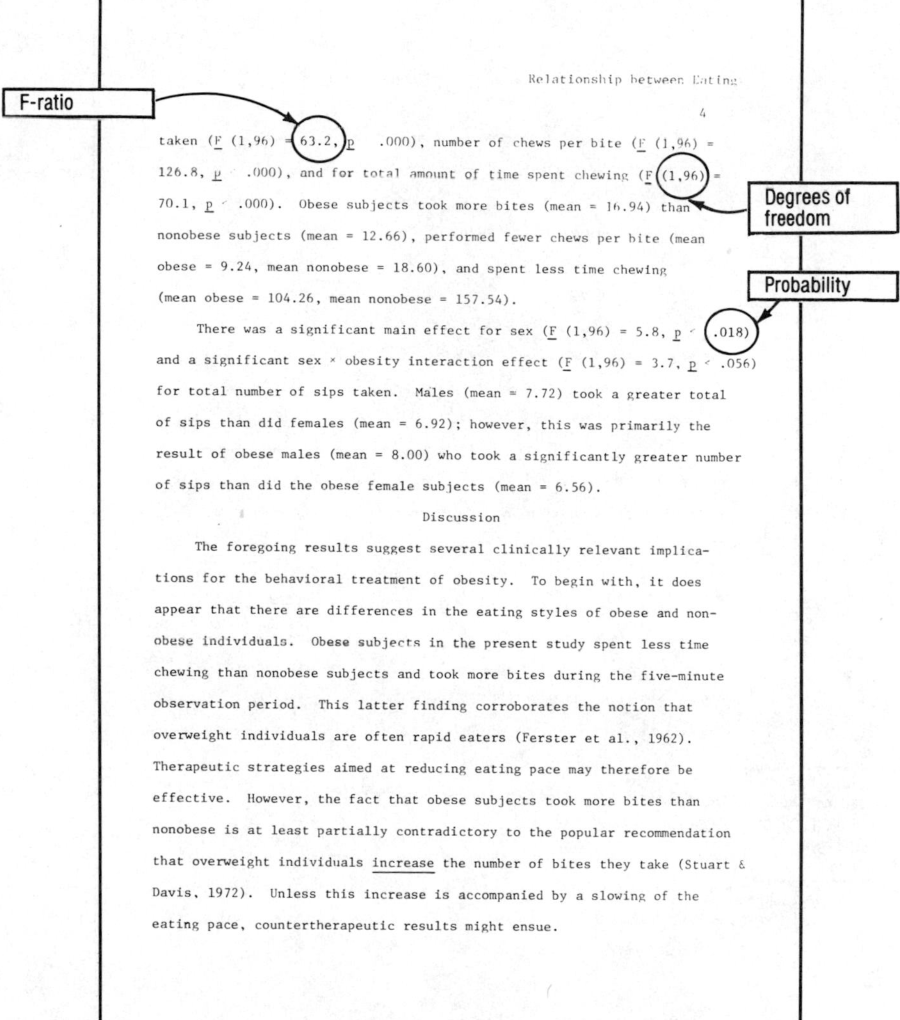

Relationship between Eating

4

taken (F (1,96) = 63.2, p .000), number of chews per bite (F (1,96) = 126.8, p .000), and for total amount of time spent chewing (F (1,96) = 70.1, $p < .000$). Obese subjects took more bites (mean = 16.94) than nonobese subjects (mean = 12.66), performed fewer chews per bite (mean obese = 9.24, mean nonobese = 18.60), and spent less time chewing (mean obese = 104.26, mean nonobese = 157.54).

There was a significant main effect for sex (F (1,96) = 5.8, $p < .018$) and a significant sex × obesity interaction effect (F (1,96) = 3.7, $p < .056$) for total number of sips taken. Males (mean = 7.72) took a greater total of sips than did females (mean = 6.92); however, this was primarily the result of obese males (mean = 8.00) who took a significantly greater number of sips than did the obese female subjects (mean = 6.56).

Discussion

The foregoing results suggest several clinically relevant implications for the behavioral treatment of obesity. To begin with, it does appear that there are differences in the eating styles of obese and nonobese individuals. Obese subjects in the present study spent less time chewing than nonobese subjects and took more bites during the five-minute observation period. This latter finding corroborates the notion that overweight individuals are often rapid eaters (Ferster et al., 1962). Therapeutic strategies aimed at reducing eating pace may therefore be effective. However, the fact that obese subjects took more bites than nonobese is at least partially contradictory to the popular recommendation that overweight individuals increase the number of bites they take (Stuart & Davis, 1972). Unless this increase is accompanied by a slowing of the eating pace, countertherapeutic results might ensue.

The dramatic difference between groups on the mastication variable also deserves comment. Although relatively little therapeutic attention has been paid to this dimension, it seems possible that increased mastication may facilitate weight reduction. This speculation is consistent with recent findings on the role of food texture and mastication in satiety (Balagura, 1973).

The strategy of counting bites (Stuart & Davis, 1972) may be contraindicated unless obese clients are given specific standards and eating behavior guidelines to pursue. At an intuitive level, the overweight person might interpret this self-monitoring task as suggesting that he should take fewer bites. Were this to result, he might inadvertently develop the maladaptive pattern of rapid, large (but few) bites. A laboratory study subsequent to the one described in this paper asked obese and nonobese individuals to eat a standardized meal in a laboratory setting. Within the next three days the subjects were asked to count the bites they took while consuming the same standardized meal. Extensive intersubject variability was encountered. Self-monitoring did not have any systematic effect on eating pace for either group of individuals. A noteworthy finding, however, was that obese subjects were significantly less accurate in their self-monitoring than nonobese subjects ($U_2 = 4.5$; $n_1 = 6$, $n_2 = 7$; $p < .05$).

One final comment has to do with the assumption that obese individuals will lose weight if they adopt the eating styles of normal persons (Stunkard & Mahoney, in press). While there is strong evidence that modifying *what* people eat (calorically) can result in weight loss, the data on modifying *how* they eat are less conclusive. Further inquiries need to evaluate the relationship between these variables.

Note: Underlined words will be in italics in printed article

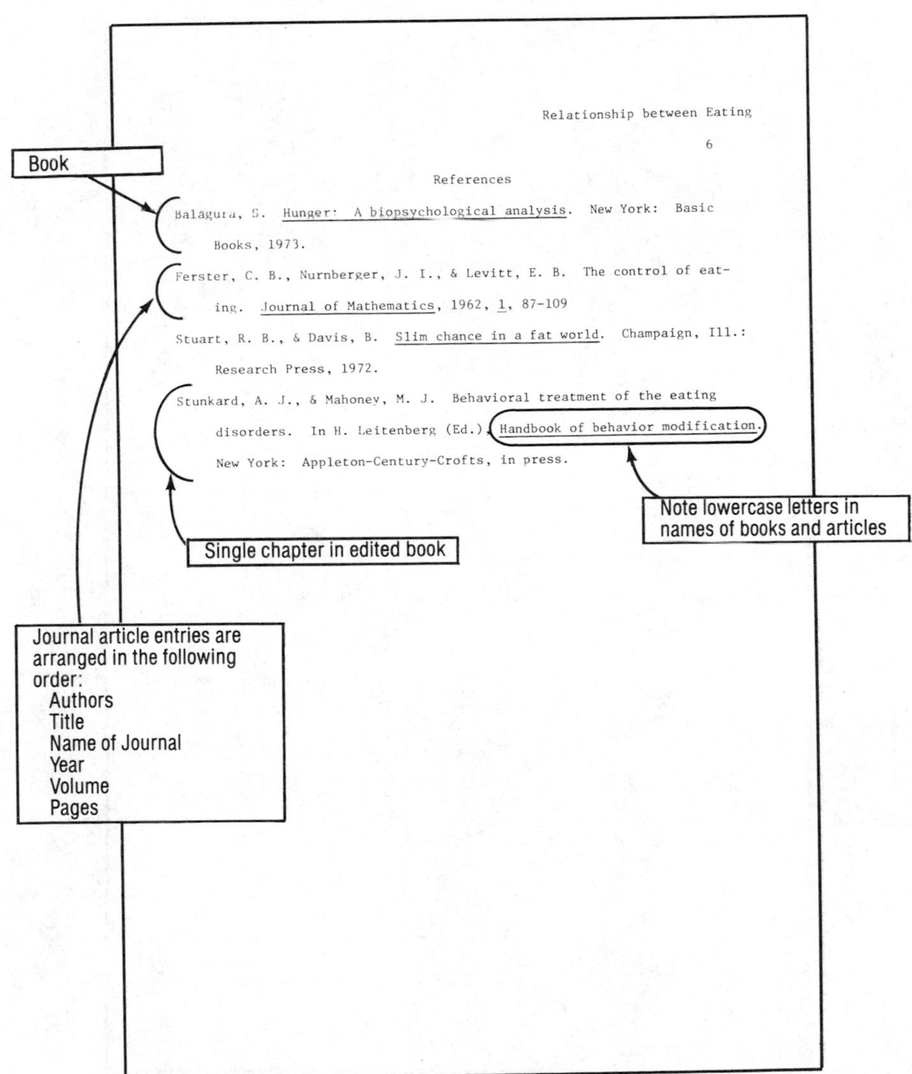
Relationship between Eating
6
References
Balagura, S. Hunger: A biopsychological analysis. New York: Basic Books, 1973.
Ferster, C. B., Nurnberger, J. I., & Levitt, E. B. The control of eating. Journal of Mathematics, 1962, 1, 87-109
Stuart, R. B., & Davis, B. Slim chance in a fat world. Champaign, Ill.: Research Press, 1972.
Stunkard, A. J., & Mahoney, M. J. Behavioral treatment of the eating disorders. In H. Leitenberg (Ed.), Handbook of behavior modification. New York: Appleton-Century-Crofts, in press.
Book
Single chapter in edited book
Note lowercase letters in names of books and articles
Journal article entries are arranged in the following order:
Authors
Title
Name of Journal
Year
Volume
Pages

Footnotes are placed on a separate page

Footnote

1. Requests for reprints should be sent to W. Edward Craighead, Department of Psychology, 512 Moore Building, The Pennsylvania State University, University Park, Pa., 16802.

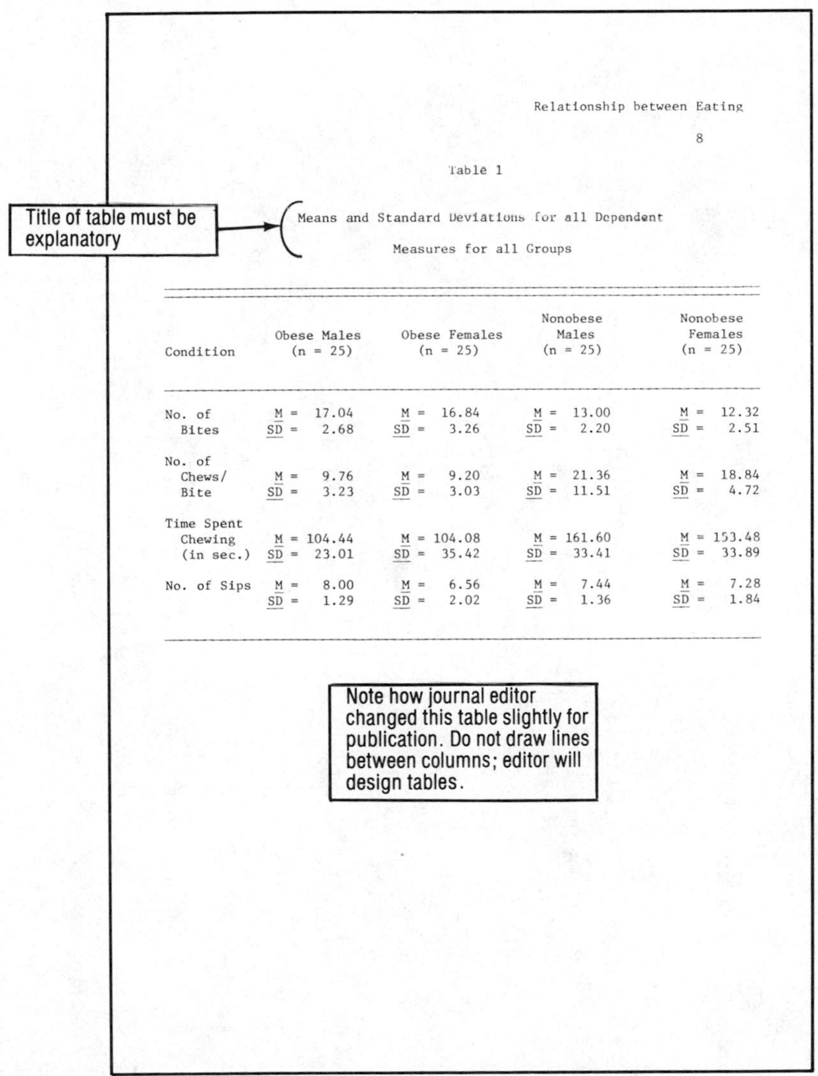

Relationship between Eating

8

Table 1

Means and Standard Deviations for all Dependent Measures for all Groups

Condition	Obese Males (n = 25)	Obese Females (n = 25)	Nonobese Males (n = 25)	Nonobese Females (n = 25)
No. of Bites	M = 17.04 SD = 2.68	M = 16.84 SD = 3.26	M = 13.00 SD = 2.20	M = 12.32 SD = 2.51
No. of Chews/ Bite	M = 9.76 SD = 3.23	M = 9.20 SD = 3.03	M = 21.36 SD = 11.51	M = 18.84 SD = 4.72
Time Spent Chewing (in sec.)	M = 104.44 SD = 23.01	M = 104.08 SD = 35.42	M = 161.60 SD = 33.41	M = 153.48 SD = 33.89
No. of Sips	M = 8.00 SD = 1.29	M = 6.56 SD = 2.02	M = 7.44 SD = 1.36	M = 7.28 SD = 1.84

Manuscript copy printed by permission of W. E. Craighead.

Bibliography

Alfred, R. The church of satan. In C. Glock & R. Bellah (Eds.), *The new religious consciousness.* Berkeley: University of California Press, 1976, pp. 180–202.

American Psychological Association. *Ethical principles in the conduct of research with human participants.* Washington, D.C.: American Psychological Association, 1973.

American Psychological Association. *Publication manual.* Washington, D.C.: American Psychological Association, 1974.

Barber, T. X. *Pitfalls in human research.* New York: Pergamon, 1976.

Barthell, C. N., & Holmes, D. S. High school yearbooks: A nonreactive measure of social isolation in graduates who later became schizophrenic. *Journal of Abnormal Psychology,* 1968, *73,* 313–316.

Baumrind, D. Some thoughts on ethics of research: After reading Milgram's "Behavioral study of obedience." *American Psychologist,* 1964, *19,* 421–423.

Bohm, D. Further remarks on order. In C. H. Waddington (Ed.), *Towards a theoretical biology* (Vol. 2). Edinburgh: Edinburgh University Press, 1969.

Bolgar, H. The case study method. In B. B. Wolman (Ed.), *Handbook of clinical psychology.* New York: McGraw-Hill, 1965, pp. 28–39.

Boring, E. G. *A history of experimental psychology* (2nd ed.). New York: Appleton-Century-Crofts, 1950.

Bransford, J. D. *Human cognition.* Belmont, Calif.: Wadsworth, 1979.

Bransford, J. D., & Johnson, M. K. Contextual prerequisites for understanding: Some investigations of comprehension and recall. *Journal of Verbal Learning and Verbal Behavior,* 1972, *11,* 717–726.

Bridgman, P. W. *The logic of modern physics.* New York: Macmillan, 1927.

Broad, W. J. Imbroglio at Yale (I): Emergence of a fraud. *Science,* 1980, *210,* 38–41.

Bronowski, J. *Science and human values.* New York: Harper & Row, 1965.

Brown, G. S. *Laws of form.* New York: Julian, 1972. In paperback, New York: Bantam Press.

Brunswik, E. *Systematic and representative design of psychological experiments.* Berkeley: University of California Press, 1947.

Campbell, D. T., & Stanley, J. C. *Experimental and quasi-experimental designs for research.* Chicago: Rand McNally, 1963.

Carlsmith, J. M., Ellsworth, P. C., & Aronson, E. *Methods of research in social psychology.* Reading, Mass.: Addison-Wesley, 1976.

Chamberlin, T. C. The method of multiple working hypotheses. *Science,* 1965, *148,* 754–759. (Reprint of article originally published in *Science,* 1890.)

Cobb, L. A., Thomas, G. I., Dillard, D. H., Merendino, K. A., & Bruce, R. A. An evaluation of internal-mammary-artery ligation by a double-blind technic. *The New England Journal of Medicine,* 1959, *260,* 1115–1118.

Cohen, M., & Nagel, E. *An introduction to logic and scientific method.* New York: Harcourt, 1934.

Cook, S. W. A comment on the ethical issues involved in West, Gunn, and Chernicky's "Ubiquitous Watergate: An attributional analysis." *Journal of Personality and Social Psychology,* 1975, *32,* 66–68.

Cook, T. D., & Campbell, D. T. *Quasi-experimentation: Design and analysis issues for field settings.* Chicago: Rand McNally, 1979.

Cunningham, M. R. Weather, mood, and helping behavior: Quasi-experiments with the sunshine samaritan. *Journal of Personality and Social Psychology,* 1979, *37,* 1947–1956.

Edgington, E. S. A new tabulation of statistical procedures used in APA journals. *American Psychologist,* 1974, *29,* 25–26.

Evans, I. M., & Robinson, C. H. Behavior therapy observed: The diary of a client. *Cognitive Therapy and Research,* 1978, *2,* 335–355.

Eysenck, H. J. Behavior therapy—dogma or applied science. In M. P. Feldman & A. Broadhurst (Eds.), *Theoretical and experimental bases of the behavior therapies.* London: Wiley, 1976.

Ferguson, G. A. *Statistical analysis in psychology and education* (4th ed.). New York: McGraw-Hill, 1976.

Fry, L. W., & Greenfield, S. Examination of attitudinal differences between policemen and policewomen. *Journal of Applied Psychology,* 1980, *65,* 123–126.

Galen. De praenotione. In D. C. G. Kuhn (Ed.), *Opera omnia,* cap. vi (Vol. 9). Lipsiae: Officina Libraria Car. Cnoblochii, 1827, pp. 630–635.

Gaul, D. J., Craighead, W. E., & Mahoney, M. J. Relationship between eating rates and obesity. *Journal of Consulting and Clinical Psychology,* 1975, *43,* 123–125.

Giannetti, R. A., Johnson, J. H., Klingler, D. E., & Williams, T. A. Comparison of linear and configural MMPI diagnostic methods with an uncontaminated criterion. *Journal of Consulting and Clinical Psychology,* 1978, *46,* 1046–1052.

Glass, G. V., & Stanley, J. C. *Statistical methods in education and psychology.* Englewood Cliffs, N.J.: Prentice-Hall, 1970.

Glasser, R. J. *The body is the hero.* New York: Random House, 1976.

Gottmann, J. M. N-of-1 and N-of-2 research in psychotherapy. *Psychological Bulletin,* 1973, *80,* 93–105.

Gould, S. J. The finagle factor. *Human Nature,* 1978, *1,* 80–87.

Guilford, J. P., & Fruchter, B. *Fundamental statistics in psychology and education* (6th ed.). New York: McGraw-Hill, 1978.

Harris, M. E., & Ray, W. J. Dream content and its relation to self-reported interpersonal behavior. *Psychiatry,* 1977, *40,* 363–368.

Hass, H., Fink, H., & Hartfelder, G. The placebo problem. *Psychopharmacology Service Center Bulletin,* 1963, *2,* 1–65.

Hearnshaw, L. S. *Cyril Burt, psychologist.* Ithaca, N.Y.: Cornell University Press, 1979.

Herodotus. In F. R. B. Godolphin (Ed.), *The Greek historians.* New York: Random House, 1942.

Holt, R. R. Experimental methods in clinical psychology. In B. B. Wolman (Ed.), *Handbook of clinical psychology.* New York: McGraw-Hill, 1965.

Holton, G. *Introduction to concepts and theories in physical science.* Reading, Mass.: Addison-Wesley, 1952.

Horner, M. S. Toward an understanding of achievement related conflicts in women. *Journal of Social Issues,* 1972, *28,* 157–176.

Jones, E. E., & Nisbett, R. E. *The actor and the observer: Divergent perceptions of the causes of behavior.* Morristown, N.J.: General Learning Press, 1971.

Kazdin, A. E. Methodological and assessment considerations in evaluating reinforcement programs in applied settings. *Journal of Applied Behavioral Analysis,* 1973, *6,* 517–531.

Kelman, H. C. *A time to speak.* San Francisco: Jossey Bass, 1968.

Keppel, G., & Saufley, W. H. *Introduction to design and analysis: A student's handbook.* San Francisco: W. H. Freeman & Co., 1980.

Kerlinger, F. N. *Foundations of behavioral research* (2nd ed.). New York: Holt, Rinehart & Winston, 1973.

Koestler, A. *The act of creation.* New York: Macmillan, 1964.

Kraft, C. L. A psychophysical contribution to air safety: Simulator studies of visual illusions in night visual approaches. In H. L. Pick, H. W. Leibowitz, J. E. Singer, A. Steinschneider & H. W. Stevenson (Eds.), *Psychology: From research to practice.* New York: Plenum Press, 1978.

Krantz, D. S. Naturalistic study of social influences on meal size among moderately obese and nonobese subjects. *Psychosomatic Medicine,* 1979, *41,* 19–27.

Kuhn, T. *The structure of scientific revolutions* (2nd ed.). Chicago: University of Chicago Press, 1970.

Lakatos, I. *The methodology of scientific research programs.* Cambridge: Cambridge University Press, 1978.

Landers, D. M., Obermier, G. E., & Patterson, A. H. Iris pigmentation and reactive motor performance. *Journal of Motor Behavior,* 1976, *8,* 171–179.

Lehner, P. N. *Handbook of ethological methods.* New York: Garland STPM Press, 1979.

Loftus, E. F., & Fries, J. F. Informed consent may be hazardous to your health. *Science,* 1979, *204,* 4388.

Lorenz, K. *King Solomon's ring.* New York: Thomas Y. Crowell, 1952.

Lorenz, K. The fashionable fallacy of dispensing with description. *Naturwissenschaften,* 1973, *60,* 1–9.

McCall, R. B. *Fundamental statistics for psychology* (2nd ed.). New York: Harcourt, Brace, Jovanovich, 1980.

Maher, B. A. A reader's, writer's and reviewer's guide to assessing research reports in clinical psychology. *Journal of Consulting and Clinical Psychology,* 1978, *46,* 835–838.

Maher, B. A. Stimulus sampling in clinical research: Representative design reviewed. *Journal of Consulting and Clinical Psychology,* 1978, *46,* 643–647.

Mahoney, M. J. *Scientist as subject.* Cambridge, Mass.: Ballinger, 1976.

Maslow, A. H. *The psychology of science.* New York: Harper & Row, 1966.

Maslow, A. H. *Motivation and personality* (2nd ed.). New York: Harper & Row, 1970.

Maslow, A. H. *The farthest reaches of human nature.* New York: Viking Press, 1971.

Mead, M. *Coming of age in Samoa.* New York: Morrow, 1928.

Mesulam, M., & Perry, J. The diagnosis of love-sickness: Experimental psychophysiology without the polygraph. *Psychophysiology,* 1972, *9,* 546–551.

Milgram, S. Behavioral study of obedience. *Journal of Abnormal and Social Psychology,* 1963, *67,* 371–378.

Milgram, S. *The individual in a social world: Essays and experiments.* Reading, Mass.: Addison-Wesley, 1977.

Miller, G. T. *Living in the environment: Concepts, problems, and alternatives.* Belmont, Calif.: Wadsworth, 1975.

Miller, N. E. Learning of visceral and glandular responses. *Science,* 1969, *163,* 434–445.

Milner, B. Amnesia following operation on the temporal lobes. In C. W. M. Whitty & O. L. Zangwill (Eds.), *Amnesia.* London: Butterworths, 1966, pp. 109–133.

Mitroff, I. I. Norms and counter-norms in a select group of the Apollo moon scientists: A case study of the ambivalence of scientists. *American Sociological Review,* 1974, *39,* 579–595.

Mitroff, I. I., & Fitzgerald, I. On the psychology of the Apollo moon scientists: A chapter in the psychology of science. *Human Relations,* 1977, *30,* 657–674.

Newcombe, N., & Arnkoff, D. Effects of speech style and sex of speaker on person perception. *Journal of Personality and Social Psychology,* 1979, *37,* 1293–1303.

Newton, I. *Mathematical principles.* Andrew Motte translator (1729), revised translation Florian Cajori. New York: Greenwood, 1969.

Orne, M. Demand characteristics and the concept of quasi-controls. In R. Rosenthal & R. L. Rosnow (Eds.), *Artifact in behavioral research.* New York: Academic Press, 1969.

Orne, M. T., & Evans, F. J. Inadvertent termination of hypnosis on hypnotized and simulating subjects. *International Journal of Clinical and Experimental Hypnosis,* 1966, *14,* 61–78.

Ornstein, R. E. *The psychology of consciousness* (2nd ed.). New York: Harcourt, Brace, Jovanovich, 1977.

Petrinovich, L. Probabilistic functionalism: A conception of research methods. *American Psychologist,* 1979, *34,* 373–390.

Platt, J. R. Strong inference. *Science,* 1964, *146,* 347–353.

Popper, K. R. *The logic of scientific discovery.* New York: Basic Books, 1959.

Popper, K. R. *Objective knowledge.* Oxford: Oxford University Press, 1972.

Premack, D., & Woodruff, G. Does the chimpanzee have a theory of mind? *The Behavioral and Brain Sciences,* 1978, *1,* 515–526.

Raebhausen, O. M., & Brim, O. G. Privacy and behavioral research. *American Psychologist,* 1967, *22,* 423–437.

Ravizza, K. Peak experiences in sports. *Journal of Humanistic Psychology,* 1977, *17,* 35–40.

Ray, W. J., Katahn, M., & Snyder, C. R. Effects of test anxiety on acquisition, retention, and generalization of a complex verbal task in a classroom situation. *Journal of Personality and Social Psychology,* 1971, *20,* 147–154.

Resnick, J. H., & Schwartz, T. Ethical standards as an independent variable in psychological research. *American Psychologist,* 1973, *28,* 134–139.

Roechelein, J. E. Sex differences in time estimation. *Perceptual and Motor Skills,* 1972, *35,* 859–862.

Rosenhan, D. L. Being sane in insane places. *Science,* 1973, *179,* 250–258.

Rosenthal, R. How often are our numbers wrong? *American Psychologist,* 1979, *33,* 1005–1008.

Rosenthal, R., & Fode, K. L. The effects of experimenter bias on the performance of the albino rat. *Behavioral Science,* 1963, *8,* 183–189.

Rosenthal, R., & Lawson, R. A longitudinal study of the effects of experimenter bias on the operant learning of operant rats. *Journal of Psychiatric Research,* 1964, *2,* 61–72.

Rosenthal, R., & Rubin, D. B. Interpersonal expectancy effects: The first 345 studies. *The Behavioral and Brain Sciences,* 1978, *1,* 377–386.

Rubin, Z. Lovers and other strangers: The development of intimacy in encounters and relationships. *American Scientist,* 1974, *62,* 182–190.

Runyon, R. P., & Haber, A. *Fundamentals of behavioral statistics* (3rd ed.). Reading, Mass.: Addison-Wesley, 1977.

Salk, J. *The survival of the wisest.* New York: Harper & Row, 1973.

Schnelle, J. F., & Lee, J. F. Quasi-experimental retrospective evaluation of a prison policy change. *Journal of Applied Behavior Analysis,* 1974, *7,* 483–496.

Schumacher, E. F. *A guide for the perplexed.* New York: Harper & Row, 1977. In paperback, Perennial Library, 1979.

Scoville, W. B. Amnesia after bilateral mesial temporal-lobe excision: Introduction to case H. M. *Neuropsychologia,* 1968, *6,* 211–213.

Scoville, W. B., & Milner, B. Loss of recent memory after bilateral hippocampal lessions. *Journal of Neurology, Neurosurgery, and Psychiatry,* 1957, *20,* 11–21.

Shotland, R. L., & Straw, M. K. Bystander response to an assault: When a man attacks a woman. *Journal of Personality and Social Psychology,* 1976, *34,* 990–999.

Sidman, M. *Tactics of scientific research.* New York: Basic Books, 1960.

Simon, J. L. *Basic research methods in social sciences* (2nd ed.). New York: Random House, 1978.

Solomon, R. L. An extension of control group design. *Psychological Bulletin,* 1949, *46,* 137–150.

Strupp, H. H., & Hadley, S. W. Specific vs. nonspecific factors in psychotherapy. *Archives of General Psychiatry,* 1979, *36,* 1125–1136.

Tart, C. T. States of consciousness and state specific sciences. *Science,* 1972, *176,* 1203–1210.

Thomas, L. *The medusa and the snail.* New York: Viking, 1979.

Tinbergen, E. A., & Tinbergen, N. *Early childhood autism—an ethological approach.* Berlin: Paul Parey, 1972.

Tinbergen, N. *The animal in its world.* Cambridge, Mass.: Harvard University Press, 1972.

Wallas, G. *The art of thought.* New York: Harcourt Brace & Co., 1926.

Walsh, R. N. Reflections on psychotherapy. *Journal of Transpersonal Psychology,* 1976, *8,* 100–111.

Walsh, R. N. Initial meditative experiences: Part I. *Journal of Transpersonal Psychology,* 1977, *9,* 151–192.

Walsh, R. N. Initial meditative experiences: Part II. *Journal of Transpersonal Psychology,* 1978, *10,* 1–28.

Wason, P. C. Self-contradictions. In P. N. Johnson-Laird & P. C. Wason (Eds.), *Thinking.* Cambridge: Cambridge University Press, 1977.

Watson, J. D. *The double helix.* New York: Atheneum, 1968.

Webb, E. J., Campbell, D. T., Schwartz, R. D., & Sechrest, L. *Unobtrusive measures.* Chicago: Rand McNally, 1966.

West, S. G., Gunn, S. P., & Chernicky, P. Ubiquitous Watergate: An attributional analysis. *Journal of Personality and Social Psychology,* 1975, *32,* 55–65.

Whitehead, A. N. *Science and the modern world.* New York: Macmillan, 1925.

Wicklund, R. A. Influence of self-awareness on human behavior. *American Scientist,* 1979, *67,* 187–193.

Winer, B. J. *Statistical principles in experimental design.* New York: McGraw-Hill, 1971.

Index

Abscissa, 54
Absolute zero, 152
Abstract, 256
Affirming the consequent, 39
Alternative dependent variables, 218
Analysis of factorial design, 154–157, 183
Analysis of variance, 143–158
APA guidelines to ethics, 239–242
Apparatus, 259
Aristotle, 5, 136
Aristotelian approach to science, 254
Assessment of articles
  guidelines, 271–275
Authority
  defined, 4
  ideas and, 4–5, 13, 22
  empiricism and, 5
  problems with, 5

Barber, T., 196, 204
Behavior
  experience and, 20
  method of studying subjective reality, 18–19
  objective, 19
Between-subjects design, 141–167, 173–175, 179
  completely randomized, 141–142, 148
  multilevel completely randomized, 142–147
  versus within subjects, 141, 171, 176
Biased data collection, 189–193
  personal equation, 189
Biased interactions with subjects, 193–194
  self-fulfilling prophecies, 194
  ways to avoid, 194–195
Bimodal distribution, 54
Biofeedback, 199
Blind experimenters, 195
Blocking, 184
Bransford, J. & Johnson, M., 101–104, 116, 135, 143–145
Bridgman, P., 7

Campbell, D. & Stanley, J., 111, 117, 133, 135, 205, 210, 213, 215
Categorical measurement, 50
Causality, 33
Cells, 150
Chamberlin, T., 283–285, 293
Chance variation, 60, 103, 105–108, 137, 158, 159, 170, 175
Common sense, 6, 14, 110
  ideas and, 22
  problems with, 6
  use of, 14
Communicating results, 255–271
Confidentiality and ethics, 239
Confirmatory logic, 39
Confounds, 99, 110–111
  controlled by
    counterbalancing, 125, 129, 176–177

Confounds (continued)
elimination, 122
matching, 122, 127–128, 170, 179–181
criterion for use of, 180
variables used for, 179
randomization, 122, 129–132, 142, 170
hypothesis and, 99, 119, 147
variables, 33, 99, 108
defined, 110–111
Construct
defined, 21
Context of experimentation, 101–103
Control
confounds by
counterbalancing, 125, 129, 176–177
elimination, 122
matching, 122, 127–128, 170, 179–181
criterion for use of, 180
variables used for, 179
randomization, 122, 129–132, 142, 170
designs and, 131–136
differential order effects, 177
examples of, 166
experimental design, 131–136, 277
experimental logic, 136–139
group, 30
internal validity, 133–134
no treatment, 199
practice effects, 176–177
quasi, 200
through subject assignment/selection, 120–131
Cook, T. & Campbell, D., 111, 116
Counterbalancing, 125, 129
matching, 8, 125, 129
Craniometry, 190
Creative thinking, 283–284
Croesus, 9–10, 12–14, 16, 23
Cultural biases, 203

Darwin, C., 25, 27, 224
Debriefing
ethics and, 247, 251–252
Deception, 238, 243–251
debriefing and, 247, 251–252
ethics, 238, 243–251
obedience to authority and, 245–247
Deduction, 37
hypothesis and, 77
Degrees of freedom, 61–63, 158–159
defined, 62
variance and, 159
Demand characteristics, 200–203
Denying the antecedent, 40
Dependent variables, 32, 276
alternative, 218
Depression, 73–74
Descriptive statistics, 56–65, 67–69
Design
between subjects, 141–167, 173–175, 179
control, 131–136
counterbalancing, 125, 129
ex post facto, 216–218
factorial, 32, 140, 147–169. *See also* Factorial design
interrupted time series, 210–212
matched subject, 170, 179–184
steps in, 182
mixed, 178–179
analysis of, 178–179
multiple time series, 212–215
naturalistic observation, 206, 208, 224–231
data analysis and, 228
data collection and, 226
functions of, 224–225
problems with, 228–229
reactive behavior, 226
selective perception, 227
strengths and weaknesses, 230
techniques, 208
unobtrusive measures, 226–227
validity and, 207, 226
nonequivalent before-after, 215–216
posttest-only control group, 133
pretest-posttest control group, 133
quasi-experimental, 207–218
techniques, 208
validity and, 207
randomized block, 181, 184
blocking, 184
leveling and, 184
stratifying and, 184
single-group pretest-posttest, 209
single subject, 208, 218–224
advantages and disadvantages, 219, 222

Design (continued)
case study, 218–221
limits of, 223–224
multiple baseline, 223–224
reversal, 221–223
Solomon four-group, 134–135, 139
time series, 208–210
two group, 149, 183
cells, 150
interaction effects, 150, 157, 159
main effects, 149–150
within subjects, 170–184
advantages and disadvantages, 175–177
versus between subjects, 141, 171, 176
examples of, 171–175
repeated measures and, 177
sensitivity of, 176
Differential order effects, 177
Diffusion or limitation of treatments, 116
Disconfirmatory logic, 40
Disconfirmatory reasoning, 40
Discussion sections, 264–267
Dispersion, 59
Distributions
bell-shaped, 56
bimodal, 54–56
normal, 55–56
skewed, 55–56
Double blind experiment, 199

Ecology, 187–188
validity and, 100, 188–189. *See also* Validity, ecological
Einstein, A., 6, 84, 86, 283–284
Elimination procedure, 122
Empiricism
authority and, 5
defined, 17, 23, 25
Equal interval measurement, 52
Error
term, 60, 105–108, 137, 158–159, 172–173
variation, 60, 103, 105–108, 137, 158–159, 170, 175
Ethics
anonymity and, 239
APA guidelines and, 239–242
confidentiality and, 239
debriefing and, 247, 251–252
deception and, 238, 243–251
defined, 233
harm and, 239
informed consent and, 237
internal review committees and, 242–243
law and, 236
privacy and, 238
psychological experiments and, 233–234, 236
rights and, 234–236
science and, 232, 253, 285–286
validity of, 285
values and, 232–233, 283, 285–286
voluntary participation and, 237–238
Experience
subjective, 18
Experimental group, 30
Experimental method, 26, 29–35
beyond, 276–278
defined, 25–26
definitions within, 30–33
design and control, 131–136, 277
ethics and, 233–234
exploratory use, 34
group, 130
hypotheses, 72
logic of, 136–137
science and, 1, 25
uses of, 34–35
Experimenter effects, 189–194
biased data collection, 189–193
biased interactions with subjects, 193–194
ways to avoid bias, 194–195
Exploratory method, 34
Ex post facto designs, 216–218
External validity, 120–121. *See also* Validity, external
Extraneous variables, 108
Extrasensory perception, 7

Factorial design, 32, 140, 147–169
advantages of, 147–148, 167
analysis of, 154–157, 183
evaluation of, 153
examples of, 151–153, 161–169, 174–175, 183
interaction in, 157–169
main effects in, 154–157, 160–169
steps in, 155–160
Factors, 149
Falsificationism, 42

Field research design, 224–231. *See also* Naturalistic observation
Field studies, 224–231. *See also* Naturalistic observation
Fisher, R., 104, 181
F-ratio, 104–107. *See also* Statistics, *F*-ratio
  variance and, 159
Frequency distribution, 53–56
  defined, 53
Frequency polygon, 54
Freud, S., 6

Galen, 10–13, 16, 23, 37
Galileo, 5, 136
Generalizability, 36–37
Genovese, K., 78, 248
Graphs, 65–66, 161–169
  bar, 65–66
  examples of, 161–169
  line, 65–66

Hawthorne effect, 196–197
Herodotus, 9–10
History, 111–112
Holt, R., 268–269, 275
Humanistic science, 2
Hypnosis, 200–202
Hypothesis, 24, 30, 75
  chance, 119
  confound, 99, 119, 147
  deductive reasoning and, 77
  defined, 24
  evaluation of, 153
  experimental, 72
  formulation of, 80
  inductive reasoning and, 75–76
  multiple working, 284
  null, 99, 104, 119, 147
    acceptance, 159
    F-ratio and, 106, 109, 147
    rejection of, 100, 109, 159
  questions related to, 98
  reliability and, 94–95
  testing, 147
  validity of, 94–95

Ideas
  acceptance through
    authority, 4–5, 12, 22
    common sense, 6, 22
    reason, 6, 22
    science, 6–7, 22
    tenacity, 3–4, 22
  experiments and, 77
  refinement of, 225
Illumination
  stage, 86
Incubation
  stage, 85–86
Independent variable, 32, 99, 148–151, 276
  effects of, 104
Index Medicus, 89–90
Individual differences
  error variance and, 108
Induction, 39, 75–76
  hypotheses and, 75–76
  logic of, 37–39
  validity and, 76
Inference, strong, 83
Inferences, 35–36
Inferential statistics, 69
Informed consent, 237
Instrumentation, 114
Interaction effect
  defined, 150
  examples of, 161–169
  factorial design, 161–169
Internal validity, 36, 76, 100, 120–121, 138, 187, 205. *See also* Validity, internal
  control of, 131–136
  threats to, 111–116
Interrater reliability, 190
Interrupted time series design, 210–212
Interval measurement, 50, 52, 58, 67–69
Introduction, 256–259
Intuition and revelation, 82–85

Journals, 86–87

Kant, I., 223
Kekulé, 84–85
Knowledge
  descriptive, 224
Kuhn, T., 44, 288

Lakatos, I., 280
Law and ethics, 236
Leveling, 184
Limitations in psychology, 282
Loftus, E. & Fries, J., 244–245

Logic, 6, 110
confirmatory, 39
deduction, 37
disconfirmatory, 40
experimentation and control of, 136–139, 166
factorial designs and, 152–160
induction, 37–39
naturalistic method, 207
propositional, 35, 37
reason and, 35
reversal design, 222
tool, as a, 40
use of, 14
Logical syllogism, 6
Lorenz, K., 28, 225

Maher, B., 271–275
Main effects, 149–150
Matched subject design, 170, 179–184. *See also* Design, matched subject
Matching
control procedure, 180–181
experimental procedure, 181–183
Matching procedure, 122
counterbalancing and, 125, 129
disadvantages of, 128
Maturation, 112
Mean, 56–57
technical use of, 58
Mean square, 159
variance and, 159
Measurement
absolute zero, 152
categorical, 50
equal intervals and, 52
frequency, 54
central tendency of, 56–59
variability of, 59–65
graphing, 65–66, 161–169
hypothesis development, 92–94
interval, 50, 52, 58, 67–69
mean square, 159
nominal, 50, 58, 67, 69
ordinal, 50–51, 58, 67–69
quantitative versus qualitative, 51
ratio, 50, 52–53, 58, 67–69
scales of, 49–53
sum of squares, 159
variance, 159
Median, 57
technical use of, 58
Methods
experimental, 29–35. *See also* Experimental method
section, 259–263, 267
Milgram, S., 245–247
Mixed design, 178–179. *See also* Design, mixed
Mode, 51–58
technical use of, 58
Modus ponens, 39
Modus tollens, 40
Mortality, 115
Multileveled completely randomized design, 142–147
Multiple time series design, 212–215
Myths of science, 282

Naturalistic method, 26–29
characteristics of, 28–29
Naturalistic observation, 25, 206, 224–231, 276–278
data analysis and, 228
data collection and, 226–227, 230
reactive behavior, 226
selective perception, 227, 230
unobtrusive observation, 226–227
experimental method and, 277
functions of, 224–225
problems with, 228–229
strengths and weaknesses, 230
techniques, 208
validity and, 207, 226, 230
Newcombe, N., 81–82, 92, 94, 114, 257
Newton, Sir I., 7–9
rules of reasoning, 8–9, 44, 283–284, 286
Nominal measurement, 50, 58, 67, 69
Nonequivalent before-after design, 215–216
Nonsystematic variation, 104
No treatment control, 199
Null hypothesis, 99, 104, 119, 147
acceptance of, 159
F-ratio and, 106, 109, 137
rejection of, 100, 109, 159

Observation, naturalistic, 49. *See also* Naturalistic observation
Operational definition, 7, 31, 72–75
of depression, 73–74

Operational definition (continued)
  problems with, 72
Ordinal measurement, 50-57, 58, 67-69
Ordinate, 54
Orne, M., 200-202, 204

Paradigms, 44-45, 203
Parsimony, 281
Peirce, C., 3, 22
Personal equation, 189
Philosophy of science, 42, 280
Placebo factors, 199-200
Plagiarism, 192
Platt, J., 83, 135, 218
Popper, Sir K., 42, 280, 288
Post hoc, 25
  tests, 143
Posttest-only control group design, 133
Practice effects, 176
  control of, 176-177
  defined, 176
Preparation stage, 85
Pretest-posttest control group design, 133
Primary variance, 107
Procedure, 259
Process of science, 283-286
Proposal preparation, 268-269
Propositional logic, 35
Pseudopatients, 226
Psychological Abstracts, 87-89
Psychological processes
  ways to study, 17-18
Publications, 254-275
  abstract, 256
  discussion, 264-267
  guidelines for assessing, 271-275
  introduction, 256-259
  methods, 259-263, 267
  preparation, 255-268
  proposal preparation, 268-269
  results, 263-264
  review of, 270-271
  submission of, 268-271
  title, 267
Purification of ideas, 6-7

Qualitative measurement, 51
Quantitative measurement, 51
Quasi-control, 200
Quasi-experimental design, 207, 208-218. *See also* Design, quasi-experimental
  ex post facto, 216-218
  interrupted time series, 210-212
  multiple time series, 212-215
  nonequivalent before-after, 215-216
  time series design, 208-210

Random
  number table
    use of, 123
  sampling versus control, 130-131
  selection, 104, 122
Randomization
  control and, 129
Randomized block design, 181, 184. *See also* Design, randomized block
Range, 59
  exclusive, 59
Rape, 77-79
Ratio measurement, 50, 52-53, 58, 67-69
Reactive behavior, 226
Reason
  ideas and, 6, 22
  logic and, 6
  problems with, 6
Reasoning
  rules of, 8-9
Relevance of research, 286-288
Reliability
  hypotheses and, 94-95
  interrater, 190
  personal equation and, 189-190
  validity and, 190
Repeated measures, within-subject design, 177
Research
  basic strategies, 1
  laboratory versus field, 278
  methods, 277-278
  obstacles, 278
  process of, 283-285
  programmatic, 278
  psychological limitations, 282
  relevance of, 286-288
  significance of, 287
  tools, 280-281
  transcendence, 288-292
  value of, 285-288
Replication
  defined, 12
Results
  argument and, 254

Results (continued)
  communication of, 255–271
  examples of, 264
  inquiry and, 254
  preparation of, 255–268
  section, 263–264
  sharing, 254–258, 270–275
Rights of scientists, 234–236
Rights of subjects, 234–236
  to anonymity, 239
  to confidentiality, 239
  to debriefing, 247, 251
  ethics and, 234–236
  to informed consent, 238
  to not be harmed, 239
  to privacy, 238

Scales of measurement, 49–53
Schumacher, E., 17, 23
Science
  acceptance of ideas, 6–7
  appearance and behavior of, 17
  approaches, 283, 287
  Aristotelian parts of, 254
  communication of, 46
  creativity and, 283–284
  ethics, 232–253, 285–286
  evaluation of, 45
  experience and, 7, 13
  goals of, 188, 205
  humanistic approach, 2
  limitations of, 280
  meaning of, 1, 25
  methods of, 1, 25
  myths of, 282
  philosophy of, 42, 280
  process of, 283–286
  publications, 255–271
  self-corrective nature, 7, 23
  statistical significance, 287
  tools of, 86–92, 280–281
  value of, 2, 285–286, 288
Science Citation Index, 91–92
Scientific knowledge, 2
Scoville, N. & Milner, B., 220–221
Secondary variance, 107–108
Selection, 114–115
  maturation interaction, 115–116
Selective perception, 227
Self-fulfilling prophecies, 194
Semmelweis, 11–14, 16, 23
Sensory experience
  appeal to, 17
Shotland, L., 77, 79–81, 85, 89, 94, 116, 257, 261
Significance
  statistical, 263
  statistical versus scientific, 287
Simple randomized design, 141–142
Single-group pretest-posttest design, 209
Single-subject design, 208, 218–224. *See also* Design, single subject
  advantages of, 219
  advantages and disadvantages of, 222
  case study, 218–221
  limitations of, 223–224
  multiple baseline, 223–224
  reversal, 221–223
Single-subject experiment, 11
Skinner, B., 6
Skinner box, 19, 194
Social biases, 203
Social science citation index, 91–92
Solomon four-group design, 134–135, 139
Standard deviation
  defined, 64
Statistical regression, 114
Statistics
  analysis of mixed designs, 178–179
  analysis of variance, 143–158
    summary table, 159
  decision process, 99
  degrees of freedom, 61, 158–159
  descriptive, 56–65, 67–69
  error term, 60, 105–108, 137, 158–159, 172–173
  F-ratio, 104–107, 109–110, 119, 159, 173, 176, 179
    control and, 136–137
    null hypothesis and, 106
  inferential, 68–69
  interactions, 156, 159–165
    examples, 161–169, 184
  interpretation, 103–107
  main effects of, 149–150, 159–165
    examples of, 161–165
  mean, 56–57
  median, 57
  mode, 57–58
  naturalistic observation and, 228
  post hoc tests and, 143
  range and, 59

Statistics (continued)
  reporting, 263–266
  scientific significance and, 287
  significance of, 263
  standard deviation, 64
  sum of squares, 60
  variability, 59
  variance, 60
    between groups, 104, 158
    within groups, 104, 158
Stratifying, 184
Strupp, H. & Hadley, S., 146
Subject factors, 195–199
Subjects, 259
Subject variable, 165–166
Sum of squares, 60, 159
  computation method, 63–65
  defined, 60
  deviation method, 61–62
Systematic variation, 103–104
  due to confound, 104
  due to independent variable, 104

Tenacity
  defined, 3
  ideas and, 3–4, 22
  problems with, 4
Testing, 112
  null hypothesis, 147
Thomas, L., 290–291
Time series design, 208–210
Tinbergen, N., 27, 225
Title of article, 267
Tools of science, 86–92, 280–281
Transcendence, 288–292
Treatment, 32
  effect, 32, 108
  main effects of, 149–150
  variance, 60, 104–107, 109–110, 137, 158, 172
Two-group design, 149, 183. *See also* Design, two group
Type I errors, 107
Type II errors, 107

Unobtrusive observation, 226–227

Validity
  defined, 36
  ecological, 100, 188
    cultural and social biases, 203–204
    demand characteristics, 200–203
    experimenter effects, 189–194
    interrater reliability, 190
    personal equation, 189
    placebo factors, 199–200
    subject factors, 195–199
  ethical/moral values, 285
  external, 36, 101, 120–121, 187, 205
  generalizability, 36–37
  hypothesis, 94–95
  induction, 76
  internal, 36, 76, 100, 120–121, 138, 187, 205
    control, 131–136
    threats to, 111–116, 207
  naturalistic observations, 226
Values in science, 2, 285–286, 288
  ethics and, 232–233, 283, 285–286
Variability. *See also* Measurement, frequency
  defined, 59
Variables
  confounding, 33, 99, 108
    defined, 110–111
  dependent, 32, 276
    alternative, 218
  extraneous, 108
  independent, 32, 99, 148–151, 276
    effects of, 104
  subject, 165–166
Variance, 60, 159
  analysis of, 143–158
  between groups, 104, 158
  calculation of, 64–65
  control, 127
  defined, 60
  degrees of freedom, 159
  effects of change, 108
  error (chance), 60, 105–108, 137, 158, 159, 170, 175
    reduction of, 179–180
  formula for, 61
  mean square and, 159
  primary, 107
  secondary, 107–108
  sources, 158
  treatment (between), 60, 104–107, 108–110, 137, 158, 172
    F-ratio, 159
  within, 60, 104–107, 109–110, 137, 158, 170, 172

Variance (continued)
    F-ratio, 159
Variation
  chance, 103
  error, 103
  nonsystematic, 104
  systematic, 103
Verification stage, 86
Voluntary participation, 237–238

Wallas, G., 85, 96
Whitehead, A., 6
Within-groups variance, 60, 104–107, 109–110, 137, 158, 170, 172
  F-ratio and, 159
Within-subjects design, 170–184. *See also* Design, within subjects

X-axis, 54

Y-axis, 54